Beside
the
Still Waters

Volume Two

Indexed

Vision Publishers
Harrisonburg, Virginia

Copyright © 2006 by Still Waters Ministries
Copyright © 2006 by Vision Publishers, LLC

ISBN: 1-932676-06-6

All Scripture references are from the
King James Version of the Holy Bible.

Published by Vision Publishers, LLC
A subsidiary of EVC Enterprises, Inc.
Harrisonburg, Virginia

Cover Design: Lonnie D. Yoder

For additional copies or comments contact us at:
Vision Publishers
P.O. Box 190
Harrisonburg, VA 22803
Phone: 877/488-0901
Fax: 540/437-1969
e-mail: visionpubl@ntelos.net
(see order form in back)

Still Waters Ministries is supported by tax-free donations.
The bi-monthly devotional booklets are
distributed free of charge.

For more information on Still Waters Ministries
or to give a gift of money, write to:
Still Waters Ministries
270 Antioch Road
Clarkson, KY 42726
Phone: 270/242-0459
Fax: 270/242-3529

A royalty payment from the sale of these
books will go to Still Waters Ministries.

Introduction

Some caterpillars can be identified by the plants they feed on. The caterpillar of the cabbage butterfly feeds on cabbage and the caterpillar of the alfalfa butterfly feeds on alfalfa. The monarch butterfly is sometimes called the milkweed butterfly because the caterpillar feeds on milkweed plants. People, too, can be identified by the diet they choose. If others could see the things you feed on, how would they identify you? Would they call you a sharp businessperson, a great orator, an aspiring athlete, or would they notice that you are a dedicated Christian?

"You are what you eat" is a good old saying. Eating carrots will not turn a man into a carrot, but it is impossible to be physically healthy without a healthy diet. The Christian's spiritual health is likewise dependent on a healthy spiritual diet. It is impossible to stay healthy as a Christian while feeding on the junk food of the world. If you would avoid spiritual ill health, you must feed your mind on the things of God every day.

For that reason, I am excited to introduce this second volume of 366 selected *Beside the Still Waters* devotional readings. I trust this book will help you maintain a healthy habit of daily coming into the presence of God and feeding your soul on Him. May the scraps of the world seem dull and tasteless beside the delicacies of God's Word!

On behalf of Still Waters Ministries, I extend a hearty thank you to everyone who has contributed in making this book possible. Above all, we thank God for the opportunity to place this book in your hands. We hope you enjoy it!

Henry Yoder, Editor
Still Waters Ministries

Jubilee

*The Spirit of the Lord is upon me, because he hath anointed
me to preach the gospel to the poor . . . to preach
the acceptable year of the Lord.*
Luke 4:18a, 19

What a great expectation! What a year to look forward to! The thrill of the great Jubilee when all lands returned to their original owner, debts were canceled, and slaves were freed. After you have made all your mistakes, and adverse circumstances have plunged you into poverty, you are now given the opportunity to start all over again. No one should have become extremely rich nor extremely poor, because of the year of Jubilee. This was a command to the children of Israel under the old dispensation. We are now living in New Testament times.

Jesus, however, quoted here an interesting verse from the book of Isaiah. Are you poor and needy? Jesus came to bring you good news. Are you broken-hearted and your life torn apart? Jesus came to heal you. Are you a captive bound with many chains? Jesus came to set you free.

Like a bride who shines forth with joy when she is united with her bridegroom, so we can experience, in Christ, the thrill of starting a new life, a new beginning, a new leaf.

Bible Reading: Isaiah 61
One Year Bible Reading Plan:
Matthew 1
Genesis 1, 2

This is the Christian's year of jubilee, the acceptable year of the Lord. What a great expectation!

Roger Rangai, Lott, TX

Salvation produces a change within that breaks the chains of sin.

Eagle or Chicken

*They shall mount up with wings as eagles; they shall run
and not be weary; they shall walk and not faint.*
Isaiah 40:31b

A man once found an eaglet and placed it in the barnyard with his chickens. The eaglet grew and became quite accustomed to barnyard life.

One day a man who studied the habits of birds came by. He watched, fascinated, as the farmer tossed grain into the barnyard. The young eagle, along with the chickens, scampered hurriedly after it. The man picked up the eagle and held it high, perched on his fingers. "Okay, eagle," he said, "you are not a chicken; you are an eagle. Open your wings and fly."

The eagle looked up to the sky, then down at the chickens, and jumped back down to eat grain. Again, the man scooped up the eagle, this time climbing up on the barn roof, and repeated his command. Again, the eagle jumped down.

The next morning, the man took the eagle up a hill and faced east to behold a lovely sunrise beaming its warm, glowing colors. "Okay, eagle," he said as he raised the eagle high. "You are not a chicken; you are an eagle. Open your wings and fly."

The eagle excitedly watched the sunrise, until its very eyes seemed to glow. Then it lighted off his fingers and was airborne. The man watched the eagle fly into the sunrise until it was a mere speck in the sky.

As we live in this world, we are so often tempted to satisfy ourselves with this world's "chicken feed" when we can soar like the eagle to heavenly places in Christ Jesus!

"If ye then be risen with Christ, seek those things which are above, where Christ sitteth on the right hand of God. Set your affection on things above, not on things on the earth" (Colossians 3:1, 2).

> **Bible Reading:** Hebrews 11:13-16; Ephesians 4:1-7
> **One Year Bible Reading Plan:** Matthew 2
> Genesis 3—5

Roger Rangai, Lott, TX

Evil communications corrupt good manners.

With Christ We Have Everything

And ye are complete in him.
Colossians 2:10

One day while working at a job, someone made this remark to me: "If you have family and health, you have a lot." I readily agreed with him. Certainly, I have much to be thankful for.

But then, upon further reflection on this man's statement, I was inspired with another thought, "If we have Christ, we have everything." Maybe I don't have everything I want, or could wish for. But with the Lord Jesus as my Savior and Master, what else do I need? David says, "The Lord is my shepherd, I shall not want." And Paul affirms, "But my God shall supply all your need according to His riches in glory by Christ Jesus" (Philippians 4:19).

In today's Bible readings, would you notice with me some of the many things we have in Christ? We have grace and peace, a living hope, an incorruptible and undefiled inheritance, God's keeping power, "all things that pertain unto life and godliness," "exceeding great and precious promises," and being "partakers of His divine nature."

Many more things could be mentioned from other Scriptures, such as the privilege of coming to God in prayer, of fellowship with fellow believers, and the indwelling presence of God's Spirit. Whether or not we have health, family, money, or abundance of earthly things, in Christ we truly have everything, both now and for eternity.

Let us always be thankful for these blessings and privileges, which we have received from our loving Lord. Let us faithfully and readily share with others the good news of His great love.

Bible Reading: 1 Peter 1:1-8;
2 Peter 1:1-8
One Year Bible Reading Plan:
Matthew 3
Genesis 6—8

Mark Kropf, Cataldo, ID

When Christ is truly our life and our all, then He is all we need.

Just One Look
From You, Lord

Behold, he cometh with clouds; and every eye shall see him.
Revelation 1:7a

Heavenly Father, it is with remorse that I look back at the times when I have taken lightly my walk with You. As I look into Your Word, it pierces my heart. Especially when I can recall other times that I enjoyed gazing into Your face with sweet peace and assurance that I was in Your will.

So may Your eyes be upon me today, Lord; to guide and instruct, to comfort and bless. And, if necessary, chasten and correct me, so that in the end, I may enjoy a closer walk with You.

A closer walk with You! O, Father, this is my prayer! May my heart always pant for You as the hart pants after the water brooks. May our fellowship be so close that I will need just one look from You, Lord, and I shall heed Your slightest bidding.

And so, heavenly Father, fill me with Your Holy Spirit, that when You look upon me today, tomorrow, and most of all at the great judgment day, I shall meet Your gaze and not be ashamed. In Jesus' name, Amen.

Bible Reading: Psalm 32:8-11; Luke 22:56-62
One Year Bible Reading Plan:
Matthew 4
Genesis 9–11

Roger Rangai, Lott, TX

When it seems hardest to pray, we should pray the hardest.

To Whom Are You Looking?

Looking unto Jesus the author and finisher of our faith.
Hebrews 12:2a

Recently, a chorus gave a program at our church. As they sang, their faces reflected the joy of the message in the songs. From where I sat, I could see the singers, as well as the face of the director. I soon noticed something very impotant. He was in constant communication with the members of the chorus, and their eyes constantly were focused on him. By his signals, they knew what song was next, when to increase or decrease. By keeping their eyes on him, they were not distracted by faces in the audience, noises of children, or even someone trying deliberately to get their attention—to make them laugh or otherwise lose their focus. Remaining focused on their leader sent the message that group harmony was important.

I was impressed with a distinct parallel. Christ is my leader. He is in constant communication with me. If my eyes remain focused on Him, I will see His signals when to increase or decrease. I will see the direction in which He is leading me. If my eyes stay fixed on my Leader, I will not see those things that might distress me and cause me to lose my peace. If my eyes are on Jesus, I will not be distracted by those who would like to see me get sidetracked. The world will see that my heart is steadfast to follow Him, and that I will not be moved. It will do no good to try to lure me away from Him and from my comrades.

If I love Jesus and want to keep perfect harmony in the body, I will keep my eyes focused and fixed on Him.

Bible Reading: Colossians
3:1-17
One Year Bible Reading Plan:
Matthew 5:1-26
Genesis 12–14

Jan L. Heisey, Taylorsville, MS

Turn your eyes upon Jesus; Look full in His wonderful face;
And the things of earth will grow strangely dim.
In the light of His glory and grace.
—Helen Lemmel, 1922

Crowds and Sycamore Trees

For the Son of man is come to seek and to save that which was lost.
Luke 19:10

Why couldn't Zacchaeus see Jesus? Besides being short, he had a crowd pressing against him. We all face obstacles when we try to see Jesus. What is the crowd that presses against you? For some, it is the radio, TV, drink, drugs, or immorality. Others are pressed by their jobs and other legitimate cares of life.

Another thing that presses against us is our own carnal nature. Our selfish nature may keep us from seeing Jesus, and we begin to feel like Zacchaeus; we can't see Jesus because the crowd gets in the way. Do we give up in despair, or do we look around to find a sycamore tree? If we have faith, we will soon find one. Important "sycamore trees" are God's Word, prayer, hymns, and faithful brethren. Think of more "trees" in your life that have helped you to see Jesus.

Are you a "sycamore tree" for others who want to see Jesus? The only way many people in this world ever see the Gospel is in the lives of Christians. Are you willing to share a few words for the Lord? Can you point those lost in the crowd to the One who can save their souls? Give an encouraging word to the discouraged. Lend a helping hand to the burdened. We need to remember our first calling in life is to serve God—which means serving others.

Today the crowd will press you. Remember, God still has "sycamore trees." And don't forget to look for ways in which you can be a "sycamore tree" for others.

Bible Reading: Luke 19:1-10
One Year Bible Reading Plan:
Matthew 5:27-48
Genesis 15—17

Daniel Kuhns, Farmington, NM

Am I a part of the crowd or a sycamore tree?

God's Mercy

But thou, O Lord, art a God full of compassion, and gracious,
long suffering, and plenteous in mercy and truth.
Psalm 86:15

Have you ever done the infamous mosquito dance? You jump up from whatever you are doing with a very determined look on your face and clap your hands repeatedly in several directions. You then look around and see someone staring at you like you are crazy. With a triumphant glow, you show the spectator the lifeless squashed blot on your palms by way of explanation. Perhaps you have caught yourself grinning from ear to ear when you are able to smash two flies with one devastating blow of your fly swatter.

When I think of how easy it is for me to execute my judgment and wrath to destroy the things that cause me aggravation, I cannot help but think of our wonderfully merciful God.

Time after time the Israelites murmured against God and committed wickedness and sin. God, for the sake of one, stayed His judgment and did not destroy the people.

I am very thankful that One stands in the gap for me. Jesus Christ pleads for my soul and is my advocate and intercessor.

Friend, are you saved by the precious blood of the Lamb? We are all worthy of unmerciful judgment. However, God has proved Himself to be full of compassion and mercy by providing a way of escape.

Willie Joe Oaks, Jr., Montezuma, GA

Bible Reading: Exodus 32
One Year Bible Reading Plan:
Matthew 6
Genesis 18, 19

It is of the Lord's mercies that we are not consumed.
—Lamentations 3:22

Life's Railway

Blessed be God which hath not turned away
my prayer nor his mercy from me.
Psalm 66:20

We were traveling by Amtrak, and one of the girls in our group, not having traveled much, often asked why we didn't get to see the engineer of the train. After completing our 2,500 mile journey, she mentioned again not having seen the engineer. "He brought us all this way, and I have not seen him, nor have I been able to thank him. Surely we owe him a thank you for bringing us safely to our destination."

Many times our train slowed down, and moments later another train whizzed by in the opposite direction on a short span of double track. If it were not for careful planning, we could have collided head on with another speeding train. Even though we knew that trains were coming in the opposite direction, we laid back at night and went to sleep in complete trust that our engineer would see us safely through.

Are we able in life's journey to sit back, fully trusting that God is in control of everything? Or are our lives filled with worries and the cares of this world?

As we were never able to see the engineer, so we cannot see God. We could not thank the engineer, but we can thank God for guiding and protecting us. Life's railway is full of dangers and snares. Without a faithful engineer, we would be destroyed by these obstacles. Second Thessalonians 3:3 says, "But the Lord is faithful, who shall stablish you and keep you from evil." We can rest in the assurance that God will keep this promise, and we can thank Him many times before we get to the end of our journey.

Ben Troyer, Baltic, OH

Bible Reading: John 20:1-18
One Year Bible Reading Plan:
Matthew 7
Genesis 20—22

If we worry, we don't trust; if we trust, we won't worry.

He Cares

Casting all your care upon him; for he careth for you.
1 Peter 5:7

Because of his Christian testimony and religious activities, David Klassen was being held in solitary confinement in the barrens of Siberia. One can easily understand his occasional periods of discouragement and loneliness.

One day, however, he was cheered in an unusual manner. When he received his meager bowl of soup, he discovered that a little leaf had found its way into his ration. He had already offered thanks for the food, but when he found the leaf, he immediately stood up and thanked the Lord again for this special little portion of His creation. It struck him that everything else in the prison was man-made, the iron doors, the bars, the walls, but God had made this little leaf and permitted it to be carried into the prison, where it served as a means of comfort and encouragement to a despairing prisoner.

When we cast our burdens upon the Lord, we acknowledge our frail humanity, and we trustingly submit our cares and concerns into the hands of the One who holds the future. No burden is too heavy for His divine understanding. No anxiety or problem is too complex for His keen discernment and ultimate solution. Remember, He cares!

Bible Reading: Psalm 27
One Year Bible Reading Plan:
Matthew 8
Genesis 23, 24

I look to Thee in every need,
And never look in vain;
I feel Thy strong and tender love,
And all is well again.
The thought of Thee is mightier far
Than sin and pain and sorrow are.
—_Samuel Longfellow, 1864_

Mahlon Gingerich, Millersburg, OH

Unnecessary cares of life can hinder your progress. Unload them!

Building on Christ

*For other foundation can no man lay than
that is laid, which is Jesus Christ.*
1 Corinthians 3:11

Recently, we replaced the floor in our living room. The old joists had rotted and were not supporting the floor properly. I thought of several comparisons between our house and our spiritual lives.

Having a place to put the new joists was essential for us. Placing them on the ground would not have worked. The floor may have looked fine at first, but after a heavy rain, or perhaps a freeze, the error would have been obvious.

Our foundation must be on Jesus Christ. Building our lives and expecting them to stand without Him is foolish! Sure, we can get by on our own for awhile, but the storms and extremes in life will be sure to tell what we are really standing on. Check your foundation. What is the basic element in your life that everything comes back to? Is Christ the motivating factor that causes you to believe and live as you do?

We need structure, too. We could not cut, place, and nail our joists wherever and however we wanted to. To best support the floor, and withstand lots of foot traffic, the joists must be placed according to the building code.

Again, I thought of the need for structure in my life. I cannot simply think, respond, or act as I want. God has put laws into motion. These laws, when followed, help me endure the tests of time, temptation, and the degeneration of man.

The structures God places in our lives, homes, and churches are not hindrances. Rather, God uses those structures to help us continue to build on the foundation—Jesus Christ.

Michael Webb, Grabill, IN

Bible Reading: 1 Corinthians 3
One Year Bible Reading Plan:
   Matthew 9:1–17
   Genesis 25, 26

True freedom is not having our own way.

In This Day Rejoice!

This is the day which the Lord hath made;
we will rejoice and be glad in it.
Psalm 118:24

The day dawns bright and clear with a cloudless sky. The sun chases away the early morning chill, and its pleasant rays gently warm us and bring a sense of cheer. Birds sing; cattle graze contentedly in the meadows; children play on the soft green grass amidst the trees, while a soft breeze whispers through a leafy canopy overhead. Somehow our key verse seems a perfect quote on a day like this. "Just splendid!" we say.

Then follows a day when not a ray of sunshine penetrates the thick clouds that hang over the mountains and valley. A cold rain falls most of the day, and mid-afternoon seems more like evening. A sense of gloom permeates the atmosphere. Somehow, our verse just doesn't seem to fit this day as well. However, let's take a closer look!

The Psalmist says the Lord is his strength and song and has become his salvation. He speaks of the gate of the Lord being opened to the righteous, and he recalls the day when the rejected stone became the head stone of the corner! Yes, in this day rejoice! It was a wonderful day of salvation when the doors were swung wide open to "whosoever will." Those who sat in darkness saw a great light, and the blind were made to see. Yes, praise be to God for His unspeakable gift of salvation, which delivers us from guilt and condemnation! Praise Him that His grace is sufficient for us poor failing mortals. Yes, in this day rejoice! Then we shall have cause to rejoice in every other day, whether it contains sun or shadow.

Bible Reading: Psalm 118:14-29
One Year Bible Reading Plan:
Matthew 9:18–38
Genesis 27, 28

David Keeney, Waynesboro, VA

The presence of God can transform prisons into palaces.

Lesson From a Spider

And we know that all things work together for good
to them that love God, to them who are the called
according to his purpose.
Romans 8:28

This morning we awoke to rain accompanied by high wind. Pulling the curtain back to get a view, I discovered that a beautiful black and yellow garden spider had woven its web on the outside window frame. With the glass in between, I watched it for a moment. It seemed unconcerned about the storm, sitting motionless, clinging to its swinging web.

When there was a lull in the wind, it began to repair and enlarge its handiwork, then again ceased as the wind returned.

May we take a lesson from this frail creature. We, too, cling to the fragile web of life and are beset at times with the tempests of trials and discouragement. Sometimes, it seems as though the storm will be our ruin.

Instead of allowing our hearts to fill with fear and despair, let us look up to our heavenly Father with the confidence of a little child. Let us trust that He in His sovereignty knows what is best and patiently wait for the storms to pass by. Then we can calmly go about our work, as God directs.

Lord, You know what is best. Teach us to accept as for our good whatever You send. Help us not to allow circumstances to be our ruin, but rather to rest in Your promises that You will be with us to the end.

David Keeney, Waynesboro, VA

Bible Reading: Psalm 16
One Year Bible Reading Plan:
    Matthew 10:1–23
    Genesis 29, 30

God is in control!

God Is Faithful

Great is thy faithfulness.
Lamentations 3:23b

While driving to church one Sunday morning, I was feeling rather discouraged. As I crested the hill, I noticed the gospel sign on a brother's mailbox post. It read: "God Is Faithful." Only three words, but, oh, what a message they contained! This message, reminding me that God is faithful and true, lifted my spirits and gave me fresh courage. He will keep and fulfill His promises to us.

We can look to faithful brethren for help and for an example. But they are only human. With time they may disappoint us. We remember those who once were faithful pillars in the church, brethren who cried out against sin and were seemingly infallible, yet they proved unfaithful.

But not so with our God. He is not made of flesh and blood as man is. He is not vulnerable to the temptations and snares of the devil. It is impossible for Him to let us down and disappoint us.

We can depend on Him. What He said thousands of years ago is still true today and will be throughout eternity. How would it be if we did not know whether God was going to be in the mood to help us or be with us tomorrow? Might he take a day off, and His grace be insufficient for our needs?

Praise God! Our Lord is not so! He is faithful, unchangeable, and dependable. Therefore, we can face tomorrow and whatever the future holds with a calm trust. We need not be of those whose hearts fail them for fear (Luke 21:26).

Bible Reading: Hebrews 6:9-20; 1 Corinthians 1:8, 9
One Year Bible Reading Plan:
Matthew 10:24–42
Genesis 31, 32

Mark Coblentz, Flemingsburg, KY

God never sends a burden to weigh us down
without offering his arm to lift us up.

January 14_____

Be Courageous

With him is an arm of flesh, but with us is the Lord
our God to help us, and to fight our battles.
2 Chronicles 32:8a

How often do we battle with circumstances in our lives instead of trusting God to work them out? We may face something that looks impossible, and we become discouraged. When we are facing battles there are certain things we need to do, and then, we need to commit it all to God, as the king of Judah did in today's Scripture reading.

When Hezekiah heard that the king of Assyria had come up to make war against the cities of Judah, he was not afraid or dismayed. On the contrary, he took counsel with his princes, then strengthened himself and built up the wall which was broken. He made weapons and shields, then he encouraged the people.

When we face the impossible or have a battle to fight, let us likewise seek counsel from a brother. Let us strengthen ourselves through God's Spirit in the inner man (Ephesians 3:16). We can do this by claiming God's promises. Let us build up that which was broken. If we have broken God's command or fallen short, let us restore that through repentance (1 John 1:9). Let us put on the whole armor of God for our warfare (Ephesians 6:11). We need also to give encouragement to others when they need it. Then we can rest assured that God will take care of it all. We don't have anything to fear during trials and battles. We can feel God's presence and experience growth in our spiritual lives.

Bible Reading: 2 Chronicles 32:1-22
One Year Bible Reading Plan: Matthew 11
Genesis 33—35

Joey Gingerich, Blanch, NC

Speak kind words, and you will hear kind echoes.

Give Me This Mountain

*Nay, in all these things we are more than conquerors
through him that loved us.*
Romans 8:37

Before my earth-dimmed vision rises a dark, formidable obstacle. Giants dwelling in its dark shadows are ready to thwart my meager attempts to conquer its heights. A mountain, a habit difficult to break, defeat in temptation, a strained relationship, physical sickness, pressing responsibilities, loneliness, sorrow upon sorrow. The list of the insurmountable woes of humanity goes on.

Listen to Caleb in opposition to an overwhelming majority say, "Let us go up at once, and possess it; for we are well able to overcome it." Caleb could see the brook Eschol, the huge clusters of grapes, the flowing milk and honey. Caleb does not fear the giants living there: "They are bread for us: their defense is departed from them, and the Lord is with us: fear them not." In his old age he courageously said, "Give me this mountain" — the domain of the giants.

Have ease and luxury influenced us to expect an easy spiritual journey? "And they overcame him by the blood of the Lamb" (Revelation 12:11a). "By the word of truth, by the power of God" (2 Corinthians 6:7a).

We have available the whole armor of God. We dare not avoid the enemy. "For we wrestle not against flesh and blood, but against principalities, against powers, against the rulers of the darkness of this world, against spiritual wickedness in high places" (Ephesians 6:12).

Let us go forth in the name of Christ conquering those dark mountains of sin. May we, like Caleb, refuse the way of least resistance.

As trials loom before us, let us say with Caleb, "The Lord is with us: fear them not."

Robert Nissley, Alpha, KY

Bible Reading: Numbers
14:1–10; Joshua 14:6–15
One Year Bible Reading Plan:
Matthew 12:1–21
Genesis 36, 37

---

*Must I be carried to the skies on flowery beds of ease,
while others fought to win the prize?*
—Isaac Watts, 1720

Rats Running Rampant

*In the day when God shall judge the secrets
of men by Jesus Christ according to my gospel.*
Romans 2:16

In the yellow glow of the lantern, a movement above me to my right caught my eye. I watched a bit and saw nothing. Then, I glimpsed it again. Rats! I suspected that there was one or so in the chicken house, but seven or eight? Warily, I fed the chickens and gathered the eggs, but rats were on my mind.

The next day, upon closer inspection, my eyes were opened. The evidence was everywhere. How could I have been so blind? I set out poison. They took it. Tray after tray disappeared. Now dead rats began to pile up. Finally, with a brother's help, I removed the barn and uncovered the underground tunnels and nests, killing rats as they appeared. We had won. Still, if someone would have told me before that 60 rats lived under that 8x12 mini-barn, I would hardly have believed them.

As I pondered the incident, I thought about sin in our lives. How often it is hidden in our hearts, and in the deep recesses of our minds. We think that we can fool others. They cannot see; they do not know. But hidden sin is finally irrepressible. Eventually, it will come to light. And then, what shame, what loss!

Let us be awake and alert to our own faults first of all and to the signs of laxness, discouragement, or bitterness in other's lives, before sin mushrooms to epidemic proportions. After all, God sees. He knows, and some day He will righteously judge and reveal the secrets of men's hearts. How much better to free ourselves today and experience the cleansing of the blood of Jesus Christ!

Bible Reading: Joshua 7
One Year Bible Reading Plan:
  Matthew 12:22–50
  Genesis 38—40

Raymond Fisher, Chuckey, TN

_____

The longer sin remains hidden, the uglier it becomes.

A Christian "Get Rich Quick" Plan

But godliness with contentment is great gain.
1 Timothy 6:6

Chain letters, sweepstakes, and the lottery entice people to become rich in a moment. As Christians we reject such enticements and choose to work honorably to sustain our families and provide for temporal needs.

A fellow believer once said to my dad, "If you want to get rich quick, just take a trip to Central America; you'll come back a rich man." Here is a "get rich quick" formula that no Rothschild can equal. 1) Surrender yourself to Christ and become an heir of eternal riches that render earth's treasures mere toys in comparison. 2) Invest in heavenly treasures through support of the church and sharing in the needs of others. 3) Count your blessings; there is always someone less fortunate than you. 4) Be a pilgrim and a stranger. Remember, pilgrims travel light; earthly riches are a burden. 5) Become actively involved with the needs of suffering humanity and join in the harvest of eternal souls. 6) Be at peace with God, your fellowman, and yourself. 7) Be willing to fill a servant's place; it will bring a rest to your soul that is priceless. Pride and peer pressure are miserable companions. Be yourself and seek only God's glory.

Bible Reading: Matthew 6:19–20
One Year Bible Reading Plan:
Matthew 13:1–32
Genesis 41

While this formula does little to increase your bank account or provide luxuries, you will be gathering riches untold for the kingdom. Best of all, you can take these along when you leave this world behind.

David Keeney, Waynesboro, VA

The best riches are poverties of desires.

21

One Small Kindness

In her tongue is the law of kindness.
Proverbs 31:26b

Actually, this title is a misnomer, for kindness is never small. Did not the Lord Himself take note of a cup of cold water given to some thirsty soul? Not only did He take note of it, but He also promised that this gesture of consideration for the needs of another would definitely be rewarded.

We were asked to provide lodging for a large family from northern Indiana on a certain evening. They were to have supper with kinfolks in the community, then come to our house for the night. However, because of mechanical problems with their van, they arrived much later than planned. My wife and I sat up and waited and waited. Finally, leaving a note that they and their driver could have the upstairs, we, with a guilty conscience, retired for the night.

They came late, and very early the next morning they left again. Their destination was a distant community where they were to have breakfast with relatives. And we, host and hostess, to our dismay, had guests in our home overnight and never got to meet them.

Later that day my wife had occasion to go upstairs, and when she came back down, she said, with a note of admiration in her voice, "They even took time to make their beds." Not only that, they left a nice thank you note expressing their appreciation. How nice, how very nice of them! Indeed the day was a little brighter for their kindness. I was reminded of the Hebrew writer's statement, "The less is blessed of the better."

For many people, kindness is to do good to them which do good to you. But the Lord says, "As we have therefore opportunity, let us do good unto all men" (Galatians 6:10).

Bible Reading: Matthew 5:38–48
One Year Bible Reading Plan:
Matthew 13:33–58
Genesis 42, 43

Jerry Yoder, Auburn, KY

Cultivating kindness is a most important part of your life.

Refreshment From the Lord

I will cause the shower to come down in his season.
Ezekiel 34:26b

Why is the picture in Joel 1 so gloomy? Why the commandment to sanctify a fast? Because the meat and drink offerings had been withheld from God. Why were they withheld? Maybe the people were serving other gods; maybe they had come up with another plan they thought was better; maybe they were careless.

We do not offer up meat and drink offerings, but we are commanded to offer up sacrifices to God. "Present your bodies a living sacrifice" (Romans 12:1). We are to sacrifice material things for the well-being of our brother: For "I am full . . . having received . . . a sacrifice" (Philippians 4:18). "But to do good and to communicate forget not; for with such sacrifices, God is well pleased" (Hebrews 13:16). "The four and twenty elders fell down before the Lamb, having every one of them harps, and golden vials full of odours, which are the prayers of saints" (Revelation 5:8). God longs for these sacrifices, and indeed, he deserves them.

Perhaps we also, in a spiritual sense, experience that barren and desolate feeling of drought sometimes. We may feel like something has been stolen from our Christian lives. Then we need to check on the activities at the altar of sacrifice in our hearts. What are we doing with those sacrifices that are specifically commanded in the Scriptures?

Today we live in a land of ease and plenty, in a land of casual Christianity. The temptations around us are subtle and alluring.

Bible Reading: Joel 1:9–20
One Year Bible Reading Plan:
Matthew 14:1–21
Genesis 44, 45

How would the prophet Joel fit into our circles? How well would he be accepted? Let us bring in the sacrifices so we can experience blessing and refreshment from the Lord.

Roger Rangai, Lott, TX

As the hart panteth after the water brooks,
so panteth my soul after thee, O God.
—Psalm 42:1

Riches

He that loveth silver shall not be satisfied with silver;
nor he that loveth abundance with increase; this is also vanity.
Ecclesiastes 5:10

Mr. Starling sits high in the old pear tree near the garden. He is quite proud of himself. He has the biggest nest on the farm. He owns the whole collection of sticks, hay, twine, paper, string, and feathers. Better yet, he has some offspring that have developed an excellent pair of lungs. He himself is quite adept at screeching. He considers himself owner of all local bird feeders and houses, and feels free to help himself wherever he wishes. He doesn't mind dirtying any machinery; why should he? That's his privilege.

As he sits pondering his great riches, a small window slides open, and the barrel of a gun slides out. Poof! A small bullet comes straight for his puffed-up chest. A second later he falls to the ground—a worthless heap of feathers that even a hungry cat refuses.

Are we like that starling? We operate contentedly, buying, selling, making gain, improving our homes, and providing luxuriously for personal satisfaction. "Oh, but the Lord intended for us to be happy on earth. We need to be good stewards," we say, as we sink into our padded recliners, look at the daily news, and sip our hot coffee. I can just hear the rich man in the Bible saying the same thing.

The Lord intended our gain to be used for people who are more needy than we. We are on the earth to establish heavenly riches, not earthly. We could die any moment. What will these things mean to us then?

Sure, we need to provide for our families, but we must draw the line between luxury and needs.

Where would we be if our beloved Jesus would have been too busy making money on His carpenter jobs to lay down His life for His friends?

> **Bible Reading:** Luke 16:19–31
> **One Year Bible Reading Plan:**
> Matthew 14:22-36
> Genesis 46–48

Edward Lambright, Campbell Hill, IL

In heaven, gold is merely pavement.

The Trees Clapped Their Hands

For ye shall go out with joy, and be led forth with peace:
the mountains and the hills shall break forth before you into
singing, and all the trees of the field shall clap their hands.
Isaiah 55:12

I listened to the songs in the night. There were crickets tirelessly keeping rhythm, katydids dialoguing their dids, and branches of tree frogs blessing the air with their harmonizing warbles. The air was vibrantly charged with the sound of God. I looked up into the heavens and gazed in wonder at the sparkling stars sprawled across the sky like salt forced out of a shaker. I marveled as the clouds like sheep with their too long wool in early spring crept upon the stars. The moon blushed down at me, then shyly crept behind the closest cloud. I looked into the face of God there in that light-sprinkled darkness.

I listened to Him in the awesome splendor of His glory. Slowly, like a lazy fog having nowhere else to go, the awareness of His glory settled upon me. The radiance of His love touching the earthly is a mystery. I listened to the night sounds around me, but did not worship the crickets, the katydids, or the tree frogs. I did not worship the moon or the gentle breeze. I worshiped the great I Am, the Creator of all, there in the darkness of the night filled with His presence. There was no music, nor people shouting praises, just the humble sounds of nature as God designed it. There was no movement, except a playful breeze teasing my hair. That gentle breeze moved the leaves in delight as they gently clapped their hands. God is honored as a little speck of human dust reverences Him here in this majestic universe. He looks at the crickets, the katydids, and the tree frogs, and calls them good. He looks at the frail creature called man and calls him very good.

Alvin Mast, Millersburg, OH

Bible Reading: Job 38
One Year Bible Reading Plan:
Matthew 15:1–20
Genesis 49, 50

The fool has said in his heart, there is no God.

Living Water

He that believeth on me, as the scripture hath said,
out of his belly shall flow rivers of living water.
John 7:38

I have been advised to walk for my health. I like to walk on a mountain road where there is no traffic. One of my favorite walks takes me by a spring coming out from under a large rock. Even in the driest weather, I have never seen this spring dry. It reminds me of the rock in the wilderness which gave water when the children of Israel were thirsty. This rock is a type of Christ, who gives spiritual water to those who thirst for Him.

In today's Bible reading Jesus speaks to the woman of Samaria whom He met at Jacob's well. In the conversation, Jesus tells her, "If you knew the gift of God, and who it is that asks you for a drink, you would ask Him and He would give you living water." The woman could not at this time understand what He meant by "living water." Neither could she understand when He told her that the water He gives would be in her a well of water springing up into everlasting life.

That living water which Jesus gives is still available today. The words Jesus spoke to the woman are still true today. The water that He gives shall be a well of water springing up into everlasting life.

Have you been to Jesus for a drink of that life-giving water?

Joe Kurtz, Belleville, PA

Bible Reading: John 4:1-24
One Year Bible Reading Plan:
  Matthew 15:21–39
  Exodus 1—3

Let him that is athirst come. And whosoever will,
let him take the water of life freely.
—Revelation 22:17

I Know Him

I am the good shepherd, and know my sheep, and am known of mine.
John 10:14

Recently a brother told me of a man whom he knew from another city. He spoke of the man, his family, his work, his home, and other details. At the conclusion of our conversation, I was shown a photograph of the man in question. "Oh, I know him!" I exclaimed. We worshiped at the same church many years ago and were involved in youth activities and Bible study groups together.

On reflection, I have concluded that my exclamation was inaccurate. "I knew him," would have been more accurate. Fifteen years have elapsed since I last met Alex. Much has changed. We have changed. Basically we are the same people, but there have been changes in our lives. Both of us are married with growing families, both a little heavier, one with hair tending to gray, the other with hair tending to disappear. I'm sure some of our ideas have changed also. I no longer know Alex, and Alex no longer knows me. Once, however, we did know each other.

Do we know the Lord as intimately today as we once did? Do we presently know Him, or can we only say that we once knew Him? What was the apostle's cry? "That I might know Him." Not that he might know about Him, or know of Him, but that he might know Him, personally.

Do we share this cry and this longing with Paul? Is this the hunger of our hearts? Is this what we are thirsting after? Are we earnestly striving to know Him as Lord and Savior? Oh, I pray so. Let each of us "lay aside every weight, and the sin which does so easily beset us, and let us run with patience the race that is set before us. Forgetting those things which are behind and reaching forth unto those things which are before," that we might all the better know Him.

Bible Reading: John 10:1–18
One Year Bible Reading Plan:
Matthew 16
Exodus 4—6

Peter McGrath, Victoria, Australia

To know Him is to love Him.

Smile!

A merry heart doeth good like a medicine:
but a broken spirit drieth the bones.
Proverbs 17:22

British scientists have found through research that happy thoughts and pleasant smells can boost your health, while bad thoughts and smells have the reverse effect. Scientists measured the production of the antibody immunoglobulin, which is found in saliva and protects against respiratory infections. It is increased by up to 60% when a person smiles and is happy. Smile! It does more than just increase your face value.

I have no idea what the research cost to come to this conclusion, but my mind immediately went to Proverbs 17:22. I find it interesting to see man studying our makeup and coming to conclusions that are recorded in Scripture.

A merry heart not only protects us from respiratory infections, but also from depression and a host of other afflictions. An anonymous writer put it this way: "Cheerfulness removes the rust from the mind, lubricates our inward machinery, and enables us to do work with fewer creaks and groans."

For some it seems to be so easy to laugh and smile. Of others, you wonder if they ever have known a happy moment. Which type of person do you enjoy being with the most? Are you trying to be that kind of person?

How can we have a merry heart? It begins in the mind. We need a renewed mind. Always having a merry heart does not mean we will never be sick, but it helps tremendously when we recognize that God is in control of our lives and knows what we are going through. What a testimony we are to others, when we rejoice in the Lord!

Mark Webb, Hicksville, OH

> **Bible Reading:** Proverbs 15:13–17
> **One Year Bible Reading Plan:**
> Matthew 17
> Exodus 7, 8

_____

Rejoice in the Lord alway, and again I say, rejoice.

The True Mark

For thus saith the LORD unto the house of Israel,
Seek ye me, and ye shall live.
Amos 5:4

The thermometer read twelve degrees on that crisp morning several years ago when I left for work. Arriving at the construction site, I decided to finish the last pieces of vinyl siding.

Cutting several pieces inside the house, I took them outside, where they soon turned brittle from the cold. Everything went well, until one of the last pieces. While nailing it, I had to be careful not to hit another piece in a tight corner.

With intense concentration, I started tapping the nail in, when "crack," my hammer hit the siding instead of the nail. Tearing it off, I tried another piece, only to have it happen again. Only then did I realize what the problem was. Instinct told my hand to strike where my eyes were focused. Snapping in the third piece, I now focused on the nail head only. With several sharp blows it was driven home.

During dangerous or difficult times in life, to focus on Christ is most imperative, but precious time is often wasted worrying about surrounding dangers. Help me, O Savior, in my journey home, to live by these words: "Trust in the Lord with all thine heart; and lean not unto thine own understanding. In all thy ways acknowledge him, and he shall direct thy paths" (Proverbs 3:5, 6).

To be sure, we need to be concerned about the dangers of this world, but let us not be overwhelmed by them. Let us remember that "God is our refuge and strength, a very present help in trouble. Therefore will not we fear, though the earth be removed, and though the mountains be carried into the midst of the sea" (Psalm 46:1, 2).

Bible Reading: Matthew
6:19-34
One Year Bible Reading Plan:
Matthew 18:1–20
Exodus 9, 10

Timothy Yoder, Cochranton, PA

Concenrate on the light at the end of the
tunnel, not on the surrounding darkness!

This One Thing I Do

*Brethren, I count not myself to have apprehended: but this one
thing I do, forgetting those things which are behind and reaching
forth unto those things which are before, I press toward the mark. . . .*
Philippians 3:13, 14

The carpenter set to his work with great zeal! At last, he was able to begin materializing the plans for his house! Much planning and deliberating had been done, until finally he caught the vision of how the completed structure should look. He then carefully counted the cost, and with the finished building in view, deemed it well worth the price. He paid careful attention to laying a good foundation, and now *progress* was the watchword.

All went well, until he discovered that he had sawn off his rafters too short. In dejection he exclaimed, "Might as well give it up; no use to go on after such a grave mistake!"

Before you call this man a fool, let's look again. We sometimes experience a restless, deliberating battle between the Spirit and our flesh. As the eye of faith sees the ends of the two roads, we conclude it is worth the cost to follow Christ. At the foot of His cross, we plead His mercy, and by His grace we become a new person. We set forth with zeal to do His bidding, but, alas! We do not go far before we make some grave mistakes. What do we do now? "No use to go on after such a big blunder!" the tempter suggests.

Then comes to mind Paul's comforting words, "Brothers, I don't count myself as one who has already attained or were already perfect, but this one thing I do, forgetting those things which are behind and reaching forth to those things which are before, I press toward the mark for the prize of the high calling of God in Christ Jesus." In our failures, let us cast ourselves again on God's mercy and there find grace to press on.

| Bible Reading: Philippians 3:8–16; 1 John 2:1-6 |
| One Year Bible Reading Plan: Matthew 18:21–35 / Exodus 11, 12 |

David Keeney, Waynesboro, VA

Failures are teachers when permitted to instruct.

Prepared Stones

And not only so, but we glory in tribulations also.
Romans 5:3a

In today's Bible reading text, we have part of the account of Solomon building the temple. First, he had to gather building materials. These building materials had to be prepared before they could be used.

Let us focus on the stones. Verse 17 says that the stones were great and costly, and verse 18 that they were prepared stones. In 1 Kings 6:7, we read that the stones were made ready before they were brought to the building site so that no sound of hammer, axe, or any tool of iron was heard in the house.

I think we can take a lesson from this account. As we yield ourselves to God, He is faithful to do His part in preparing us for heaven.

As Solomon's men shaped and prepared the stones, here and there a big chunk might have to be broken off; but for the most part, the stones were prepared one chip at a time. My own experience has been that I am more apt to respond improperly to the small things God sends my way than to major challenges.

If we do fail, let us not become discouraged. Remember, like costly stones, we are bought with a price—the precious blood of Christ. As we allow Him to cleanse us from our sins, God is faithful to do His work in our lives to prepare us for the time when no sound of hammer or tool will be heard. That is a time when we will be with Him in glory where there will be no trials and testings, and nothing that defileth or worketh abomination, or maketh a lie. Only those will be there who have their names written in the Lamb's book of life (Revelation 21:27).

Bible Reading: 1 Kings 5:13—6:7
One Year Bible Reading Plan:
Matthew 19:1–15
Exodus 13—15

Leon Yoder, Auburn, KY

Heaven is a prepared place for a prepared people.

Search and Find

Ask, and it shall be given you; seek, and ye shall find;
knock, and it shall be opened unto you.
Matthew 7:7

Search and you will find—if you search with perseverance the object you are looking for. We must have much courage, inspiration, and perseverance in order to obtain our desired object. However, we must also look in the right place for what we seek. We would not look for fish in the Sahara Desert, an apple on an orange tree, or a gold ring on a peasant.

The silver dollar-sized hummingbird nest can be found, provided you know where to look. The hummingbird prefers to build its nest in beechnut and maple trees, usually on the lowest branch overhanging a clearing, logging trail, road, or creek. If you know these facts, you have a good chance of finding a nest. The person who does not know what a hummingbird nest looks like could look at one and think it was another of those innumerable knots that are ever-present on branches.

How do we search for peace and joy in our Christian lives? Do we know the means of finding them, or do we miss opportunities because we do not recognize them? It can be a joy to show courtesy to others in small ways. How often do we miss the opportunity to compliment another, to help a needy person, or to give a warm smile? Do we meet those golden opportunities but pass them off as only another knot on the branch?

Peace and joy can be found if we search for them with perseverance. Let us know the means and search for them.

Harvey D. Yoder, Marion, MI

Bible Reading: Matthew 7:1-20
One Year Bible Reading Plan:
Matthew 19:16–30
Exodus 16—18

Better is it to search and fail than to fail to search.

God Incarnate

*Behold as the eyes of servants look unto the hand of their masters,
and as the eyes of a maiden unto the hand of her mistress, so our eyes
wait upon the LORD our God until that he have mercy upon us.*
Psalm 123:2

Would it be too much to say that ever since the ascension, Jesus has looked for other bodies in which to continue the life He lived on the earth? Would it be too much to say that the Church serves as an extension of His incarnation? Isn't that God's primary means of establishing His presence in the world? The Church is where God lives.

During Jesus' life on the earth, He brought healing, grace, and the good news of God's love to a few. The Church can now bring the same to all men. It might be easier to accept that God was incarnate in Jesus of Nazareth, than that He is in the people of our own church. Yet, according to God's Word, that is what we are to believe. Jesus did His part and then left. Now it is up to us.

One of the last parables that Jesus gave before His death is found in Matthew 25. In it He reminds us for the last time that we are to continue the work that He started. Would it not be easier to serve Jesus if we could only see Him? But what a surprise to learn that by tangible acts of love and kindness to people, we are actually serving God! Our focus must be on Jesus. Our delight is in doing His will.

Bible Reading: Matthew 25:31–46
One Year Bible Reading Plan:
Matthew 20:1–16
Exodus 19—21

Marvin Gingerich, Meadville, PA

But by love serve one another.

Manifestations of God's Grace

Grace be unto you.
1 Corinthians 1:3a

Have you experienced God's grace? Human attempts to fully explain this spiritual phenomenon are futile. The eternal treasures and divine mysteries of God's grace are hidden in His character. God planned that divine grace be experienced—not explained.

In our Bible reading text taken from 1 Corinthians, verse five indicates that grace has an enriching effect on our lives. Just suppose God did not enable us to teach and learn spiritual things. But through grace "ye are enriched by Him in all utterance and in all knowledge."

Verse six suggests that grace enables us to have ready a convincing testimony for everyone. Have you ever been surprised at the uncharacteristic boldness with which you spoke up for the Lord? Score one for God's grace. Conversely, if you struggle with speaking up for the Lord, let divine grace assume control.

According to verse seven, God's grace supplies us with everything necessary for Christian service "that ye come behind in no gift." The thrilling thought in this verse is that grace doesn't shortchange us in equipping us for service. "We can't afford it." "Our budget won't allow it." "We'll have to make do." Such discussions are never heard in the budget office of the Trinity.

Furthermore, though we are earthbound and naturally fear the unknown, grace enables us to anticipate "the coming of our Lord Jesus Christ." Through His grace we can remain faithful and be found blameless at His return.

> **Bible Reading:** 1 Corinthians 1:1–9; Titus 2:11–14
> **One Year Bible Reading Plan:** Matthew 20:17–34
> Exodus 22–24

Ken Kauffman, Falkville, AL

To the praise of the glory of his grace, wherein he hath made us accepted in the beloved.
—Ephesians 1:6

The Greatest Disappointment

_Jesus said unto him, If thou wilt be perfect, go and sell that
thou hast, and give to the poor, and thou shalt have
treasure in heaven: and come and follow me._
Matthew 19:21

People face many disappointments every day. Some are great,
and some are smaller. One of a man's greatest disappointments
comes when he gives up what he really wants for what he wants
right now. I really want to lose weight, but right now I am going to
eat this piece of chocolate cake. I really want to visit my sick neighbor, but it is such a nice day, I am going to work outside instead.
Perhaps you really would like to hand out tracts on a Sunday afternoon, yet a nap would feel so good.

Our Bible reading for today gives us an example of this. The
young ruler really wanted eternal life, but he wanted his possessions right now. That young man made a foolish choice. How often
do we shortchange ourselves in this same way?

Imagine how much your neighbor would have enjoyed a thirty
minute visit with you. Certainly, if one person would repent and
believe in Jesus Christ, it would be worth missing a nap! Many
people are searching for something to fill the void in their hearts
but have not heard about Jesus, simply because we are too busy to
tell them.

Bible Reading: Matthew
19:13-30
One Year Bible Reading Plan:
Matthew 21:1–22
Exodus 25, 26

Every day we must choose
how we will spend our time, and
every choice will affect us, and
those around us. If we follow
God's direction, He will never
fail to show us the best path.
May God richly bless you today
and evermore.

Matthew Miller, Sugarcreek, OH

_I desire to have both heaven and hell ever in my eye, while I
stand on this isthmus of life between two boundless oceans._

Caleb: Another Spirit

*As my strength was then, even so is my strength
now, for war, both to go out and to come in.*
Joshua 14:11b

The story of the twelve spies sent to the land of Canaan is very interesting. These twelve men spent forty days together in that land, and they all saw and experienced the same things. They brought back some of the bounty of the land, and all agreed that it was a land flowing with milk and honey.

But a division about the land of Canaan arose among the spies. Ten of the twelve men were certain that the inhabitants of Canaan were too many and too powerful for the Israelites to defeat. They feared the walled cities that would have to be conquered. They described the giants in the land, and how the spies were as grasshoppers in their sight.

In spite of the bad report of the ten spies, courageous Caleb tried to calm the people's fears and told them that they were well able to overcome all obstacles that might be in their way. That wasn't enough to convince the people, however. It grieved Caleb and Joshua so much that they both tore their clothes and defended God's position, but to no avail. The people would have stoned them had not the Lord intervened.

Has there been a time in your life when following the ten spies was the easiest course to take? Remember that those ten men all died in the wilderness, but Caleb and Joshua were allowed to go into the promised land. Numbers 14:24 tells us that Caleb followed God fully because he had another spirit. May we also fully follow God, as Caleb did, and make our way out of the wilderness and into the promised land.

Bible Reading: Numbers
14:17—15:10
One Year Bible Reading Plan:
Matthew 21:23-46
Exodus 27, 28

Terry Lester, Montezuma, GA

Who is on the Lord's side?

As the Heart Beats

As the hart panteth after the water brooks,
so panteth my soul after thee, O God.
Psalm 42:1

Paul uses "fellowship of the mystery," "principalities," "powers," "heavenly places," and "eternal purpose," as if we would readily understand such terms. He takes for granted that as believers in Christ we understand the wisdom of God in the most intimate things of God's heart.

The deer's thirst for water compelled him to find it, so he becomes familiar with the watering hole because of his frequent visits there. As we thirst for the water of life, we are compelled to find it. Once we find it, we become familiar with it because of our frequent visits there.

Though our hearts throb after God, we often crash into the wall of intellectual reasoning. After listening to God's tender message, the will is softened. Then we must tear down vain reasoning, so that the heart has a path to the heart of the One it desires. As we frequent the heart of God, we become familiar with Him. Paul understood the mystery to be revealed in the heart of God, and as he frequented His heart, he began to fellowship in it.

Let us allow our hearts to find the heart of God, for there is our dwelling place. As we frequent the heart of God, purpose will be burned into our lives, love will blossom and cast its radiant glory, and contentment will shine like a glistening diamond, for all to behold. Our frequent visits will produce joyous conversation, deliberate goodwill, and consistency of healthy desires. May our heavenly place become firmly rooted in the very heart of God. For this cause I bow my knees unto the Father of our Lord Jesus Christ.

Alvin Mast, Millersburg, OH

Bible Reading: Ephesians
3:1–14
One Year Bible Reading Plan:
Matthew 22:1–22
Exodus 29, 30

Walk quietly and hear the heart of God.

Follow the Gleam

*But if we walk in the light, as he is in the light,
we have fellowship one with another, and the blood
of Jesus Christ his Son cleanseth us from all sin.*
1 John 1:7

A visitor to the great annual flower exhibition in London saw that one of the prizes was taken by a magnificent bloom of a geranium in an old tin can. It was exhibited by a small child from an apartment building which had no garden. One of the judges asked the little girl about the success of her flower. She simply related that a lady had given her a slip from a geranium plant. Retrieving an old can from a trash barrel, she scraped off the dirt without and within, filled it with soil, and planted the slip in it. "Then," said the little girl, "in the morning I put it in the east window, and in the afternoon I removed it to the west window; I just keep it in the sun."

We all "walked in darkness" (Isaiah 9:2), like the can in the trash barrel, but Jesus has lifted us out of the "horrible pit." We must allow God to scrape off the dirt without and within ourselves and plant new life within. We must "fear [God's] name and then shall the Sun of righteousness arise with healing in his wings; and ye shall go forth, and grow up . . ." (Malachi 4:2).

Jude exhorts us to "keep ourselves in the love of God." God is the light and by following Him, we are made radiant. Others will then ask how this can be in such a dark world. Our answer should be in Jesus' own words, "I [Jesus] am come a light into the world, that whosoever believeth on me should not abide in darkness" (John 12:46).

Benuel Stoltzfus, Parkesburg, PA

Bible Reading: John 3:11-21
One Year Bible Reading Plan:
Matthew 22:23–46
Exodus 31—33

"He that followeth me . . . shall have the light of life."

The Power of God

Declare his glory among the heathen, his wonders among all people.
Psalm 96:3

"[There is] one God and Father of all, who is above all and through all, and in you all" (Ephesians 4:6). There is only one God, for He is above all else and He is the only one who dwells in you. He does not give what belongs to Him to anyone else. No one is like Him, for He is greater than all.

We heard thunder most of one night. Then, ominous clouds rolled in, dark and threatening, with lightning flashing all around. It was an awesome sight to behold. I went out into the thunder and lightning and the darkness. There I was—a feeble, frail, helpless human exposed to the awesome power of God. What could I, a mere man, do against such awesome power? I could do nothing against Him, so I acknowledged my frailty and lifted my hands toward heaven. I raised my voice there in the blackness and in the thunder of His presence and worshiped Him.

May our thoughts toward Him be pleasant thoughts. For in His power and in His presence one can only think of Him in such a manner. In His presence is fullness of glory, and that fullness is expressed toward us as far as the mind can comprehend. Let us stretch our minds in the magnificent revelation of His majesty. I desired to see His power in all of its glory, and He allowed me a glimpse of it as the lightning flashed all around me. The lightning and thunder stood alone in power. Nothing can equal it, adequately describe it, nor duplicate it. God stands alone in majesty, power, and glory. He is God. Amen.

Bible Reading: Psalm 96;
Job 37
One Year Bible Reading Plan:
Matthew 23:1–22
Exodus 34—36

Alvin Mast, Millersburg, OH

Man does what he can, and God what He will.

February 5

The Sacrifice of Praise

By him therefore let us offer the sacrifice of praise to God
continually, that is, the fruit of our lips giving thanks to his name.
Hebrews 13:15

In Old Testament times, there were various sacrifices required of the people by God. There were also voluntary sacrifices made. One required sacrifice was the sin offering to make an atonement for sin. A voluntary offering was the peace offering.

Today we no longer offer sacrifices for sin, because Jesus has made that sacrifice for us once for all. We are encouraged to offer the sacrifice of praise to God continually, giving thanks to His name.

Why consider praise to God a sacrifice? Is this not something that we just love to do, without being compelled? I think the reason may be because the tongue of man is inclined to speak things that are dishonest, unkind, or hurtful to others.

The tongue that praises God must sacrifice those carnal things in order to praise God acceptably. The heart that controls the tongue must be sacrificed along with the tongue. "But the tongue can no man tame, it is an unruly evil full of deadly poison" (James 3:8), "and the heart is deceitful above all things and desperately wicked: who can know it" (Jeremiah 17:9)?

When the heart and tongue are sacrificed to praise God continually, there is no time left for them to be used for anything else. If we could spend every minute of our lives and all of eternity in praising the Lord for the sacrifice He made for us, it would never pay for the gift of salvation that was so freely provided for all mankind.

Bible Reading: Hebrews 13:8–21
One Year Bible Reading Plan: Matthew 23:23–39
Exodus 37, 38

Alvin Coblentz, Carrollton, OH

When everything seems to be going wrong, try praising God!

The Great Commission

*Therefore said he unto them, The harvest truly is great,
but the labourers are few; pray ye therefore the Lord of the
harvest, that he would send forth labourers into his harvest.*
Luke 10:2

When Martin Luther set out on the work which shook the world, his friend Myconis told him, "I can best help where I am. I will remain and pray while you toil." He prayed day by day; but as he prayed, he became uncomfortable.

One night he had a dream. He dreamed that the Savior himself approached and showed him His hands and feet. He saw the fountain where he had been cleansed from sin. Then the Savior said, "Follow me." He took him to a lofty mountain and pointed eastward. Myconis saw a plain stretching away to the horizon. It was dotted with white sheep—thousands and thousands of them. One man was trying to shepherd them all. The man was Luther. The Savior pointed westward. Myconis saw a great field of corn. One reaper, lonely and exhausted, persisted in trying to harvest it all. Again Myconis recognized his friend Luther.

When Myconis awakened, he said, "It is not enough that I should pray. The sheep must be shepherded, and the fields must be reaped." He then went out and shared his friend's labors.

Bible Reading: Mark 16
One Year Bible Reading Plan:
Matthew 24:1–22
Exodus 39, 40

May God awaken in us a greater love for our fellow man as well as a greater compassion for a lost and dying world. May we go forth sharing in the labor of the harvest.

Melvin Yoder, Gambier, OH

Faith without works is dead.

Lives That Inspire

Let your light so shine before men, that they may see your
good works, and glorify your Father which is in heaven.
Matthew 5:16

We all notice people who have made a significant contribution to society. We tend to think of them as heroes. Secretly we admire them. We would like to have the same recognition. But it is a selfish desire to seek praise from men. God is asking us to have a much higher goal as we serve Him—living godly lives that inspire others to do the same. Not to bring glory to ourselves, but to Him who is worthy of all honor and praise. The life God has given us is not for self-glorification or self-gratification; it is meant to glorify God. If we secretly desire to draw attention to ourselves, we should think on Jesus Christ. In His life, Christ glorified the Father in heaven. There were no selfish motives hidden beneath His behavior. His constant focus was to draw people to the Father.

Let us refocus our lives in such a way that we will be known as people who glorify the Father in heaven. May we live lives that draw people to Christ, because they see quality fruit hanging on our "limbs." May they find fruit they can partake of and find satisfying. Can we say with the apostle Paul, "Be ye followers of me, even as I also am of Christ" (1 Corinthians 11:1)?

Bible Reading: 1 Peter 3
One Year Bible Reading Plan:
  Matthew 24:23–51
  Leviticus 1—3

Dennis Eash, Free Union, VA

Your life is an open book; what do men read?

God Uses Broken People

*The sacrifices of God are a broken spirit; a broken and a
contrite heart, O God, thou wilt not despise.*
Psalm 51:17

Some things are of little value to man unless they are broken.
Wheat cannot be made into bread unless it is broken. Food must be
broken down to release the energy it contains. Before God can use
people, they must be broken of their own will and be willing to be
used.

Throughout history we find examples of people who were useful to God once they were broken and willing.

Joseph trusted God and did not rebel against the circumstances
in which he was placed, and he was used to save his family and
Egypt from famine.

Paul was struck down in his tracks, on the way to Damascus,
by the One he was working so hard against. He became one of the
greatest evangelists the world has ever known.

Peter forsook the Jewish concept of uncleanness and obeyed
the call of God to help a group of Gentiles find the Savior.

Jesus Himself gave us the perfect example of a willing spirit,
aligning His will with the Father's to save a lost world from sin and
give it hope.

Are we willing to be used, to give ourselves so others can benefit? To be used of God, we must realize that we are nothing, and of
ourselves can do nothing. It is only as we totally deny ourselves
and give everything into the Master's hand that He is able to mold
and shape us for His glory. We may think that what we have to give
is not worth much, but we must remember that God can start with
nothing and make anything. We
must be available and take those
opportunities that He brings.
They may seem small, but there
is no telling how far the effects
may reach.

Bible Reading: Acts 10
One Year Bible Reading Plan:
Matthew 25:1–30
Leviticus 4—6

Galen Lengacher, Summersville, KY

The first lesson in Christ's school is self-denial.

The Exemplary Life

Let no man despise thy youth; but be thou an example
of the believers, in word, in conversation, in charity,
in spirit, in faith, in purity.
1 Timothy 4:12

We are either good or bad examples. Which kind of example are you?

What about our example as husbands and fathers? When we speak or act harshly toward our wives, at times right in front of our children, we fail to remember that some day our sons, too, will be fathers and husbands. They may then act the same way we have, or even worse. We will be partly to blame for the example we have given them.

How about our responses to our children? Sometimes they do things that really get under our skin. If we get angry and say unkind things and even sometimes discipline them in that state of mind, what kind of example is that?

How about on the work site, in the classroom, or away from Mom and Dad? When the bishop or deacon is not around, what kind of example do we set to those around us?

Can the world see Jesus when they look at our lives? Are we faithful in the spiritual fight: in word and in deed, in faith, and in charity?

Bible Reading: 1 Timothy 4
One Year Bible Reading Plan:
  Matthew 25:31–46
  Leviticus 7—9

Mark Meighn, Hattieville, Belize

We are a book. Others read us.

The Brevity of Life

So teach us to number our days, that we
may apply our hearts unto wisdom.
Psalm 90:12

When I was a child, time seemed to go so slowly. I could hardly wait to grow bigger and taller. When a new sibling was added to the family, I became well aware that "I'm much bigger than the baby!"

Some children can't wait to enter the first Sunday school class. Soon it's first grade in school, and next it's a growing anticipation to graduate.

The "growing pains" often continue through the adolescence and then slack off about age twenty to twenty-four. In many people's experience, the anxiety lessens when they enter into marriage. There comes a shift when family responsibilities mount, and twenty-four hours in a day seem too few to accomplish all we would like to accomplish. And so soon time just flies by. We hardly realize where it went.

My father talked that way. I have been doing so, and yes, my older sons and daughters are expressing themselves in like manner. An eighty-year-old with waning health once exclaimed, "I don't understand how I got old all of a sudden!"

Did you ever think about the duration of life prior to the flood in Noah's time? Some men lived to reach nine hundred and sixty years or more. Now our years are seventy to eighty.

A person who has lived eighty years has lived 960 months, not 960 years. Is it any wonder that time seems so swiftly to move us toward eternity?

Bible Reading: Genesis
5:18-27; Psalm 90:1-12
One Year Bible Reading Plan:
Matthew 26:1–19
Leviticus 10—12

The shadows are getting longer as we near the sunset of life. Let us do the work that God has assigned to us that we might finish our course with joy.

Willis Halteman, Carlisle, PA

_____

What we have to do, let's do quickly, for life is short.

The Ego Trip

For if a man think himself to be something,
when he is nothing, he deceiveth himself.
Galatians 6:3

The Ohio Department of Education used to run eighth grade Scholarship Tests when I went to school. As I recall, it was a pretty important event for us eighth graders, and we put forth extensive effort to make a decent score.

I had practically forgotten about this, until I recently found a certificate of award in my files, which I had received back in 1964. I pulled it out and proceeded to read it aloud to my family. The certificate stated that I had placed 21st in our county for this special test. When I finished reading, my daughter promptly took the wind out of my sails by asking, "How many eighth graders were there, twenty-two?"

You know, it's so easy to fall into the self-inflated "ego trap." Unthinkingly, we present a view or relate experiences which really prove no other point than self-glorification. Oh, no, we wouldn't like that term. Perhaps we just got carried away relating a story about what we did in our younger days. Do we enjoy the attention we get by imitating someone, or criticizing their shortcomings? Others may have a tendency to elaborate on their unique understanding of certain Scriptures, and so on. What you are saying isn't all that bad, but the end result is self-glorification.

It's easy to recognize these subtle characteristics in someone else, but with a little realistic effort, we can see our own tendencies and take a lesson from this observation. We can deflate our own balloon by meditating on the key verse and similar ones. May this condition us so that we are not even "desirous of vain glory."

Bible Reading: Proverbs 16:1–26
One Year Bible Reading Plan:
Matthew 26:20–54
Leviticus 13

Mahlon Gingerich, Millersburg, OH

_____

The hardest secret for a man to keep is his opinion of himself.

46

Take Correction

Reprove not a scorner, lest he hate thee: rebuke a wise man, and
he will love thee. Give instruction to a wise man, and he will be
yet wiser: teach a just man, and he will increase in learning.
Proverbs 9:8, 9

There is one thing we can do to accelerate our spiritual growth more than almost any other thing: learn to take correction from the Bible, the Spirit of God, and from His people.

This may be hard for us to do. When the preacher gets up and preaches about something we already know, some aspect of life we have already submitted to the Lord, or something that we have experienced that has brought us great joy and peace of heart, then we think he is great. We appreciate him because he makes us feel comfortable. But the moment he stands up and begins to preach about something we are doing wrong, we take offense.

God says that is foolish! He says in Proverbs 1:7 only fools strike out at or despise correction. We should not be like that. When our minister or anyone else in the body of Christ has a word of correction for us, we should receive it gratefully.

We should appreciate it when some wise person points out some of our mistakes. Instead of reacting, we need to examine our motives and make corrections where necessary to get our lives in line with the Word of God.

It may not be easy to take correction. But if we will make up our minds to take correction and remain teachable, we will be able to grow in spiritual things much more quickly.

Do we believe our ways are best, and we have all the answers? If we think we have already "arrived," we most certainly will not keep going on. Let us remember that the next time someone corrects us. Let us love that person and thank him for speeding along our spiritual progress.

"Then shalt thou walk in thy way safely, and thy foot shall not stumble" (Proverbs 3:23).

Daniel Mast, Apple Creek, OH

Bible Reading: Proverbs 3:1–24
One Year Bible Reading Plan:
  Matthew 26:55–75
  Leviticus 14

Direction is a matter of fact; ideas are a matter of opinion.

The Fountain of Youth

*For which cause we faint not; but though our outward man
perish, yet the inward man is renewed day by day.*
2 Corinthians 4:16

Many of us who are middle aged or senior have secretly wished to be a few years younger again. Our aches and pains are a little more persistent, and our pace has slowed down considerably. We are sometimes even slightly insulted when someone guesses us to be older than we are. We cherish the thought of being young and capable.

This mentality is probably as old as time. In the early 16th century, explorers in Spain heard many wonderful stories about the new world, which is now America. A Spanish sailor name Juan Ponce de Leon believed the story about a wonderful fountain whose water could make people young again. In 1513 he sailed off to find this Fountain of Youth. It took many weeks to sail the vast Atlantic. Many more weeks were spent stalking and searching the land, which is now Florida. Of course, all the searching was in vain. Ponce de Leon never found these magic waters.

No, we will never find a magic formula to keep our bodies from aging. But the Bible tells us that though our outward man perishes, yet the inward man is renewed day by day. The formula to renewing the inward man is no secret. It is not a bit of magic. It is simply keeping the inward man nourished daily with God's Word of truth.

Yes, there is a "fountain of youth" for the inward man. God satisfies the mouth with good things, so that youth is renewed like an eagle's (Psalm 103:5). "For with thee is the fountain of life: in thy light shall we see light" (Psalm 36:9). "The law of the wise is the fountain of life, to depart from the snares of death" (Proverbs 13:14).

When we come to the cross at Calvary, we can experience the fountain of grace. We will then rejoice as the inner man is renewed, and we will be less concerned with the aging process and the perishing of the outward man.

> **Bible Reading:** 2 Corinthians 4
> **One Year Bible Reading Plan:**
> Matthew 27:1–31
> Leviticus 15—17

Ben Troyer, Baltie, OH

Age is like love; it cannot be hidden.

Closed Hearts

_And saith unto them, My soul is exceeding sorrowful
unto death: tarry ye here, and watch._
Mark 14:34

We were traveling home from Pennsylvania after attending a seminar on counseling. On the way home, we passed a restaurant with many large red hearts in the windows. They were decorations for Valentine's Day. One large heart was hanging on the door. Above this heart was a sign that said, "Closed." Immediately, I thought, "Closed Hearts!"

When we do not feel what others are feeling to the point that it moves us to action, we have closed hearts. If we feel justified that we wrote out a check to feed the hungry but fail to be sensitive to their real needs, we have closed hearts. When we tell others that we feel for those who are sorrowing but do not go and weep with them, we have closed hearts. If we do not rejoice with our brother when he is rejoicing, we have closed hearts. When someone fails, and we sit back thinking, "I told you so," it indicates a closed heart. Knowing of a need a brother or sister has, and hoping they won't ask me for help, shows a closed heart.

Opening our hearts to others makes us vulnerable to rejection and betrayal. However, God desires that we show compassion, forgiveness, and love as Christ did. Christ opened His heart to Peter, even after Peter denied that he even knew Him! May God enable us to open our hearts to the people He brings our way! Let us even go out of our way to help meet the genuine needs of the people in our churches and communities.

Bible Reading: 2 Corinthians
1:3–12; 2:1–5
One Year Bible Reading Plan:
Matthew 27:32–66
Leviticus 18, 19

What sign is above my heart? Open or Closed?

Mark Webb, Aroda, VA

Lord, let me see the people!

Fallen Trees

For there is nothing covered, that shall not be revealed;
neither hid, that shall not be known.
Luke 12:2

During a recent storm in our area, we had very high winds. We didn't realize the severity of the storm until we surveyed some of the damage it had done. A few people lost their roofs, an empty grain bin was overturned, and a semi-truck was blown over. It was an amazing sight to see all of the limbs and even large trees that had been felled by the wind. Trees that had stood tall and strong for decades were now lying split and splintered on roads and front lawns.

As I observed the trees, I noticed that almost all of them were rotten or decaying in the center. From the outside they looked like healthy trees. Before the storm split them open for all to see, no one would have guessed that there was anything wrong with them. But then came the test and revealed what was inside.

Jesus rebuked the scribes and Pharisees and called them hypocrites because, although they appeared righteous, they were corrupt inside.

What about you and me? How deep does my Christianity go? Is it just an outward thing that I do to impress others? If that is all the further it goes, I will be just like those trees that had no inner strength to stand when the storm came.

We need the kind of experience that Paul had. Even though his outward man took a beating—troubled, perplexed, persecuted, and cast down, this was his testimony: "For which cause we faint not: but though our outward man perish, yet the inward man is renewed day by day" (2 Corinthians 4:16). Is this your testimony? It can be.

Jeff Martin, Hicksville, OH

> **Bible Reading:** Luke 11:35—12:2
> **One Year Bible Reading Plan:**
> Matthew 28
> Leviticus 20, 21

What will the storms of life reveal about you?

Thinkest Thou That I Cannot?

*But put ye on the Lord Jesus Christ, and make not
provision for the flesh, to fulfill the lusts thereof.*
Romans 13:14

"Thinkest thou that I cannot?" These words of Jesus in Matthew 26:53 provoke deep feelings within us. Jesus plainly stated that there were things that He could do while living on earth that He would not do. "Thinkest thou that I cannot," is a blessed statement of testimony to us. It is a great example for us to follow. If He would have done what He had the ability to do, the Scriptures would not have been fulfilled.

How often we miss the will of God by engaging our natural ability rather than the faith which works by love. Ability is as close to us as the flesh, but faith is as close as God. We dare not do everything we are capable of lest we bare the arm of flesh, and the shield of faith fall by the wayside. We must remember that if we strive for masteries in the kingdom of God, we must do it legally (2 Timothy 2:5). Illegal activity in the kingdom of God brings dire consequences, which we can ill afford to experience. I may be able to persuade people to see things my way, but should I? I may be able to buy it, but is it approved by God? I may be able to beat him, but is it pleasing to the Father (1 Corinthians 10:23)?

The ability to accomplish anything must be the result of a moving by the Holy Spirit according to Hebrews 11:6. Natural ability without this motivation is like the noise of steel banging on steel (1 Corinthians 13:1-3). Yes, we may have the ability, but are we strong enough to harness that ability so God can steer it? Jesus did it, and Paul did it, but what about us?

Bible Reading:
Romans 14:7–18
One Year Bible Reading Plan:
Mark 1:1–22
Leviticus 22, 23

Alvin Mast, Millersburg, OH

*The greatest strength is not to do what we can,
but to not do what we should not.*

A Sermon Lived

Thus did Noah; according to all that
God commanded him, so did he.
Genesis 6:22

One picture is worth a thousand words! How true. It is better yet to see the reality with our own eyes. A story can be written ever so true to life, with vivid, descriptive words. Yet nothing sends it home as much as if the reader has been there or seen it.

One sermon lived is worth a thousand preached! A preacher may speak ever so eloquently, and with fiery zeal, yet nothing sends it home as much as if the listener can say, "Indeed, he believes it, because he lives it!"

The Bible calls Noah a preacher of righteousness, and yet we do not have any of his sermons recorded for us.

But the sermon of Noah's living faith in the Word of God, which he preached for 120 years, spoke volumes. Every day that the ark was under construction Noah lived out a dramatic sermon of judgment to come that surpassed that of the most gifted orator.

Why? Because Noah lived out what he believed and taught by preparing the ark in exact obedience to God's direction.

How is it with us? We are called to be ambassadors in Christ's stead. We are the only gospel some people may ever read and the only sermon they may ever receive. Does our life speak of judgment to come, of living for eternity, and of laying up treasures in heaven? Or do the sermons we live have a hollow ring to them? The world desperately needs a sermon lived today!

> **Bible Reading:** Genesis 6:5–22; Hebrews 11:7
> **One Year Bible Reading Plan:**
> Mark 1:23–45
> Leviticus 24, 25

David Keeney, Waynesboro, VA

_____

One demonstration is worth a thousand lectures.

Uprooting the Sycamine Tree

_Jesus said unto him, If thou canst believe, all things
are possible to him that believeth._
Mark 9:23

The sycamine tree of the New Testament is the black mulberry.
Its edible fruit is similar to the fruit of fig trees. The root system of
a large sycamine tree is impossible to uproot, even by an experienced dozer operator.

Spring Valley Grocery was a small, simple but busy country
store. Brother Alvin, the owner, was enthusiastic and aggressive.
He deeply loved the souls of his employees and customers.

But Alvin noticed a definite problem at the store. Fruits and
groceries were mysteriously disappearing. Quietly he made it a
matter of earnest, fervent prayer and fasting. Though tried, he sincerely loved the soul of the unknown thief.

After some time, Alvin confronted and kindly rebuked an employee named Jay. Jay brokenly confessed stealing the groceries.
Alvin freely forgave him and rejoiced over the penitent sinner.

In the next month, Alvin confronted Jay three times for repeated
offenses. Jay confessed each time. By now Alvin realized that Jay
had a "sycamine tree" in his life. He began to doubt the sincerity of
Jay's confessions, yet he chose to discard those doubts and instead
pray, "Lord, increase my faith." Consistently Alvin prayed for Jay
and assured him of his love and forgiveness. Eventually, Jay gained
victory over this sin.

Through faith in the power of God, and a consistent spirit of
meekness and compassion toward an erring but penitent brother, sycamine trees of sin can be uprooted. Leaf, branch, stump, root, and all may be cast out.

Bible Reading: Luke 17:1–7;
Matthew 17:14–21
One Year Bible Reading Plan:
Mark 2
Leviticus 26, 27

David Stoltzfus, Spencer, WI

_God can mightily use a Christian who stays
cool in a hot place, and hot in a cool place._

53

What Am I Pursuing?

I press toward the mark for the prize
of the high calling of God in Christ Jesus.
Philippians 3:14

"Look at that dog!" my wife Joan exclaimed over the noise of the machinery. She was driving our small Massey tractor pulling a flat bed wagon, as I was running the skid loader to pick up the many round bales in the field.

I grinned and shook my head, rolling my eyes. Many times I had observed the same scene when Jethro, the farm dog, eagerly accompanied me to the fields. There he ran, with his head pointed to the sky and his mouth hanging open, frantically pursuing several small birds. If the birds flew too high, especially bigger birds, he simply chased their shadows. He did this for hours!

"If he keeps that up, he's going to have a heart attack!" Joan added further. "I know what you mean," I answered, "and yet, to my knowledge, Jethro has never once caught a bird, in spite of all his desperate attempts." As I went on to spear the next bale, my mind also went on. How many times are we like that?

Most of us have goals and ambitions. But maybe we should pause a few minutes to think about our pursuits. Do they have real purpose, such as living for the happiness of those around me? Am I pursuing God with all my heart, constantly striving to get in step with Him? Or am I like Jethro, vainly chasing something that I will never likely achieve?

The more time and energy we pour into nonessentials, the less time we have for more important things. It is so easy to get sidetracked by unimportant things in this fascinating world. Let us pursue worthwhile things!

Bible Reading: Philippians 3:10–21
One Year Bible Reading Plan:
Mark 3:1–21
Numbers 1, 2

Edward Brechbill, Chambersburg, PA

_____

Until the pain of staying the same exceeds
the pain of change, you will remain the same.

God's Rewards

*And everyone that hath forsaken houses, or brethren or sisters,
or father or mother, or wife, or children, or lands, for my name's sake,
shall receive an hundredfold, and shall inherit everlasting life.*
Matthew 19:29

Why do I serve? What is my motivation for writing, giving to the church, being a good father, and loving my wife and family? Put more bluntly, what do I expect for my efforts?

We ask the same question when we seek a job. How much money will I make? What are the benefits? What's in it for me? In today's passage, Peter asks Jesus the same question: "What then will there be for us?"

Jesus' answer tells what's in it for us when we serve God and His kingdom:

—Whatever we give up, we will receive a hundred times as much.

—We will inherit eternal life.

—Many who are first shall be last; the last shall be first.

These rewards are wonderful and generous. Do they motivate your service to God, or do you only think of how God will punish you if you don't serve Him?

We must daily ask the Lord to reveal to us our motivation for serving Him and to help us purify our reasons. Ask Him to help you accept the rewards promised in His Word, and not only to serve because you fear His punishment. Do you believe that God graciously promises not only eternal life because we have accepted Jesus as Lord and Savior, but also to give us a hundredfold more than what we gave up to serve Him?

Dale Hochstetler, Wolcottville, IN

**Bible Reading: Matthew
19:16–30
One Year Bible Reading Plan:**
Mark 3:22–35
Numbers 3, 4

Heaven: rewarded to those faithful in this life.

Devotion and Service

But one thing is needful; and Mary hath chosen that good part.
Luke 10:42a

Mary, Martha, and Lazarus, special friends of Jesus, lived in Bethany. Jesus always expected a welcome there, and when they had needs, they felt free to call on Jesus.

The sisters' personalities were different. Martha was a bustling person, determined to make a difference in life by what she did for others. It was her delight to get together a meal to serve her friends.

By contrast, Mary was a quiet, reserved person, content to leave the bustle to her sister and listen to Jesus. She loved to sit at His feet and listen to His gracious words.

Both sisters were admirable in their devotion to the Master in Luke 10. But when things did not happen as Martha thought they should, she became irked by what she thought was Mary's laziness. How could Mary sit there so placidly and leave Martha with such a load? In her perturbed spirit, she chided the Master: "Dost thou not care that my sister hath left me to serve alone?"

Jesus' answer gives us an insight into devotion. Devotion does not encumber us. It is not burdensome. If we allow our labor to trouble us, then we have lost the spirit of devotion that should fuel our service to the Lord. If we are worried about our work and begin to find fault with other's service, we have lost the love that is the heart of devotion.

Devotion needs to precede and accompany service. Service without devotion lacks the motivation that makes it acceptable to God. Devotion without service lacks that which makes it a blessing to others.

John 12 again highlights Mary's devotion and Martha's service, but this time, Martha's service is also coupled with devotion. May we learn the same.

Bible Reading: Luke 10:38–42; John 12:1–11
One Year Bible Reading Plan:
Mark 4:1–20
Numbers 5, 6

Delmar Eby, London, KY

Your life is God's gift to you;
what you do with it is your gift to God.

Let Your Light Shine

*Let your light so shine before men, that they may see your
good works, and glorify your Father which is in heaven.*
Matthew 5:16

You step into a dark room, flip the light switch . . . , and nothing happens. The room is still dark! What do you do first? You try to find the source of the problem! First, you check to see if the light is connected to the power source. Next, you check the bulb to make sure it is in working condition and secured tightly. If you have not found the problem by now, you begin to look for other things, like a short in the cord.

Spiritual life is a light. How well does your light work? Are you lighting the path for others, or is the world around still dark? You may ask, "But how do you expect little me to light such a big world?" We do not expect one street light to light up an entire city, do we? No, but when many street lights work together, each one lighting his little "world," the entire city is lit up. It is the same in our spiritual lives. If we each do our part, we can light up the world for Jesus!

Maybe sometimes we find that our light is not working properly. We need to take time to find the problem. Are we connected to the power source, Jesus Christ? A short could indicate a number of problems. Maybe our devotional life is lacking, or our prayer life, or the way we relate to others needs attention.

Let us be dependable lights for Jesus. With each person in his or her rightful place, lighting up his or her little world, the whole world can soon be aglow with the love of God.

Matthew Hochstetler, Woodburn, IN

Bible Reading: Matthew
5:13–16; Ephesians 5:8–14
One Year Bible Reading Plan:
Mark 4:21–41
Numbers 7

*I am only one—but I am one. I can't do everything—
but I can do something. What I can do, I ought
to do, and by God's grace, I shall do.*

Returned Missionaries

. . . and confessed that they were strangers
and pilgrims on the earth.
Hebrews 11:13b

Our definition of a returned missionary: Someone who has returned home after a term of missionary service in a foreign land. A good definition. But wait a minute! What is "home" and what is the "foreign land"?

We recently returned "home" from a term of missionary service in a "foreign land." That makes me a "returned missionary," right? But where is home? Yes, it is nice to be back where the language is not a struggle, and we are surrounded by friends and family. Yet this place which should feel like home, actually feels strange to me. It is strange to see ten-year-old children that I last knew to be eight years old. It is strange to see men with gray hair who should still have dark hair. It seems strange to walk into a store and speak English to the clerks, instead of Russian. Most of all, it seems strange to be away from our good friends on the other side of the world. This place that should feel like home, actually seems like a strange place. Where is home? It surely isn't on this old globe.

If this isn't home, then it must be a foreign land. That means I'm still a missionary in a foreign land and not a "returned" missionary at all.

Will we ever be returned missionaries? Yes, someday I will go home! I'll be there with Jesus, and there will be no more missionary work to do. Until then, we will continue to be missionaries—strangers and pilgrims in a foreign land. Join me in the journey.

> **Bible Reading:** Genesis
> 12:1–10; Hebrews 11:8–15
> **One Year Bible Reading Plan:**
> Mark 5:1-20
> Numbers 8—10

Henry Yoder, Clarkson, KY

I'm just nobody telling anybody about
Somebody who can save everybody.

Sheep or Goats?

And he shall separate them one from another,
as a shepherd divideth his sheep from the goats.
Matthew 25:32b

As a young boy, Matthew 25 irked me. We had goats at our place, and the Bible seemed to condemn them! But after growing up, I realized that Jesus' parable was a metaphor of the difference between eternal life and death.

Are we "sheep" so in tune with our Shepherd that the needs and misfortunes of others catch our attention quickly? Or are we being "goats," with time only for ourselves, simply too busy to notice the needs around us? Consider the needs mentioned in Matthew 25: giving food to those who find it difficult to provide their own; giving a drink to a thirsty worker; opening your home when lodging is needed; and donating clothing to those in need.

The last point brings it close home—visiting those in prison. There is a young man with whom I went to school, who recently, as a result of bad habits, was sent to a juvenile detention center. I have not yet taken the time to visit him. We can write letters to missionaries or those in voluntary service. If writing letters is not your talent, you can at least pray for them or send a box of things to them. The possibilities are endless.

It is very important, though, that we do these deeds with the attitude of those at the right hand of the Father. They were not concerned with receiving credit for their kindness. They were unselfish. An elder once said that perhaps one reason the Lord does not visit us with more glory is that then we would be tempted to touch it. May God bless you today as you, like a meek sheep, serve Christ by serving others.

Bible Reading: Matthew
25:31–46
One Year Bible Reading Plan:
Mark 5:21–43
Numbers 11—13

Timothy Yoder, Sarasota, FL

If the Lord is your Shepherd, then you are the Lord's sheep.
He has the right to shear you when He deems best,
and you have no right to bleat.

Flexibility

Love worketh no ill to his neighbor:
therefore love is the fulfilling of the law.
Romans 13:10

The alarm shatters the stillness of the night and wakens us to a new day. We rise and begin to prepare ourselves for the tasks that await us today. We begin by praying and reading God's Word. As we view our schedule for the day, we wonder how we will find time to fit in all the things we have planned.

We need flexibility — submitting our schedules and plans for the day to God's direction; learning to look at interruptions as God's appointments. Most of our schedules and plans can be prioritized; some of the things we have planned for the day may not be all that important, especially in the light of eternity.

Our world is overflowing with people who have needs. Jesus always took time to meet others' needs. Unless we recognize who our neighbors are, we will miss wonderful opportunities to serve the Lord. In some ways, the modern conveniences of our day have helped us to better meet the needs around the world. We learn of people's needs in other countries and easily travel to go and aid them. In other ways, conveniences hindered us from becoming involved in the needs of our next door neighbors. We are so busy that we overlook people. How flexible am I when I see someone stranded along the highway? Do I take time to listen to those who are hurting? Am I willing to take a meal to a shut-in? Remember to be flexible with the time God gives you today.

Mark Webb, Aroda, VA

Bible Reading: Luke 10:25–37
One Year Bible Reading Plan:
Mark 6:1–32
Numbers 14, 15

_____

Lord, may you make my appointments throughout this day!

Come to Seek and to Save

Are they not all ministering spirits, sent forth to minister
for them who shall be heirs of salvation?
Hebrews 1:14

In 1960, Roger Woodard became the first person to survive a plunge over Niagara Falls. That afternoon, he and a friend were boating above the falls, when their motor failed. A strong wave overturned the boat, throwing both into the swift water. Roger's friend vanished while Roger, wearing a life jacket, was swept over the falls. The tourist boat *Maid of the Mist* happened to be at the bottom of the falls. The captain heard Roger crying for help, and a life ring was thrown to him. Roger grabbed it and was hauled to safety. A year later, when he accepted Christ as his Savior he said, "I guess the Lord saved me the first time so I could be saved the second time."

God has the right to pass condemnation and judgment upon us because of our disobedience and sinful nature, even as He did during the time of Moses at the rebellion of Korah. He said, "Separate yourselves from this congregation that I may consume them in a moment" (Numbers 16:21).

But God, through Jesus Christ, has not dealt with us according to our sins and misdeeds. He has granted us much mercy and grace. He willingly sacrificed His only begotten Son. He sends His Spirit to work in our lives, His ministering angels watch over us, and the longsuffering of God waits for us to respond to Him.

Lord, help me today to be keenly aware of your protection, which I do not deserve. Help me to be more grateful, that I may escape the condemnation and judgment which I really deserve, because of your love and the sacrifice of your Son, Jesus Christ.

Bible Reading: Luke 19:1–23
One Year Bible Reading Plan:
Mark 7:14–23
Numbers 21, 22

Willard Hochstetler, Hicksville, OH

To be an heir of God one must be a child of God.
Is He still waiting to adopt us?

63

Power Source

I am the vine, ye are the branches . . .
for without me ye can do nothing.
John 15:5

One of the handiest items in my tool box is a cordless screwdriver. It is one of a new generation of power tools that renders obsolete the old fashioned wrist-wrenching labor of turning a screw by hand. Put the bit into the screw head, push a button, and the job gets done. There is only one drawback to this handy tool. It is totally dependent on an outside power source and must be charged regularly. Without a charger, it is an unusable tool.

The same is true of us. We need an outside power source if we are going to serve God effectively where He has placed us. Using the analogy of a vine and branches, Jesus told His disciples that without continual contact with Him, they would be ineffective and unproductive. We maintain our spiritual strength by spending time with Jesus. Our faith is renewed through prayer, praise, confession of sins, and obedience to the Word of God. We need regular times alone with the Lord, as well as continual renewal of our trust in Jesus throughout the day.

Let us never forget what Jesus told His disciples: "Without me you can do nothing." We need to spend time with Jesus, even though we have a busy schedule.

Bible Reading: John 15:1–17
One Year Bible Reading Plan:
Mark 7:24–37
Numbers 23, 24

William Miller, Middlebury, IN

Spending time with Christ makes you Christ-like.

The Value of One Soul

For the wages of sin is death; but the gift of God
is eternal life through Jesus Christ our Lord.
Romans 6:23

One day I met a one-armed, elderly man in an area where a mission would later become established. Lewis was offered Christian literature but rejected it furiously. He lived in a very modest dwelling by a mountain side. The heat from his wood-burning stove almost drove you backwards when you stepped into his room during the winter.

One day I asked Lewis about his missing arm. "Well," he said, "one night, when I was young and wild, I was stealing a ride on a freight train. While trying to hold on between two railroad cars, a sudden jolt caused me to loose my grip, and I fell down between the cars. I landed on the ties with my arm flung over the rail, and the wheel of the train severed it. I lay there as thirteen cars passed over me."

I pondered—"So close to death but still such hardness of heart, can it be?" Yes, it was real! We maintained our contact with this newly-found friend, and soon a small church was established close to his house. His stony heart began to soften. He attended church services and later received Christ and was baptized.

Lewis, a former cigarette smoker, developed physical problems. His larynx (voice box) became infected and had to be surgically removed, leaving him mute. Thereafter, if we couldn't read his lips, he communicated by pencil and paper.

Finally, Lewis was called home to his eternal reward. "Precious in the sight of the Lord is the death of his saints" (Psalm 116:15).

There are multitudes of souls in a condition similar to Lewis's. Years ago, I heard an evangelist say that an average of eighty-three souls per minute are going to Christ-less graves. What a staggering figure! Let us be busy seeking the lost while it is called today!

Bible Reading: John 1:29–51
One Year Bible Reading Plan:
Mark 8
Numbers 25—27

Willis Halteman, Carlisle, PA

We are either missionaries or a mission field.

March 2

Lost and Found

Rejoice with me; for I have found my sheep which was lost.
Luke 15:6b

Alex Herr waded slowly in the clear water of Pine Creek in northern Pennsylvania. He stopped occasionally to cast his fishing line, in hopes of catching a trout in the mountain stream. Suddenly an object on the pebbled creek bottom caught his eye. What at first appeared to be a holder for fishing hooks turned out to be a banking wallet. Upon opening it, he found it contained a number of hundreds and fifty dollar bills, plus personal checks.

Imagine the owner's surprise when Alex took the wallet to the enclosed address. The woman was overjoyed at the sight of what she thought was hopelessly lost. Her husband had taken the money to the bank, intending on the way back to meet his wife, who had taken a girl's group canoeing. However, the bank was closed, so he carried his wallet in his hip pocket, and it slipped out while he was canoeing.

We rejoice when lost valuables are recovered. How much more when precious souls that are hopelessly lost turn to the Lord and are gloriously saved! There is much joy in heaven when one sinner repents. Likewise, there ought to be much joy among believers throughout the household of faith. Truly, one of our greatest joys in heaven will be worshiping the Lord with the redeemed.

> **Bible Reading:** Luke 15
> **One Year Bible Reading Plan:**
> Mark 9:1–29
> Numbers 28, 29

Willis Martin, Wellsboro, PA

A soul gained is for eternity, but the whole world gained is only for a moment.

A Work for You

Meet for the Master's use, and prepared unto every good work.
2 Timothy 2:21b

When we look at others' talents and abilities, some of us may feel discouraged. We may feel that we are just not gifted as others are. What little we can do may not seem very important compared to the labors of a gifted preacher, a prolific writer, or a foreign missionary. Perhaps because of circumstances, we feel cramped in our service to God.

The Bible tells of a boy who had only five loaves and two fishes. How would one small lunch meet the great need of five thousand hungry people? But this lad gave what he had. When we dedicate to God what we have, He is able to use our little to do great things.

We may not be able to sing like Silas or preach like Paul, but God has a plan and purpose for each of our lives. He can use us as vessels for His glory. Surely, there are some ways in which we may be instrumental in touching someone's life or helping to lift the load of a weary fellow pilgrim. Have you considered writing a letter of encouragement, or visiting the lonely, reaching out to someone with a helping hand, or taking one of the many other opportunities available to show love and compassion? Do not forget the powerful ministry of intercessory prayer.

God has you and me here for such a time as this. He is more concerned about our faithfulness and commitment than our ability. Our behind-the-scenes service for Christ may go unnoticed by others, but God, who sees all, will not "forget your work and labor of love." Let us be faithful in our small corner. We will in due time hear the blessed words of our Master, "Well done, thou good and faithful servant, enter thou into the joy of thy Lord."

Mark Kropf, Cataldo, ID

Bible Reading: Matthew 25:14–46
One Year Bible Reading Plan:
Mark 9:30–50
Numbers 30, 31

Ready for service, lowly or great, ready to do His will.

Following Christ

And he saith unto him, Follow me.
And he arose, and followed him.
Matthew 9:9

What does it mean to be a disciple of Christ? He is not here with us in physical form. We cannot literally follow Jesus down the dusty paths of Galilee, as did the disciples of old. We do not usually hear His voice in an audible way, nor do we see Him with our natural eyes.

How then can we respond to Christ's call to "follow me"? Certainly it involves more than going to church, being baptized, treating people nice, or being a good neighbor. To follow Christ begins with a new birth and with turning from sin and receiving Christ as our personal Savior. We must fully surrender to Christ, making Him Lord of our lives in daily commitment.

To follow Christ involves obeying His commandments. Loving, devoted obedience and submission to God and His Word are evidences of true discipleship. Self must be denied and the world forsaken. We must take up the cross of Christ, thereby identifying our lives with His and bearing His reproach. We must have fellowship with the Lord in prayer as we sit at His feet and feed on His Word. A daily prayerful, reverent meditation and reading of the Scriptures brings us into a living encounter with the living Word.

Following Christ involves following His example and exemplifying His life. As we walk daily with our Savior, we should reflect the evidence of a Christ-controlled, Christ-centered life. As we abide in Him and He in us, fragrant fruit such a love, joy, peace, and meekness will radiate from our lives through His indwelling Spirit.

Bible Reading: Matthew 16
One Year Bible Reading Plan:
Mark 10:1–31
Numbers 32, 33

Mark Kropf, Cataldo, ID

Following Jesus is a pilgrim journey,
not a sight-seeing luxury tour.

Faith Without Works

Even so faith, if it hath not works, is dead, being alone.
James 2:17

Some years ago, four men attended a business meeting. The meeting ran late, and the men hurried to catch the train home. As they hurried through the depot, one of them bumped the table of a boy selling apples. The apples rolled in all directions, but the men hurried on to catch their train. Once on the train, one of them said to his companions, "Call my wife and tell her that I will be a few hours late. I must go back and make things right with that boy." Back at the depot, the man gathered up the apples, and noticed that some were damaged and could not be sold. As he apologized, and handed the boy twenty dollars, he noticed that the boy was blind. As the man walked away, the boy called after him, "Are you Jesus?"

Our Scripture reading reminds us that faith without works is dead. This man's faith produced works, which were evident to those around him.

Does my faith produce godly works? Do my words and actions draw attention to Jesus? Our presence should have a powerful influence on those around us. May we resolve with each passing day to become more Christlike.

Bible Reading: James 2:10–26
One Year Bible Reading Plan:
Mark 10:32–52
Numbers 34—36

Melvin L. Yoder, Gambier, OH

By their fruits you shall know them.

Interpersonal Relationships

And be ye kind one to another, tenderhearted, forgiving
one another, even as God for Christ's sake hath forgiven you.
Ephesians 4:32

The Bible gives us much instruction concerning interpersonal relationships. How we relate to others has a direct bearing on our relationship with God and even affects our eternal destiny.

God did not intend for us to live a hermit's life on some isolated mountain. It is God's plan that we interact with other people, living, working, and sharing with them in the joys and sorrows of life.

Our relationships with others can be among the greatest joys on earth—a foretaste of heaven. There is the close bond of loving friendships wherein flows a mutual exchange of trust, acceptance, and appreciation. There is the blessed fellowship with fellow believers and the beauty of harmonious home relationships. But we also may experience the sadness and stress of strained relationships due to misunderstandings, selfishness, or lack of open communication. We can be sure that God brings no one into our lives to whom we cannot respond in a loving, Christian way by His all-sufficient grace.

In today's reading, we discover two great priorities—loving God and loving our neighbor. It is on the foundation of loving God with all our heart, soul, and mind that we can truly love our neighbor as our self. The first step in solving any interpersonal relationship problem is to examine our own life before God. The Bible makes it clear that our relationship with God directly affects our relationships with our fellow men.

By God's grace our hearts can be free of bitterness, anger, resentment, and ill will. May love, forgiveness, kindness, forbearance, and meekness fill our hearts and control our responses. By God's help we can enjoy harmonious, peaceful relationships.

Bible Reading: Luke 10:25–42
One Year Bible Reading Plan:
Mark 11:1–19
Deuteronomy 1, 2

Mark Kropf, Cataldo, ID

Kindness is the oil that keeps the friction out of life.

Do I Really Love My Husband?

*Wives, submit yourselves unto your own husbands,
as it is fit in the Lord.*
Colossians 3:18

We have all heard about families in which the father abuses his authority. Operating as a dictator, the father controls, hurts, or neglects his family. "Wife and children submit!" is the motto he carries.

You may not be the wife of a dictator, but if you are a wife, you are the wife of an imperfect husband. When your husband's imperfection shines through, you may tend to lose your trust in him.

Your husband tells you he wants supper at 5:00 sharp, so you make sure you have it all ready for him. Five o'clock comes and goes, and he does not show up. You begin to feel frustration. The children become fussy, and one of them crawls on a chair, reaches up on the table, and pulls down a plate, which clatters to the floor. Your frustration rises a bit. Then the burnt aroma of hamburgers wafts from the kitchen. Your frustration rises another notch as you hurry to turn off the stove.

"Where is he?" Why does he not come? He is not being faithful in loving me." These and many more are the thoughts the tempter throws at you to get you to turn from loving and trusting your husband to doubting and harboring anger.

If you only love and submit to your husband when he loves as he should, you are no better than the publicans (see Matthew 5:46).

When your counter is full of dishes and he is buried in a book, the children are fussy as a result of being neglected by Dad, and you feel just plain neglected, rejected, and used, do you let your natural desires to rebel, blame, and accuse take hold? Or is your life lost in the love and power of Christ, in which you love with a zeal and submit with delight in spite of your husband's imperfections?

Marcus Troyer, Belle Center, OH

Bible Reading: Colossians 3:12–25; Romans 13:1–7
One Year Bible Reading Plan:
Mark 11:20–33
Deuteronomy 3, 4

A happy marriage is the union of two forgivers.

March 8

Do I Really Love My Wife?

Husbands, love your wives, and be not bitter against them.
Colossians 3:19

Throughout the New Testament we find statements about the importance of husbands loving their wives. The Scriptures seldom mention the need for wives to love their husbands. This points to the fact that husbands tend not to be as loving as they should be.

I have only been married for nine months, but already I understand that women as a rule are more sensitive than men. This first became clear to me when my wife made a bean salad that I had said I really liked. She made a nice big bowl of it. Near the end of the meal, I said, "It looks like we'll have bean salad for a while." My comment said to her, "I'm tired of bean salad already." I needed to more carefully consider my words.

Forgetting to give our wives a hug before leaving for work may say, "He doesn't love me anymore." Perhaps we forget because our mind is already on our work, but we must be careful to remember our wive's needs.

It is a challenge to walk in the footsteps of Jesus, giving my life to my wife as Jesus gave His for the Church. Impatience and frustration can creep in so easily and cause a wife to feel rejected and unloved. May our heart's desire and motive always be pure with love, so that our wives can trust us more deeply.

It is true that marriage gets better with age, but marrying and living happily ever after is a false concept.

Bible Reading: Ephesians 5:9–33
One Year Bible Reading Plan:
Mark 12:1–27
Deuteronomy 5—7

Marcus Troyer, Belle Center, OH

Bitterness leads to loneliness, but love leads to intimacy.

Are You Listening?

I love the Lord, because he hath heard my voice and my supplications.
Psalm 116:1

With the unrelenting cacophony of sound filling the world, is it any wonder that we have lost the art of listening? In our effort to preserve some degree of sanity, we have stopped our ears to the hawkers of the worldlings' wares: the music, merchandise, and services.

Because of this, our sense of hearing has become dull, if not deadened. It is only with genuine effort that we are able to hear what people say. But a good listener is blessed with the ability not only to hear, but also to understand.

It takes time and effort to listen. Often, we are not really listening, we're waiting our turn to talk.

The best listeners are those selfless individuals who really care about the other. They take the time to listen to the burden of the other's heart. Often they say very little, except an occasional h-m-m-m, or some other expression that lets the other know they have their undivided attention.

Oh how I love that person! He or she provides a relief valve for the troubles that press in on me. That listening ear has contributed to my mental well-being in a real way. Those dreadful giants—fear of the unknown, problems without answers, a completely helpless feeling—when presented to a listening ear, are exposed for what they are—figments of the imagination. Unexpressed, however, they retain their ability to overwhelm.

The nicest thing about being a listener, a really good one, is that it doesn't take someone special. Somehow, however, through the experience, you become someone special. Not because of who you are, but because of what you have done.

Jerry Yoder, Auburn, KY

> **Bible Reading:** Job 2:11—3:10
> **One Year Bible Reading Plan:**
> Mark 12:28–44
> Deuteronomy 8—10

Lend a man your ears, and you will open the door to his heart.

Be Yourself

Fear thou not; for I am with thee: be not dismayed; for I am thy God.
Isaiah 41:10a

You are sick of following the crowds. Your strength has been drained trying to keep up with your peers. Frustration attends as you try to do "what my friends expect of me."

Well, be yourself. Not to carry out a selfish agenda. But realize and accept that God has made you. Allow God to use your life for His glory.

"Why hast thou made me thus?" Many have felt this question rise within them at one time or another. I know I have. My looks leave much to be desired. In my background there are things I would rather forget. Some present situations are less than desirable.

But we must not question why God made us as we are. We must learn to live with ourselves. How do we achieve this? Realize that God made each one of us. Believe that God has a specific plan for your life. Submit your life to God's control and allow Him to lead you. As you abide in Him, He will give you grace daily to be yourself—God's way.

Being yourself involves much more than the world makes of it. They are on their own, floundering in sin, grasping for pleasures. Their paths become obscure and gains evaporate into nothing. Soon, all is gone, and they are left by themselves—despairing.

Thank God, it is not so with us! We are led by the Spirit of God. We are provided for out of His storehouses. As God leads, His will becomes plainer and our lives more full. When this life is over, we shall find complete fulfillment in being united with Christ. Thank God for the fulfillment we receive in living our lives His way!

Bible Reading: Isaiah 41
One Year Bible Reading Plan:
Mark 13:1–13
Deuteronomy 11—13

Josh Bechtel, Estacada, OR

A new heart creates a new life.

Who Will Serve?

For David, after he had served his own generation
by the will of God . . .
Acts 13:36a

Everyone was waiting expectantly for me. I had the ball, and the whole game hinged on my serve. In volleyball the game cannot be played unless the ball is served.

"David, after he had served his own generation by the will of God . . ." David knew that if you are going to get the ball rolling, someone has to serve; so he chose to serve. I can't think of a better thing for people to say about me after my death, than that I served my generation by the will of God.

"And Mary said, 'Behold the handmaid of the Lord.' " The mother of Jesus was blessed among women and highly favored by God (Luke 1:28, 42). She was not a supernatural woman to be worshiped, but she was blessed because she chose to serve her generation by the will of God. We, too, can be blessed by serving our generation by the will of God (Revelation 22:14). We are called the elect, the chosen of God, to serve in this generation. We are ambassadors, and it is our privilege to serve by the will of God.

Many people strive to serve their generation, but only a few serve by the will of God. Let us be faithful and bless our generation by the will of God. We can do nothing less, for on the one hand we are bound by duty, and on the other we are constrained by love.

When I served the ball, it greatly affected the game. Others joined in and contributed to the effort by being faithful to the rules of the game. Who will get the ball rolling? Let us serve; others will join in.

Alvin Mast, Millersburg, OH

> **Bible Reading:** 2 Corinthians 5
> **One Year Bible Reading Plan:**
> Mark 13:14–37
> Deuteronomy 14—16

He that is greatest among you shall be your servant.

March 12 _____

Identify With Your Target

Pleasant words are as a honeycomb,
sweet to the soul, and health to the bones.
Proverbs 16:24

There's a saying that goes something like this, don't judge another man until you have walked in his moccasins. We must learn to identify with a person, before we try to speak to him about needs in his life.

About a month before turkey season was to open in Pennsylvania, I started noticing billboards along the road. Each bore a picture of a turkey and said, "Identify your target before you shoot."

Often we judge people, or say things to them without knowing all the details of a situation. Our words, like arrows, go down into the innermost parts, wounding the victims, even possibly killing them spiritually.

Several years ago our Eastern Youth Fellowship Meeting's theme was "Don't Shoot the Wounded." How sad it is when there are people who have been already wounded by hardship, personal failure, or loss, yet Christians come along and throw additional barbs at them, driving the wounds deeper and deeper until they become so painful that the victim succumbs. If we learn to identify with the hurting or wounded, we will be more careful about what we say. We won't be guilty of shooting the wounded.

I asked an elderly lady why she had so many friends. She replied, "I taste my words before I let them pass through my lips." Let our speech be seasoned with the salt that preserves others, and not with the poison that wounds them.

Bible Reading: James 3:1–12
One Year Bible Reading Plan:
Mark 14:1–25
Deuteronomy 17—19

Joe Miller, Belleville, PA

_____

The kindly word that falls today may bear its fruit tomorrow.

The Separated Heart

_And be not conformed to this world: but be ye
transformed by the renewing of your mind._
Romans 12:2a

The world offers many things with which to fill our hearts. Too often, when we think of separation, we think of our lifestyle rather than our hearts. God would have us fill our hearts with Himself and His desires, allowing this to lead us into a lifestyle separated.

About half of the Netherlands lies below sea level. The building of dikes and the draining of sea-water to create usable land requires a lot of hard work. Once the Dutch get the water out, they have to keep the dikes in good repair and watch for leaks. Water that seeps in has to be pumped out. The Dutch have to keep in mind at all times that they are below sea level. Unless they continually watch and maintain the dikes, the sea will once again overcome them.

We are in the same situation. Our hearts are totally useless until the world is separated out by the atoning blood of Jesus and by God's Word. We must keep a sharp eye out for gaps in the dikes, which will cause a lack of separation from the world. If we allow gaps to grow in our spiritual dikes, the world will quickly fill our hearts. When our hearts are full of the things of this world, there is no room for God and His Word.

Bible Reading: Romans 12
One Year Bible Reading Plan:
Mark 14:26–50
Deuteromony 20—22

The challenge is always to remember that we are surrounded by the sea level of the world; and it takes continual maintenance to keep it out.

Jeff Carpenter, Kingston, ID

A separated life requires a God-filled heart.

Are You a Servant?

Not with eye service, as menpleasers; but as servants of
Christ, doing the will of God from the heart.
Ephesians 6:6

Joseph encountered envy and hatred with his brothers. His dreams predicted his future rise to greatness, but Joseph did not consider their importance or try to understand them, so he flaunted them before his family, including the brothers who already hated him.

The tension between them, and his brothers' anger continued to mount. Joseph was sold into slavery.

Joseph lacked discernment. One day he would exercise dominion over his brothers, but his actions proved that he wasn't ready for the job yet. He had yet to be prepared for the responsibility of leadership, and that preparation would come as he learned the role of a servant. Servant leadership requires discernment, sensitivity, and maturity.

This is true for husbands and wives, leaders in the church, and supervisors with employees. The cry in our generation is for leaders with servants' hearts.

Joseph had to develop the character of a leader through the lessons and experience of being a servant. The challenge for us is the same. Are we using our positions for ourselves, or are we allowing God to use us in our positions?

Bible Reading: Genesis 37
One Year Bible Reading Plan:
  Mark 14:51–72
  Deuteronomy 23—25

Lester Zehr, Grabill, IN

Service is love in overalls.

Compassion in Action

_But when he saw the multitudes, he was moved with
compassion on them, because they fainted, and were
scattered abroad, as sheep having no shepherd._
Matthew 9:36

People need compassion more than anything else. They need someone to reach out to them with the compassion of God.

Compassion is a deep yearning that responds to the needs of people. It is much deeper than sympathy. Sympathy can just sit around feeling sorry for people. Compassion must do something for them. It stands to reason that people who regularly enjoy fresh touches of love from the hand of God should in turn extend similar acts of grace and kindness to other people. We should be conduits of God's love.

Occasionally we receive touches of grace and compassion from God, but we forget to pass them on. We have received good gifts from Him: salvation, guidance, forgiveness, answered prayer, and sometimes, a miraculous provision in our lives. But we just absorb it all without passing it on to others. As a result, our compassion quotient drops.

You may ask, "How do I activate compassion within me?" Notice how much time Jesus spent alone with the Father. Whenever He encountered a need, He met it.

Bible Reading: Mark 6:32–56
One Year Bible Reading Plan:
Mark 15:1–26
Deuteronomy 26, 27

Jesus has sent His followers to touch a love-starved world with His compassion. If we don't do it, who will?

Daniel Mast, Orrville, OH

_Compassion heals people—both the ones
who give it and the ones who receive it._

Operation World

Then saith he unto his disciples, The harvest truly is
plenteous, but the labourers are few.
Matthew 9:37

Let's face it. If we are to remain faithful to God's calling, we are going to be in the battle called *Operation World*. Jesus died for the sins of the whole world. Are we satisfied with the old excuse that we need to build up for our future? You cannot even spell "Gospel" or "God" without spelling "Go" first. We must remember that we are not here for ourselves, but for the good of others. When I get discouraged, I usually find it is because I have forgotten to help others.

If we want to revolutionize the world, we will have to be better than the revolutionaries. Revolutionaries are often more persevering, dedicated, obedient, and more willing to lay down their lives for their cause than we are for Christ. Let us keep our feet upon the path and our eyes upon the goal, and we will have the true victory and reward. May we truly see the millions whose hearts are hungry and whose feet are headed for destruction.

Our first responsibility is to our immediate neighbors. If we cannot testify to them, we will not get far. Put your trust in God and be willing to speak for Him to all you meet along life's way.

> **Bible Reading:** Matthew 10
> **One Year Bible Reading Plan:**
> Mark 15:27–47
> Deuteronomy 28

Jerry Miller, Molalla, OR

_____

The fields are ripe for the harvest.

Today

For today I must abide at thy house.
Luke 19:5b

The Holy Ghost does not have to use many words to be understood. From our Bible reading in Hebrews 3:7, listen to the thoughts of God: "Today if ye will hear his voice." God is always today, and He dwells in the fullness of today.

God thinks and speaks to us today, for there may be no other day for us. Exhort one another. Edify one another; raise yourself up today, for Christ is coming back in that magnificent, noteworthy today. He is the historical Christ who inhabits eternity and dwells in our hearts today. He said, "Before Abraham was, I am." He is the Christ of today, of Whom we are made partakers if we hold the beginning of our confidence steadfast unto the end. He is now our confidence, our beginning, and our end. We are made one—we in Him since He is the Head, and we together in the body. We are made one body of His flesh and of His bones, if we hold fast the principle of our subsistence.

Think upon Him today. Meditate upon Him today; for today we must hear His voice. Do you have an evil heart of unbelief? Do you have an Israelite heart of stone as in the temptation? Do not despair. Recover yourself, for it is still today.

Today we will comfort the feeble minded, support the weak, and be patient toward all men. Today we can rest from our stubbornness, our selfishness, our greed, and lusts. Today we sit at the feet of Jesus because He has finished the work.

Bible Reading: Hebrews 3
One Year Bible Reading Plan:
Mark 16
Deuteronomy 29, 30

Alvin Mast, Millersburg, OH

What you put off today, you'll probably put off tomorrow too.

Loose Him and Let Him Go

Brethren, if a man be overtaken in a fault, ye which are
spiritual restore such an one in the spirit of meekness;
considering thyself lest thou also be tempted.
Galatians 6:1

Lazarus was dead. The sisters wondered why Jesus had not arrived in time to heal him. After a delay to draw attention and glory to God's miraculous power, Jesus finally did arrive. But it was too late. Too late by human standards, that is.

Jesus came and wept with the grieving family. How well He knew that the sisters did not understand!

They came to the grave, and Jesus commanded in a loud voice, "Lazarus, come forth!" Lazarus came forth from the grave, but he was still bound by his grave clothes.

Who loosened him? Jesus said, "Loose him, and let him go." Why did not Jesus unwind the clothes?

We also are lifeless. Jesus calls while we are yet dead in sin. We hear and stand up, for Jesus has given us spiritual life. But we are still bound in our grave clothes. We are helpless to remove them ourselves.

Do we see the new birth as a dramatic experience where our grave clothes are miraculously removed? Jesus is able, no doubt. But the people He's working with sometimes need help from their brethren to loosen their bands. This is growth—sanctification. We are truly and wholly justified through Jesus, but sanctification is the growing process whereby we become more Christlike. Without our brethren and ministry to direct us with God's holy Word and the Holy Spirit, sanctification will stay at a standstill.

One reason this is of extreme importance is that we can see where these needs are not supplied. The individual is still helplessly bound and cannot make progress. He may have experienced that very important step of accepting Christ, but without further aid, he will remain bound.

Jesus said, "Loose him." That command stands for you and me today.

John Hochstetler, Worthington, IN

Bible Reading: John 11:14–45
One Year Bible Reading Plan:
Luke 1:1–23
Deuteronomy 31, 32

Nothing is too hard for God.

Professor or Possessor?

So are the paths of all that forget God;
and the hypocrite's hope shall perish.
Job 8:13

"Just one more gallon, or even part of a gallon of paint, should finish this storage barn!" I thought, as I strode into my employer's shop to find more.

I found a can with the correct label and picked it up. Judging by its weight, it should be plenty to finish. I returned to my brush and pan.

Imagine my dismay when upon opening the can I found only an assortment of scrap! The can had all the outward appearances of the real thing. It was even the right weight, but inside were objects of little value.

Am I a possessor or merely a professor? Do I only appear to be a Christian in the eyes of men, or is my heart filled with the real thing—the indwelling presence of God?

The professor is concerned with what people think of him; the possessor with what God thinks. The professor wonders what his public image is; the possessor desires only to reflect the image of Christ. The professor needs to wear a mask and use fine convincing words. What miserable bondage! How much better to wait on God and let Him be our defense! What freedom to walk in the light, to be the person God knows and meant us to be, to acknowledge willingly our undoneness, to confess our faults and pray one for another, and to fill the servant's place!

Our ego may often be deflated, and our public image may at times be marred. But as God looks down into our hearts, He will see a broken heart, contrite and meet for the Master's use, instead of one He must reject, saying, "Thou hypocrite!"

David Keeney, Waynesboro, VA

Bible Reading: Job 8
One Year Bible Reading Plan:
Luke 1:24–56
Deuteronomy 33, 34

The empty wagon rattles the loudest.

*March 20*_____

Proud Flesh

Only by pride cometh contention.
Proverbs 13:10a

Some time ago as I was working, my wrench slipped and smashed my fingernail. As you might expect, I had a very painful finger the rest of the day. Gradually the pain subsided. By the third day it was gone. However, I noticed a small area where the skin was growing out over the nail. As time went on, this area grew and became puffed up. It did not really hurt unless I bumped it. As careful as I tried to be, it seemed I was always bumping that finger.

At our church we are blessed to have a brother who is a medical doctor. Brother Laverne often gets cornered for a bench-side consultation after church. When I showed him my finger, he said that the little puffed up painful area was called "proud flesh." H-m-m. Proud flesh. Puffed up. Very painful when bumped. Sounds familiar!

The Lord was telling me that this is how pride works in my life. It causes me to be easily offended. Someone may try to give me some good counsel or correct me, and Ouch! it hurts my pride!

The older I get, the more I realize that pride is one of my biggest problems. Why is it so hard to say "I'm sorry" or "I was wrong"? We often confess other sins in our lives, but how often have we heard anyone confess that they are proud? I guess we are too proud to admit it!

So, the next time someone bumps you a little, and you find that it causes a very sore spot, check to see if it might be a case of "proud flesh." If so, go to the Great Physician. Only He can give you a humble spirit instead of "proud flesh."

Jeff Martin, Hicksville, OH

| Bible Reading: Ezra 28:1–10; James 4:5–10 |
| **One Year Bible Reading Plan:** Luke 1:57–80 Joshua 1—3 |

Blessed are the meek—not the proud.

Foundation Inspection

_Therefore whosoever heareth these sayings of mine and
doeth them, I will liken him unto a wise man._
Matthew 7:24a

We are all familiar with the story of the wise man and the foolish man. The rock, which the wise man built upon, is Jesus Christ, our Rock of salvation. If our salvation is based on our church membership, our history or genealogy, or any basis other than the blood of Christ, we are building on sand; and our house will surely fall.

How do we respond when someone inspects our foundation? If someone questions our conversion, our trust and faith, or our motives, how do we respond? If we are rebuked for sin or an inconsistency in our life is revealed, what do we think?

When we are based on the Rock, Jesus Christ, we need not have any fear or resentment when we are inspected. We can welcome opportunities to share our belief. We will know that our foundation is solid and not be ashamed. We will gladly share our experiences, victories, or failures with fellow believers.

Our part in church activities can make our foundation look good. But what if someone probes a bit? If we become angry or upset, we must check our lives. When our foundation or motives are built on sand (carnal desires or human reasoning), we will become defensive or fearful of exposure. As a school teacher, I frequently encounter work poorly done. The pupil reveals whether his error was done in innocence or carelessness simply by his openness to correction.

Let us check our lives, inspect our foundations, and make corrections where necessary. Then we need not be ashamed if someone "digs" around our foundation.

Bible Reading: Ephesians 3
One Year Bible Reading Plan:
Luke 2:1–24
Joshua 4—6

Earl Beachy, Flat Rock, IL

We are building for eternity.

Talents

Moreover it is required in stewards, that a man be found faithful.
1 Corinthians 4:2

Some time ago I stopped at a fast-food restaurant. Along with my food I received a handful of coupons worth more than the food I had just purchased. Recently I found these coupons, unused, in the desk drawer. The expiration date indicated that these valuable coupons were now worthless. Had I used them, they would have been worth something, but since I stuck them into a drawer and forgot about them, they were worthless.

Did you know you have a talent? God has given every believer a talent (or gift), and to some he has given more. But many times we think that because someone else has more visible talents than we do, ours are not worth as much. If we hide our talents in a "drawer," never using them, they become worthless. But, if we exercise the talents God has given us, we can bring Him honor.

Notice in Jesus' parable that the second servant received the same blessing as the first, even though he did not gain as many talents. All the master required was faithfulness. God also requires us to be faithful in our use of the talents He has given us for His honor and glory. Let us be faithful with the responsibility He has given us.

> **Bible Reading:** Matthew 25:14–30
> **One Year Bible Reading Plan:** Luke 2:25–52
> Joshua 7, 8

Matthew Hochstetler, Woodburn, IN

_____

Invest your talents in God's retirement plan—it is out of this world.

Do We Take Time to Pray?

And whatsoever ye shall ask in my name, that will I do,
that the Father may be glorified in the Son.
If ye shall ask anything in my name, I will do it.
John 14:13, 14

I recently visited a good friend of mine who was feeling very ill. After a short visit, I departed without offering to pray for her. Even though her illness was not serious, later on that day I asked myself why I did not offer to pray for my sister. It bothered me so much that a few hours later I revisited her and ended the visit the way I should have the first time, with prayer. We often pray earnestly for someone only when their sickness appears to be terminal.

As a result of this incident, I was impressed by the thought of prayer as the Christian's most powerful weapon. We can call on God anytime, anywhere. Anything we ask according to His will, believing, we shall receive (Matthew 21:22). Why then are we afraid to ask? Is it a lack of faith in God? Are we using this weapon to its utmost capacity, or do we doubt God?

Let us remember that God's promises never fail. The only way we can fully understand how prayer works is to get deeply involved in it. There is a hymn that says prayer is the Christian's vital breath. Take a deep breath and inhale God's love toward you, and in return exhale your love toward others.

Bible Reading: Acts 16:16–32
One Year Bible Reading Plan:
Luke 3
Joshua 9, 10

Rupert Rodriguez, Belize City, Belize

He pleads for me . . . I'll ask of Him.

Considering Others

Thus saith the Lord of hosts; Consider your ways.
Haggai 1:7

My job of pouring footers brings me into contact with many excavators, most of whom do careless work. This in turn makes my work harder. However, I kept noticing the neatness and precision of one excavator. I finally called him to thank him for doing such good work. Then I asked him, "What do you do to get your employees to do such good work?" Troy Varney said this, "On rainy days we have meetings and discuss safety issues, and then we discuss ways we can make it easier for those who follow us."

This businessman's concern was an inspiration to me. Shouldn't this be my goal? Should it not be the goal of every child of God? Think of how nice it would be, if everyone had this concern for others. What would happen in our homes, schools, churches, and workplaces if this were the reality? Today's Scripture reading brings out the responsibilities of various people. If each does his part well, it makes life easier for someone else.

Take time personally or as a family to think of ways you can help someone else, instead of being a hindrance. Ask yourself: Do I make life pleasant for those who live and work with me? Do I have an understanding heart with those I relate to? Do I live my life with regard for others? Do others desire to follow after me?

Bible Reading: Colossians 3:17—4:6
One Year Bible Reading Plan:
Luke 4:1–32
Joshua 11—13

Duane Eash, Gambier, OH

Are you making it easy for yourself or for someone else?

Humility and Pride

For God resisteth the proud, and giveth grace to the humble.
1 Peter 5:5b

A lot of our youth seem to lack humility, and not only youth, but also older folks. Decisions are based on thoughts like, "What will others think of me?" and, "If he can have it; I can too." Such thoughts reveal pride that should not be part of a Christian's life. We try to draw attention to ourselves by our hairstyles and clothes, but true beauty comes from humility before God and men. Much disunity and strife in the church also originate in pride. We need to forget ourselves and to put God and others first.

We think of a superiority complex as stimulated by pride, and an inferiority complex as the absence of pride. But both focus on self. Humility puts self last.

Moses was a proud man who became humble. He killed the Egyptian because he figured he was the one to lead God's people! But God sent him into the desert for forty years. When God said, "I'm ready," Moses asked Him, "Who am I, that I should go unto Pharaoh?" Moses had learned humility.

Bible Reading: James 4:6–17
One Year Bible Reading Plan:
Luke 4:33–44
Joshua 14, 15

When we allow God to work in our lives, we will not focus on ourselves so much, but on others.

Jadon Yoder, Franklin, KY

Knowing God makes us humble;
knowing ourselves keeps us humble.

To Love the Fallen

And the greatest of these is charity.
1 Corinthians 13:13b

Recently I was visiting with a sister in my church, and in the course of the conversation she said, "In my younger years, I was with the wild group. We did things we shouldn't have done. But, you know, they accepted me for what I was."

Most of us have witnessed situations in which some members, youth, or children have behaved themselves in an unseemly manner.

What is our response to such situations? Do we avoid the offenders? Do we try to make them feel uncomfortable in our "godly" presence?

God hates sin, and so must His children. But God also loves and yearns for the souls of men. And so will His children. As children of God, we need to be a reflection of His love. Being mindful of the fact that God always loves us as we are, in spite of our shortcomings, we also must love our fellow men. God sent His Son to die for us, and He accepts us as we are. "Beloved, if God so loved us, we ought also to love one another."

It is worth noting the humility and acceptance Jacob showed toward his brother Esau, even though he himself had the birthright, was rich and powerful, and was blessed of God. Jacob not only accepted Esau, he gave him thousands of dollars worth of gifts, called himself "thy servant," and acknowledged Esau as "my lord." It was Jacob's love and humility that broke Esau's heart, not his disapproval of Esau's behavior. Let us win the fallen by showing them love—not only by reminding them of their fallen state.

Bible Reading: Genesis 33:1–15
One Year Bible Reading Plan:
Luke 5:1–16
Joshua 16—18

Earl Beachy, Flat Rock, IL

We may not love the sin, but we must love the sinner.

Our Children Need to Be Loved

*And he took them up in his arms, put his
hands upon them, and blessed them.*
Mark 10:16

In our frenzied society, it seems hard to take time for the really important things in life: wives and children and our devotion to God. Jesus tells us what our priorities should be: "But seek ye first the kingdom of God, and his righteousness: and all these things shall be added unto you."

Our children are really God's. He just lends them to us, that we might bring them up in the nurture and admonition of the Lord. That is kingdom work. To nurture our children is to help them develop right thinking. This takes time. One element missing in many children's lives is proper physical touch. In our key verse, we see that Jesus used appropriate touch with the children.

I vividly remember instances in my childhood, when the teacher belittled me in front of the class, or when the big boys mocked me. I went to my mother and told her about it. She would take me on her lap, give me a hug, and say, "I love you anyway." I am convinced that this helped me to understand and accept God's love.

Our children will view God in the same way that they view us as parents. We can tell our children that God is love, but they also need us to show them. "We teach some things by what we say, more things by what we do, but most lessons by what we are."

Bible Reading: Isaiah 40:3–11; Matthew 18:1–14
One Year Bible Reading Plan:
Luke 5:17–39
Joshua 19, 20

John Otto, Evart, MI

Do your children know they are loved?

Who Is My Neighbor?

Love worketh no ill to his neighbor;
therefore love is the fulfilling of the law.
Romans 13:10

The day arrived for the loggers to come. They pulled in with their big trucks and chain saws. The trees were identified and the work began.

My neighbor John came over to see how the work was progressing, for our properties met at the place we were working. The loggers wondered, "How about these trees that would be easiest to fell over onto John's land?"

John quickly replied, "No problem, you can even drive your truck back to load."

Similar instances came up. Finally, one of the loggers exclaimed, "How is this? It's not often that neighbors get along so well!" Jesus Christ makes the difference!

Who is my neighbor? Is it not anyone in need, to whom we can reach out and help? There are needs all about us. Let us especially be mindful of those needs close to us. Our wives, husbands, children, brothers, sisters, and parents all need our encouragement and support. At times a helping hand, or merely a listening ear, is all that is needed. Whatever it may be, let us deny ourselves of our own interests for the sake of maintaining a family circle where love abides. We also have brothers and sisters in Christ. We also need to practice self denial toward them.

Bible Reading: Luke 10:25–37
One Year Bible Reading Plan:
Luke 6:1-26
Joshua 21, 22

Leland Yoder, Linneus, MO

Being neighborly does not sacrifice godly principles.

Sharing the Gospel

Go ye therefore, and teach all nations.
Matthew 28:19a

As I look at the world around me today, I feel a great burden for those who do not know Christ. I want to do all that I can for those who are still lost in sin.

In our Bible reading today, Jesus commands us to spread the Gospel to all parts of the world. Have we told our friends and neighbors about God's love? Are we so concerned that we help and encourage those who have been called by God to give themselves in service for Him? Are we praying for those working in foreign lands and for those who are suffering for the sake of the Gospel?

The disciples were commanded to go to Jerusalem and wait for the Holy Spirit. After receiving the Holy Spirit, they went with power and boldness preaching the Gospel to everyone. God gave them power to cast out devils and heal people because they believed on Him.

We need to be out witnessing, trying to lead to Christ those who are lost. Jesus is returning! Let us pray and do all we can to bring others to a saving knowledge of Jesus Christ. A song writer says, "As long as just one soul is yet astray, Lord, weep through me." We should be concerned about those who have not yet given their hearts to God. Are you willing to allow God to speak through you and be a witness for Christ?

Bible Reading: Matthew 28:16–20; Mark 16:15-20
One Year Bible Reading Plan: Luke 6:27–49
Joshua 23, 24

Marlin Coblentz, Hicksville, OH

_____

Witnessing for Christ is the first step in leading others to Him.

Leaving the Comfort Zone

And everyone that hath forsaken houses, or brethren, . . .
for my name's sake, . . . shall inherit everlasting life.
Matthew 19:29

Man is a self-serving creature, best described by a sage who advised, "Get all you can, can all you get, then sit on the can." Ephesians affirms this miserly picture: "No man yet hateth his own flesh, but nourisheth and cherisheth it."

Our heavenly Father is aware of our selfish proclivity, and He has provided a remedy: death, the way of the cross. This cross business is not a one time ordeal. The cross is the avenue whereby we are ushered into His divine presence.

The Bible is a record of those who left the comfort zone voluntarily, and the Lord himself is our best example. To leave the comfort zone is an invitation extended to all ages. It has no social or racial barriers. It is, in fact, open to anyone who will listen. Hearing, however, is only the first step. There must be a response.

Abraham heard the call of God when he was 75 years old. His instructions were to leave the idolatrous society in which he was living. He left. He had faith in God, and he obeyed Him. These two responses are the keys that open the door from our comfort zone into eternal bliss.

Bible Reading: Matthew 19:16–30
One Year Bible Reading Plan: Luke 7:1–30
Judges 1, 2

Jerry Yoder, Auburn, KY

_____

Hammering tempers steel but crumbles putty.

Lazy Christians

*But whoso hath this world's good, and seeth his brother
have need, and shutteth up his bowels of compassion
from him, how dwelleth the love of God in him?*
1 John 3:17

Our faith in God should move us to respond out of love to the needs we see around us. However, we live in an age of worldwide communication. Into our homes come newsletters informing us of needs from all parts of the world. There are physical needs for food, clothing, and shelter. There are spiritual needs for salvation, Christian literature, and Bibles. What is the correct way to respond to these needs?

We must begin with prayer. A true sincere prayer takes work. To pray for a specific need instead of just mentioning the needs of the world in general terms requires more effort of us. However, the blessing of praying specifically strengthens our faith, as we see God answer our prayers. We miss this blessing when we pray only in general terms.

Do you remember the story of the group praying at a church meeting for a family that had a need? They asked one boy where his father was. Just then he pointed at a wagon coming up the road, and replied, "Here comes my father with the answer to our prayer." His father had a load of groceries for the family in need. A true genuine prayer will move us to action. How can I make a difference in even one of the needs that I am aware of? Let us do all we can to meet the physical and spiritual needs of others.

Bible Reading: James 2:14–26
One Year Bible Reading Plan:
Luke 7:31–50
Judges 3—5

Mark Webb, Hicksville, OH

*Let's say, "Be warmed and filled,"
and then take part in making it happen.*

95

April 1

Let God Guide

And thine ears shall hear a word behind thee,
saying, This is the way, walk ye in it.
Isaiah 30:21a

Have you ever stopped and wondered what really matters most in life? What would you say? Is it to be wealthy and well to do? To have a fine farm, a big business, or a late model vehicle? Am I seeking first the kingdom of God and His righteousness?

We are all sometimes tempted to seek first other things apart from God's will and righteousness, aren't we? May God help us to remember who we really are and where we are really going.

According to Ecclesiastes 5:10, earthly things can never satisfy. The devil wants us to believe that those things would make us happier, but circumstances should never determine whether or not we are a rejoicing people.

Let us commit our lives into the hands of the Almighty and be content with the way He orders our lives. He yearns to guide us in the ways of truth and righteousness. He did not leave us to grope in darkness, even if at times it seems like we do not know for sure which way He would have us go. What peace of mind to know God is leading! May God grant wisdom to each of His pilgrims on life's way today!

> **Bible Reading:** Judges 6:36–40;
> Matthew 6:19–34
> **One Year Bible Reading Plan:**
> Luke 8:1–21
> Judges 6, 7

Dale Troyer, Linneus, MO

Is God in your plans today?

Instant Potatoes or Mighty Oaks

But let patience have her perfect work,
that ye may be perfect and entire, wanting nothing.
James 1:4

We live in an age of instant everything. We want our meals done now. We demand instant information and communication. Everything we need is only a phone call away. We order parts and expect to see UPS the next day. The busy signal on the phone irritates us, because it hinders us from making contacts, and our work cannot go on.

This instant mentality has hindered our seeking after God, to know Him as our personal Lord and Master. We want maturity in sanctification, patience in tribulation, and forbearance with our fellow brethren right away. Our lifestyle of "hurried everything" is a detriment to our search for knowing God. How often do we spend only a few minutes with God in our closet and expect to come out as shining stars or pure gold? Moses, Daniel, and Joseph did not attain closeness with God like we obtain instant potatoes in a microwave. These men of God went through tests of time, experienced defeat, and through patient endurance came out as shining vessels that God was able to use.

A meal prepared from scratch is always better than those that are only microwaved. So our spiritual fruit is more beautiful if we are willing to allow the time it takes to grow. The strength of the mighty oak comes through enduring winds, rainstorms, hot sun and freezing weather. Our roots will not grow deeper than the time we invest in the Word of God.

Bible Reading: James 1, 5:7–11
One Year Bible Reading Plan:
Luke 8:22–56
Judges 8, 9

Dennis Eash, Free Union, VA

Personal Bible study helps our roots to grow deeper.

Life Through Death

*Verily, verily I say unto you, Except a corn of wheat fall into
the ground and die, it abideth alone: but if it die,
it bringeth forth much fruit.*
John 12:24

Once, many years ago, a kernel of corn lay in a corn crib surrounded by thousands of others like itself. As the long winter
months passed, the kernel dreamed of what it would like to do
someday. One day it confided to a neighboring kernel, "You know,
someday I should like to produce corn to feed the world."

Months later, the kernel was taken from the corn crib and carried to a distant field. It protested, "No, no, this wasn't in my plans.
I wanted to feed the world." But the farmer did not hear the kernel's
cries.

To its horror, the kernel of corn felt itself being pushed into the
cold, damp earth. There it was buried alive by the hard, unfeeling
planter. It raged to itself, "This will never work! How can I feed the
world from this deserted field?"

As the days passed, the kernel felt its shell become soft from
the damp earth. It fought valiantly against death, crying out, "No!
My work is not completed." At last, however, the kernel of corn
had to admit defeat. It bowed its head, and died.

In several days something amazing happened. A tiny green
sprout burst through the decaying shell, pushed up through the
moist soil, and raised its head to the sun. Months later, the corn
stalk that sprang from the tiny kernel of corn produced hundreds
of beautiful kernels of corn. It had helped to feed the world, but not
in the way it had thought.

You and I are like that kernel of corn. We too have plans, dreams,
and goals for our lives. How-
ever, unless we give up our ideas
and our own wills to God, He
can never produce in us the fruit
that He desires.

Matthew Mast, Mountain View, AR

Bible Reading: John 12:20–33
One Year Bible Reading Plan:
Luke 9:1–36
Judges 10, 11

It is in dying that we are born to eternal life.
—St. Francis of Assisi

One Day at a Time

In all thy ways acknowledge him, and he shall direct thy paths.
Proverbs 3:6

I saw a poster that said, "I've been trying to live one day at a time, but lately several days have attacked me at once." Have you ever felt that way? I have. What is it that makes it so hard to trust God one day at a time? Is it not because, with our human limitations, we cannot see one minute into the future? However, God holds the future in His hand, and He sees the whole picture. Because we fail to trust God for the future, we begin to worry.

I am told that 40% of the things people worry about never happen. Thirty percent are things that have already happened; and we cannot change the past. Twelve percent are thoughts about our health. Worry has never cured any health problem. Ten percent are petty things that really do not matter. That leaves 8% for legitimate concerns. Prayer does 100% more good for these than worry does.

So why worry when we have a heavenly Father who knows the future? Although we do not always understand, God does have a purpose, and as we learn to trust Him, we can enjoy each day as it comes.

We have no promise of tomorrow. If tomorrow never comes, then all the worry about it has done nothing but make us miserable today. Matthew 6:34 says, "sufficient unto the day is the evil thereof." Today has enough trouble. Do not add to it tomorrow's.

Pray to God and trust Him with all your heart. He is able to do even more than we could ask or think (Ephesians 3:20). Enjoy this day; this will be your only chance to enjoy it. If tomorrow does come, the Lord will still be there to take you through.

Jesse Troyer, Crossville, TN

Bible Reading: Matthew
6:19–34
One Year Bible Reading Plan:
Luke 9:37–62
Judges 12—14

Why worry when you can pray?

Our Blessed Redeemer at Calvary

In whom we have redemption through his blood, the
forgiveness of sins, according to the riches of his grace.
Ephesians 1:7

We praise God, our heavenly Father, for His divine plan of redemption. Many people have heard about Calvary, "the place of the skull," and thousands of Holy Land tourists visit there every year. But the significance of the events that took place on that hill nearly two thousand years ago are often not realized by many of those who merely view its location.

What wondrous mercy and grace Christ Jesus demonstrated through His death on the cross! Because Jesus was led to the hill of Golgotha and crucified, lost man is assured of a way to eternal reconciliation. The Roman cross, intended to be an instrument of cruel death, instead became the instrument of new life and hope for the human race.

God loved and valued each one of us so dearly that He was willing to pay the greatest price imaginable for our salvation. May our Lord be exalted as our lives praise Him for conquering sin and death and bringing salvation to all who receive Him as Redeemer and Lord. The gulf between God and man was bridged with Christ's sacrificial atonement at Calvary. Praise His Name!

Bible Reading: Ephesians 1:1–14
One Year Bible Reading Plan:
Luke 10:1–24
Judges 15—17

Ervin Yoder, Victoria, Australia

A hill with three crosses. One cross where a thief died in sin.
One cross where a thief died to sin.
A center cross where a Redeemer died for sin.

Panting After God

_For he satisfieth the longing soul, and filleth
the hungry soul with goodness._
Psalm 107:9

Once we bought a load of young steers. They were trucked up from Pennsylvania and arrived here late one evening. We did not sleep well that night because the steers were constantly bawling, as if in desperate need. They had access to hay and water, so that was not the problem. I wondered if it was because of their new surroundings. The real problem, I later found out, was that they had just been weaned. No wonder they were bawling!

We should have a longing like this for God. The word _pant_ means "to long for eagerly; to yearn." The first verse in our Bible reading describes a deer yearning for a brook to satisfy his thirst. Like the psalmist here, there are times when I feel cast down and ask, "Where is my God?" This is often the result of a trial or struggle that God has brought into my life. Oh, for a drink from the living God! I need the reassurance that God knows and cares about me.

God cares about us. He knows what we are going through. I suspect that as those steers were bawling for their mothers, somewhere there were some disturbed cows yearning for their young. So God longs for us to come to Him, so that He can satisfy our needs. No matter what we face, we have reason to praise Him.

Bible Reading: Psalm 42
One Year Bible Reading Plan:
Luke 10:25–42
Judges 18, 19

John Beiler, Munnsville, NY

Know God—know peace. No God—no peace.

He Is Risen

And if Christ be not raised, your faith is vain; ye are yet in your sins.
1 Corinthians 15:17

Praise God for the resurrection! The foundation of the gospel message is that Jesus died and arose from the grave. Death could not hold Him.

In the fifteenth chapter of 1 Corinthians Paul establishes the fact of the Resurrection with prophetic Scriptures and eyewitness accounts. He names six post-resurrection appearances. Once over 500 people saw Him alive after He rose. Someone has said that the resurrection of Christ is the most documented fact of history.

As it was in Paul's day, so it is today. Many still refuse to believe in the resurrection of Christ and in the "general resurrection" of all humanity. Paul says that the Corinthians were limiting God. Could God raise up Christ but no one else?

I am impressed with Paul's reminder of man's hopelessness in the absence of the Resurrection. He conveys the thoughts, "faith in vain"; "believed in vain"; and "grace in vain." Also, he says if there is no resurrection, then we are "false witnesses"; "perished"; and "most miserable." The gospel without the Resurrection is quite powerless and hopeless.

Praise God! In Colossians 2:12 we are told that we are risen with Him through faith in the operation of God! I am grateful for the power of Christ's resurrection in my life today. I am also looking forward to that great resurrection day when I will see my Savior face to face.

Bible Reading: 1 Corinthians 15:12–28
One Year Bible Reading Plan:
Luke 11:1–28
Judges 20, 21

Rodger Byers, Free Union, VA

Life is real, life is earnest, and the grave is not its goal;
Dust thou art, to dust returnest, was not spoken of the soul.
—Henry Wadsworth Longfellow

Is There a God?

The fool hath said in his heart, There is no God.
Psalm 53:1a

As I completed the paperwork for a tiller sale, I commented to the customer that selling this leftover unit was an unexpected blessing. At my comment, he responded with contempt.

He informed me that although he respected my beliefs, he is convinced that there is no God. My face must have betrayed the shock and disbelief I felt. As I struggled to organize my thoughts, I inwardly called upon God to guide me. I felt a prompting to listen rather than speak. I did ask him one question: "Did you ever believe in God?"

He affirmed that he had at one time. Then, in a voice choked with sorrow and bitterness, he told me of losing his son to a sudden and tragic death. He told me of all the injustice he had seen across the world while serving for thirty-three years in the Navy.

When he was finally silent, I realized this man who had held a position of prestige in the Navy, found his own strength and wisdom inadequate before an almighty God. I reached across the counter and took his hand. I told him I cared, and that I would be praying for him. As his shoulders shook and tears coursed down his cheeks, I realized that deep down inside he knew there is a God!

Thank you, Father, for prompting me to listen (Psalm 46:10). Thank you for reminding me that you are the only true God (Acts 17:22-34). Thank you most of all for sending your only Son, who gave His life, so that we could find forgiveness (John 3:16).

Lavern Stoll, Conneautville, PA

Bible Reading: Isaiah 44
One Year Bible Reading Plan:
Luke 11:29–54
Ruth 1—4

Is God my God?

103

April 9

Thou Wilt Keep Him
in Perfect Peace

Thou shalt not be afraid for the terror by night;
nor for the arrow that flieth by day.
Psalm 91:5

As I sat meditating on Psalm 91, my thoughts went to the storm that recently threatened our country.

Everywhere I went, I saw people who made me wonder if their god had died. They just sat around, or walked about with forlorn faces. They never smiled. All I could hear was, "Mitch, Mitch."

The Psalmist said that we should not be afraid of the terror by night and the arrow that flieth by day.

I had to wonder if people had stopped to consider who was in control of all things. Allow me to go a little further. What were the Christians doing? Many were praying. But praying for what? That the storm would vanish into thin air? Really, what were we praying for?

If we took more time to think about God, and did not only think about Him in adverse times like these, we would not forget that He is Creator of heaven and earth and all that is in them. He who sits on the throne of heaven knows our frame. We are but dust, and He knows our frailty. Best of all, He knows how to take care of His own.

> **Bible Reading:** Psalm 91
> **One Year Bible Reading Plan:**
> Luke 12:1–34
> 1 Samuel 1—3

Let us give Him thanks and praise, for He is worthy! God is in control.

Mark G. Meighn, Belize City, Belize

The storm cannot hide His blessed face.
—Ballington Booth, 1855-1940

Resurrection Power

I am he that liveth, and was dead; and,
behold, I am alive for evermore, Amen.
Revelation 1:18a

A Muslim and a Christian were discussing their beliefs. They agreed that both Mohammed and Christ were prophets. Where then was the difference? The Christian illustrated it this way: "I came to a crossroads and I saw a dead man and a living man. Which man did I ask for directions?" The Muslim quickly answered, "The living man, of course." "Why, then," asked his friend, "do you send me to Mohammed who is dead, instead of Christ, who is alive?"

The Christian faith is distinguished from all other religions on the basis of the empty tomb—the glorious, miraculous resurrection of Jesus Christ from the grave.

The Resurrection has been called the "best established fact in all history." Yet down through the centuries, the critics and skeptics of Christianity have tried their best to disprove this historical fact, which is the foundation of our salvation, the very core of our faith. But what can they answer to the age-old question, "If a man die, shall he live again?"

Praise God that because we serve a living Lord, Who is our risen Savior, we have a hope that is beyond the grave. Day by day we experience in our lives the presence, the power, the life, the victory, and the peace of the resurrected Christ.

Let us remember that to the lost world around us, the greatest witness of the Resurrection is the transforming work of Christ in our lives. Who can change a person from a sinner estranged from God, to a saint on the highway of holiness, at peace with his Maker? May those looking on see that we are truly a new creation; that "all things are become new." In Christ, we have a new life, a new Master, and we are in a new kingdom, with a new destiny.

Bible Reading: 1 Corinthians 15:1-20
One Year Bible Reading Plan:
Luke 12:35–59
1 Samuel 4—6

Mark Kropf, Cataldo, ID

How do I know He lives? He lives within my heart.

*April 11*_____

Walk Close and See More

And when I saw him, I fell at his feet as dead.
Revelation 1:17a

John wrote the words, "I saw" over a dozen times in Revelation. Who did John see?

John was once a young boy trained in the Jewish tradition. He became a fisherman on the Sea of Galilee. He heard John the Baptist preach and announce, "Behold the Lamb of God" (John 1:36). In response to that proclamation, he became a disciple of Jesus Christ. Later he left his fishing business and followed Jesus.

John heard Jesus preach the Sermon on the Mount. He saw the beginning of miracles in Cana. He heard Jesus refer to Himself as "the Living Water," "the Good Shepherd," "the Bread of Life," and "the Way, the Truth, and the Life." John witnessed the Master's healing touch on the lame man by the pool and on the man born blind. He saw the Lord feed five thousand people with five loaves and two fish. He saw Lazarus raised from the dead. He saw Jesus take the role of a servant and wash the disciples' feet. He witnessed Jesus "become obedient unto death, even the death of the cross" (Philippians 2:8). John's own eyes saw the risen Lord with the nail scars in His hands. He rejoiced to see his risen Lord.

John was a faithful follower and an intimate friend of Jesus Christ. When he was abandoned on the Isle of Patmos, his close fellowship with Christ did not cease. It blossomed. His relationship was so close that God revealed to John greater things about Himself. He walked so closely to Jesus that he "saw" more of Him.

This gives me great encouragement. If I walk in an intimate, obedient, loving relationship with Jesus, He will show me more of Himself. Commit yourself to obeying Christ and the Scriptures and trust Him to show you more of Himself.

Bible Reading: Revelation 1:12–20; John 1:35–42
One Year Bible Reading Plan:
Luke 13:1–21
1 Samuel 7—9

Simon Schrock, Fairfax, VA

_____

Step by step loving obedience is the path to an intimate relationship with Jesus Christ.

Jesus Is Greater Than the Temple

. . . in this place is one greater than the temple.
Matthew 12:6

Jesus was well aware of the Pharisees' misplaced devotion. They had corrupted the original intent of the Sabbath by introducing a cumbersome catalogue of stifling rules. They had become worshipers of formality and rules. They had left off worshiping the God of the temple and venerated the temple instead. In essence, they had become "externalists," working themselves and their constituents into a frazzling fray of binding rules.

They had neglected their inner life. Neglect of the inner life is often evidenced by an inordinate attraction to rules and emphasis on external controls and restraints.

We do well to judge ourselves by the same measure of criticism we level at the Pharisees. What is my primary motivation? Rules or a compelling love for Jesus? Wherein is my security? In external controls, or in my position as a child of God?

External controls that function as an application of Scriptural principles have great value for the true-hearted believer. We voluntarily subject ourselves to such controls when we unite with a body of believers. It is also important that we individually adopt guidelines for our personal lives. But it is crucial that we have the proper perspective on rules and controls. Rules do not bring salvation; Jesus does. Regulations do not bring peace; Jesus does. External controls fall far short of transforming us; but Jesus can. A standard of discipline fails to fill me with love; Jesus does.

Bible Reading: Matthew
12:1–21
One Year Bible Reading Plan:
Luke 13:22–35
1 Samuel 10—12

Jesus is greater than formalities, regulations, and rules. Devotion to Him should be the greatest motivating factor in our lives.

Ken Kauffman, Falkville, AL

Wherefore God also hath highly exalted him,
and given him a name which is above every name.
—Philippians 2:9

Risen With Christ

If ye then be risen with Christ, seek those things which are above, where Christ sitteth on the right hand of God.
Colossians 3:1

What does it mean to be risen with Christ? For something to resurrect, it first must die. Just as Jesus' body died, so we too must die to our carnal nature. In Romans 6:11, Paul says, "Reckon ye yourselves also to be dead indeed unto sin." Selfish desires, fleshly lusts, worldly passions, pride, and evil thoughts must no longer be a part of us. Our whole life must be taken to the cross and put under the lordship of Jesus Christ. His blood must be applied to our hearts. Then, and only then, can we experience His resurrection power.

After the old man dies, the new man comes forth; and with him come the attributes of Jesus. The fruit of the Spirit—love, joy, peace, meekness, faith—is seen and felt by those around us. We cannot hide it. Our goals and purposes change. No longer do the things of this world control us. God's Spirit and His will become the motivating force in our lives. God's Word becomes valuable to us. We see beyond this life and view things in the light of eternity.

We like to say we are risen with Christ, but are we really? Remember, this resurrection is proven by our actions. "By their fruits ye shall know them."

> **Bible Reading:** Colossians 3:1–17
> **One Year Bible Reading Plan:**
> Luke 14:1–24
> 1 Samuel 13, 14

With Christ now let me risen be, and seek those things above;
For Jesus died to set me free, and bought me with His love.
No longer do these worldly sins, in my life find a place;
I've brought them all to Calvary—begun the godly race.
So now within my heart must dwell, the Word of Christ each day;
I need its light to be my guide, to walk the narrow way.

Philip Kauffman, Boswell, PA

Only one life 'twill soon be past;
Only what's done for Christ will last.

Jesus Is Greater Than Jonah

And, behold, a greater than Jonas is here.
Matthew 12:41

Jesus reminded the "evil and adulterous" sign-seeking scribes and Pharisees of the story of Jonah. He declared that the Ninevites would rise up as a standard of judgment against them and condemn them. The Ninevites had repented at Jonah's preaching. Now, "a greater than Jonas" was there, and they were refusing to repent.

When I was a lad, the John Deere 6030 was the undisputed champion among the tractors in our neighborhood. It was unequaled in power. When the neighborhood men would bring their tractors for a friendly neighborhood tractor pull, it would easily outperform our biggest "horsepower-adjusted" tractors. The 6030 was the greatest!

Then a neighboring farmer's 4-wheel drive tractor was brought into the competition. Suddenly, the 6030 looked puny! It quickly lost its lofty perch in our esteem, and we unequivocally transferred our loyalty to the stronger tractor.

There is no doubt that Jonah was a great preacher. For a large city with over half a million people to experience such wholesale repentance is a great tribute to his effectiveness as a preacher. Very few preachers have been more effective since then.

But, a "greater than Jonas is here." We sometimes elevate men of God too high. God has unique ways of reminding us that a "greater than Jonas is here." "Jonah" will let you down. (Remember his pouting and God's rebuke?) Jesus won't let you down.

Is Jesus greater in your esteem than any other person? His name is infinitely greater than any "Jonah."

Bible Reading: Matthew 12:22–41
One Year Bible Reading Plan:
Luke 14:25–35
1 Samuel 15, 16

Ken Kauffman, Falkville, AL

Jesus is not humanity deified. He is not Godhead humanized.
He is God. He is man. He is all that God is, and all
that man is as God created him.
—Spurgeon

Peace

The peace of God, which passeth all understanding
shall keep your hearts and minds through Christ Jesus.
Philippians 4:7

Peace is an undisturbed state of mind; the absence of mental conflict; serenity, calm, quiet, tranquility.

Men who are peacemakers love and desire peace. They take no delight in commotion, strife, and quarreling. They shy away from these things as much as possible. Where peace has been disrupted, by God's help, they seek to restore it. They not only strive to keep peace with God and man themselves, but they are also concerned that all men might have this peace.

We need not be offended about anything. If we respond in a loving and kind way to being hurt, we will find redeeming power both for ourselves and others. We should meditate often on the words in our Bible reading: "Great peace have they which love thy law, and nothing shall offend them."

This is a wonderful promise. When we love the law of God, a great peace fills our hearts. We do not often refer to peace as "great." We say peace is deep, precious, wonderful, but seldom great. There is a special emphasis here on the strength of the peace that fills our souls when we are not offended.

Let us compare our lives with the perfect example of peace that Jesus left us. Peace in adversity, peace with God, peace with His own purpose and action, peace with His position, peace with others, and peace regarding the future.

Bible Reading: Psalm 119:162–176
One Year Bible Reading Plan:
Luke 15:1–10
1 Samuel 17, 18

Bert Raber, Chuckey, TN

Prince of peace, control my will;
Bid this struggling heart be still.
Bid my fears and doubting cease,
Hush my spirit into peace.
—Mary A. S. Barber

Spiritual Equations

And Jesus said unto them, I am the bread of life:
he that cometh to me shall never hunger;
and he that believeth on me shall never thirst.
John 6:35

Here is the dilemma. An outdoor seminar is being held in the wilderness with over five thousand people in attendance. The people are hot, tired, and hungry; and there is no McDonald's in sight.

Jesus asks Philip to calculate the amount of food needed to feed the crowd. After some quick math, Philip answers that two hundred pennys worth of bread will not supply everyone a taste. Philip's calculations were mathematically correct, but he left Jesus out of the equation. Jesus did not panic when He was faced with this problem. He already knew how He was going to handle the situation. He only wanted to see if Philip would remember to figure God into the equation.

How many times are we faced with a "larger than life problem" that looks impossible to us? Rather than bringing it to God, we analyze it and say, "This is what I need to do. This is the solution to my problem." How it must hurt God when we leave Him out of the equation!

Let us simply bring our "loaves and fishes" to Jesus and allow Him to supply the meal. No problem is too large or small for God to handle; however, some people are too "big" to hand them over to God. Let us not leave God out of the equation.

Merlin Mast, Scotland H. M., Belize

Bible Reading: John 6:1–14; 30–40
One Year Bible Reading Plan:
Luke 15:11–32
1 Samuel 19—21

God sends no one away empty, except
those who are full of themselves.

April 17

The Eyes of the Lord

The eyes of the Lord are in every place, beholding the evil and the good.
Proverbs 15:3

I was wading off the Philippine coast in the South China Sea one warm afternoon in January. Unknown to my friend Edwin and I, a typhoon had struck some of the islands south of our mission location. The resulting turmoil of the waves kept us close to the shore, but not close enough. An extra large wave suddenly bowled me over and covered me completely. When I regained my footing, I was horrified to realize that my eyeglasses were missing! I spent several futile minutes feeling over the ocean floor but soon realized my glasses were gone for good. Being very nearsighted, I was thankful to have Edwin lead me by the sleeve to public transportation, and home.

On that day of partial blindness, I realized how important my eyes were. Most people, if forced to surrender one of their five senses, would give up sight last!

Consider another pair of eyes. A most unusual pair of eyes. In our Bible reading today, King Asa is reminded that the eyes of the Lord miss nothing, and that God was displeased with Asa's lack of trust in Him. Consider three facts about God's vision.

God's vision is telescopic. From His throne in heaven God sees the tiny sparrow fall.

God's vision is microscopic. God knows the number of hairs on our heads. Many people have around 100,000 hairs. It is mind-boggling to think of the minute detail God perceives.

God's eyes can shear through any glossy veneer of pretense with which we might cover ourselves! He told Samuel, "Man looketh on the outward appearance, but the Lord looketh on the heart." He exposes the innermost recesses of the heart, every thought, desire, and motive.

May we be challenged to walk in the fear of God, so that as His all-seeing eyes fall upon us, we will be blessed with His smile of approval.

Titus Hofer, La Crete, AB

Bible Reading: 2 Chronicles 16
One Year Bible Reading Plan:
Luke 16:1–18
1 Samuel 22—24

His wisdom ever waketh, His sight is never dim.
—Anna Laetita Waring, 1850

The Church of Ephesus

Nevertheless I have somewhat against thee,
because thou hast left thy first love.
Revelation 2:4

The Lord commends the Ephesian Christians' diligence in duty, patience in suffering, and zeal against that which is evil. Then comes a rebuke: "Thou has left thy first love." Those who had some good in them also had much amiss in them.

God is love, and we must love Him more than anything else. We must give God priority in our lives. Man's first affections toward Christ are usually lively and warm. We must take care not to allow these lively affections to cool. When new churches begin, love for God and each other runs high. It is like marriage. As time moves on, the first love may cool off.

What is the root of the problem? We let something come between ourselves and God. We become too busy either in church work or in trying to make a living. These things begin to rob us of our devotion to God, and our love cools off.

Jesus saw the need to spend all night in prayer to God. He rose up early in the morning to have a time of devotion to His Father. This is the secret to keeping our love for God aflame in our hearts. If we try to survive without having that kind of relationship with God, we may have to hear the same rebuke that was given to the church at Ephesus.

The greatest commandment is still in effect today: "And thou shalt love the Lord thy God with all thy heart, and with all thy soul, and with all thy mind, and with all thy strength: this is the first commandment" (Mark 12:30).

Bible Reading: Revelation 2:1–7
One Year Bible Reading Plan:
Luke 16:19–31
1 Samuel 25, 26

Simon Overholt, Auburn, KY

God deserves our first love. Keep it aflame.

The Church in Smyrna

*I know thy works, and tribulation, and poverty, (but thou art rich)
and I know the blasphemy of them which say they are
Jews, and are not, but are the synagogue of Satan.*
Revelation 2:9

"I know thy . . . poverty (but thou art rich)." Some who are poor outwardly are inwardly rich—rich in faith and good works. Where there is spiritual plenty, outward poverty may be better borne. "I know thy tribulation." Jesus Christ took particular notice of the Smyrnan's troubles. He knew the wickedness and the falsehood of their enemies: "I know the blasphemy of those that say they are Jews, but are not." There were those who pretended to be people of God, when indeed they were the synagogue of Satan.

God knows the trials of His people. He warns us about future trials and troubles. If we abide by His counsel, we do not need to fear any trial. They come to try us, not to destroy us. God promises us a glorious reward if we endure to the end.

I would rather spend time in prison for the cause of the Gospel than reject my Lord and spend eternity in hell. Heaven will be worth any suffering we might have to go through in this life. "Yea, and all that will live godly in Christ Jesus shall suffer persecution" (2 Timothy 3:12). "Yet if any man suffer as a Christian, let him glorify God on this behalf" (1 Peter 4:16). Jesus Christ suffered so much for us; should we not be willing to suffer for Him? When we get to heaven, there will be no more pain or suffering.

Simon Overholt, Auburn, KY

Bible Reading: Revelation 2:8–12;
1 Peter 4
One Year Bible Reading Plan:
Luke 17:1–19
1 Samuel 27—29

Let us be willing to suffer for Jesus.

The Heretical Church

*Repent, or else I will come unto thee quickly and will
fight against them with the sword of my mouth.*
Revelation 2:16

The church of Pergamos was infected with men of corrupt
minds, and Christ resolved to fight against them by the sword of
His mouth. The Word of God is a sword; it is a weapon both offensive and defensive. Offensively it is ready to attack. Defensively it
is ready to defend.

Christ took notice of the trials and difficulties the church at
Pergamos encountered. He commended their steadfastness: "You
hold fast my name. You are not ashamed of your relation to me but
count it an honor that my name is upon you. You have not denied
nor departed from the Christian faith." There was a faithful martyr
in Pergamos who sealed his faith with his blood. The others were
not discouraged nor drawn away from their steadfastness, but Christ
reproves them for allowing false teachers to remain in their midst.

Filthiness of the spirit and filthiness of the flesh often go
together. To continue in communion with people of corrupt doctrine and practice brings guilt upon the whole society. When God
comes to punish the corrupt members of a church, He rebukes that
church itself for allowing them to continue in its communion.

The Word of God will take hold of sinners, sooner or later, either
for their conviction or for their
confusion. "Be ye not unequally
yoked together with unbelievers;
for what fellowship hath righteousness with unrighteousness?
And what communion hath
light with darkness?"

Bible Reading: Revelation
2:12–18
One Year Bible Reading Plan:
Luke 17:20–37
1 Samuel 30, 31

Simon Overholt, Auburn, KY

If thine eye be single, thy whole body shall be full of light.

The Church of the False Prophets

I know thy works, and charity, and service, and faith, and thy patience, and thy works; and the last to be more than the first.
Revelation 2:19

The church of Thyatira was in peril. They were being influenced by corrupt doctrine, idolatry, and immorality. Jesus speaks to them hardly a word that is not a stern rebuke. "Eyes like a flame of fire" — fire destroys. "Feet like fine brass" — molten metal burning out all the dross, separating the pure from the impure. He reminds them that He is omniscient.

They had turned to works rather than love, service, and faith. They had allowed Jezebel to lead them away by flattery and promises; their fornication and idolatry caused the severity of the wrath of God to threaten them.

"Whatsoever a man soweth that shall he also reap." God is long-suffering, patient, and merciful, but He will not always strive with man.

Some in Thyatira did not embrace the false doctrine. Jesus knows His own. He said he would strengthen them, give them power over their adversaries. "But that which ye have already, hold fast till I come." Jesus said concerning their works that their last works were better than their first, just the opposite of the church of Ephesus, who had lost their first love. God is interested in how we start out, but more interested how we end up. "And ye shall be hated of all men for my name's sake: but he that endureth to the end shall be saved" (Matthew 10:22). May our last works be better than our first.

Let us hold fast our faith in a good conscience till He comes, then all the difficulty and danger will be over. Oh, the great reward to the persevering victorious believer! "I will give him the morning star." Christ is the morning star. He brings day with Him into the soul, the light of grace and of glory. "He that hath an ear, let him hear what the Spirit saith unto the churches."

Bible Reading: Revelation 2:18–29
One Year Bible Reading Plan:
Luke 18:1–17
2 Samuel 1—3

Simon Overholt, Auburn, KY

Know the truth, and you will not be deceived by false doctrine.

Sardis—A Dying Church

*Be watchful, and strengthen the things which remain, that are
ready to die: for I have not found thy works perfect before God.*
Revelation 3:2

In its beginning the church of Sardis was a flourishing church.
It seems, however, that the leaders had the same frame of mind as
Nebuchadnezzar, who boasted, "I have built . . . the house of the
kingdom by the might of my power, and for the honor of my majesty" (Daniel 4:30). When leaders begin to get proud of their accomplishments, God will pull back His hand and let them go on
their own. Then their church becomes like the church of Sardis, a
dying church. We cannot live on the past reputation of our forefathers.

If our churches want to survive, we first must be humble. If
there has been anything accomplished for the Lord, we must give
Him all the glory. Oh, how Satan would like for us to become proud,
thinking that we have done great things for God's kingdom. "But
he giveth more grace. Wherefore he saith, God resisteth the proud,
but giveth grace unto the humble" (James 4:6).

When a church becomes a dying church, who is to blame? One
thing is certain, a church will never rise above its leaders. Jesus
said to the church of Sardis, "I know your reputation as being alive
and active, but you are dead, now wake up!" They died spiritually.
When this takes place, the church loses its compassion for lost souls
and its fellowship with God and one another. There are no spiritual fires burning, but loose living, neglected services, and a lack of
enthusiasm. Jesus said, "Hold fast and repent, or I will come on
thee as a thief. . . . Thou hast a
few names even in Sardis
which have not defiled their
garments: and they shall walk
with me in white: for they are
worthy. . . . I will not blot [their]
name out of the book of life."

Bible Reading: Revelation 3:1–6
One Year Bible Reading Plan:
Luke 18:18–43
2 Samuel 4—6

Simon Overholt, Auburn, KY

May we be dead to the world but alive to Christ.

April 23

The Loyal Church

I know thy works: behold, I have set before thee an open door,
and no man can shut it: for thou hast a little strength,
and hast kept my word, and hast not denied my name.
Revelation 3:8

Philadelphia was a city in the Roman province of Asia, in the western part of what is now Turkey. It was founded by Cumenes, king of Pergamum in the second century B.C. and named after his brother Attalus whose loyalty had earned him the name *Philadelphus.* The letter to the angel of the church in Philadelphia probably alludes to some of the circumstances of the city. As Philadelphus was renowned for his loyalty to his brother, so the church of Philadelphia inherits and fulfills his character by its steadfast loyalty to Christ. The church was loyal to God's Word. They did not compromise with the world, but kept God's commands regardless of the cost.

They may have been called "old-fashioned," but the church of Philadelphia remained faithful to God.

"Thus saith the Lord, Stand ye in the ways, and see, and ask for the old paths, where is the good way, and walk therein, and ye shall find rest for your souls" (Jeremiah 6:16). But they said, "We will not walk therein." Are we looking for a new path which offers pleasure: fun, sports, eating, and drinking? Do we seek the freedom to do as we please or have we chosen to turn our backs on these things and be loyal to God's Word?

Bible Reading: Revelation 3:7–12
One Year Bible Reading Plan:
Luke 19:1–28
2 Samuel 7—9

Simon Overholt, Auburn, KY

God needs more loyal people.

118

Forgive, As I Forgive

But if ye forgive not men their trespasses,
neither will your Father forgive your trespasses.
Matthew 6:15

Let us take a look at the parable Jesus taught in answer to Peter's question, "How many times do I need to forgive my brother?"

The king in the parable had a servant who owed him 10,000 talents. If they were gold talents, they would equal $262,800,000 today. Oh, the impossibility of it all! It would be preposterous even to consider paying off such a debt. The servant knew this and begged for patience, "I will pay it all." The king knew he could not, so he simply was compassionate and canceled the debt. He released him, extended grace, and forgave.

Something inexplicable happened. The servant found someone who owed him 100 pence, approximately $15. Taking this fellow servant by the throat, he said, "Pay me." The same words, "I will pay it all," echoed in his ears. But no pardon was issued. He cast the fellow servant into prison. Later the king held him accountable for what he had done.

Does this short parable apply to me? I do not want it to, but it does. I owed God a debt of the same magnitude as the ungrateful servant's. It could not be paid. Jesus erased that debt by giving His precious lifeblood. I am free, but if I am forgiven so much, why can I not forgive my brother for some trivial $15 debt?

We need to remember that we are all servants, not kings. One reason we may find it difficult to forgive is that we try to assume the King's position and elevate ourselves above a brother. This is pride. We do not want to forfeit our salvation because we are not able to release our brother.

Bible Reading: Matthew
18:21–35
One Year Bible Reading Plan:
Luke 19:29–48
2 Samuel 10—12

John Hochstetler, Worthington, IN

To forgive and "remember" takes the grace of God.

April 25

One Body—Many Members

So we, being many, are one body in Christ,
and every one members one of another.
Romans 12:5

"A fire!" My daughter called excitedly, looking out the kitchen window. I ran outside and saw our landlord's hay barn in flames. My wife called the fire department and soon, the whole farm was filled with activity. Several fire trucks arrived with many volunteers. The pumping reservoirs were set up, fire hoses were hooked up, and water began to gush onto the flaming hay barn.

I marveled at how everyone worked together to accomplish one goal. Each volunteer fireman had a task to perform which contributed to putting out the fire. There were also many support groups involved. There were men with tractors to carry the hay from the barn to the field. The farm's irrigation system was used to supply the water. A crane was brought in to hold up the roof of the barn while the hay was taken outside. Ice, drinks, and food were provided for all of the volunteers. Everyone worked together so beautifully. Finally the danger was past, the mission was accomplished, and everyone went his separate way.

It made me think of the body of Christ. We are many members in one body. Each of us has a specific role to fulfill so that the church may function as one body. Just as every firefighter cannot drive the fire truck, not everyone in the church can be a minister, a bishop, or a deacon. However, each member is important to the body of Christ. If the church would function as well as those firefighters, then God would be glorified and the body of Christ would be strengthened. Friend, what is your role in the body? Remember, it is important.

Bible Reading: Romans 12:1–5;
1 Corinthians 12:12–27
One Year Bible Reading Plan:
Luke 20:1–26
2 Samuel 13, 14

Terry Lester, Montezuma, GA

There is a great work to be done: but it
takes unity, not competition, to perform it.

God's Workers

For we are laborers together with God.
1 Corinthians 3:9a

In Nehemiah chapter three we are told that the different sections of the wall and gates of Jerusalem were repaired by appointed groups or families. Every individual had a special work to do.

Nehemiah chapter four describes the people's willingness to work, in spite of opposition. Their prayer life was up-to-date, and their devotion to God and His work had first priority. They set a watch so that the enemy could not come upon them unawares. They labored at their work "from the rising of the morning, till the stars appeared" (Nehemiah 4:21).

It is important that we realize our position as workers together with God in building the church of Jesus Christ. To visualize the consequences of one member not accepting his or her God-given responsibility, think about a typewriter with one key not functioning properly.

Xvxn though my typxwritxr is an old modxl, it works quitx wxll xxcxpt for onx kxy. I havx wishxd at timxs it would work pxrfxctly. It is trux that thxrx arx forty-six kxys that function wxll xnough, but onx kxy not working makxs thx diffxrxncx.

Sometimes it seems to me that a church or organization is somewhat like my typewriter, if all the people do not work properly. I may say to myself, "I am only one; I won't make or break the church." But it makes a difference because in order to be effective, an organization needs the participation of every member. So remember my typewriter and say to yourself, "I am a key member of the church, and I am needed very much."

Ervin Yoder, Victoria, Australia

> **Bible Reading:** Nehemiah 4
> **One Year Bible Reading Plan:**
> Luke 20:27–47
> 2 Samuel 15, 16

Do not pray for easier lives; pray to be stronger men!
Do not pray for tasks equal to your powers,
pray for powers equal to your tasks.

_April 27_____

Exercising Gifts

But covet earnestly the best gifts: and
yet shew I unto you a more excellent way.
1 Corinthians 12:31

God created our bodies in a marvelous way. Recently a young man entertained us for a few minutes with his juggling skills. As he proceeded through the various stages of his act, I was amazed at his coordination. As he juggled two or three balls, along with an apple, he ate the apple, bite after bite.

This took complete concentration and the working together of his whole body. His eyes, hands, mouth, and feet all worked together in one coordinated activity.

Christ's body is similar. God has put together in the church many different individuals with different insights and gifts. He expects a working together for the profit of the whole body (1 Corinthians 12:7). There is no place for inferiority (1 Corinthians 12:15-17). Neither is there room for superiority (1 Corinthians 12:21-23). Exercising our gifts without charity, however, is worth nothing (1 Corinthians 13:1-3).

Paul gives us a great example of exercising charity rather than promoting a gift in 1 Corinthians 8. He writes that meat offered to idols can be eaten with a free conscience. However, another brother may not have this understanding, and as he follows the example of the one who eats with a free conscience, his own conscience becomes defiled. Thus, by exercising our knowledge, we have sinned. Paul writes that he would rather do without meat than to cause a brother to sin.

Let us follow Paul's example and exercise our gifts with charity to profit the whole body.

Merle Miller, Free Union, VA

Bible Reading: 1 Corinthians 12:4—13:8
One Year Bible Reading Plan:
Luke 21:1–19
2 Samuel 17, 18

Knowledge puffeth up: but charity edifieth.

I Need You

*Not forsaking the assembling of ourselves together, as the
manner of some is; but exhorting one another: and so
much the more as ye see the day approaching.*
Hebrews 10:25

Last summer we had a logging company clear cut 25 acres of
woods on our property. They took all the trees and brush except 25
to 30 large trees that would not make good logs and were too big
for the shredder.

Shortly afterward, we had a heavy thunderstorm with wind
gusts of 100 miles an hour. The unsheltered trees scattered through
the clearing suffered intense damage from the high winds. Many
were uprooted, some had their entire tops broken off, and others
had large limbs torn off. All were affected.

Christians cannot make their pilgrimage from the cross to the
crown on their own strength or wisdom. Jesus said, "Without me,
you can do nothing." This truth cannot be overemphasized. Without the continual guidance of the Spirit, we would surely fall!

We also need fellowship with, and admonition from, fellow
pilgrims. Our trees would have received less damage had the rest
of the trees still been there. The church offers the Christian support
in the storms of secular influence. This does not mean we will not
be tried, or that the winds will not blow, but that we will receive
help.

There is no individual so infallible that he cannot learn from
others. This is true of us as groups of Christians. It is shameful that
Anabaptist churches have frac-
tionalized as much as they have.
We might as well make the best
of it and learn from each other.
Let our hearts be open enough
to realize one goal, and may we
joyfully await His appearing.

Bible Reading: Hebrews
10:15–27
One Year Bible Reading Plan:
Luke 21:20–38
2 Samuel 19, 20

Kenton Martin, Carson City, MI

A coal by itself may glow for awhile, but will soon be out.

What Are You Eating?

*As newborn babes, desire the sincere milk of
the word, that ye may grow thereby.*
1 Peter 2:2

I raise turkeys and have made some interesting observations while caring for these amusing creatures. Even when they are only a day old they are very curious. They will follow me when I walk through the building. They will also try to eat anything shiny, especially the staples that hold their cardboard pens together.

They also have a great appetite, which is good, because we could not hand feed thousands of them. Unfortunately, there are some which never find the feed, and of course by the third or fourth day we can tell which ones they are. We carry them out to the compost pile.

As they grow, their appetite and curiosity combine to stimulate their interest in eating the shavings on the floor. I cannot imagine that they are very tasty! Some tend to eat shavings when they do not feel well enough to get up and go to the feed. The result is the same as those who do not eat at all, because they become impacted and digestion stops.

Spiritually, we are much like these turkeys. God has put within each of us an appetite for Him. Perhaps, at times, we try to fill that appetite with shiny and attractive easier reading, instead of going to His Word, the real food. Just as the lazy turkeys eat shavings, we sometimes feel like it takes too much effort to read God's Word, especially when we are not "feeling well" spiritually. The evil one provides plenty of shavings for us to pick up self pity, mental arguments with that difficult person, and much more. The result is the same as for the turkeys, only spiritual death has far greater consequences than a turkey's death. Let us fill ourselves with God's Word.

Dan Miller, Stuarts Draft, VA

Bible Reading: Psalm 119:9–32
One Year Bible Reading Plan:
Luke 22:1–30
2 Samuel 21, 22

*Unless there is within us that which is above us,
we shall soon yield to that which is about us.*
—Peter Forsythe

Open Your Eyes Before Your Mouth

He that keepeth his mouth, keepeth his life.
Proverbs 13:3

The warm July sun beat down. The cool, blue water of the pasture pond invited us to cool off in its refreshing ripples. As we were swimming and splashing around, I heard one of my friends begin coughing and spitting out water. Realizing that he was in no great danger, we laughed, asking him what his problem was. "Aw," he said, "I was under water coming up, and I opened my mouth before my eyes."

My friend's mistake of opening his mouth before he was sure his head was out of the water resulted in a mouthful of pond water. Too many times in my journey through life, I find myself making a more serious mistake of opening my mouth before my eyes. We should speak carefully and prayerfully and beseech God's help in guarding our tongues (Psalm 141:3). Then we should roll up our sleeves and work together with God in this area. This involves guarding against the pasture pond mistake. Most regrettably, insensitive conversations take place because our mouths have opened while our eyes are still shut, so to speak.

We have no way of knowing what the people we meet have experienced before our paths cross. Perhaps their day has been a turmoil of stressful situations. They may have faced a close accident or a severe temptation. Now you meet. Open your eyes! Be observant. Be sensitive to their feelings. Everyone you meet is fighting a battle and deserves the thoughtful regard of a Christ-controlled tongue.

There is much, much more than a mouthful of pond water at stake when we open our mouths. Others are influenced, eternity is affected. "For by thy words thou shalt be justified and by thy words thou shalt be condemned" (Matthew 12:37).

Bible Reading: Proverbs 10:10–32
One Year Bible Reading Plan:
Luke 22:31–53
2 Samuel 23, 24

Joshua Yoder, Clarkson, KY

"Careful with fire" is good advice we know;
"Careful with words" is ten times so.

————————————————————

Ye Shall Know Them
By Their Faults

I thank my God upon every remembrance of you.
Philippians 1:3

A slip of the tongue can be revealing and instructive. Recently we were reading in Matthew 7 for family devotions. When we came to verse 16, "Ye shall know them by their fruits," the person reading accidentally substituted the word "faults" for "fruits." It seemed funny at the time, but as I pondered the misstatement, I began to think that there may be more significance to it than it seemed at first.

Try this experiment: take a list of your church members. Briefly think of each one in succession. Notice the first thought that comes into your mind for each one. Is it a fault or a fruit? If we emphasize each other's fruits, it will foster appreciation for the brotherhood. It will make it easier to encourage each other, and we will be more likely to follow their good example.

However, if we focus on each other's faults, we will become cynical, and eventually we will consider everyone a hypocrite. We will become discouraged, as we become more and more disillusioned with the church. James writes, "Confess your faults one to another." He does not say, "Confess other's faults one to another." While we do have a responsibility to be sensitive about sin in the church, we err when we become too critical of one another. Each of us will have some faults as long as we are on this side of eternity. Let us know our brothers and sisters by their fruits, not by their faults.

Enos Stutzman, London, OH

> **Bible Reading:** Philippians 3:12—4:9
> **One Year Bible Reading Plan:**
> Luke 22:54–71
> 1 Kings 1, 2

———————————————————

It is more fruitful to be fruit finders than fault finders.

You Can't Do That!

. . . the Lord saveth not with sword and spear: for the battle is the Lord's, and he will give you into our hands.
1 Samuel 17:47

We often hear the words, "You can't do that," when someone thinks there is something God wants them to do, but others think it is too radical. Suppose they would have said those words to Noah when he was building the ark? "Build a boat on dry land?" "You can't do that!" Moses stood up against Pharaoh to lead his people out of bondage. "You can't do that!" Jonah preached to a whole city that repented in three days. "You can't do that!" Can David kill Goliath with a sling and a few stones? "You can't do that!? The Bible is full of accounts of ordinary people, who with God's help did extraordinary things. We need to be like David. He saw a need, and with God's help he destroyed a stronghold of Satan's.

Too many times we run when the stronghold looks too big for us. But we need to remember that it is God who fights our battles and that He uses ordinary people to do it. If we are to win the world from Satan, we need to do more than defend. We need to attack. And when people say, "You can't do that!" we need to ask, "Is this God's work?" God will always honor obedience and perseverance. He will never condemn a willing heart that is truly devoted to Him.

Bible Reading: 1 Samuel 17:32–58
One Year Bible Reading Plan:
Luke 23:1–26
1 Kings 3—5

Jerry Miller, Molalla, OR

God honors obedience.

Who Is Truly Great?

But it shall not be so among you: but whosoever
will be great among you, let him be your minister.
Matthew 20:26

When I was in the fourth grade, my friends and I often spent lunch time discussing which brand of tractor was the best. Each boy was sure that his father's or uncle's tractor was the best. He was certain that his favorite brand made the biggest, strongest tractors.

The drive to have the fastest, most powerful car, a high-ranking job, or the most expensive fashionable clothes does not die as we grow older. It is rooted deep within the human heart. That drive is the desire for greatness.

The Bible tells us how to become truly great. In the eyes of the world, these Biblical directions to greatness are paradoxical, even ridiculous. The world seeks prominence, riches, popularity, and aggression as the sure way to greatness. The Bible declares that ministering is the key to true greatness. Human thinking counts this utter foolishness.

Joseph is an excellent example of the truth that greatness lies in servanthood. No matter what state he was in, Joseph invariably rose to greatness through loyal service. He came to Potiphar's house as one of the lowest slaves but rose to become chief steward because he was a conscientious worker. The same thing happened when he was cast into prison. Word of his reliable service also reached Pharaoh's ears. When someone was needed to oversee storing up food for the coming years of famine, Pharaoh appointed Joseph.

Just as a tractor's greatness is only truly judged by its service to its owner, so a person's greatness is judged by his service to God.

Bible Reading: Matthew
  20:20-34
One Year Bible Reading Plan:
  Luke 23:27–38
  1 Kings 6, 7

Michael Jantzi, Kiev, Ukraine

_____

No man is small who does a small job in a great way.

Fear

Fear ye not therefore, ye are of more value than many sparrows.
Matthew 10:31

What puts a feeling of fear into our hearts when we think of the future? Is it not the realization that our future is really beyond our control? We would like to have control over what is going to happen in the rest of our lives. But we all know that only God has this privilege. We may compare our desire for control to the teenager's longing to control his own life. Many people think that we should allow teenagers to make all of their own choices; but we see the consequences.

We need to place our lives into God's hand in complete trust and quit striving to have control. Fear will then flee. A child is afraid to go into a long, dark hall, but he is no longer afraid when his daddy comes, takes his hand, and goes with him. We, too, are standing in a hallway. We do not know what is down the hall to surprise us. However, we know the God who is holding our hand, and we need not worry. Let us take consolation from the words of Jesus in Matthew 10, and realize what a magnificent God we serve. He cares so much about us that He keeps track of the number of the hairs on our heads. We have no room for fear.

Bible Reading: Matthew
10:16–31
One Year Bible Reading Plan:
Luke 23:39–56
1 Kings 8, 9

Jeff Carpenter, Kingston, ID

The way to take fear out of living is to put faith in the Lord.

Of Mortar and Love

Love worketh no ill to his neighbor:
therefore love is the fulfilling of the law.
Romans 13:10

An elderly man who had done much masonry work was asked this question: "When you lay blocks, does the mortar hold the blocks together; or does it hold them apart?" He quickly replied, "Both."

The Bible says Christians are members one of another. Like blocks in a wall, we have close contact with each other; and it takes mortar (love) to keep all the blocks in place.

Mortar does two things.

It holds the blocks together. How beautiful it is to see Christians who have a concern for each other, born not of a critical attitude, but of love that has an interest in the others' spiritual well-being. A love like that draws people together. When we go through a valley experience, or when we confess and repent of sin in our lives, or perhaps a non-Christian says something against a brother to see how the rest will respond, true brotherly love draws us together like the mortar between the mason's blocks.

Mortar also holds the blocks apart. Each one of us has faults, which tend to irritate others. It takes love to overlook those irritations and instead remember the virtues of each other.

It is my understanding that a good mason keeps a close watch on the bond, or the thickness of the joint. He wants it to be consistent, not too thick and not too thin. He wants the same thickness in all the joints. May God's love shed abroad in our hearts radiate out to the brotherhood.

> **Bible Reading:** 1 John 4:7-21
> **One Year Bible Reading Plan:**
> Luke 24:1–35
> 1 Kings 10, 11

Leon Yoder, Auburn, KY

Charity is the bond of perfectness.

Grace in Vain?

Receive not the grace of God in vain.
2 Corinthians 6:1b

Several months ago, we took an orphan kitten into our home. My first impressions of the unfortunate little critter that was found in the chicken barn were not very good. He was a scrawny, feisty, rather ugly kitten with a persistent and annoyingly loud mew. Abandoned, his chances of survival were zero.

But, through a staff girl's compassion, "Tigger" was brought into our house. He was warmed, fed, loved, and generally provided with everything he needed to grow strong and healthy.

The kitten so enjoyed our house that he later became very resistant toward our efforts to help him graduate to the outdoors. Sadly, his uncooperative attitude in this area led to an untimely death, as Tigger attempted to dash into our garage before the overhead door closed. The goodness we extended to the kitten was in vain.

Today's key verse urges us to be careful that we don't receive God's grace—the favor and abundant kindness shown to us without regard to our worth or merit—in vain. "But I'm a Christian," you're saying. "How could God's grace be in vain in my life?"

Paul tells us in 1 Corinthians 3:9 that not only are we fellow laborers with God, but we are also His husbandry and His building. That means I am the field needing cultivation! I am the building being built!

A consistent Christian life is evidence that God's grace is not being received in vain, but is accomplishing its intended purpose. Even in very difficult circumstances, we are ministers of God, living evidence of His gracious work. May we grow in grace so that we receive not the grace of God in vain.

Bible Reading: 2 Corinthians 6
One Year Bible Reading Plan:
Luke 24:36–53
1 Kings 12, 13

Curtis Miller, Free Union, VA

We are both His fellow workers and His work project.

*May 7*_____

Leave the Past Behind

But this one thing I do, forgetting those things which are
behind, and reaching forth unto those things which are before.
Philippians 3:13b

Sometimes we have failures and disappointments and aches and pains that just don't seem to go away. Most of us know what it's like to suffer from them, but too few of us know just what to do about them. So we limp along, hoping that somehow they will magically stop hurting.

But it never happens that way. In fact, the passing of time often leaves us in worse condition, not better. Instead of putting these painful failures behind us, we often dwell on them until they become more real to us than the promises of God. We focus on them until we become bogged down in depression, frozen in our tracks by the fear that if we go on, we will only fail again.

My friend, if depression has driven you into a spiritual nose-dive, break out of it by getting your eyes off the past and onto your future—a future that has been guaranteed by Christ Jesus through the precious promises in His Word.

Forgive and forget those failures in the past! That is what God has done. If He does not remember them any more, why should you?

The Bible says that God's mercies are new every morning. If you will take God at His Word, you can wake up every morning to a brand new world. You can live a life that is full and rewarding.

So do it! Replace thoughts of yesterday's mistakes with Scriptural promises about your future. As you do that, hope will start taking the place of depression. The spiritual aches and pains that have crippled you for so long will disappear. Instead of looking behind you and saying, "I can't,"
you will begin to look ahead and
say, "I can do all things through
Christ who strengthens me!"

Daniel Mast, Orrville, OH

Bible Reading: Philippians 3
One Year Bible Reading Plan:
John 1:1–28
1 Kings 14, 15

The greatest sweets are bittersweets.
The greatest beauty is always watered by tears.

132

The Importance of My Brother

*So all the men of Israel were gathered against
the city, knit together as one man.*
Judges 20:11

It is too often a foreign experience to have someone give in to someone else. It may be that it comes closer to home than we would like to think.

Am I willing to give in to my brother's idea?

In this day of the independent spirit, we do well to recognize that the arch-enemy of our souls is behind this spirit which seems to be invading our churches and long ago made an inroad into our world. This spirit has caused many to be trampled on, or pushed off the path to heaven.

Let us look at one of the marvels of God's creation—the mountain goat. What happens when two goats are coming together on a path so narrow that there is absolutely no room to pass? Will one back up to a wide spot in the trail? Maybe one will push the other off the mountainside? No, indeed! When they come together, one meekly lies down on the trail, while the other gently steps over, and sometimes on, him.

If an animal has this instinct to promote the good of his fellow being, how much more should we, with the aid of the Holy Spirit, be willing to lay down our will for the good of our brother!

Bible Reading: Psalm 133;
Ephesians 4:1–16
One Year Bible Reading Plan:
John 1:29–51
1 Kings 16—18

David Lee Yoder, Russellville, KY

May Christ be the hub of our wheel.

The Tongue

Whoso keepeth his mouth and his tongue
keepeth his soul from troubles.
Proverbs 21:23

The tongue is a very important part of our body. We could do without teeth if we had to, but how could we do without a tongue?

On the other hand, the tongue probably gets us into more trouble than any other member of our body, unless we allow God to tame it. A wise tongue may not be able to heal diseases, but it can heal people's discouragements and sorrows. A wise tongue heals broken or wounded relationships like a soothing medicine.

The average man speaks 20 to 25 thousand words a day. The average person spends at least 1/5 of his life talking. In a single day one person says enough words to fill a 50 page book. In one year the average person's words would fill 132 books, each containing 400 pages. From the time a person says the first "good morning" until he says the last "good night," he engages in approximately thirty conversations a day.

With all that conversation, we really have to be careful of what we say. We cannot recall any of those words, though we may repent of some of them and ask for forgiveness. An anonymous poet has well expressed the importance of even one of those 25,000 words.

Bible Reading: James 3
One Year Bible Reading Plan:
John 2
1 Kings 19, 20

A careless word may kindle strife.
A cruel word may wreck a life.
A bitter word may hate instill;
A brutal word may smite and kill.

A gracious word may smooth the way,
A joyous word may light the day.
A timely word may lessen stress;
A loving word may heal and bless.

Lonnie Peachey, Woodville, NY

He that hath knowledge spareth his words.

Life From Death

*Verily, verily, I say unto you, Except a corn of wheat fall into
the ground and die, it abideth alone: but if it die,
it bringeth forth much fruit.*
John 12:24

I enter the seed room of the greenhouse where I work. I open the seed packet and sprinkle a few tomato seeds into my palm.

Visions of juicy tomato sandwiches dripping with mayonnaise enter my mind. I try to imagine bushels of luscious tomatoes being produced by these few shriveled seeds. It seems impossible!

Now I walk over to the germination table and pull a tiny tomato seedling from its cell. I pull away the roots and soil until I can see the place where growth began. Wonder of wonders, the seed is a rotten husk, but there is life springing from death!

I move from the world of tomatoes into the realm of my personal struggle. Self, that hard crust enclosing my spirit, must "fall into the ground" and decay. Paradoxically, if I would really live, I must first die. Then only can the life of Christ spring up in my spirit and produce the kind of fruit that delights the Husbandman.

This is a difficult, lifelong process that involves humiliation, self-denial, darkness, obscurity. But, thank God, Christ did not propose anything to His disciples that He was not willing personally to exemplify.

Jesus' discourse in John 12 was punctuated by His own suffering and death. Just a few days after He outlined these principles of self-denial, the perfect Seed was laid into the ground and the stone was rolled in place.

But three days later, *Life* burst forth from death in a glorious "germination" that shook the universe. Out of death grew a beautiful organism, the Church of Jesus Christ, and His true followers are still dying to live.

Bible Reading: John 12:20–36
One Year Bible Reading Plan:
John 3:1–21
1 Kings 21, 22

Ken Miller, Stuarts Draft, VA

Death—the gate of life.
—Bernard of Clairvaux

A Porcupine Lesson

Forbearing one another, and forgiving one another, if any man have
a quarrel against any: even as Christ forgave you, so also do ye.
Colossians 3:13

Today our family went to our local church as usual. Beside us and all around us were fellow church members. We know them very well. We see them at almost every church service. We see them at work projects and ball games. We labor together to support our school. We get together summer evenings and make ice cream. Our children catch lightning bugs together. We've laughed together and cried together. We know them very well.

Needless to say, they also know us very well. They have seen us at our best and worst. They know our faults and idiosyncrasies. But they love us and accept us anyway. Surely this is evidence of the grace of God!

Several porcupines faced a fierce storm together in the far north. As the temperatures plummeted, their only hope of survival was to band closely together. During that long, frigid night they may have needled each other occasionally. But they also realized they needed each other for their own survival. Today let us learn from the humble porcupine! Have you been dwelling on things that "needle" you about a brother or sister? We all have some sharp edges that God needs to further sanctify. Rather than focusing on the needles, let us appreciate the contribution that our brothers and sisters have made to our lives. We really do need each other!

Have you shared a word of appreciation with any of them lately? Do it today!

Jim Yoder, Clarkson, KY

> **Bible Reading:** Hebrews 3:1–13
> **One Year Bible Reading Plan:**
>   John 3:22—36
>   2 Kings 1—3

Love your neighbor as yourself.

First Responder

But a certain Samaritan, as he journeyed, came where he was:
and when he saw him, he had compassion on him.
Luke 10:33

Most of our communities have emergency medical technicians who provide us with emergency ambulance services.

Many of these technicians have training as a first responder.

An accident across the road from our shop brought one of these first responders at the scene, long before the ambulance itself arrived. This specially trained responder provided medical assistance in the first few, life-saving minutes after an accident.

Just as a community benefits from such technicians, how much more the church from spiritual "first responders"? Are we prepared to respond to the needs of those around us? Our fellow church members, our own family members, and others we work with have special needs.

The call to "bear ye one another's burdens, and so fulfill the law of Christ" is a call for us to be first responders (Galatians 6:2).

In the same way that our communities' first responders need training and education, so do we in the church of Jesus Christ. We need a close relationship with Christ and an experience of Him, from which we can share.

If we wait around for the bishop, ministers, or deacons to respond, we may well lose precious time. Our call is to be available and "ready always to give an answer to every man that asketh you a reason of the hope that is in you with meekness and fear" (1 Peter 3:15).

An emergency may face us today. Are we ready to respond?

Ernest Hochstetler, Abbeville, SC

Bible Reading: Luke 10:25–42
One Year Bible Reading Plan:
John 4:1–30
2 Kings 4, 5

First responders are people that are standing by.

Fire!

*And the tongue is a fire, a world of iniquity: so is the tongue
among our members, that it defileth the whole body, and
setteth on fire the course of nature; and it is set on fire of hell.*
James 3:6

This past summer we had a drought that lasted for quite some
time. We were warned not to start fires of any kind. Although extra
precautions were taken, several fires were started and got out of
control. The damage caused was severe.

Fire is useful in many ways; without it, life would be complicated. Yet, we also realize that if it gets out of control fire can cause
untold damage.

So it is with our tongue. We can do much good with our tongue,
by cheering people and witnessing for Christ. If, however, we do
not allow God to control our tongue, terrible damage can also be
done by it. We can cause things to happen through the use of our
tongue that have consequences far more serious than the consequences of fire. How sad if we should say something that caused
someone to turn away from God and be cast into eternal hell fire!

James tells us that no man can tame the tongue. God alone can
control our tongue, but it is up to us to allow Him to do so. "Set a
watch, O Lord, before my mouth; keep the door of my lips" (Psalm
141:3). We can speak good words, and give a flowery testimony,
but unless we have the love of God in our hearts, it is nothing
(1 Corinthians 13:1). Let us use
our tongues to God's honor and
to His glory. Surely God gave us
a great gift when He gave us our
tongues, and it should be our
pleasure to dedicate the use of
the tongue to His service!

Bible Reading: James 3
One Year Bible Reading Plan:
John 4:31–54
2 Kings 6—8

Philip Cross, Millwood, KY

Is God our fire chief?

Hidden Wives

He that covereth his sins shall not prosper: but whoso
confesseth and forsaketh them shall have mercy.
Proverbs 28:13

The following story appeared in the editorial column of our local weekly newspaper.

"Some years ago, the most married man in the world was found in Yugoslavia. It happened this way: A young woman confided to her girl cousin that she was soon going to be married. She told her cousin that the bridegroom was so shy and timid he wanted to keep the marriage a secret. The cousin became curious. She got a glimpse of the bridegroom after the secret wedding and recognized him as her own husband! He had also married her secretly, claiming to be shy and timid.

That was only the beginning. A total of fifty women came forward and claimed that the same man had married each of them. In each case, he was the same bashful bridegroom. They called him Ivanhoe, the Terrible, breaker of women's hearts. He was a traveling salesman and went from wife to wife by plane. He supported all fifty of them, and told each that his duties as a traveling salesman kept him away much of the time.

They put him in jail, and he begged to stay there. He would rather be in prison than face those fifty wives."

While we may not be hiding fifty wives, there may be other things we try to hide from others (and God)—things that we are ashamed of, or that we know to be wrong. If it were possible for this man to hide fifty wives from each other, at least for awhile, how easy is it for us to hide some sin in our lives?

Let us remember that though we may be able to hide sin from our brothers and sisters, we cannot hide it from God.

Matthew Hochstetler, Leo, IN

> **Bible Reading: 1 Corinthians 3**
> **One Year Bible Reading Plan:**
> John 5:1–24
> 2 Kings 9—11

For some, conscience is the fear of being found out.

May 15

Contagious Attitudes

I will give thee thanks in the great congregation:
I will praise thee among much people.
Psalm 35:18

Have you ever noticed how yawns are contagious? One person yawns, then another, and soon, several people are yawning. In our Bible reading today, ten men spread a negative attitude to several million. This contagious bad attitude caused the children of Israel to wander in the wilderness forty years.

We need to be careful not to harbor wrong or negative attitudes in our hearts, because these attitudes will soon spread to our brethren if we are not careful!

The good news is that good, positive attitudes are also contagious. Instead of having negative attitudes, we can spread good will to others. If someone around us has a happy, positive attitude, we are likely to catch the enthusiasm too. Likewise, if we are joyful and positive, those around us will also rejoice.

Take cheer! Like David, let us purpose in our hearts to thank and praise God among many people, so they will catch the attitude and spread it on to those around them. We should take time to praise God. If we do, our joy will overflow, and others will also become joyful.

If you are plagued by a negative "virus," keep up your cheer and you may be able to stop that "virus" and start a good attitude going around. Joshua and Caleb were far outnumbered, but they did not give up. They rent their clothes and prayed. When a negative attitude is going around, pray for help and guidance to keep on spreading your little bit of joy. It may catch hold and spread!

> **Bible Reading:** Numbers 13:25–33; 14:1–10
> **One Year Bible Reading Plan:**
> John 5:25–47
> 2 Kings 12–14

Douglas Kauffman, Falkville, AL

Brighten the corner where you are . . .
it may brighten the whole room!

A Pig Is a Pig

As a jewel of gold in a swine's snout, so
is a fair woman which is without discretion.
Proverbs 11:22

What is your first thought when you think of a pig? For some reason pigs have a bad name. My thoughts of pigs aren't very pleasant: muddy and dirty, greedy, noisy, bad smelling, and just overall bad mannered. Are we being fair to automatically put all pigs in this category? Let us give them a chance to prove themselves. Give them a nice, clean pen, brush them till they look nice, feed them in a glass dish, and even talk nice to them for a couple of days; and then see if they won't improve their dignity.

How foolish! You could dress up a pig and put a jewel in its nose, but underneath you still have a pig. It will still make a slop out of its pen and still grunt. You have not changed the inside.

When Jacob deceived his father, his neck and arms were hairy, and the meat he brought was an Esau specialty, but the real person was still Jacob. The Gibeonites tricked Joshua with moldy bread, old wine bottles and ragged shoes, but when the story came out, they were still Gibeonites.

The key verse reminds me of a hypocrite, the person who looks good on the outside but is full of bad on the inside. The good looks and gold jewelry do not change the real thing. The answer is not to dress up the pig or cover up the bad points on a person but to change the character underneath. Let us allow Jesus to change our hearts so that our character matches the words we say.

Bible Reading: Joshua 9:3–27
One Year Bible Reading Plan:
John 6:1–21
2 Kings 15—17

Luke Schwartz, Harrodsburg, KY

Just polishing the outside will not brighten the inside.

Are You Painted?

*Therefore if any man be in Christ, he is a new creature: old
things are passed away; behold, all things are become new.*
2 Corinthians 5:17

Recently I was reminded again what paint can do to improve
the looks of something. My wife and I did a face lift on one of the
rooms of our house. It had old, brown paneling on the walls, and
the ceiling was brownish looking with smoke and age. We went to
work on it.

First, we took the old trim off, and then we textured the ceiling.
But that stain leaked through. So I decided I would fix that. I bought
some Kiltz stain block and put it on. Sure enough, it worked. With
another coat of paint, it was nice and white.

You should have seen all the nail holes and cracks in the walls.
We got the caulk and nail putty out and went to work filling all
those ugly holes. After we painted over it, you could not see them.
It looked pretty good. The whole room looks like a different room
now, but, you know, underneath it is still the same room, no matter
how often we paint it.

It takes more than a good paint job to be a Christian. The scribes
and Pharisees tried that by looking good on the outside. They convinced themselves they were doing right. But Jesus said they were
full of dead men's bones and all uncleanness.

It is so easy to have the right speech and act right most of the
time. We get this feeling we are making it. But it takes more than a
paint job. It takes a new heart to become a new creature in Christ
Jesus. How is it with you? Are you a real Christian, or a painted-up
one?

"A good man out of the good treasure of his heart bringeth
forth that which is good; and an
evil man out of the evil treasure
of his heart bringeth forth that
which is evil: for out of the abundance of the heart his mouth
speaketh" (Luke 6:45).

Michael Mast, Russellville, KY

Bible Reading: Matthew
23:25–39
One Year Bible Reading Plan:
John 6:22–44
2 Kings 18, 19

It takes a change of heart to be a new creature!

The Man After God's Own Heart

Lead me in thy truth and teach me: for thou art the God
of my salvation; on thee do I wait all the day.
Psalm 25:5

David refused to murder Saul for his own benefit because he understood that God's dealing with Saul was not his personal responsibility. "The Lord shall smite him, or he'll die in battle, or his day shall come to die." With these expressions David allowed God to guide his life and fulfill God's plan. Rather than following human reasoning, he simply accepted God's will for his life. Yet in all this, we see a burden for Saul's soul. In our Bible reading, David opened his own life for examination. "Why are you seeking me? If I have sinned tell me, so I can confess it and offer an offering to the Lord, so that my relationship may be restored. Why do you seek to destroy me? If I have done evil, allow me to repent before I die." By carefully maintaining his life, he was able to ask Saul these questions; and Saul could not find fault with him. This exposed Saul's ignorance and foolishness.

What does this mean to us? David is a good example for us. Consider the time he was living in. He was living under the Old Testament Law, with a few other teachings that his parents taught him. One thing we know is that he sought the Lord's will rather than exalting himself.

May we make it our goal to seek to help our brothers. Like David, rather than condemning them, let us seek to strengthen our brothers. If there is a need, let us do as David did and seek our brother's spiritual good. David was a man after God's own heart; are you?

Bible Reading: 1 Samuel 26
One Year Bible Reading Plan:
John 6:45–71
2 Kings 20—22

Joe Sommers, Flemingsburg, KY

Be not overcome of evil, but overcome evil with good.
—Romans 12:21

A Brotherhood

So built we the wall; and all the wall was joined together
unto the half thereof: for the people had a mind to work.
Nehemiah 4:6

We took a trip to North Carolina to help with a disaster service project. We were helping repair houses that were damaged by Hurricane Floyd. It was a rewarding feeling to be able to help those people in need. What a blessing to see the tears of joy in their eyes, as their homes took shape again!

Are we thankful to be part of a brotherhood where we still help one another? In Ezra and Nehemiah we read that the people had a mind to work.

Two weeks ago my neighbor lost his barn to a fire. Yesterday we were over to help, and the project is nearly completed already. Many hands make light work! I believe this is also part of the Lord's commandment that we love one another. Are we not too often concerned about having our own homes, farms, and businesses in top shape before we think we have time to help some struggling brother who can hardly make ends meet? I am reminded of Jesus' teaching in Luke 10:27 when the lawyer asked Him what he should do to inherit eternal life. Jesus told him to love his neighbor as himself. The lawyer then trying to justify himself, asked, "Who then is my neighbor?" After the story of the good Samaritan, Jesus said, "Go, and do thou likewise."

Let us continue to have a love for our fellowmen, knowing that Christ lived a life of service to others. "And whatsoever ye do in word or deed, do all in the name of the Lord Jesus" (Colossians 3:17).

Bible Reading: Ezra 5
One Year Bible Reading Plan:
John 7:1–31
2 Kings 23—25

Irvin Kruemer, Wallenstine, ON

Let us do good unto all men.

Needed: Watchmen

Watchman, What of the night?
Isaiah 21:11

During Bible times, the night was divided into several watches. The Jews divided the night into three watches, but the Romans had four. Watchmen were on guard during each watch. The watchmen would inform the city of the time of night. They would also warn of enemies or other dangers.

Being a spiritual watchman today is not at all popular. Many people do not want to be reminded about the time in which we live. It is too disturbing to them. However, we have a command from God to go into all the world and preach the Gospel. With the Gospel message, we must also remind men of death, hell, and judgment.

There are many scoffers and false prophets in our day. What a responsibility we have to stand up and warn those who have been deceived! Although there will be but few that heed the warning, it is our obligation. Just as the watchman was held responsible if he failed to warn of danger, so will we be held accountable if we fail to warn our friends and neighbors. If there was a bridge out, you would not just hope that other drivers would see it in time; you would do all you could to stop traffic from driving off the bridge! How much more should we warn people of the coming judgment on sin!

Be a faithful watchman!

Mark Webb, Hicksville, OH

Bible Reading: Ezra 3:16–27; Jude 20–25
One Year Bible Reading Plan: John 7:32–53
1 Chronicles 1, 2

Do you know what time it is? It is time to serve the Lord.

Esteem Them Very Highly

And to esteem them very highly in love for their work's sake.
And be at peace among yourselves.
1 Thessalonians 5:13

Do we honor, respect, and regard with value those who are over us in the Lord? Most ministers would probably prefer not to talk too much about this subject, but we need to be reminded at times.

We know that there are various offices in the church, and it is important that they be fulfilled scripturally. It is also very important for us to support leaders and fulfill our roles properly and scripturally. Equally, it is important to pray for those in the ministry. How well we are fed spiritually is in part our responsibility. Paul asked to be prayed for. "Pray for us, that the word of the Lord may have free course, and be glorified" (2 Thessalonians 3:1). "Praying always . . . for all saints; and for me, that utterance may be given unto me, that I may open my mouth boldly, to make known the mystery of the gospel" (Ephesians 6:18, 19).

When Jesus spoke to Peter in John 21, He told Peter, "Feed my sheep." Let us be thankful for those who bring us spiritual food and remember to faithfully pray for them, that they will give us a balanced diet. Let us think about the responsibilities ministers have and respect them. We may not always understand everything or maybe even see eye to eye on everything, but we are still admonished to esteem them highly for their work's sake.

Mark Miller, Millersburg, OH

Bible Reading:
1 Thessalonians 5
One Year Bible Reading Plan:
John 8:1–20
1 Chronicles 3—5

Let us therefore follow after the things which make for peace,
and things wherewith one may edify another.
—Romans 14:19

The Deep Things of God

But God hath revealed them unto us by his Spirit: for the
Spirit searcheth all things, yea, the deep things of God.
1 Corinthians 2:10

Most of us are intrigued by mysteries. Mysteries fascinate with their captivating plots. Paul writes about "the wisdom of God in a mystery" (1 Corinthians 2:7). He says that "eye hath not seen, nor ear heard, neither hath entered into the heart of man, the things which God hath prepared for them that love him" (1 Corinthians 2:9). Some people have applied these words to heaven, and this is not a wrong application. But verse ten tells us that "God hath revealed them unto us by His Spirit." This intrigues me. Through the Holy Spirit the deep things of God (mysteries) can be discovered by the believer.

As I meditate on God's Word, I learn more about the deep things of God. It is there that I see my shortcomings. It is there that confession is made. It is there that blessings come down.

"The Spirit searcheth all things, yea, the deep things of God." As I seek to know more of the deep things of God, my soul overflows with praise. For God, as Isaiah writes, is able to measure the waters in the hollow of His hand, and yet, He reveals Himself to us as we search His deep things. Our challenge is to apply them to our lives so that we may grow. How often I have failed! But the desire is there. The Psalmist says, "As the hart panteth after the water brooks, so panteth my soul after thee, O God" (Psalm 42:1).

> **Bible Reading:** 1 Corinthians 2
> **One Year Bible Reading Plan:**
> John 8:21–36
> 1 Chronicles 6, 7

Allan Miller, Sarcoxie, MO

You can see God best on your knees.

Termites

Take us the foxes, the little foxes, that spoil the vines:
for our vines have tender grapes.
Song of Solomon 2:15

Termites are little wood boring insects that eat clothes, books, furniture, and even whole houses.

Recently I discovered termites were eating my dresser! Did I see them? No, all I could see were little piles of sawdust in the corners! Termites are often that way. They often seriously damage, or even destroy, whole houses without the homeowner realizing it! Of course, a smart homeowner will check his home and furniture periodically for termites. Nipping the problem in the bud goes a long way toward protecting a home from termites.

Do we have termites in our lives? Maybe a small, seemingly insignificant sin? An evil thought? A wrong attitude? Do we exterminate these termites immediately? Or do we sweep up the dust piles and hope no one will notice? One wrong thought or attitude left unchecked can turn into a root of bitterness. A root of bitterness can destroy a person's spiritual life.

There is a young woman in our community who at one time made a commitment to serve Christ. She started instruction class, but somewhere she lost out and today is selling her body at the cost of her soul. "How terrible," we say, but the problem probably started with a small sin in her life, and the damage from the termites has consequences of eternal proportions.

How can we avoid termite damage in our lives?

First we must realize our own humanity: we all are vulnerable to the invasion of termites. But by renewing our relationship with God daily and spending time in prayer, and by honestly examining our lives, we can destroy the termites before they build a home.

Bible Reading: Joshua 7:1–15
One Year Bible Reading Plan:
John 8:37–59
1 Chronicles 8—10

Vernon Miller, Masaya, Nicaragua

Truth and light rejected lead to hardness and bitterness.

Clay

But we have this treasure in earthen vessels, that the
excellency of the power may be of God, and not of us.
2 Corinthians 4:7

Recently we visited a restored historic village for a family out-ing. One of the most interesting displays was the pottery shop. A man was there with his foot powered potter's wheel. He put a lump of clay on the wheel and began to turn it with his feet. As the wheel was turning, the potter began to shape his lump of clay very skill-fully with his hands. Occasionally he would add just a little water and the clay would take on whatever shape the potter wished it to take. Once he did not like how the clay was turning out, so he flat-tened it out and began again. Finally, that once flattened lump of clay was shaped into a nice pitcher.

I made observations that day. The potter had to have his wheel, so that it would turn the clay. And the potter said he used a special clay for the pottery craft. Any old lump of mud would not do, because it would crack during the firing process. But the most important thing I noticed were the hands of the potter. With his supple fingers the potter could shape the clay into any vessel he chose.

God is the potter, and we are the clay. Our lives are turning on God's wheel, and He is ever so carefully shaping us into vessels for His service. The shaping pro-cess may be painful, but the Master Craftsman knows how He wants us to turn out, so that when the fires of life come, our vessels will not crack. How is your vessel? Is God still shaping it?

Bible Reading: Genesis
1:26—2:7; Jeremiah 18:1–6
One Year Bible Reading Plan:
John 9:1–23
1 Chronicles 11—13

Terry Lester, Montezuma, GA

Be a vessel of honor

I Can Play Loud!

And whatsoever ye do, do it heartily, as to the Lord, and not unto men.
Colossians 3:23

A group of school children wrote letters to the President of the United States for a class project. One young lad made this generous offer: "Dear Mr. President, I would like to play my trumpet for you. I cannot play so good, but I play loud!"

Let's face it. Most of us are pretty average. We will probably never be gifted church leaders. An Ira Sankey or Fannie Crosby? That's not me. Our attempts at writing will never measure up to Daniel Kauffman or Adam Clarke. Most of us qualify as "regular folks" or "common material."

But take courage! God has done some remarkable things with "common material." Here are some examples.

Who carried God Incarnate in her womb? A Jewish maiden named Mary. Who was chosen to raise Jesus in his home? A village carpenter named Joseph. Who killed Goliath? A young shepherd boy. What did he use as a weapon? Five round stones. Who let the spies down over the wall? A harlot named Rahab. Who provided food when Jesus fed the five thousand? A lad who gave his lunch. And have you considered the twelve disciples? They were Galileans.

The man who had only one talent and buried it had another option. He could have exercised his talent heartily "as unto the Lord." No doubt he would have received the same blessed commendation from the Lord as the more gifted servants received.

I do not know if the little trumpet player ever got to play for the President. Although he lacked talent, his zeal and willingness are to be admired.

Bible Reading: Matthew 25:14–30
One Year Bible Reading Plan: John 9:24–41
1 Chronicles 14—16

Jim Yoder, Clarkson, KY

Ability is wonderful, but God is more interested in your availability.

The Subtlety of Darts

*Above all, taking the shield of faith, wherewith ye shall
be able to quench all the fiery darts of the wicked.*
Ephesians 6:16

The huge hollow maple tree swayed to and fro as the wind blasted against it. As the wind became stronger, the tree creaked, groaned, teetered, and then, with a thunderous roar, crashed to the ground. The tree had started from a tiny seed. First, it was only a tender seedling. Rain had at intervals watered it, quenching its thirst. Minerals and other nutrients had fed it, satisfying its hunger. The tree had taken root and grown into a sturdy, towering maple. During a thunderstorm, lightning dismembered one of its boughs. The wound lay open, inviting the darts of precipitation. The wound festered, and the tree started to decay. The storm tested its endurance, and it crashed to the ground.

This tree is like the local church. The church needs a food source upon which to feed. If each individual member absorbs the love of God, the church becomes strong. Each must carefully maintain his spiritual life, or with time, the church will decay. The wounds that result from the darts that the devil hurls at us must be sealed and healed. These darts have many names. Wrong attitudes, envy, false accusation, and gossip are labels that some bear. Another subtle one is evil surmising.

When we feed on God's love, and forgiveness freely flows among us, we can overcome these darts. Wounds can be continually healed, and the church will withstand every storm.

Harvey D. Yoder, Marion, MI

Bible Reading: Ephesians 6
One Year Bible Reading Plan:
John 10:1–21
1 Chronicles 17—19

Soldiers void of armor are short-lived.

Complaining

But godliness with contentment is great gain.
1 Timothy 6:6

Sometimes, if we complain loud enough and long enough, we get what we want. "The squeaky wheel gets the grease." It may make us feel good to complain. We feel we are better than people we are complaining about. But when we complain, we tell people that we lack something. We lack a grateful spirit. We forget all that God has done and is doing for us. We also tell others that we lack faith. We do not believe His promises to care for us and provide answers for our problems if we ask Him.

Complaining damages friendships. No one wants a friend who continually talks about what is wrong. Complaining also makes our troubles worse. We become discouraged and lose hope. Worst of all, complaining leads us away from God. Romans 1:21 tells about people who knew God but did not glorify Him or give thanks to Him. As a result, their foolish hearts were darkened. Numbers 16 tells of God's people complaining. As a result, 14,700 complainers were destroyed by a plague. Complaining, from God's point of view, is serious. How can we stop complaining?

The first step is to admit we cannot do it ourselves. Jeremiah 17:9 tells us, "The heart is deceitful above all things, and desperately wicked." We must confess to God and ask Him to take full control of our minds and tongues. We must realize that complaining is sin and ask God to forgive us and change us. Then we need to fill our minds with good things, as Philippians 4:8 tells us. It is very important to read God's Word daily. When we feel discouraged, we should read Isaiah 41:10. The more we tell God our complaints, the less we feel like complaining to others. Let us replace complaining with prayer and thanksgiving.

Eli Yoder, Stuarts Draft, VA

Bible Reading: Philippians 4:4–19
One Year Bible Reading Plan:
John 10:22–42
1 Chronicles 20—22

The more I know Jesus, the more contented I become.

A Clean Heart

Create in me a clean heart, O God;
and renew a right spirit within me.
Psalm 51:10

In the aftermath of a flood, there is a lot of despair. Being involved in restoring flooded houses, I see a parallel between this and our lives. There is much more involved in restoration than just hanging wallboard, installing new carpet, and painting. Before we even think of doing any of these, there must be a total clean out. All debris, ruined furniture, walls, and floors have to be removed, until you have an empty shell of a house that can dry out and be restored, refurnished, and made livable again.

Are we sometimes guilty of trying to restore our lives without allowing Christ to remove the garbage of sin? Do we try to hide some trash and filth behind a good front and a good life? God is willing to completely remodel our hearts only as we let go of selfish attitudes, motives, and desires. Christ, the master rebuilder of lives, does the work; but we must choose to allow Him to rebuild.

I remember a comment a poultry service man made about thoroughly cleaning out a poultry house. He said, "You cannot sanitize dirt." You must remove it all first, then sanitize and disinfect the house. We cannot clean sin, but we can let go of it, and Christ will give us the victory as we lay all at His feet.

In our weakness, we need to cry out to God for His mercy and forgiveness. Is my all on the altar? Is He in full control of all of my life?

Bible Reading: Psalm 51
One Year Bible Reading Plan:
John 11:1–16
1 Chronicles 23—25

Phil Schrock, Stuarts Draft, VA

Only God can clean hearts.

The Resigned Life

*Out of the mouth of babes and sucklings hast thou ordained
strength because of thine enemies, that thou mightest
still the enemy and the avenger.*
Psalm 8:2

When we go through certain things in life, we sometimes ask, "Why?" Why is God allowing me to pass through these trials? We may sit and complain about our lot. So quickly we overlook our blessings, never even stopping to thank God. We fail to resign ourselves to His will.

My son had to have an operation for acute appendicitis. Just before he went into the operating room, he entered into serious prayer with his Father in heaven. He prayed that his Father would take away the pain and help him through this ordeal. He prayed for help to be brave, and if it was God's will to have the operation, then he wanted to give himself up totally to Him. He also prayed that if he should die during the operation, he might go home to be with his heavenly Father. This brought tears to our eyes. It touched the hearts of his mother and myself to hear such faith from a child.

The Apostle Paul gave a tremendous testimony, saying, ". . . Christ shall be magnified in my body, whether it be by life, or by death. For to me to live is Christ, and to die is gain." As we go through life and face circumstances that are not favorable to us, let us resign ourselves to His will.

Bible Reading: 2 Timothy 4
One Year Bible Reading Plan:
John 11:17–46
1 Chronicles 26, 27

Mark Meighn, Hattieville, Belize

Yes, my heart says amen to thy will, Lord.

Christ Our All in All

_I am the vine, ye are the branches: He that abideth in me,
and I in him, the same bringeth forth much fruit:
for without me ye can do nothing._
John 15:5

King Solomon tried many things to find happiness. After they were all exhausted, he discovered that his efforts were vanity and vexation of spirit.

Where do we try to find joy and happiness? In the things we do? In the things we buy or the places we go? Can these things really make us happy? Look at the things the world does to find happiness, and you will see that it is not working; there is no joy in it.

Trying to find happiness in material things, or in things we do, does not work. Before I was converted, I was always trying to find fulfillment in the things I did. But after each experience, there was still an empty spot in me. So I looked for more. It was a never ending battle. I always ended up wondering, "Is there anything a person can do to find real joy in life?"

That answer is in Jesus Christ. He is the only one Who can fill every need in every heart. He will never let us down. Sure, there are going to be trials and struggles in this life, but leaning on Jesus is really the only way.

I'm thankful that we can abide in a place where Christ is our all. All the riches, amusements, and worldly pleasures cannot bring us the joy, happiness, and fulfillment that the love and care of our risen Lord and Savior can.

Dustin Nichols, Newberry, IN

Bible Reading: Ecclesiastes 2
One Year Bible Reading Plan:
John 11:47–57
1 Chronicles 28, 29

Jesus + you = happiness

Eyes or Memory

This one thing I do, forgetting those things which are behind,
and reaching forth unto those things which are before . . .
Philippians 3:13

A man who was quickly losing his eyesight because of a degenerative nerve condition, was told by the surgeon that an operation would restore his failing vision, but there was a very real danger that he would lose his memory. After serious consideration, the man consented to proceed with the operation. "I would rather have my eyes to see what is ahead," he said, "than my memory to remind me of those things which are in the past."

Life can be enjoyable, but it can also bring us sorrow and hardships. The loss of a loved one, financial setbacks, or cruel, harsh words can cause grief or depression. Today's Scripture reading encourages us to forget those things which are behind us and to reach out to those things which are before us. We need not be discouraged because of past hurts and lost opportunities. Each day brings with it grace and strength for that day. Someone has said, "The most creative power given to the human spirit is the power to heal the wounds of a past it cannot change."

Bible Reading: Philippians 3
One Year Bible Reading Plan:
John 12:1–19
2 Chronicles 1—3

Melvin L. Yoder, Gambier, OH

God does not take away trials or carry us over them,
but He strengthens us through them.

A Church Worth Reviving

. . . And upon this rock I will build my church;
and the gates of hell shall not prevail against it.
Matthew 16:18

The church of Jesus Christ is the extension of God's arm on earth. It is God's intention that His wisdom would be manifested to principalities and powers in heavenly places by the church (Ephesians 3:10). The church on earth is supposed to reflect the image of Christ. He is the Chief Cornerstone of our building, and we are fitly framed together and are growing into a holy temple in the Lord.

Jesus said that if two or three are gathered in His name, then He is in the midst of them. If Jesus is in our midst, then we have His power available to us. But that power seems to be lacking today. Christ's church needs to be revived.

All of the elements are in place for revival to happen. Jesus is the same as He was in the first century, when the early church grew and spread so rapidly. Jesus is the same as He was in the 16th century when a spiritual fire broke out in Europe, and a revived church of true believers sprang forth with much zeal and power. The church does not need to redefine Jesus or the teachings of the apostles and prophets. What the church needs to do is to return to the Cornerstone, to the Rock of our salvation, to our risen Lord and Savior, Jesus Christ, and ask Him to revive our hearts with a yearning for Him. When the church accomplishes this, then we will have a tremendous impact on our world.

Bible Reading:
Ephesians 2:1–22
One Year Bible Reading Plan:
John 12:20–50
2 Chronicles 4—6

If the gates of hell cannot prevail against the church, then is it not worth reviving?

Terry Lester, Montezuma, GA

Revive us again, fill each heart with Thy love.
May each soul be rekindled with fire from above!
—William P. MacKay 1839-1885

Deeply Rooted

*As ye have therefore received Christ Jesus the Lord, so walk ye
in him: Rooted and built up in him, and stablished in the
faith, as ye have been taught, abounding therein with thanksgiving.*
Colossians 2:6, 7

A few years ago there was an earthquake in Seattle, Washington. Since Seattle is in an earthquake prone zone, the city has strict building codes. Because builders followed those codes, most of the earthquake damage was done to buildings that were nearly 100 years old.

We, too, have a building code for our Christian lives. Today's key verse teaches us that we should have a root system that goes deep and will stand the test of time so that when we tremble under the pressures of life, we may be able to stand.

This root system can only become deeply rooted when we have our daily source of nourishment from God's Word. Our spiritual lives will then be strong and sturdy, we need never fall.

The Bible tells of a wise man who built his house upon a rock. When the rains descended and the floods came, the house was able to stand the test.

Satan has many different ways to hinder our root systems from going deep. Peer pressure, dishonesty, the love of money, pride, and covetousness are a few things that hinder the Word of God from going deep into our hearts, developing strong spiritual roots.

May we be like a seed put into good soil. The rain and the warm sunshine cause it to spring forth and bear precious fruit, some thirty-fold, some sixty-fold, and some one hundred-fold.

Bible Reading: Colossians 2
One Year Bible Reading Plan:
John 13:1–17
2 Chronicles 7—9

Eddie E. Miller, Sugarcreek, OH

---

*On Christ the solid rock I stand;
all other ground is sinking sand.*
—Edward Mote, 1797-1874

Victory Over Sin

*But thanks be to God, which giveth us the
victory through our Lord Jesus Christ.*
1 Corinthians 15:57

The boa constrictor that a man had trained from a baby was now 18 feet long. The trainer would allow the snake to wrap around him, and by the snap of a finger, order it to release its hold. But one day something went amiss. Before an audience, the snake went mad and refused to release. Tighter and tighter became its hold until the deadly serpent crushed his trainer to death.

The bondage and power of sin can bind a person in its awful grip. It may seem so harmless, but it becomes a taskmaster. On every hand, we can see the blight and consequences of sin—pain, debauchery, remorse, and shattered lives. Sin is deceptive. It promises happiness, fulfillment, and liberty; but it brings a smitten conscience, emptiness, and bondage.

Praise God that through Christ we can experience deliverance and live in daily victory over sin. God is faithful to forgive and to cleanse as we repent of, confess, and forsake all sin. "The wages of sin is death, but the gift of God is eternal life through Jesus Christ our Lord." We can enjoy peace, pardon, and power to live the overcoming life here; and in the life to come be forever with the Lord in our eternal home.

As we travel through this sin-stained earth, let us endeavor to keep ourselves unspotted from the world. The pleasures of sin are only for a season, but the unspeakable joys of heaven are forever. Let us lay aside the sin that so easily hinders us in our heavenly race, as we ever look to Jesus, through Whom we are more than conquerors.

Mark Kropf, Cataldo, ID

Bible Reading: Romans 6
One Year Bible Reading Plan:
John 13:18–38
2 Chronicles 10—12

Victory in Jesus, our Savior, forever.
—E. M. Bartlett, 1939

*June 4*_____

Clouds

And now men see not the bright light which is in the clouds:
but the wind passeth, and cleanseth them.
Job 37:21

At times when dark clouds hover low above us, it's hard to visualize the bright sun shining above the clouds. Yet the source of light is just as close to us on a cloudy day as on a clear, sunny day. When the sun comes out following a cloudy, rainy day, we witness the growth in vegetation thriving before us. Who can perform such magnificent works but our almighty Creator? We can only marvel at its splendor. What a purpose God has in clouds! They play an important part in His nourishment of the earth and the provision for mankind.

At times our lives seem full of adversities and trials. We cannot visualize the blessings these sufferings may bring. All we see are the clouds hovering above us. We cry to God to help us through these situations in life, yet the clouds remain. Do we fail to believe that God is at work behind the clouds?

We ask, "Why all these cloudy days?" This is the way we grow and prosper, being formed and molded by God's purpose for our lives. If we let these clouds have their perfect work in our lives, we will shine for Christ and bloom forth as true servants of God. What a purpose God has in clouds: our spiritual nourishment! "Now no chastening for the present seemeth to be joyous, but grievous: nevertheless afterward it yieldeth the peaceable fruit of righteousness unto them which are exercised thereby" (Hebrews 12:11).

Bible Reading:
Hebrews 12:1–17
One Year Bible Reading Plan:
John 14
2 Chronicles 13—16

Wayne Miller, Salem, IN

A desert is the result of too much sunshine.

Linked Together in Christ

And every one members one of another.
Romans 12:5b

Some years ago at the Seattle Special Olympics, nine contestants who were physically or mentally disabled assembled together at the starting line for the 100 yard dash. At the gun, they all started out, not exactly in a dash but with a relish to run and win the race. All, that is, except one boy who stumbled on the asphalt, tumbled over a time or two, and began to cry. The other contestants slowed down and looked behind them. Then they all turned around and went back. Every one of them. One girl with Downs Syndrome bent down and kissed the crying boy and said, "This will make it better." Then all of them linked arms and walked together to the finish line.

This touching incident illustrates a spiritual truth. We need each other. We cannot run the race of the Christian life alone. We need to be linked together with fellow pilgrims as we travel together through the rough wilderness of our earthly journey. We need the encouragement, counsel, correction, discernment, and support of a spiritual brotherhood.

There may be times when we would be inclined to take our own way or choose our own path. The path may seem right. But rejecting the counsel of concerned parents and godly brethren puts us in a perilous spiritual vulnerability. We must be careful not to step out from under the umbrella of protection that God has provided through the church. It is for our own spiritual welfare that we submit ourselves "one to another in the fear of God" (Ephesians 5:21).

Bible Reading: 1 Peter 5
One Year Bible Reading Plan:
John 15
2 Chronicles 17—19

Mark Kropf, Cataldo, ID

The Christian life is a chorus not a solo.

Bird Talk

For a bird of the air shall carry the voice,
and that which hath wings shall tell the matter.
Ecclesiastes 10:20b

On our way to the Canadian North on Route 17 along Lake Superior, we saw a large statue of a Canada goose, the national bird of Canada. Some Canada geese have spent the last few summers in our area, where they find water ponds and grain fields. They raise their young, then fly south in the beginning of November.

Let us notice the characteristics of this intelligent bird. They are willing to descend with their fallen mates. When a goose drops out of formation, two others will follow it to the ground. They protect the fallen one, feed it, and nurse it back to health. Only if the fallen one dies do the others leave and follow another formation.

The geese fly in a "V" formation to break the air for those behind. They encourage each other by honking. Whenever a goose strays from the formation, it soon returns, because it is far easier to travel together in the broken air. When the leader grows tired, instinct tells another goose to take the lead position. No resentment is shown toward the lead goose. They all share the task.

If we have as much sense as geese, we will stand with each other in difficult times and urge each other to continue on. Let us consider one another and stimulate one another to love and good works as we see the great day approaching, when we will migrate to the promised land.

Bible Reading: Psalm 104:1-24; 11:1
One Year Bible Reading Plan:
John 16:1–15
2 Chronicles 20—22

Leonard N. Jantzi, Brunner, ON

The closer Christians get to Christ,
the closer they get to one another.

Christ to the Rescue

And he said unto Jesus, Lord, remember me
when thou comest into thy kingdom.
Luke 23:42

Is the crucifixion only a historical fact in our minds, or does it stir our hearts to faith, as it did the thief on the cross? Let us consider this man.

The Bible does not say that he previously knew Christ, saw the miracles He performed, or heard His teaching. Yet this man had faith. What spoke to this thief, we do not know. Perhaps it was Christ's prayer, "Father, forgive them for they know not what they do."

The people and the rulers stood around the cross and derided Christ, saying, "He saved others, let him save himself." The other thief railed on Him, saying, "If thou be the Christ, save thyself and us." The believing thief rebuked him and said, "Doth thou not fear God, seeing thou art in the same condemnation, and we indeed justly, but this man has done nothing amiss?" He feared God, justified Christ, and recognized that his own condemnation was just. It caused him to have faith in the Son of God.

For many years, God spoke to Abraham. Abraham had experience to support his belief. God worked in Moses' life for years: in the courts of Pharaoh, in the wilderness, in the great encounter at the burning bush. Moses had reason to believe. This thief may have met Jesus for the first time at the scene of the crucifixion. He allowed the fear of God to come upon him. He took his place among sinners and saw his only hope to be the Man on the middle cross. By faith he cried out, "Lord, remember me," to which he heard the answer, "Today thou shalt be with me in paradise." Praise God, He still honors simple acts of faith!

Whether you face a life or death crisis or a simple decision or struggle, remember the crucifixion scene. God still honors the heartfelt phrase, "Lord, remember me."

Willard Hochstetler, Woodburn, IN

Bible Reading: Luke 23:26–46
One Year Bible Reading Plan:
John 16:16–33
2 Chronicles 23—25

No man is rich enough to buy back his past.

Rescue Squad

*And he said unto them, I must preach the kingdom of God
to other cities also: for therefore am I sent.*
Luke 4:43

Here at home there is a local rescue squad that is called on in times of emergency. If a child does not come home from school and is reported missing, the rescue squad takes action very quickly. Maps are brought out, and the rescue squad grids the community in minute detail. Members of the local law enforcement agencies, the rescue squad, and other volunteers are given different areas of search. Phone calls are made to alert the community, and an intensive search begins. Four-wheel drive trucks, ATV's with spotlights, volunteers on foot with high-powered flashlights, and even small aircraft are called in. No stone is left unturned while the whereabouts of the child are unknown. Eventually the child is found, and there is much rejoicing in the community and elsewhere.

Suppose a member of our church is reported spiritually missing. Do we have a well-trained "rescue squad" in place for the search to begin? Let us sound the alarm, gather together for prayer and fasting, bring out our spiritual spotlights and leave no stone unturned until the missing one is recovered.

Bible Reading: Luke 4:18–30
One Year Bible Reading Plan:
John 17
2 Chronicles 26—28

Terry Lester, Montezuma, GA

Joy shall be in heaven over one sinner that repents.

Rejection

For I reckon that the sufferings of this present time are not worthy to be compared with the glory which shall be revealed in us.
Romans 8:18

Have you ever felt rejected? Did someone say something to you that hurt you? Perhaps it came down through the grapevine that you said something bad that you never said. One time you said something you wished you had never said, or did something you now regret, but people will not forget. Maybe someone has ridiculed you for something you could not help. It hurts, doesn't it? You feel like withdrawing from the whole human race. Have you ever wished you were a chipmunk that could burrow into the soil when winter comes along with its bitter, cold wind? You could just sleep until the spring breezes blow across the grass.

Maybe you are going through a real test right now. You feel rejected and worthless. You are sick of people misunderstanding you.

Jesus was often hurt. People said many things about Him that were not true. They accused Him falsely. Toward the last, they really got ugly. They spit in His face, they slapped Him; finally, they killed Him. It does not get any worse than that.

> **Bible Reading:** Philippians 3:8–14; 2 Corinthians 1:1–10
> **One Year Bible Reading Plan:**
> John 18:1–23
> 2 Chronicles 29—31

When you hurt badly, when you think you cannot endure any more, when you think people have treated you as badly as they possibly can, why not do as Jesus did? He stretched His arms out to each end of the cross and said, "Father, forgive them."

Alvin Mast, Millersburg, OH

When life gives you a dog that kills chickens,
make chicken noodle soup!

A Rugged Path

That there should be no schism in the body; but that the
members should have the same care one for another.
1 Corinthians 12:25

One evening while bringing in the cows, I noticed something among the cows that reminded me of people. The cow lane was not very wide. In some places it was muddy from the rain, with just a path on one side, so that the cows had to go single file. One cow did not wait her turn but did what was normal for a cow. She shoved the next cow back, which caused a chain reaction. Another cow had to stop quickly, causing the cow behind her to bump into her. So she turned around and gave her a shove. One cow made it hard for them all. If she would have waited, they all would have gotten to the barn sooner. But cows being cows, they did not know any better.

Let's think about ourselves. Jesus wants us to be considerate of others. How do we walk with our friends and brethren? Do we help wherever we can, or do we just go our own way and not help the brother sinking in despair? Do we notice if someone is hurting and struggling? What do we plan to do with our riches after we have them all hoarded up for ourselves? We cannot take them with us into eternity. After all, these material goods are God's, so why not share with others? Let us cheer one another along the rugged road of everyday life.

Reuben Miller, Holton, MI

Bible Reading: 1 Corinthians 13
One Year Bible Reading Plan:
John 18:24–40
2 Chronicles 32, 33

Love thy neighbor as thyself.

Unfeigned Love

Seeing ye have purified your souls in obeying the truth through the Spirit unto unfeigned love of the brethren, see that ye love one another with a pure heart fervently.
1 Peter 1:22

Almost two thousand years ago, brother Peter said that we should love each other fervently with a pure heart. Beloved, as we look around the world, we must stop and ask ourselves, "Is there any love, even in our churches? Is there love?" Can I look my brother or sister in the face and say, "Brother, I love you from a pure heart"? If so, then why is there tumult and strife among us? Let us be honest with ourselves, our love for each other is fading out. Can I see my brother receiving blessings from the Lord without thinking, "Why him and not me?" The Apostle Paul admonishes us to rejoice evermore with the prospering brother.

Will I allow myself to be used as a door mat or a floor rag? Me? Never! I must lift up my self-esteem. No, I cannot let myself be trampled on.

The man after God's own heart (David) said, "Let me be a servant for the Lord." Being a servant, we dare not say how the Master is to use us. If my love for God means to be used by God, then by all means I, yes, even I, am to be used by my brother. That is what unfeigned love means.

Is there a limit to my forbearance with an often offending brother? Can I allow myself to be pushed around? Do I draw a line after the fourth or fifth time and say, "This is enough. No more"? Love unfeigned bears with the brother's shortcoming. That is longsuffering.

Mark G. Meighn, Belize City, Belize

Bible Reading: 1 Peter 1
One Year Bible Reading Plan:
John 19:1–22
2 Chronicles 34—36

Let me be more and more like Thee, O Savior.

Stop!

Finally, brethren, pray for us, that the word of the Lord may have free course, and be glorified, even as it is with you.
2 Thessalonians 3:1

Several years ago I let my horse trot through a stop sign on our way to church. My young daughter looked up at me and asked, "Daddy, what does that stop sign say?" I explained to her that s-t-o-p spells *stop*. But she persisted, "But, Daddy, what does it mean?" I had to humbly admit that it means to stop.

I felt condemned, as for several years I had been easing through this stop sign without really stopping. I had convinced myself that because of the clear view, it was not necessary to come to a complete stop.

In reality, I was teaching my children disregard for the law. I was teaching them not to take stop signs too seriously—that they do not really mean what they say. I could have reasoned with them that it is a matter of interpretation, but that sign did not need to be interpreted. It meant what it said—*stop*. The only way to ease my conscience was to stop.

My children are about grown now, but at times I wonder if they would say that I apply the Scriptures in the same way that I regarded the stop sign. Perhaps things which are plain and easy to be understood, we wrest to our own destruction.

Sometimes it is easy to say that Scriptures that are clear and plain are a matter of interpretation, when really, they need only to be applied.

Needless to say, I became more conscious of stop signs from that day on. I find it much more difficult to apply that same principle in my spiritual life. The spirit indeed is willing, but the flesh is weak.

Bible Reading: James 2
One Year Bible Reading Plan:
John 19:23–42
Ezra 1, 2

Bill Miller, Conneautville, PA

God said it, I believe it, that settles it.

The Best Wine Last

Every man at the beginning doth set forth good wine;
and when men have well drunk, then that which is worse:
but thou hast kept the good wine until now.
John 2:10

Jesus was a guest at a wedding. When the hosts ran out of wine to serve, Jesus gave very simple directions to remedy the situation. When the servants filled the water pots with water, Jesus miraculously transformed it into wine. The governor of the feast, ignorant of what had taken place, inquired why the best wine was served last.

Why was it so strange to the governor of the feast that the best wine was provided last? It was contrary to the custom of the time for weddings. When men's appetites were keenest, the best was served. After their appetites were diminished, the poorer quality was served, and they hardly recognized it. When Jesus miraculously changed the water into wine, He provided a much better tasting beverage than that which they had at first.

This story provokes an insight into the way God works. It also provides guidance for our response to the directions He gives to us. Both His work and our work are necessary to continually experience the best wine.

What is the best wine that Christ provides for us? The Gospel, which followed the Old Testament law, is a much better covenant. Just meditate on the book of Hebrews and see for yourself. God saved the best wine until last!

Likewise, personal spiritual growth leads us on to a deeper and fuller experience with God. Our spiritual progress enables us to taste even better wine.

God is so much that way. We always have something better to look forward to. A bright heavenly future lies before all who obediently fill their water pots with the water of faith. And the best wine has been saved until last, when we will enjoy it forever.

Bible Reading: John 2:1–17
One Year Bible Reading Plan:
John 20
Ezra 3—5

Delmar R. Eby, London, KY

When we walk with the Lord, the best is yet to come.

Fearing God

We ought to obey God rather than men.
Acts 5:29b

Pharaoh, king of Egypt, commanded the Hebrew midwives to kill all the baby boys they delivered and to allow the girls to live. The Hebrew midwives feared God. They recognized that Pharaoh's command was direct disobedience to God. They chose to obey God, rather than Pharaoh.

Today we are under pressure to limit the size of our families. Some rulers of our day encourage abortion, and in some countries they command that it be done. When does life begin? Who gives life? Do we choose whether a child should live or die? What should be our response to these issues? Because of the ideas promoted on television, in the newspapers, and in magazines, we fail to look at this issue as seriously as we should. We have become calloused to death, especially the death of the unborn. The concerns of increasing world population, limited resources, and seeing children as a bother instead of a blessing have affected our thinking.

Our response should be to fear God as the midwives did. God wants His people to multiply and be strong. We should be evangelizing, as well as raising up children for the Lord. God will bless us as we follow His commands, not being influenced negatively by our society. A question to ponder: Is God permitting abortion to fill heaven with souls that we are refusing to have because of our selfishness?

Bible Reading: Exodus 1:1–22
One Year Bible Reading Plan:
John 21
Ezra 6—8

Mark Webb, Aroda, VA

Jesus loves the little children.

The Answer Is Yes

*And if ye call on the Father, who without respect of persons
judgeth according to every man's work, pass the
time of your sojourning here in fear.*
1 Peter 1:17

Recently someone called our office. I picked up the receiver.
"Is this the Akamba (a bus company) office?" a voice inquired. "No,
this is the Lamp & Light Bible correspondence course office," I corrected. "Sorry, I called the wrong number," he apologized and hung
up.

In the Bible, we find people who tried to call, but their prayers
were not answered.

In 1 Kings 18, four hundred prophets of Baal called from morning till evening, but got no answer. Simon the sorcerer, instead of
calling, attempted to buy the Holy Spirit with money. On the other
hand, people of God, like Elijah, Peter, and Stephen, did not need
to make a show or call extra long to be heard. They called, and God
answered them, even beyond their expectations. Their secret? They
were connected to the right place.

It does not matter who you are, what you are, what you have,
or where you live. Anyone is qualified to call the greatest office,
greatest and perfect home, greatest business, and greatest power
the world has ever known. The Lord Jesus Christ, King of kings,
and Lord of lords is His name.
He made the first call. Men need
only answer it.

> **Bible Reading:** 2 Samuel
> 22:1–22
> **One Year Bible Reading Plan:**
> Acts 1
> Ezra 9, 10

"In my distress I called upon
the LORD, and cried to my God:
and he did hear my voice out of
his temple, and my cry did enter into his ears" (2 Samuel 22:7).

Collins Okoth, Nakuru, Kenya

---

*Call services are available any time around
the globe by the blood of Christ.*

June 16

The Effect of the Spirit

Thou hast made known to me the ways of life;
thou shalt make me full of joy with thy countenance.
Acts 2:28

The rain had lazily drifted in, a few drops at a time, as if teasing us. The tiny drops sat bewilderingly on the parched earth for a few dry moments, then crept into the soil. A few other drops splashed down to take their place. These too disappeared. The clouds peered down—then, with a roar, a mighty stream of rain pummeled the ground as if avenging its fellows. The rain continued for most of the day, sometimes beating the ground mercilessly, at other times teasing the grass with a drop here and there. Now an occasional drop drips from leaf to leaf, joyously playing the last tap.

At Pentecost, the believers were all with one accord in one place when suddenly there came a sound like a rushing, mighty wind. They were all filled with the Holy Ghost. The Spirit of God had "blown" from heaven and filled them.

When the Holy Ghost comes to dwell in man, He manifests Himself so strongly that it is impossible to hide Him. The effect on the group in the upper room was that they spoke in other languages as the Spirit gave them utterance. Sometimes He comes in a small whisper. The manifestation is not loud and boisterous, but with quietness. The result is not an earth-shattering noise, but a peaceful witness in the heart.

The quietness of the Spirit as He fills us is as forceful as when He filled those in the upper room. The witness is the same. It produces fruit unto everlasting life. It is up to God to decide how He fills you with His Spirit. It is up to you to decide that you will live in a way that He is manifested and glorified.

> **Bible Reading:** Acts 2
> **One Year Bible Reading Plan:**
> Acts 2:1–13
> Nehemiah 1—3

Alvin Mast, Millersburg, OH

Living the Christian life without the Spirit
is a vain attempt at living the impossible.

172

Freed!

If the Son therefore shall make you free, ye shall be free indeed.
John 8:36

About noon one day I lay in my cell staring at the tile ceiling. Suddenly I heard voices coming down the hall. It was the jailor and the centurion, and let me tell you, they did not sound happy! They were talking about the prisoner that they had to release this year over the time of the feast. My hopes didn't rise a fraction. I would never be released. I knew that! No chance!

The men stopped in front of my cell and stared through the bars at me. I thought that they were trying to rub it in, so I turned and looked at the wall. Then I heard the keys rattle in the door. The door swung open, and the jailor said, "Barabbas, you're free." Free? I couldn't believe it!

Yes, Barabbas was free. And like Barabbas, you and I were in prison—the prison of sin where Satan is the jailor. One day we were also released.

What Barabbas did with his life after he was freed from prison I do not know, but I do know what we can do with our freedom. We can go out from our prison telling others about the saving grace of the Lord Jesus Christ, and how He freed us from sin.

If you are still in prison, cry out to the Lord, because your deliverance has already been provided for. When you cry out, your door will be opened, and you will be free!

Kevin Coblentz, Hicksville, OH

Bible Reading: Matthew
27:12–26
One Year Bible Reading Plan:
Acts 2:14–47
Nehemiah 4—6

Believe on the Son, and you shall be free indeed.

June 18

Skipping Stones

Verily I say unto you, Except ye be converted, and become as little children, ye shall not enter into the kingdom of heaven.
Matthew 18:3

It was a beautiful fall day. The employees had the one rope machine ticking and the other one spinning. Orders were being processed one after another. In the middle of all this, I found myself on the creek bank skipping stones with our seven-year-old son, Marcus, who has Down's syndrome. Here I was skipping stones with a child. I felt rather foolish, but doing Marcus's favorite thing made him so happy!

How we love it when Jesus, through the Holy Spirit, comes down to our level and helps us when we preach, work, or are in fear or need. Yes, then we get joyful!

I realized that the contrast between Jesus coming down to me and me coming down to Marcus is much greater. That took away my foolish feelings and replaced them with joyful blessings.

Fathers, please sacrifice your valuable time today and help your children do their favorite things. Watch their eyes overflow with happiness. Remember that Jesus made a much greater sacrifice for you on the cross than when you give what you think is valuable time to your children. Furthermore, the only way your children feel loved, accepted, and needed is to communicate with them heart-to-heart.

As a child looks up to his parents, so are we to communicate with our Savior Jesus Christ. That's what He is telling us in our key verse today.

Christ said, "He who has ears to hear let him hear."

Bible Reading: Matthew 25:31–46
One Year Bible Reading Plan:
Acts 3
Nehemiah 7, 8

Andrew M. Troyer, Conneautville, PA

Take time for your children; Christ takes time for you.

Our Salvation

*Lo, I come to do thy will, O God. He taketh away
the first, that he may establish the second.*
Hebrews 10:9

It surely must have been a dreadful experience for the Egyptians to have the first nine plagues come. Now the children of Israel prepared to obey the command to kill the Passover lamb and paint their door frames with blood to escape the death penalty pronounced upon the land of Egypt. The verdict was final!

Three requirements must be met: find a perfect lamb, kill the sacrifice at the correct time, and paint the door frame with the blood before the Lord appears.

These three points were also important at Calvary. The lamb was to be killed at midafternoon, between the two quarters of the last half of the day. When Jesus was crucified, there was darkness from 12:00 to 3:00 p.m. At the end of this time, Jesus cried out and said, "It is finished," and died. The earth quaked, the veil in the temple was rent from top to bottom, and many saints rose from the grave. These things happened to signal that a great reality had come to pass.

A soldier thrust his spear into Jesus' side, and out came blood and water. This blood perfected forever them that are sanctified. This blood applied to our lives takes care of our sins. Confession is important, but it is not enough. Let us apply the blood to our sins before the Lord returns.

Bible Reading: Exodus 12:1–7;
Hebrews 10:9–18
One Year Bible Reading Plan:
Acts 4:1–22
Nehemiah 9—11

Ben Coblentz, Millersburg, OH

The blood cleanses, redeems, reconciles, saves, justifies, and sancifies.

Purity By God's Grace

That the trial of your faith, being much more precious than of gold that perisheth, though it be tried with fire, might be found unto praise and honor and glory at the appearing of Jesus Christ.
1 Peter 1:7

Peter, that bold, outspoken apostle who before his conversion defended his Lord with a sword, afterwards suffered much and finally finished his earthly race upside down on a cross. He had learned much about growing in grace through tribulation when he penned these words.

The Christian is called to suffer. Do we realize this? God has no better way to glorify His name than to draw us to Himself by sending trials (or allowing them to come) into our lives.

I like the way the Dortrecht Confession of Faith sums it up. It pleads for us to allow God, by His grace, to make us fit and worthy to enter heaven. Nothing impure will enter there, so it should be our sincere and heartfelt prayer that God will, by His means, purify us so we may be fit for heaven.

Once a goldsmith was heating his gold. He stirred the liquid with his ladle and scooped the impurities off the top. Someone asked him how he knew when his product was pure.

His reply was, "When I can see my reflection on the surface."

God's method generally does not consist of one thorough heating and then we are pure. Repeated heatings are necessary to bring us to higher planes.

It is comforting to know that nothing will come our way that our Lord has not experienced before us. May our attitude toward our trials be positive. They are for our eternal welfare.

Kenton Martin, Carson City, MI

Bible Reading: 1 Peter 4
One Year Bible Reading Plan:
Acts 4:23–37
Nehemiah 12, 13

There shall in no wise enter into heaven anything that defileth.

What Do You Think?

For as he thinketh in his heart, so is he . . .
Proverbs 23:7a

In today's Scripture reading Jesus asks Peter about paying taxes, and prods him: "Peter, what do you think?" It is important what we think. We need to be careful about our thoughts. You know the familiar lines:

> Sow a thought, reap an act,
> Sow an act, reap a habit,
> Sow a habit, reap a character,
> Sow a character, reap a destiny.

Many people live in a make-believe world. They do not think rightly but believe what is really not true. Sound thinking faces facts, believes truth, and does not evade reality. "Keep thy heart with all diligence; for out of it are the issues of life" (Proverbs 4:23). Right thinking leads to healthy convictions about matters of right and wrong. It will bring confession, repentance, and a turn to right living.

Guard what enters your eyes and ears. Let nothing enter there that would pollute your mind. We live in bodies with minds prone to wrong thoughts and foolish thoughts. But by the power of God, we can have renewed minds that think on things that are true, honest, just, pure, lovely, of good report, things of value, worthy to be praised (Philippians 4:8).

Bible Reading: Matthew 17:14–27
One Year Bible Reading Plan:
Acts 5:1–16
Esther 1—3

Edward Hochstetler, Hicksville, OH

We may not be what we think we are—
but what we think, we are.

The Christian Home

Submitting yourselves one to another in the fear of God.
Ephesians 5:21

Love is the basic material that transfers a house into a home.

A family camped on a sidewalk in town had no place to live. Two women standing close by were talking about them. One said to the other, "such a nice family and no home to live in." A little boy in the family said, "Oh, we have a home, but we don't have a house to put it in." Many today have a house to live in but do not have a home. In a Christian home each lives for the others, and all live for Christ.

When a baby has trouble, it cries because it cannot talk. He wants what he wants, and he wants it now. But when an adult wants what he wants regardless of how unhappy it makes someone else, he has failed to grow up. He is an adult baby.

The love a husband and wife have for each other should be a self-sacrificing, forgiving kind of love. Self-love wrecks a home, but true love builds a home. We cannot try primarily to change others. A better home begins with me.

> **Bible Reading:** Colossians 3
> **One Year Bible Reading Plan:**
> Acts 5:17–42
> Esther 4—6

Eli Yoder, Stuarts Draft, VA

---

*Marriage is a union that cannot be organized
when both sides think they are management.*

Let Us Be Honest

Wherefore by their fruits ye shall know them.
Matthew 7:20

Today's Scripture reading reminds us that we are known by our fruits. There are also many other things that help to identify us. It has been said that a man is known by the company he keeps. Some years ago, we noticed a sign in front of a small country church that said, "A man is known by the company he avoids."

The things we read also identify us. The cabbage caterpillar feeds only on cabbage, while the walnut caterpillar feeds on the leaves of the walnut tree. The milkweed caterpillar feeds only on milkweed, and we readily identify the potato bug by his love of the potato plant.

The man who spends hours reading the sports pages does so because he is a sports fan. The literature in your home identifies what kind of thinker you are. Do you have ample time for the newspaper but give only a fleeting glance at good, sound literature, which might help you grow spiritually? We become like the books we read and the people we associate with.

Bible Reading: Matthew 7:20
One Year Bible Reading Plan:
Acts 6
Esther 7—10

Does your reading identify you as a child of God?

Melvin Yoder, Gambier, OH

The more we walk with Christ, the more Christ-like we become.

Homesick for Heaven

We have a building of God, an house not made
with hands, eternal in the heavens.
2 Corinthians 5:1b

We have been building houses for people who lost theirs in a tornado. Most of the folks have been living in the homes of family or friends, or in some other makeshift arrangement. They are anxious to move home. Many of them move home before their houses are completed. Some even move into their houses before we have the drywall hung. Most have only a temporary generator for electricity, but they are so glad to be home.

I have been thinking about our home in heaven which Jesus has gone to prepare. Are we anxious to move there? Do we sometimes enjoy our temporary setting so much that we have little desire to move to heaven? When we think of that home in heaven, we do not need to worry about it not being ready for us. We will not need a U-Haul, for we will leave all our possessions behind. We will not need electricity, for the Lamb is the light there.

When someone moves into a new house, it does not take long for things to need repair. The paint gets scratched, or someone spills something and stains the carpet. Many things happen, and the house begins to show wear. Our heavenly home will not require maintenance.

To be able to build a new house, we must have our names on a deed. To receive our home in glory, we must have our names written in the Lamb's book of life.

Bible Reading: Revelation 21:21—22:7
One Year Bible Reading Plan:
Acts 7:1–19
Job 1—3

Mark Webb, Birmingham, AL

Can you truly say, "I'm ready to move Home"?

The Spotted Garment

*And to her was granted that she should be arrayed in fine linen,
clean and white: for the fine linen is the righteousness of saints.*
Revelation 19:8

One morning after finishing my personal devotions, I was sitting in my rocking chair meditating on current events. I must have fallen asleep, because I awoke sometime later realizing I had had a dream.

In my dream I saw a woman dressed as a bride, wearing a beautiful white dress. I also saw the Lord standing beside her. My eyes suddenly were drawn to a black spot on the hem of her otherwise perfect garment. I asked the Lord, "What is the meaning of this?" Sadly he pointed to me and replied, "That spot is you. If you do not repent, I will have to blot your name out of my book."

When I awoke I began to confess and forsake some bitter and ungodly attitudes that had plagued my mind during that time.

It is hard to express the joy that came with the realization that my Lord could now remove that spot from my life.

No attitude is worth hanging onto if it keeps us out of the Lamb's book of life. We must turn it over to Him so that He can present us "faultless and blameless" to the Father.

Bible Reading: Matthew 22:1–14
One Year Bible Reading Plan:
Acts 7:20–43
Job 4—6

David Lee Yoder, Russellville, KY

To dissolve "spots," try the detergent of God's Word.

A Sure Foundation

*For other foundation can no man lay
than that is laid, which is Jesus Christ.*
1 Corinthians 3:11

It was an engineer's challenge. A 46-story bank was to be built in Hong Kong, but the construction site was found to have a bed of mud over 100 feet deep. Construction workers met the challenge with extensive digging, pumping down concrete and erecting eight huge pillars, each weighing 1,000 tons. Thus they provided an adequate foundation for the building.

My nephew, who told this story at our son's wedding, said that he really does not care about that bank, but he does care about laying the proper foundation for our marriages. When do we begin to build such a foundation? Certainly, it is essential that a Christian couple start on day one to have a family altar—reading, praying, and singing together. That is a good foundation for building a Christian home, but is it the beginning of the foundation?

I think the building materials for a solid foundation are obtained before this. What Christian virtues do young people observe in our homes which give them a vision for establishing their own Christian homes? Is the young man who is dating your daughter greeted with a smile and treated with Christian hospitality when he visits your home? Is he impressed with the "meek and quiet spirit" of his loved one's mother. Is he impressed with the manners, respect, and obedience of the other children? Is he impressed with cleanliness and orderliness? Or is he depressed with the opposites? The same applies to the girl who visits a boy's home. These young people have their eyes and ears open during this period of their lives. I know I did.

Lord, help us to remember that we are not only to have functioning Christian homes, but that we are now laying the groundwork for our children's future as well.

Bible Reading: 1 Corinthians 3
One Year Bible Reading Plan:
Acts 7:44–60
Job 7—9

Mahlon Gingerich, Millersburg, OH

Building on sand is more than unwise, it is disastrous.

Delighting in the Lord

_Delight thyself also in the Lord; and he
shall give thee the desires of thine heart._
Psalm 37:4

The snow floated straight down, more slowly than seemed possible, forming a perfectly smooth blanket of white. The beauty was more pronounced because of its rarity. Here in windswept Kansas, we hardly ever get to see such a snow, each fence post topped with its own white cap. More commonly we see road signs obliterated by sticky snow, driven my a biting wind.

Isaiah uses both rain and snow as types of the Word of God, of which God said, "[It] shall not return unto me void, but it shall accomplish that which I please, and it shall prosper in the thing whereto I sent it."

God's Word comes in different ways to accomplish His different purposes. Perhaps we could say that the rain represents His nourishing Word of instruction, doctrine, and teaching. In the torrential gales of a storm, we see His declarations of divine power. The stinging sleet is like His Word of conviction. The pummeling hail resembles His judgment.

But the gentle snow is like God's whisper, "Take time out of your busy schedule to sit in silence in My presence and fill your spirit with My delight."

All day long the gentle snow continued. I gazed at the snow as often and as long as I thought my responsibilities allowed. I wish now I would have gazed longer. Those responsibilities would have been there the next day. The snow was not.

Too often I have allowed the pressures and the burdens of the day to deprive me of the delight of communion with my Lord. My devotions become something to get out of the way so I can get on with the day. Lord, help me to delight myself in You, for You are the desire of my heart.

Bible Reading: Psalm 147
One Year Bible Reading Plan:
Acts 8:1–25
Job 10—12

Harry Shenk, Hutchinson, KS

If we are too busy for God, we are too busy.

Unforgiving

If a man say, I love God, and hateth his brother, he is a liar:
for he that loveth not his brother whom he hath seen,
how can he love God whom he hath not seen?
1 John 4:20

Do we realize what effect unforgiveness has on us, both physically and spiritually? Doctors have traced many illnesses to a patient's bitterness over something or someone they are unwilling to forgive. The body can become so tense that the immune system cannot function properly.

In today's Bible reading, Peter asked Jesus how many times he should forgive a brother who has sinned against him. Peter asked if he should forgive him seven times, which was the custom of that day. Jesus answered, "Not only seven times, but seventy times seven." That is four hundred and ninety times. No matter how many times a person sins against us, we should forgive that person.

Too often we are like the unforgiving servant. The offense may not be monetary, but what if someone hurts our feelings? Do we start to harbor bitterness against that person?

Satan would like for us to think that we can be bitter at someone and still love God. This is false. In our key verse, John condemns this kind of thought. You cannot love God and at the same time hate your brother.

The unforgiving servant discovered that it does not pay to sit in this prison cell in chains of bitterness and anger. Jesus said it best in the Lord's prayer, "And forgive us our debts as we forgive our debtors."

Bible Reading: Matthew 18:21–35
One Year Bible Reading Plan:
Acts 8:26–40
Job 13—15

Jethro Miller, Hicksville, OH

The first person who gains from forgiveness
is the person who does the forgiving.

Washing Nets

_And when they had brought their ships to land,
they forsook all, and followed him._
Luke 5:11

Peter was busy washing nets after a long night of fishing. He had worked hard, but had nothing to show for it. He may have been thinking of getting done, going home, and trying again tomorrow. He was busy working when the crowds began to gather around. The Master had come.

Suddenly Jesus stood before Peter and asked to use his boat. Peter might have thought, "I'm busy now, later would be better." Instead, he responded immediately.

Jesus had Peter's full attention as He taught. When he was finished, He spoke to Peter, "Launch out and let down the nets." Peter's faith wavered, but again he responded, obeyed and was rewarded abundantly.

Am I, like Peter, busy washing nets—fulfilling the daily duties of my life? Am I willing to allow the Lord to interrupt my well-planned schedule, or am I too busy?

Peter would have missed a great blessing if he would not have allowed Jesus to board his boat. The Lord wants to use us as well. Am I going to obey even when it seems unreasonable? Peter could have said, "There are no fish in the sea. Why launch out?" May we today, by faith, launch out into the deep where God's blessings are.

Bible Reading: Luke 5:1–15
One Year Bible Reading Plan:
Acts 9:1–22
Job 16—18

The disciples forsook all and followed Jesus. May we not revel in blessings received but follow our beloved Master on to greater heights of usefulness.

Carl Martin, Lititz, PA

_The Lord never asks us to give up something
unless He gives something better in return._

Are You a Teacher?

Be thou diligent to know the state of thy flocks,
and look well to thy herds.
Proverbs 27:23

Having taught school for several years, I am often referred to as a "teacher." I occasionally hear people remark, "I'd never be a teacher." I am a teacher since I am responsible for a group of children each day and have to make sure they learn the necessary things of life, but are we not all teachers? Each of us is responsible for the example we leave. Parents are responsible to teach and train their children.

As brothers and sisters in the church, we also teach by the example we leave to others. We are responsible to teach the world what a true Christian is. By our words and actions, the world learns what the Bible says and how a Christian lives.

Do I see my responsibility to look after the things under my care as Proverbs 27:23 says? I take this verse as a challenge to be diligent in my personal life and also in the duties to which the Lord calls me. If I am not diligent in school, the children suffer. When we are not diligent as Christians, the cause of Christ suffers.

Many of the words we say will be forgotten, but our example is not forgotten. Whether we are young or old, we need to remember that somebody follows us. Let us be diligent and faithful teachers in the duties to which the Lord calls us.

Bible Reading: Ezekiel 33:1–16
One Year Bible Reading Plan:
Acts 9:23–43
Job 19, 20

Luke Schwartz, Harrodsburg, KY

The Lord needs more teachers in an unlearned world.

Marvelous Grace of God

_Being justified freely by his grace through
the redemption that is in Christ Jesus._
Romans 3:24

Recently the grace of God took on a whole new meaning in my life. In today's Scripture reading, the Apostle Paul says, "Where sin abounded, grace did much more abound." Today we see and hear much about the sin around us, but praise be to God that His grace does much more abound.

Each of us is influenced by a variety of things. We must reckon with these influences because they affect us and shape us. The Scriptures warn us of the effects of evil influences. But as Christians, we have experienced a miraculous work in our hearts. The thing that makes the difference in our lives is the grace of God.

Grace gives us the opportunity to choose. We may have developed bad habits that are hard to overcome. We may have characteristics that beset us, or face circumstances that discourage us. It is easy to allow these habits and pressures to shape our character. But God's grace has appeared, and brings salvation to all men—the ability to choose a different course. "Put off the old man, and put on the new man" is possible because of the grace of God.

Grace forgives. Grace frees us from the guilt and condemnation of the past. If it were not for this, we would be miserable, hopeless creatures—slaves to corruption.

Grace delivers and saves. Being saved by grace, the Christian is no longer bound as a slave to sin. Praise God! "For sin shall not have dominion over you: for ye are not under the law, but under grace" (Romans 6:14).

Lester Zehr, Grabill, IN

Bible Reading: Romans
5:16—6:18
One Year Bible Reading Plan:
Acts 10:1–23
Job 21, 22

My grace is sufficient for thee.

Three Square Meals

In the mean while his disciples prayed him, saying, Master, eat.
John 4:31

I once asked a brother to go with me to another state. He said he would go if he could have three square meals, so I struck a deal with him. We had a real nice trip.

Jesus went to the city of Samaria one day. He came to Jacob's well and being wearied with his journey, He sat by the well. A woman of Samaria came to draw water, and Jesus told her, "Give me to drink." The disciples may have been like we are, concerned about three square meals. They were in the city buying food, while Jesus took time to share with the woman at the well.

He told her about another well, called Living Water. Jesus took time to lead this woman to the Living Water. As a result, she left her water pot and went into the city. She told the men, "Come, see a man which told me all things that ever I did: is not this the Christ?" Then they went out of the city, and came to Him. In the meantime, His disciples told Him, "Master, eat." But He told them, "I have meat to eat that ye know not of."

There is something more important than eating three square meals a day. It is far more important to share the saving gospel with some seeking soul and lead them to the Living Water than it is to get every bite we are accustomed to. We have saved a soul from going to a burning hell. Consider the account of the rich man in hell. He said that he had five brethren. He pleaded that someone from the dead would testify unto them, lest they also come into this place of torment.

> **Bible Reading:** John 4:1–42
> **One Year Bible Reading Plan:**
> Acts 10:24–48
> Job 23—25

Simon Overholt, Auburn, KY

A soul saved from hell is another soul for heaven.

Where Are You Looking?

I will lift up mine eyes unto the hills, from whence cometh my help.
Psalm 121:1

The job seemed endless. I was working alone. The hot Nicaraguan sun beat down on my sweat-soaked clothes. A pile of packed dirt and stones was in front of me. I had no skid-steer or tractor with a loader, only a pick and a shovel. The small trailer hitched behind the tractor waited to be loaded. When it was full, it would be driven down to the new house and shoveled into wheelbarrows. Then it would be wheeled inside and dumped onto the uneven floor to get ready for concrete. But that was not all. A sledge hammer must be used to break the large stones to make the ground more level. My energy diminished with every shovelful thrown onto the trailer.

Then a saying that I had read a few days before flashed through my mind. "Obstacles are what you see when you take your eyes off the goal." A new vision started forming in my mind. I saw a level floor with rugs and household furniture arranged in an orderly way. That boosted my energy. I am helping to build a house! The goal gave me courage against overwhelming obstacles.

So it is in all of life. Milking cows, making mini-barns, washing dishes, changing diapers, or whatever daily task we face, can become drudgery. But instead of looking at the obstacles, we can choose to think, "We're occupying till our Lord comes!"

We choose where we look. Looking backward stops our progress (Genesis 19:26). Looking Christward saves (John 3:14, 15). Looking at difficulties brings discouragement and depression (Matthew 14:29, 30). Looking heavenward glorifies (Acts 7:55).

Timothy Coblentz, Wallingford, KY

Bible Reading: Philippians 3:7–21
One Year Bible Reading Plan:
Acts 11
Job 26—28

Goals make the difference between a pilgrim and a tramp.

Contributors to the Cause

Thou therefore endure hardness as a good soldier of Jesus Christ.
2 Timothy 2:3

In 1975 the U.S. Postal Service issued a four-stamp series bearing this message: "Contributors to the cause." Portrayed on each stamp was a hero of the American Revolution.

One of these heroes was Haym Solomon, who pledged his entire fortune to General Washington. He was responsible for raising most of the money needed for the war, yet died penniless. His obituary read: Gentleman, scholar, patriot, a banker whose only interest was the interest of his country.

Then there was 16-year-old Sybil Ludington who rode through the night alone on horseback to call her father's men to action.

Most of us have read of Paul Revere's midnight ride and Patrick Henry's famous words, "Give me liberty or give me death!"

These and many more like them had a common cause—freedom from England. They worked either behind the scenes or on the front lines to contribute their best to the cause of liberty. Their all-out commitment to their earthly cause goes down in the pages of history as a challenge to Christians today.

We have enlisted as soldiers in the army of God and have a common cause—the cause of Christ! Ours is a heavenly General who has commissioned us to carry out His work! The enemy forces are closing in; time is running out!

How dedicated are we to this cause? Souls are on the brink of endless ruin. Would we be willing to give up our entire fortunes and our lives for this cause?

The Word of God and every principle conveyed to the hearts of men, whether written, spoken, or exemplified, is Gospel ammunition against the forces of evil.

Hear the battle cry, "Rise up, O men of God, be done with lesser things. Rise up and fight!" Are you a contributor to the cause?

Bible Reading: 1 Corinthians 9:24–27; 2 Corinthians 11:16–33
One Year Bible Reading Plan:
Acts 12
Job 29, 30

David Keeney, Waynesboro, VA

All gave some, some gave all.

When Things Go Wrong

And not only so, but we glory in tribulation also:
knowing that tribulation worketh patience.
Romans 5:3

Most of us are acquainted with adversity. And most of us don't appreciate it. We regard it as an enemy as old as Job, who lamented, "Man that is born of woman is of few days and full of trouble" (Job 14:1).

There is, however, a positive side to trouble. It was Thomas Edison, standing in the ashes of the fire that destroyed his laboratory, who spoke these inspiring words, "Wonderful! All our mistakes have been burned up and we can start over."

Even in nature, life depends on resistance. A fish, without the buoyancy of water or the thrust of the current, would be unable to swim. Birds, without the lift provided by the air against their wings, would remain earthbound.

In its metamorphosis from larvae to caterpillar and finally into the beautiful creature we call a swallowtail butterfly, the vital principle of struggle and resistance is striking. In its final stage, there is so much visible effort as the fully developed butterfly struggles to emerge from the chrysalis, that a sympathetic observer is tempted to come to its aid and slit the cocoon open with a sharp knife. This, however, would be a good deed gone awry. Without the benefit of the effort involved, its wings, which were intended for flight, would be mere appendages. The poor little creature, deprived of the life-supporting benefit of struggle, would be doomed.

"When things go wrong." How dare I entertain such a thought? The Word says, "All things work together for good."

Jerry Yoder, Auburn, KY

Bible Reading: Job 5:1–7
One Year Bible Reading Plan:
Acts 13:1–24
Job 31, 32

Many are the afflictions of the righteous,
but the Lord delivers him out of them all.
—Psalm 34:19

191

Be Quiet

*Be still, and know that I am God: I will be exalted
among the heathen, I will be exalted in the earth.*
Psalm 46:10

The moon appeared to gaze down at me in delight. Its radiance cast a long shadow to my side which walked with me. The moon seemed to say, "I am glad you are out tonight." I was glad to be out. The night sounds serenaded me as I walked there in the light of the moon. The gravel crunched too loudly under my feet. The sounds of my footsteps seemed so out of place amidst the sounds of nature. I stopped. The sounds of nature were magnified.

I was reminded of the song that says, "Be still and know that I am God." In our busyness, days gallop along, and we forget to be quiet. Seconds leap into minutes, and minutes disappear into hours. Hours glide into days, and days stealthily sneak into years. Years turn us into regretting older people, regretting that we did not take time to be still and know God.

The sound of footsteps are so out of place in God's world. God is looking for those who will quit walking their way and walk His way. So many people—so many footsteps. Too many people going their own way.

Activity is no substitute for a relationship with the Lord Jesus Christ. Many people hustle about doing all kinds of good things without God. Do not allow yourself to become so busy with good activities that you rob your family and God of your time. Stop and clasp a small child's hand, smell a flower, crawl through the grass, sit beside a stream, kneel quietly in your closet. Listen quietly until you hear God, then go your way a changed person.

Alvin Mast, Millersburg, OH

Bible Reading: 1 Kings 19
One Year Bible Reading Plan:
Acts 13:25–52
Job 33, 34

Why are you doing what you are doing?

Honest Confession

Confess your faults one to another, and pray one for another,
that ye may be healed. The effectual, fervent prayer
of a righteous man availeth much.
James 5:16

Several years ago I was in town one evening. It was a dark night, and the thunder rolled in. As the storm broke, the rain descended in torrents. I chose to pull over into an empty lot in front of a business and wait for the rain to pass. While turning around, I hit a stop sign which was set in concrete. Instead of bending, the post snapped off at the concrete surface. I could have simply gone on and ignored it, but I knew that it would always bother me. I drove to the police station and explained what had taken place. I told them that I wanted them to know that the stop sign was down, and that I wished to pay for having it put up again.

The officer thanked me and assured me that workers would be sent out the next morning to erect the sign. He said they appreciate it when people tell them about such things, and they do not want me to pay for fixing it. He said other people simply drive off and do not tell them.

Driving to the station and explaining what happened took some time and effort, but it gave me an opportunity to share a few thoughts on Christian stewardship. The officer seemed very appreciative and thanked me for coming in.

I went home knowing that all was clear. I had to wonder, why is it so hard to confess and admit mistakes and wrong deeds? Nothing is of greater value than a clear conscience. May we resolve to clear our record daily and enjoy the peace that God wants us to have. Confession is the way to healing and forgiveness.

Bible Reading: James 5
One Year Bible Reading Plan:
Acts 14
Job 35—37

Melvin L. Yoder, Gambier, OH

Complete honesty in little things is not a little thing at all.

Habits

Abhor that which is evil; cleave to that which is good.
Romans 12:9b

We are creatures of habit. Good habits have to be developed, while bad habits form without effort and are not easily broken. There are simple habits like good personal hygiene, such as brushing your teeth and washing your hands. Other habits, such as regular church attendance, daily devotions, and continuous heartfelt worship, praise, and prayer, contribute to our spiritual well-being. Loving responses, deeds of kindness, and edifying speech are godly habits characteristic of the Spirit-filled life.

We may not be enslaved to sinful habits like smoking, drinking intoxicating beverages, or using illicit drugs, but what about habits like evil speaking, bitterness, unforgiving attitudes, wrong thoughts, or gluttony? Such habits are also wrong and displeasing to God.

Do you find yourself struggling with a habit that may be causing you spiritual defeat? Praise God, there is victory and freedom in Christ through His shed blood. Here are some suggestions that may help you gain the spiritual victory God desires.

1. Truly repent of and confess all known sin.

2. Confide in someone you can trust, and make yourself accountable to that person until you are free.

3. Be honest and open with others about your temptations and struggles. We need the prayers and encouragement of fellow saints. We need each other in our pilgrimage to heaven.

4. Do not neglect your devotional life. Spend time daily with God and His Word. Fasting is a helpful practice, along with earnest prayer.

5. Claim the promises of God's Word.

6. Put on the whole armor of God. "Be strong in the Lord, and in the power of His might."

We are in a spiritual warfare. God has made every provision for our victory if we do our part by meeting the conditions of His Word. Through the power of Jesus, we can be "more than conquerors."

Mark Kropf, Cataldo, ID

Bible Reading: Romans 6
One Year Bible Reading Plan:
Acts 15:1–21
Job 38, 39

O victory in Jesus, my Savior, forever.
—Eugene M. Bartlett, 1939

Little Things

Take us the foxes, the little foxes, that spoil the vine.
Song of Solomon 2:15a

I know of a giant oak tree. It stood majestically strong and tall. It looked healthy and well. What a surprise, when during a high wind, it crashed to the ground. Upon closer observation, I discovered that ants—hundreds of them—had attacked the tree.

What an irony! The little ant, maybe ½ inch long, toppled a giant oak 50 feet tall. According to those numbers, the ant was one twelve hundredth the size of the tree!

I cannot help but wonder what went through Achan's mind that day in Jericho. "Oh, well, what's a little gold and silver? What's wrong with a couple of Babylonian garments? It's such a little thing."

Fast forward. We, too, are confronted with Achan's temptation. A few "little ants" nibble at us. "Ah, what does it matter? It's such a little thing." "That thought was just a little envious—it's such a little thing!" "I didn't take my gaze off of that immodest woman as soon as I could have." "I raised my voice just a little bit—it's such a little thing." What "little ants" are nibbling at you?

It is very important that we see the consequences of little things! It is through little things that we allow Satan to gain a foothold in our lives. Little things open the door for us to become deceived, and little things have a way of becoming big things. Remember this the next time you are tempted.

Bible Reading: Joshua 7
One Year Bible Reading Plan:
Acts 15:22–41
Job 40—42

Galen Stutzman, London, OH

He that is faithful in that which is least is faithful also in much.
—Luke 16:10

Are You Secure?

*Trust in the Lord with all thine heart, and lean not unto thine
own understanding. In all thy ways acknowledge him,
and he shall direct thy paths.*
Proverbs 3:5, 6

Over the last several years I have noticed how much people long for security. Our carnal nature does not like to lose anything! You know how it is: my tools, my car, my horse, my toys, my life, my children, etc. You fill in the blanks.

The owner of one home I helped trim out spent $60,000 on an alarm system. Another man has loaded guns in every room of his house. He feels very secure when he's asleep because there is a loaded gun within his reach. Another man has both! If someone opens a window, a pager will tell him exactly which window it is.

But let's move closer home. Are we insured to the max? Do we need to make sure our vehicles are insured, so that in case of an accident we do not have to pay anything? Do we insure our houses so that if they burn down, we can totally rebuild without touching our savings account?

The government requires some forms of insurance, such an auto insurance; and the banks require us to have insurance before we can get a loan to build a house. But what are we placing our trust in? Do you trust the insurance company or the Lord Jesus Christ? I am reminded of Elisha and his servant, Gehazi. When Gehazi feared for his life, Elisha told him, "Fear not; for they that be with us are more than they that be with them."

> **Bible Reading:** 1 Samuel 17:32–51
> **One Year Bible Reading Plan:** Acts 16:1–15
> Psalms 1—3

Alva Mast, Leitchfield, KY

Security—insurance or assurance?

The Disciplined Life

If any man will come after me, let him deny himself.
Matthew 16:24a

In our day temperance and self-denial are considered outdated and old-fashioned. Self-indulgence and self-gratification are the accepted norm. Godly self-control runs counter to the world's, "If it feels good, do it" or "Live it up," mentality. The idea is to get all of the fun out of life you can. What a distorted, short-range concept!

The aim of the Christian is on a higher level—to please, serve, and glorify our Savior. We make Christ the focus and Lord of our life, rather than satisfying selfish and fleshly desires. Like Moses, we take the long-range view, rejecting the fleeting, shallow pleasures of this world. The world, and everything in it, will soon pass away. As heaven-bound pilgrims, we must view everything in the light of eternity. We look for the eternal reward, that undefiled, incorruptible inheritance which will not fade away.

All around us we see the sad consequences of undisciplined, unbridled living, which ends in emptiness, disillusionment, and disappointment. But God's way to happiness, peace, and contentment is the way of sacrificial service, cross bearing, and self-denial.

Victorious Christian living requires keeping every desire under God's control. The Spirit-led, Christ-honoring life of temperance and holiness will yield rich blessings, true satisfaction, and unsurpassed fulfillment, both now and for eternity.

What is our ambition? Is it a comfortable lifestyle, pleasing ourselves, or is it dedication and devotion to Jesus Christ?

Bible Reading: Romans 13
One Year Bible Reading Plan:
　　Acts 16:16–40
　　Psalms 4—6

Mark Kropf, Cataldo, ID

---

*By God's grace we can keep a Biblical standard
in an undisciplined age.*

The Foolish Woodpecker

*Wherefore, if God so clothe the grass of the field, which
today is, and tomorrow is cast into the oven, shall he
not much more clothe you, O ye of little faith?*
Matthew 6:30

It was exciting to watch the red-bellied woodpecker that frequented our bird feeder during the cold months of January and February. Often he carried seeds from the feeder to a nearby tree and hid the seed under the bark to be enjoyed at a later time.

Then it happened! Instead of carrying the seed to the tree, he hopped outside the feeder and placed the seed in a crack of the feeder. "How foolish," I thought. "After all, we keep seed in the feeder all year. If we did not want to feed the birds, we would remove the feeder."

One morning at breakfast, I was watching the foolish woodpecker hide his precious provisions in the crevices of the feeder. Suddenly I realized God was reminding me of my own carnal tendencies. I know the "cattle upon a thousand hills" belong to God. I also understand that Jesus instructed us not to worry about clothing and food, and that He called those that worried "ye of little faith."

In our ungodly society, we are encouraged to "feather the nest" for old age. Even among professing Christians, we hear of setting aside abundance so our retirement years can be spent in pleasure and leisure, instead of living and serving for God's glory.

The world's system demands that I take care of number one. God has a different value structure. His unique order necessitates that we "do justly . . . love mercy . . . and . . . walk humbly with [our] God."

When worry crowds into my life to steal peace and trust, I want to remember the lesson of the foolish woodpecker. God has promised to take care of His children. He promises peace and consolation to those who trust in His provisions.

Henry Petersheim, Abbeville, SC

Bible Reading: Matthew 6:19–34
One Year Bible Reading Plan:
Acts 17:1–15
Psalms 7—9

If you can't help worrying, remember, worry can't help you either.

Do We Tithe?

Bring ye all the tithes into the store house, that there may be meat in mine house . . . I will . . . open you the windows of heaven, and pour you out a blessing, that there shall not be room enough to receive it.
Malachi 3:10

A year ago I had difficulty paying my taxes, so I called the IRS. A lady answered the call and asked what she could do for me. After I explained my problem, she asked, "Do you tithe?"

"What?" I asked, "Do I tithe? You mean like church offerings and such?" I was very perplexed.

"Yes," she replied.

"Well, yes, if I can, and when my bills don't swamp me too much," I answered.

Her reply to that was, "In my job I find that those who don't pay tithes are not able to pay taxes, and if you waste your 90% on luxury or a higher standard of living, it doesn't change the fact that God still requires His 10%."

I was humbled and embarrassed that God had to use the IRS lady to show me something I needed to improve in. I have found since then, that if I tithe, God enables me to pay all my bills. We must realize that God owns all that we have. In fact, He owns the whole world. David says in Psalm 37:25, "I have been young, and now am old; yet have I not seen the righteous forsaken, nor his seed begging bread." Let us be good stewards, giving to God that which is His, that He may pour out His blessings on us.

Jerry Miller, Molalla, OR

Bible Reading: Malachi 3
One Year Bible Reading Plan:
Acts 17:16–34
Psalms 10—12

Thankful giving brings happy living.

Poor—Rich Me

And having food and raiment let us be therewith content.
1 Timothy 6:8

Did you ever notice when the subject of "the rich" comes up, people usually refer to the rich as "they"? James speaks directly to the rich. Reading this passage may be a self-satisfying experience. After all, I am not rich. I cannot buy everything I want when I want it. Our refrigerator is thirty-some years old. It still has stains on it from a house fire back in 1982. It frosts over rather quickly and does not have an ice maker. Rich folks would have bought a better one long ago. Rich people should take the warning from God's Word seriously.

Beside me lies a magazine with a cover picturing a near-starved boy. It reads, "I was hungry . . ." As I leaf through it, I see a boy drinking from a cup with flies on the cup and on his forehead. There is a story of a nursing team struggling to care for 1200 children and mothers.

A Christian Aid newsletter reminds me of needs around the world. The rich, "they" ought to help these poor folks.

I look around a bit. There is my cell phone! Another phone on the wall puts me in touch with people around the world. I think of the food in the refrigerator, freezer, and canned in jars. There is a glass of tea with real ice in it, and an empty dish that had Schwan's ice cream in it.

Deep down, I know that as God looks over all His created people around the world, in His eyes He sees *me* as rich. I have food, clothing, shelter, transportation, fellowship with Christ and His church.

How shall I respond to James chapter five? I need to recognize that in God's sight I am not poor. That puts me into the class of folks that should work so we can give to the needy, rather than heaping up treasures for the last days. "As ye have done it unto one of the least of these my brethren, ye have done it unto me."

Bible Reading: James 5
One Year Bible Reading Plan:
Acts 18
Psalms 13—16

Simon Schrock, Fairfax, VA

When comparing your possessions with others,
look through God's eyeglass.

Does the Lord Know Me?

Be not deceived; God is not mocked: for whatsoever
a man soweth, that shall he also reap.
Galatians 6:7

Do I know President Clinton? "Why sure," I say, "I have seen his picture many times. I would recognize him the minute I saw him." Does President Clinton know me? Well, he probably will never know that I exist.

Do I know the Lord? "Why sure," I say, "I go to church every time there is a service. I give plenty in the offering. I go to jail services. I am doing many things for the Lord." Does the Lord know me? "Well, I hope He does."

I am afraid there are people who will say, "Lord, Lord, we were good Christians." And the Lord will say, "I never knew you."

How do we know that the Lord knows us? We find the answer in the context of today's Bible reading. Go back to the verses on the fruit. The quality of our fruit will prove if we are on the straight and narrow way. But even if our fruit seems pretty good to other men, that is no proof that we are known of the Lord. The people who cried, "Lord, Lord," had done many wonderful things in the name of the Lord.

Now look at the parable of the wise man and the foolish man. Which one did the Lord know? Why? Was it not because he did the will of the Father? The same applies to us. We must do the will of the Lord in all of our life. The one little corner that we reserve for ourselves will keep Him from knowing us.

Are we hearing the sayings of the Lord and doing them?

Bible Reading: Matthew 7:13–29
One Year Bible Reading Plan:
Acts 19:1–20
Psalms 17, 18

Daniel Kuhns, Farmington, NM

We may fool most men most of the time. But we cannot fool all men all the time. And we will never fool God any of the time.

Our Thought Life

For as he thinketh in his heart, so is he.
Proverbs 23:7

I was about thirteen years old. It was a beautiful sunshiny winter day with a thick blanket of snow on the ground. I was out walking behind the buildings in the fields, just admiring and enjoying the day. I do not know what all I was thinking, but it must have appeared that I was deep in meditation. Soon after that, I went into the house where my older sister was sweeping the floor, and my mother was baking bread.

They asked me what I was thinking, because I was walking so slowly out there. "Oh, nothing really," I told them.

"Oh, yes, you were," they told me. "If you wouldn't have been thinking anything, you would have been sleeping."

Ever since that incident, this thought comes to my mind many times: every hour and minute that we are awake, we are thinking something—either for the good or the bad.

Early in the morning, as soon as we wake up, we have an enemy to face; but we also have Jesus with us to help us be victorious. No matter what part of the day it is, Jesus is always ready to help us reject Satan's deceitful suggestions.

What is in our thoughts? Are we preferring one another, or are we criticizing one another? Are we an encouragement or a discouragement to one another? Do we have pure or impure thoughts? Do we praise God or seek honor and glory to ourselves? Do we have a forgiving attitude, or do we hold grudges one toward another?

Bible Reading: Romans 12
One Year Bible Reading Plan:
Acts 19:21–41
Psalms 19—21

Norman Farmwald, Greensburg, KY

Our attitudes rule our lives.

A Wide-Open Mouth

Open thy mouth wide, and I will fill it.
Psalm 81:10b

How can a tiny baby bird have such a huge mouth? Have you ever wondered this as you viewed a nest full of hungry birds with outstretched beaks, longing for some food? These birds have healthy appetites and are anxious to receive the nourishment their parents bring.

As a parent with young children, I have often wished their mouths would open as readily as a hungry bird's mouth. God desired this for Israel, but they frequently displayed no desire for the rich spiritual food which God had for them.

Let us consider three reasons a child's mouth does not open wide. If a child is not hungry, he has no interest in food. A healthy child who is not hungry at mealtime has probably been snacking between meals. When we spiritually "snack" on the world's food, we, too, lose our appetite for God's Word.

A child will also not open his mouth wide if he dislikes the food. The food may be very healthy and nutritious, but he has not learned to enjoy it. Perhaps he prefers junk food over healthy food. God has provided for us to receive rich spiritual nourishment through church services and personal Bible reading. However, our appetites can degenerate into a desire for worthless reading material or worldly entertainment when we should be feasting on manna from God.

Sometimes a child is too distracted to eat. As a spoonful of delicious food nears his mouth, his attention is riveted on other activities nearby, and his mouth remain closed. Partaking of spiritual food also requires quietness—both inward and outward. Only as we are still before God can we really feast on His Word.

Bible Reading: Psalm 81
One Year Bible Reading Plan:
Acts 20:1–16
Psalms 22—24

Tim Stoltzfus, Harrison, AR

Junk food or heavenly Manna? The choice is yours.

God's People

If a man love me, he will keep my words: and my Father will love him, and we will come unto him, and make our abode with him.
John 14:23b

You have heard statements like, "We're all just one big family." "We're all serving the same God." "We're all God's children." What really qualifies us to be considered part of God's people and to have Him dwell with us? People want God's approval on their lives (especially at the time of death), but are not willing to meet the conditions that He sets forth in His Word.

In Isaiah 57:15, God says, "I dwell in the high and holy place, with him also that is of a contrite and humble spirit." In 2 Chronicles 7:14, He says, "If my people, which are called by my name, shall humble themselves, and pray, and seek my face, and turn from their wicked ways; then will I hear from heaven, and will forgive their sin, and will heal their land."

God is not interested in dwelling with pride and selfishness, but rather He is interested in hearts that are willing to let Him be Lord of all. Additional tests to see if we qualify are found in reading the five chapters of 1 John. Do we confess that Jesus is the Son of God? Do we love one another? Do we obey the commandments of God in His Word?

Our Scripture readings portray God's people as separated from the world unto God. Do we find ourselves craving the glamor and pleasure the world offers, or do we see them as a threat to our relationship with God? Remember, we cannot have both. Things highly esteemed among men are an abomination to God. Let us give Jesus His rightful place in our hearts. He alone is worthy.

> **Bible Reading:** 1 Peter 2:1–12; 2 Corinthians 6:13–18
> **One Year Bible Reading Plan:**
> Acts 20:17–38
> Psalms 25—27

Omar Schrock, Laclede, MO

Jesus will have first place in our lives or no place.

Worries or Peace?

But seek ye first the kingdom of God, and his righteousness;
and all these things shall be added unto you.
Matthew 6:33

Where will the money come from for the next payment? How can I get this business paid off more quickly? Where will our next meal come from? Where will we get the money for the shoes we need so badly? How can I make more money so I can buy the truck I want so badly? Where can I invest my money to make sure it increases? What can I do with all my riches, so I can keep them? After all, a fire could burn up all our things, or someone could steal them, or . . . The list could go on.

Being overly concerned about any of these things should tell us we are not trusting God as we ought. God does not have our total devotion, which He deserves.

If God has our total devotion, material things will not matter so much. We can be poor and still serve God with a whole heart. If the Lord has blessed us with riches, we can use them to bring honor and glory to God by sharing with the needy instead of hoarding it to ourselves.

Bible Reading: Luke 12:13–34
One Year Bible Reading Plan:
Acts 21:1–14
Psalms 28—30

The key is found in verse 33 of our reading. "But rather seek ye first the kingdom of God; and all these things shall be added unto you." If we put God first in everything, He will supply all our needs.

Lowell Brenneman, Cullman, AL

_____

True peace and contentment are found only in Jesus.

205

Each Little Thought

For as he thinketh in his heart, so is he.
Proverbs 23:7a

What were you thinking about just before you began reading this? What have you been thinking about the past few days? What do you think about most of the time?

What you are is a product of what you've been thinking about. Take some time today to watch your thought life. Do you meditate upon the law of the Lord day and night? Do you think about the things mentioned in Philippians 4:8? Is God serious when the Bible tells us what we are supposed to fill our minds with? Did you ever know God to not mean what He says? God says we must think about these things if we want to be fruitful.

A little thought does not seem so bad. But each little thought is another brick in the wall of the stronghold we are building in our minds for either God or Satan. The stronghold of God is a mighty fortress of protection against the storms of life. But Satan's strongholds lock us in a dungeon of guilt, shame, and misery. He will take us captive whenever he wants to. When he says "hate" we will hate. When he says "overeat" we will overeat. When he says "complain" we will complain. When he says "fear man" we will fear man. In what ways does Satan have you chained?

To repent means to change our thinking. Today, pay close attention to what you think about. Ask yourself, "What kind of person thinks thoughts like that?" With God's help, pull down those Satanic strongholds in your mind, and build strongholds for God. Perhaps it will take several days or months until you're done. But do not give up. The strongholds that took many years or generations to erect may take time to pull down. He that perseveres and patiently brings forth fruit unto perfection will be blessed by God and saved eternally.

Philip Cohen, Summersville, MO

Bible Reading: Philippians 4
One Year Bible Reading Plan:
Acts 21:15–40
Psalms 31—33

Your mind is the gateway to your heart.

By What Means Shall We Live?

*Man shall not live by bread alone, but by every word
that proceedeth out of the mouth of God.*
Matthew 4:4

We live in a very prosperous country and a prosperous time.
People work from early morning to late evening hours. Some even
work into the night.

We buy, we sell, we plant, we build, we marry and are given in
marriage, just as they did in the days of Noah. I wonder if we do
not also eat and drink as they did back then.

Are we concerned about bread only? 1 Timothy 6:8 says, "And
having food and raiment let us be therewith content."

But we say we need much food and raiment. Do we?

Yes, we do need food and clothing and shelter and transportation and money to pay for many other things. But there are more
worthwhile things in life.

By what means shall we live then? In Luke 10:25–28, we read
about a lawyer who asked Jesus, "What shall I do to inherit eternal
life?" Jesus asked him, "What is written in the law?"

The lawyer said, "Thou shalt love the Lord thy God with all thy
heart, and with all thy soul, and with all thy strength, and with all
thy mind; and thy neighbor as thyself."

Jesus said, "You have answered right. Do this and you shall
live." He also said that He is the Living Bread. "If any man eat of
this bread, he shall live forever" (John 6:51).

Bible Reading: Haggai 1:3–11;
James 4:1–3
One Year Bible Reading Plan:
Acts 22
Psalms 34, 35

As we seek to earn bread for
ourselves and for our families,
may our main goal be to eat of
the Living Bread.

Nelson Yoder, Hartville, OH

Physical life ends soon—eternal life is forever.

Faint, Yet Pursuing

And Gideon came to Jordan, and passed over, . . .
faint, yet pursuing them.
Judges 8:4

You caught a glimpse of God's plan. You said, "Yes, Lord, I will follow wherever You lead. Give me grace to follow." Remember how excited you were when you caught that flash of destiny? A straight shot, and you expected to arrive at your grand destination.

But something has happened. God led you away from that mountain into a series of valleys. At first the way was still clear. Confidently you walked along.

Suddenly you came to a fork in the road. Two paths were well trodden and appealing. You had to strain to see the third path. The overgrowth fairly swallowed it.

"Lord, which way?" your voice trembled. (You almost knew that He would choose the jungled path.)

"Straight ahead. But follow me. I have walked this way before you."

He continues to lead you on the overgrown path today. You thrash through the brush. Branches of doubt slap your face. Impatient thorns tear into your flesh.

You are faint, yet pursuing. You still remember the goal, now seemingly so far away. A dream. You can barely discern your Lord through the brush.

You cry, "Lord! Where are you? I cannot see—I am confused. I—I thought you had a great plan. But this . . . ! I . . . I can't . . . go . . . on."

Everything becomes blurry, and you crash headlong down the path. A moan. You are too weak to call out.

But He hears! He picks you up. From somewhere the Lord produces water and bread. Groggily you eat. Revived by the water, you partake of the Bread of Life. Your body is strengthened, and soon you feel ready to resume the journey.

"Are you still willing to walk with me?"

"Yes, Lord," you whisper, "by Your grace."

"Then let us go."

Josh Bechtel, Estacada, OR

> **Bible Reading:**
> Judges 7:16—8:14
> **One Year Bible Reading Plan:**
> Acts 23:1–11
> Psalms 36, 37

When you are your weakest, God is His strongest.

Five Steps to Repentance

Bring forth therefore fruits meet for repentance.
Matthew 3:8

I have often wondered how we can apologize for something like getting angry at someone, and then turn around and do it again only a short time later. We try ever so hard to conquer a habit, but we seem to find no victory. Maybe it is because we do not really understand repentance. How do we find real victory over sin?

1. Acknowledgment. Psalm 51:3. The first thing we must do is acknowledge that we have sinned. If we do not acknowledge that we have wronged a brother when we became angry at him (or whatever else we have done) then we have missed the first step.

2. Godly sorrow. 2 Corinthians 7:10. Many times we are sorrowful simply because others have discovered our sin. "What will others think if they hear that I'm a bitter person?" Godly sorrow means we are remorseful that our sins have hurt our Lord.

3. Confession. 1 John 1:9. We may reason that we have said we are sorry, so what more is needed? Or, if ours is a private sin, we may have only confessed it to God, thinking that is enough. But it is not. I remember a time when I did something wrong that involved no one else but myself. One day I became convicted of my wrong and repented of it. Yet I did not find peace until I confessed it to a responsible person. "Confess your faults one to another."

4. Restitution. Matthew 5:24. We must also be willing to make wrongs right at any cost. Some relationships cannot be restored, but we need to be willing to do our part.

5. Forsaking it. Proverbs 28:13. If we truly repent, we will want to quit sinning. These five steps must be complete before we have really repented from sin. This does not mean we can escape the consequences for sin, but we can accept God's grace as sufficient for us and begin to overcome our sin.

James Miller, Evart, MI

> **Bible Reading:**
>   Matthew 3:1–12
> **One Year Bible Reading Plan:**
>   Acts 23:12–35
>   Psalms 38—40

It takes humility to admit we are wrong; none to insist we are right.

True Humility

And be clothed with humility: for God resisteth the
proud, and giveth grace to the humble.
1 Peter 5:5b

Humility may be described as a righteous estimate of ourselves as God sees us. It is not a cast-down, self-despising spirit, but a simple feeling of unworthiness, a sense of our own insignificance. Never does it leave room for pride and self exaltation.

A drunkard came home at midnight with a crowd of his drunken friends. He demanded that his Christian wife make supper for them. She promptly complied. After they were done eating, one, who was more sober than the rest, and knowing of her disapproval of their conduct, asked how she could respond so kindly to their unreasonable request. She said that if her husband had died in this miserable condition, he would be miserable forever. It was through this woman's act of humility to these unreasonable and corrupt men that her husband was saved.

Jesus in His humility stripped Himself of His rightful dignity when He gave Himself up as a servant and became a man. This was not the end of His humiliation; He stooped still lower, in obedience. He went to the shameful cross where He suffered much abuse by His own people. Because of His humiliation, God was so well pleased that He gave Him a position, "That at the name of Jesus every knee shall bow."

We may say it was only right for Jesus to give himself like this, but what should our attitude be to humility? "Let this mind be in you, which was also in Christ Jesus" (Philippians 2:5). Unless we are converted, we cannot experience true humility. Humility brings with it a childlike spirit that manifests itself in meekness, submission, and lowliness in heart (Matthew 11:29).

As we make our pilgrimage here, may we also be clothed with humility and take opportunities to serve others for the kingdom of God's sake.

Lester Stoltzfus, Honey Brook, PA

> **Bible Reading:** Philippians
> 2:1–11; Matthew 18:1–6
> **One Year Bible Reading Plan:**
> Acts 24
> Psalms 41—43

God hath promised to lift on high,
he who sinks himself by true humility.

Only This Manna

But now our soul is dried away: there is nothing at all,
beside this manna, before our eyes.
Numbers 11:6

Israel had been on her journey through the desert for over two years. Because of her murmuring in the wilderness, God had faithfully sent Israel bread from heaven each morning, except on the Sabbaths. There was always enough, and the manna was nutritionally complete.

But then God's people fell into lust. They remembered the fish they had back in Egypt, as well as the melons, leeks, onions, and garlic. Now they had nothing at all but this manna.

The Christian church has traveled through the wilderness of this world for many years now. Since her miraculous birth at Pentecost, God has faithfully supplied her every need and fully equipped her with the armor of God. Through His Word and the guidance of the Holy Spirit, He has supplied clear directions to the promised land.

But God's people still fall to lusting after the pleasures and fashions of this world and become dissatisfied with the heavenly manna He provides.

The Christian pilgrim, too, begins his pilgrimage with the ardent joy of seeing "old Pharaoh" drowned, his host overthrown, and Egypt left behind. Feasting on a boundless supply of manna, he feels as though he has already had a taste of heaven! But all too soon, the heat of the desert sun, the cares of this life, the deceitfulness of riches, and the lust of other things unite to dry away our souls. We are no longer content with this manna alone. But as we raise the eye of faith to the things not seen and give God the throne room of our hearts, we find that nothing in this world satisfies, and nothing is more fulfilling than the sweet manna that God still provides today!

Bible Reading: Numbers 11:4–9;
Psalm 19:7–14
One Year Bible Reading Plan:
Acts 25
Psalms 44—46

David Keeney, Waynesboro, VA

God's manna in the soul renders the pleasures of this world tasteless.

Be Metamorphic

*And be not conformed to this world: but be ye transformed
by the renewing of your mind, that ye may prove what is
that good, and acceptable, and perfect will of God.*
Romans 12:2

While traveling along slowly on a southern highway, I marveled at the thousands of newly emerged butterflies. Entomologists estimate there are about 90,000 different kinds of butterflies and moths, displaying the marvels of their Creator. They are found worldwide, from pole to pole, and from deserts to hot, wet jungles. They vary in color and size from the Queen Alexandria Birdwing of New Guinea with an eleven inch wingspread to the Western Pygmy Blue with a 3/8th inch wingspread. Amazingly, many of these fragile creatures migrate thousands of miles across continents and oceans.

Every butterfly goes through four changes in its development. This is called metamorphosis, from the Greek words "meta," implying change, and "morphe," meaning form. In the fourth and last marvelous change we see the caterpillar enter its homespun chrysalis as a homely worldly worm. According to the Creator's marvelous plan, it emerges a short time later as a magnificent butterfly. This complete form change defies explanation.

Probably on creation day five, as God brought into existence the butterfly and moth, He was looking down through the ages of time to the penning of Romans 12. The metamorphosis of the moth and butterfly illustrate God's call to His people. Do not be conformed—pressed into this world's mold or cocoon—to act, think, look, or respond as the world does, but be ye transformed—completely changed—so that you can be a living proof of God's perfection. Oh, God, let me this day again be that proof!

Bible Reading: Romans 12
One Year Bible Reading Plan:
Acts 26
Psalms 47—49

David Stutzman, Punta Gorda, Belize

---

*Becoming like the world does not help you
win the world, but the world wins you.*

The Token of God's Covenant

*For the mountains shall depart, and the hills be removed; but my
kindness shall not depart from thee, neither shall the covenant of
my peace be removed, saith the Lord that hath mercy on thee.*
Isaiah 54:10

After a heavy rain and thunderstorm, the sun came out. I left
the barn expecting to see an exceptionally bright rainbow against
the dark storm clouds, but I was disappointed. For just a moment,
the thought crossed my mind, "Surely God has not forgotten His
promise," but I quickly realized that even though a light rain still
fell and the sun shone, conditions were not right to form a rainbow.

When we see the rainbow, we are reminded of God's promise
to Noah that He would never again destroy all life with a flood. But
the rainbow should mean much more to us than that. In Isaiah
54:9, 10, God assures us, "For this is as the waters of Noah unto me
. . . neither shall the covenant of my peace be removed, saith the
Lord." His promise of a Savior to "redeem my people Israel" has
been realized, and when we see the rainbow, we are reminded anew
that God is and that all His promises will eventually be fulfilled.
He has promised that He will separate the sheep from the goats.
"According to their deeds, accordingly he will repay, fury to his
adversaries, recompense to his enemies" (Isaiah 59:18). "Therefore
the redeemed of the Lord shall return, and come with singing unto
Zion, and everlasting joy shall be upon their head: they shall obtain gladness and joy; and sor-
row and mourning shall flee
away" (Isaiah 51:11).

We have this promise, that
just as the rainbow is a token of
God's covenant with Noah, so is
it also in regards to all of God's
promises to mankind.

Bible Reading: Jeremiah
   31:15–34
One Year Bible Reading Plan:
   Acts 27:1–26
   Psalms 50—52

Osiah Horst, Cobden, ON

The rainbow—a sure sign of God's presence.

He Came; I Wasn't Ready

Watch therefore: for ye know not what hour your Lord doth come.
Matthew 24:42

It was late morning on the first day of deer season, and I had only seen a glimpse of one deer all morning. I sat in my tree stand watching the woods around me, when suddenly in a small clearing before me appeared a nice buck. I thought I was prepared, but I was not ready for immediate action. By the time I had gotten ready to shoot, he was in the thicket; and the opportunity was gone.

My disappointment was keen at first. "If only I had heard him coming or seen him sooner and gotten ready!" But it was too late.

As I continued pondering, the Lord gently reminded me of a spiritual lesson. That lesson was to be ready for Christ Jesus to return. Being ready, not just thinking I am ready and finding out too late I am not.

That day I missed a splendid opportunity. The same opportunity may never present itself again, but there will be others. It will be forever too late, however, if we fail to be prepared when Jesus comes. There will never be another chance.

While living in the hope of Christ's return, we must watch at all times (Mark 13:37). We must give diligence to make our calling and election sure (2 Peter 1:10). We can place our full confidence in Christ, who will prepare us for that day as we yield to Him (Philippians 1:6).

According to 1 Thessalonians 4, Jesus' coming will be announced with a shout, a voice, and a trumpet. 1 Corinthians 15:52 tells us it will be in the twinkling of an eye. His coming will be swift, sudden, and sure.

Are you ready for Him today? If not, getting ready is the most important thing you can do today.

Carl Martin, Lititz, PA

> **Bible Reading:** Matthew 24:36–51
> **One Year Bible Reading Plan:**
> Acts 27:27–44
> Psalms 53—55

Be ready when He comes.

Keeping the Awareness of God's Presence Alive

That the generation to come might know them, even the
children which should be born; who should arise and
declare them to their children.
Psalm 78:6

Israel's deliverance from Egypt is a recurrent theme in the Bible. Why did the Jews put so much emphasis on that experience? Did they have no new experiences with God to talk about?

Human beings are forgetful creatures. We forget where we laid the checkbook, who has the car keys, or even what day of the week it is. More importantly, we forget the experiences we have had with God. We forget how God sent the exact amount of money we needed to pay a bill, how He used a brother in the church to encourage us, or how He met some physical need at exactly the right time.

Often we do not realize that we base our current trust in God on the trust-building experiences we have had in the past. Therefore, forgetting what God has done for me in the past may have far-reaching consequences. My faith today is weakened when I forget God's goodness in the past.

God recognizes this tendency in us. He knew the Jews would forget the tremendous experiences they had in Egypt, unless they were frequently reminded. Because of this, God commanded the Jews to talk about their past often. Through these frequent repetitions, God wanted the Jews to pass on faith and trust to their children.

We have the same opportunity today. We can strengthen our children's faith by telling them how God has dealt with us and met our needs. We have the privilege and the responsibility to pass on our faith by sharing with others how God has worked in our lives. Do the stories you tell your children increase their faith?

Matthew Mast, Mountain View, AR

Bible Reading: Psalm
78:1–12, 40–54
One Year Bible Reading Plan:
Acts 28:1–15
Psalms 56—58

Remembering God's goodness always puts a song in your heart.

Empty Shells

But when ye pray, use not vain repetitions.
Matthew 6:7

I read a story of a man who lived alone in a little hut in a forest. He felt it was his duty to pray before meals and at bedtime. So, he merely repeated prayers he had learned as a boy.

One day he decided to keep count by putting a walnut in a glass jar every time he prayed. This went on year after year until he had a long row of jars completely filled. As their number increased, he became more and more self-satisfied.

Then he had a dream. Jesus stood before him and asked, "What is the meaning of all these jars filled with nuts?" He said, "Each nut stands for a prayer."

"Take a hammer and crack the nuts one by one," said Jesus.

He did as he was told and found that the kernel of each had dried up. When he had cracked all the nuts, nothing was left but a pile of empty shells. Then Jesus said, "Your prayers are empty too. You speak the words you have been taught, but your heart is not in them. Prayers are meaningful only when they come from the heart, not just from the lips!"

The Father longs for His children's heartfelt communication with Him. Vain repetitions are nothing but "empty shells."

Bible Reading: Matthew 6:5–18
One Year Bible Reading Plan:
Acts 28:16–31
Psalms 59—61

> *Prayer is the soul's sincere desire*
> *Uttered or unexpressed;*
> *The motion of a hidden fire*
> *That trembles in the breast.*
> —James Montgomery, 1818

William Miller, Middlebury, IN

Prayer is measured by its depth, not its length.

Patience

And let us run with patience the race that is set before us.
Hebrews 12:1b

It was a beautiful, late summer day, suitable for working outside. I had much to do, or so I thought. However, our little three-year-old daughter needed to see the doctor, so we went in for her appointment. The time for her appointment came and went. Five, ten, fifteen, twenty, thirty minutes, one hour and thirty minutes, and still no doctor showed up! Finally, two hours later we accomplished our goal!

During our wait, a spirit rose up within me that would not have responded in a Christlike way. I could see others in the waiting room getting impatient. In times like this may people see in us the character described in Luke 21:19: "In your patience possess ye your souls."

We often have the mentality that is so prevalent in our day. We want something, and we want it now. If we would only wait on God in faith and patience, things would work out smoothly in God's order and time. To be "patient" means bearing pains or trials calmly and without complaint.

"Knowing this, that the trying of your faith worketh patience, but let patience have her perfect work, that ye may be perfect and entire, wanting nothing" (James 1:3, 4).

Bible Reading: Job 2
One Year Bible Reading Plan:
Romans 1
Psalms 62—64

May others see in us Job's trust, who had many trials, sickness, and setbacks, but still confessed, "I know that my redeemer liveth" (Job 19:25).

David Nissley, Alpha, KY

Patience is staying sweet through good or ill.

The Road Runner

*I have fought a good fight, I have finished
my course, I have kept the faith.*
2 Timothy 4:7

The Scripture speaks of a race in which we all must partake if we want to reach heaven.

The Apostle Paul spoke about the heroes of faith in the eleventh chapter of Hebrews. He wrote of the pilgrims who looked for a better city which hath foundations, whose builder and maker is God.

He also referred to Moses, who spurned the privileges of the king's court. He chose rather to suffer affliction with the people of God and to receive an eternal reward which does not fade away.

Paul said in the Scriptures that we should lay aside every weight and the sin which so easily besets us, looking unto Jesus, the author and finisher of our faith. What are some of the things that hold us back? How about the sin of greed and not being truly thankful for the things God bestows upon us? What about lusting after something that we want and cannot have because it belongs to someone else.

Then there is the sin of rebellion and disobedience, which the Bible clearly states is as the sin of witchcraft and idolatry. Gossiping is a destructive sin. The Bible teaches us that we should not be busy bodies in other men's matters.

These are just some of the things that can hinder us in the race. Paul's testimony at the end of his life was, "I have fought a good fight, I have finished my course, I have kept the faith." Can we say the same for ourselves? Will this be our dying testimony? May God help us.

Bible Reading: Hebrews
11:6–16; 12:1–11
One Year Bible Reading Plan:
Romans 2
Psalms 65—67

Mark Meighn, Hattieville, Belize

---

*If there were no enemies, there would be no battles;
if no battles, no victory; if no victory, no crown.*

How Is Our Root System?

*For other foundation can no man lay than
that is laid, which is Jesus Christ.*
1 Corinthians 3:11

I was reminded recently how important a good root system is.
We have some bushes along the road in front of our house that I
wanted to remove. I thought that the best way to remove them would
be to cut them off at ground level with the hatchet. When I chopped
the first one a few times, I noticed the roots were just under the
surface of the ground. I could easily pull them out of the ground by
hand.

As I thought about it, I realized how readily we become like
those bushes. They appeared to be well-rooted, but it was otherwise.

If we do not nourish our spiritual lives with God's Word and
drink deeply of its truths, we also will become shallow rooted. Satan
tries to lure us away with his tactics, and we can only overcome if
we are rooted and built up in Christ.

"Rooted and built up in him, and stablished in the faith, as ye have been taught, abounding therein with thanksgiving" (Colossians 2:7).

Stephen Wagler, Beckwourth, CA

Bible Reading: 1 Corinthians 3:1–15
One Year Bible Reading Plan:
Romans 3
Psalms 68, 69

---

*Our roots go deeper as we find fulfillment
and inspiration through God's Word.*

The Age of Deception

And Jesus answered and said unto them,
take heed that no man deceive you.
Matthew 24:4

The last days, Jesus says, will be characterized by the multiplication of false doctrines and deceptive cults. How significant and arresting this warning is in the light of the amazing increase in new and exotic sects, cults, isms, and religious fantasies. Never before has there been such confusion of tongues. No matter how fantastic, fanatical, or even satanic these movements may be, they do not lack followers. There are some 350 different sects, cults, denominations, and nondenominational groups in America today, all of them quoting the Bible. They all claim the guidance of the Spirit, yet they differ with one another. Is it any wonder that men are confused and are asking, "What can we believe anyway?" "Who, after all, is right?" "Where can truth be found?"

The test is this: "Is it the Word of God or the addition of men?" The moment we accept the word of man instead of the Bible, we will be led astray. Anything added to the Word of God is false and dangerous.

Jesus said that as it was before the flood, so shall it be at the time of His second coming. The days before the flood must have been days of great deception. In spite of Noah's powerful preaching and witnessing, the world would not believe the Word of God. When the flood came, there were only eight people who were saved. There was good preaching in those days. The people had a chance to hear. We read in Jude how Enoch preached coming judgment, but the world paid little heed. Noah too was a preacher of righteousness. Jesus said as it was then, it will be again. One cannot miss the parallel. There is no lack of preaching today, and yet comparatively few are heeding the warning. Be not deceived!

Simon Overholt, Auburn, KY

Bible Reading: Matthew 24
One Year Bible Reading Plan:
Romans 4
Psalms 70—72

If you have a close walk with God, you will not be deceived.

Thoughts of Things

I will meditate in thy precepts, and have respect unto thy ways.
Psalm 119:15

As soon as we have thought a thought, we are responsible for it. A thought can never be killed—only covered with other thoughts. We are never in want of thoughts. They come upon us like the air we breathe and settle upon us like the morning dew.

Every thought is an irrevocable act of being alive. We do not think thoughts because we decide to think thoughts. No, we really have no say in the matter. No one has to tell us to think. And no one can keep me from thinking the thoughts that I wish to think. However, it is imperative that we encourage right thinking. Our thoughts must be based on things that are real. I am free to think of an elephant, but if I think of an elephant with no trunk, my thoughts have become irrational.

Thoughts that wander away from that which is real are imaginations (2 Corinthians 10:5). These thoughts can take us on a dangerous journey we cannot afford. Paul's heart cry is that we think on these things—things that are real—like honesty, things that are just, things that are pure, things of good report, of virtue and praise. We have a good teacher in Christ. He never thought upon evil. He disliked to hear about it and did not speak it. Let us imitate Him by disliking the very thought of evil. If we can refrain from thinking evil, we will hate to hear it and refuse to speak it.

Alvin Mast, Millersburg, OH

Bible Reading: Philippians 4:4–13; Colossians 3:1–17
One Year Bible Reading Plan:
Romans 5
Psalms 73, 74

Think about what you are thinking.

Yuk!

So then because thou art lukewarm, and neither
cold nor hot, I will spew thee out of my mouth.
Revelation 3:16

One morning I decided to help my wife by making breakfast. I like pancakes, so I got out the recipe book and found a recipe for pancakes. Somehow, I made the mistake of using baking soda instead of baking powder. My wife ended up making another batch of pancakes with the right ingredients. The ones I had made were just not edible. They looked all right, but the awful taste just would not go away.

Verse eight of our Bible reading reminds me of pancakes. Ephraim was a cake not turned. Imagine what a pancake would taste like that was burned on one side but gooey on the other. "Yuk!"

What is God's response when He looks at our lives? Jesus had much to say to the Pharisees for making the outside of their lives look good, while the inside was full of all kinds of uncleanness.

How often do we mix wrong things into our lives? Are the things we do or say proper for a child of God? We think we can get by with changing the requirements God has set forth for our lives. We do not allow Him to turn us over and perfect our lives. When we fail to allow God to have His way in our lives, we not only end up being repulsive to others, but also to God. May God help us to follow the directions He has given and allow Him to make us acceptable to Him.

Bible Reading: Hosea 7:1–16
One Year Bible Reading Plan:
Romans 6
Psalms 75—77

Mark Webb, Aroda, VA

Yuk! or Yum! Which will it be?

Guard Your Heart

Keep thy heart with all diligence: for out of it are the issues of life.
Proverbs 4:23

In the fall, we press cider from the apples in our small orchard. We freeze some of this cider in plastic jugs. When we are ready to use the cider, we simply set out the frozen jug and let it thaw for a tasty treat.

One day last summer, our Amish neighbors came over and asked my wife to get something from the freezer for them. As she was getting their items from the freezer in our basement utility room, she noticed that we still had one of these jugs of cider in the freezer. So she set it out on the floor, intending to come back for it a little later. However, she forgot about the cider.

Several days later, in the middle of the night, a thunderous KABOOM from the basement shook the household awake. Our two oldest sons accompanied me to the basement to investigate the cause of this midnight commotion. We noticed a tangy cider smell and followed our noses to the utility room. We were amazed to find a twisted plastic jug, and a wall coated with sticky, pungent cider.

The amazing power of the exploding cider jug set my mind to thinking about the hidden issues of the heart. Man's heart can hide issues that fester and ferment for years. They build strength as time passes but go unnoticed by others, until finally the issues reveal themselves in a destructive eruption.

Let us guard our hearts, keeping them open to God and to our brethren lest they become a place where Satan can brew his hateful stew of hidden sin and thereby destroy us and many others.

Samson Eicher, Grabill, IN

Bible Reading: Luke 6:31–49
One Year Bible Reading Plan:
Romans 7
Psalm 78

Hide His Word in your heart, and the resulting fruit will bless you and others.

The Good Shepherd

I am the good shepherd and know my sheep, and am known of mine.
John 10:14

I have enjoyed caring for sheep for many years, and it is interesting to see how fully dependent on me they have become. I provide pasture and water in summer; and when the snow covers the grass, I provide hay and grain. There is nothing more beautiful than to see sheep lying in a lush green pasture, contented and well filled.

Recently we had some excitement when several stray animals got into the pasture. Their aim was to kill and to destroy our sheep. They attacked, one in front of a sheep and the other behind. They killed two sheep before we came to the rescue. Sheep are defenseless and do not fight back. They soon give in to an attacker.

We as Christians have an adversary about us, in front and behind, trying to destroy us. He comes in a number of ways. He may come with doubts about our assurance of salvation. He may bring doubts and ill feelings between husbands and wives in an attempt to destroy their homes. He delights in bringing strife into the Church to destroy our witness to the world.

For our protection, we need to stay close to the Shepherd through communion with Him, by reading His Word and prayer. He has promised us strength and guidance if we ask, seek, and knock.

Bible Reading: Psalm 23; John 10:7–18
One Year Bible Reading Plan: Romans 8:1–18
Psalms 79—81

Laban Hochstetler, Middlebury, IN

Jesus said, "My sheep know my voice." Am I listening?

224

Be Still

Casting all your care upon him, for he careth for you.
1 Peter 5:7

It is interesting to notice the order of verses seven, eight, and nine in today's Bible reading. Peter admonishes us, after we have cast our care upon the Lord, to be sober and vigilant because the devil will come as a roaring lion. When a lion roars, he puts his mouth to the ground and makes a terrible noise. The lion's prey is confused because it cannot discern where the noise is coming from. Because of the noise and the fright, the prey cannot sit still. They run—sometimes right into the mouth of the lion.

When we are walking with the Lord and have cast our care upon Him, how do we respond to the devil's roaring? The devil's raging is intended to make us stop resting in the Lord and trusting Him. Peter tells us to resist him and be steadfast in the faith.

The devil's roar often comes in the form of desperate situations in our lives. Our first reaction is to do something—run! At such times it is a grave mistake to take matters into our own hands, even if we think we are seeing clearly. When everything in life seems to be falling apart, can we "be still and know that I am God" (Psalm 46:10)?

Our very nature and even common sense tell us we must do something. Will we give in, or will we choose the simple, peace-giving, divine solution—"Cast all your care upon Him"? If we choose the latter, we will suffer ridicule, but we will also discover the peace that passes all understanding. God will soon open the eyes of our discernment, allowing us to understand the purpose of the situation we are in.

Dave Gingerich, Ovid, MI

Bible Reading: 1 Peter 5
One Year Bible Reading Plan:
Romans 8:19–39
Psalms 82—84

When the hardest thing to do is to be still—be still!

Love Not the World

Love not the world, neither the things that are in the world.
If any man love the world, the love of the Father is not in him.
1 John 2:15

The Old Testament account of the lying prophet has always caught my attention. It never seemed quite fair to me that the man of God was deceived by the lying prophet and lost his life, while seemingly the lying prophet faced no consequences for his deception.

Nevertheless, there are a few lessons we can learn from this account. They will help us be faithful today.

First, we notice that the man of God was sent by God to Bethel, and the power of God was working through his life. When the king presented an earthly reward for his act of kindness in healing his withered hand, he steadfastly refused and immediately departed from the temptation to disobey the command God had given him.

But it seems his downfall occurred when he stopped to rest under an oak tree. Here is where the old prophet found him and tempted him to disobey God.

Today the world invites us to join them in their craze for pleasure and amusement. If we are to be faithful to God, we must be busy in His service. When we take time to relax "under the oak tree" spiritually, the world's pressures will prevail on us.

Remember that the grace of God is just as sufficient to help us to be faithful as it ever was. Let us strive for that heavenly reward!

Bible Reading: 1 Kings 13
One Year Bible Reading Plan:
Romans 9
Psalms 85—87

Delmar Miller, Caneyville, KY

Rise, ye Christian soldiers; be ye up and doing!

God Is Bigger

The heavens declare the glory of God; and
the firmament sheweth his handywork.
Psalm 19:1

We can see God's glory in the vastness of space. The spheres of the planets and the thousands of stars we see are just the beginning of space. The universe is so large we cannot grasp the size of it. Yet the planets and the stars work in the orderly way God created them.

Men have made large telescopes that can see into space hundreds of light years and more. They send satellites and telescopes into space to explore and see if they can possibly find some answers to their ridiculous questions, only to discover more things they had previously never seen.

The sun is approximately 93 million miles from the earth. If you traveled in a rocket that flew 25,000 miles per hour, you would need approximately 5 months to get to the sun. If you would actually get there, you would risk meltdown. To fly to the nearest star at the speed of light (186,000 miles per second) would require approximately four years and three months. There are countless stars beyond that.

It is exciting to think about how big the universe is. But even more exciting than that is the fact that I know Someone bigger. God is the One Who created the universe and controls it today. To know the One Who created all this by His spoken word makes man's measurements seem insignificant.

To describe how big God is with human speech would put limits on Him, and He is limitless. I cannot describe how big God is, but I can tell you that God is bigger than any obstacle you may face. When you have an assignment that you think is too hard to do, a trial that you think is too hard to bear, a sorrow that you think is too overwhelming, look to the One Who is bigger than your problems, Who can give you the strength, courage, and grace to face them.

Bible Reading: Psalm 19:1–6; Job 38:1–18
One Year Bible Reading Plan: Romans 10 Psalms 88, 89

Vernon Troyer, Clarkson, KY

God's grace is immeasurable; His mercy
inexhaustible; His peace inexpressible.

Eternal Father (Part 1)

For thus saith the high and lofty One that
inhabiteth eternity, whose name is Holy.
Isaiah 57:15a

Imagine Christianity without songs. Much of its power and vibrancy would dissipate. Songs have been a distinguishing characteristic of Christianity since its inception.

The grand hymn "Eternal Father" is an expression of adoration for God. Written by Hervey D. Ganse in 1872, this song is an impressive attempt to laud the attributes of God.

The first verse focuses on God's eternity, His infinity, and His majesty.

> *Eternal Father, when to Thee,*
> *Beyond all worlds, by faith I soar.*
> *Before Thy boundless majesty,*
> *I stand in silence, and adore.*

It should stand to reason that time-bound man can never fully comprehend eternity. Yet eternity is where God exists. Eternal is the way God thinks. Eternal is what God is. His attributes are eternal—He is eternally holy, eternally majestic, and eternally loving. All of God's purposes and dealings in time and in the lives of men are from His eternal perspective. He sees the end from the beginning, perceives things that are not yet as though they are past, and has no time limitations. Certainly God knows best because of His eternal view of the issues that face us. Oh, the folly of failing to trust Him!

God is not older than He was in Adam's day. He is eternally young. But wait! "Young" is a time concept. God is simply, but profoundly, "eternal."

Furthermore, God, with His attributes, is infinitely greater than man's loftiest concepts of Him. Surely, adoring and reverent worship should be the feeble response of our awestruck hearts. "I stand in silence and adore."

Ken Kauffman, Falkville, AL

> **Bible Reading:** Job 37
> **One Year Bible Reading Plan:**
> Romans 11:1–21
> Psalms 90—92

How often does God chuckle at our foolish attempts to reconcile
and explain eternal concepts with time-terminology?

Eternal Father (Part 2)

I will never leave thee, nor forsake thee.
Hebrews 13:5b

> _But, Savior, Thou art by my side;_
> _Thy voice I hear, Thy face I see:_
> _Thou art my friend, my daily Guide;_
> _God over all, yet God with me._

The second verse of "Eternal Father" aptly illustrates the paradoxical truths of God personally abiding with His children and His sovereign transcendence. That is, He is both a personal presence in my life and the Sovereign Ruler over the whole universe, at the same time! "God over all, yet God with me."

The song depicts God as beside us and speaking to us. Although God has no physical form, by faith and in spiritual experience His presence is a conscious reality for His children.

This verse especially directs our thoughts toward the second person of the Godhead, the Savior Son of God. "In him dwelleth all the fullness of the Godhead bodily" (Colossians 2:9). Our blessed Lord is the eternal God. Yet He meets me where I am. He is God in His own right, and yet He is "my friend, my daily Guide."

". . . they shall call His name Emmanuel" (Matthew 1:23). God with us. Emmanuel: more than just another name for Christ. For the child of God it is a fact, a divine encounter, a conscious reality, and a perpetual experience.

Bible Reading: Hebrews 1
One Year Bible Reading Plan:
Romans 11:22–36
Psalms 93—95

Ken Kauffman, Falkville, AL

In every circumstance I must remember
this truth—NEVER ALONE.

229

Eternal Father (Part 3)

What? know ye not that your body is the temple of the Holy Ghost which is in you, which ye have of God, and ye are not your own?
1 Corinthians 6:19

> *And Thou, Great Spirit, in my heart,*
> *Dost make thy temple day by day,*
> *The Holy Ghost of God thou art,*
> *Yet dwellest in this house of clay.*

The third verse of "Eternal Father" focuses on the Holy Spirit. The fact that God dwells in our lives through His Holy Spirit is a great unsolved mystery. This "house of clay" housing the boundless and infinite God? Only by faith can this truth be appropriated to our hearts. It is a spiritual phenomenon and cannot be explained by earthly vocabulary.

"I dwell in the high and holy place, with him also that is of a contrite and humble spirit" (Isaiah 57:15). The heart that is inhabited by the Holy Spirit is by necessity a humble and broken heart. A heart that is lifted up in conceit and pride will not afford a dwelling place for the Spirit of God. Such an environment is hostile toward the control and domination of this holy inhabitant, and He will not dwell therein. With such a heart, He will assume the role of holy judge.

The truth that our bodies are His temple suggests the idea of worship. Temples are typically centers of worship. Is adoring worship a perpetual characteristic of the activities of my temple?

It bodes me well to marvel greatly at the truth of the indwelling Holy Spirit. But it also obliges me to a posture of humility and a feeling of utter unworthiness, for who am I that God should choose to dwell in me? A heart with this holy mixture of awe and humble unworthiness is prepared for this holy resident.

Ken Kauffman, Falkville, AL

Bible Reading: John 14:15–31
One Year Bible Reading Plan:
Romans 12
Psalms 96—98

The truth of the indwelling Holy Spirit comforts the child of God.

What Is Truth?

Jesus saith unto him, I am the way, the truth, and the life.
John 14:6a

Humanity longs for something real and genuine. People long for truth.

Turn back the centuries and briefly join Pilate in the judgment hall as he faces both a screaming mob and a quiet, suffering individual known as Jesus. As we look into Jesus' eyes, we hear Pilate ask, "What is truth?" Our heart jumps as we realize, "Yes, I have searched for the answer to that question myself. What really is truth?"

God is truth. What God is and what God does is truth. What God is not and what God does not is untruth. Jesus Christ, being part of the Godhead, was Truth incarnate. Unknown to Pilate, he was then gazing on the most perfect expression of Truth ever to walk on earth—Jesus Christ.

Hallelujah! We can know with perfect assurance that our search is over. Our longing for truth is entirely satisfied when we ask Jesus into our heart.

Jesus has given us the freedom to be genuine. Now it is completely safe to be open. There is nothing to hide. My life is a clean mirror reflecting the satisfaction I find in knowing that I have discovered Truth. The smile I wear is a result of a conscience at peace. Now my words and actions can be real because they are motivated by a cleansed heart and the presence of Jesus within.

Praise God, the old veneer is gone! The ugly shackles of hypocrisy have been loosed by the fingers of Truth. We leave the miserable confinement of error to willingly accept the reality awaiting nearby. Today someone near you is searching for a genuine life that clearly portrays Jesus—the Way, the Truth, and the Life.

Let us be real!

Joshua Yoder, Clarkson, KY

Bible Reading: John 18:28–40
One Year Bible Reading Plan:
Romans 13
Psalms 99—102

Truth never dies.

231

Get Real!

This people honoureth me with their lips, but their heart is far from me.
Mark 7:6b

Did I hear you sigh as you wondered, "Why have I just read in a devotional book two words that I have long grown weary of hearing?" *Get real.*

By now you may pass these words off as mere "conversation fillers" to today's youth. What you may not realize is that while these words are often spoken flippantly in casual conversation, they express the heart's plea of the world today. Please be real!

The human race has become calloused and dulled by hypocrisies, half truths, generics, and fakes. Fakery is all around, expected, and "normal."

Man's carnal nature, ruled by Satan the Father of Lies, finds it impossible to be real. To be real would mean exposing the carnal heart for what it is. For a dirty, sin-stained heart to appear respectable, it must be covered with a blanket of "good deeds," a frosting of bright smiles, a varnish of cheerful, pious talking, and good moral living.

Yet the sobering fact is this: if humanity would "get real" for one day, stripping off the veneer and living its defiled heart's desire, this world would become unspeakably wicked and hellish.

The request to "get real" could be very risky and dangerous if taken literally. Well, get braced as you read on. You are asked to do just that. Yes, not only does the Bible say in Philippians 1:10 to be sincere, but also to be not as the hypocrites (Matthew 6:5, 8, 16).

Plainly, God asks us to be real. Is your life ready for this command? Are you prepared to be real?

Joshua Yoder, Clarkson, KY

Bible Reading:
  Isaiah 29:13–24
One Year Bible Reading Plan:
  Romans 14
  Psalms 103, 104

Not every one that saith unto me, Lord, Lord,
shall enter into the Kingdom of Heaven.
—Jesus

Giving

Every man according as he purposeth in his heart, so let him give;
not grudgingly, or of necessity: for God loveth a cheerful giver.
2 Corinthians 9:7

The Apostle Paul experienced things in his life that we are not faced with today. According to today's standards, he would have been the "poorest of the poor," and yet he probably felt richly blessed (Philippians 4:11, 12). Paul became a wonderful example of how we can give liberally even out of a small supply.

Our Scripture reading prescribes first the correct attitude of giving. We should give cheerfully. Verse 6 says, "He which soweth sparingly shall reap also sparingly; but he that soweth bountifully shall reap also bountifully."

First Corinthians 16:2a says, "Upon the first day of the week let every one of you lay by him in store, as God hath prospered him." There is really no set amount of giving taught in the New Testament. But Luke 21:1–4 gives an example of giving in which a rich man gave a lot, but a poor widow gave everything she had, and she was praised, even though her "everything" amounted to less than a penny.

Sometimes we see pictures in the newspaper of people giving or donating to some good or worthy cause, but, according to Matthew 6:1–4, giving anonymously will bring greater blessings.

We may also give of our time. This can be done in many different ways: by helping some brother on a project or helping rebuild in a disaster area. Many volunteer service units have needs, which are an opportunity to help.

Bible Reading: 2 Corinthians 9
One Year Bible Reading Plan:
Romans 15:1–21
Psalms 105, 106

We need to be open and willing to give in whatever way the Lord directs us to give, whether it be of our time or of our money.

Harry Bender, Hicksville, OH

_____

Freely you have received, freely give.

Poverty Versus Spiritual Wealth

My little children, let us not love in word,
neither in tongue; but in deed and in truth.
1 John 3:18

"But whoso hath this world's goods, and seeth his brother have need, and shutteth up his bowels of compassion from him, how dwelleth the love of God in him?" (1 John 3:17). Do we have compassion and love for our brother? How willing are we to share our spiritual and physical wealth with others who live in darkness?

I recently read a book about India and the dire physical and spiritual needs that they have there. They are far away, but that does not make us less responsible. We can reach them through missions. Let us empty our church treasury. It can be replenished. Tomorrow may be too late to help! I would like to pray with you, "Lord, increase our faith."

We have storehouses of spiritual wealth. We freely experience everlasting life in Christ Jesus. It is only by God's grace and mercy that we have this. Are we willing to share our faith with others? Do we realize how great the need is to bring the gospel to a lost and dying world? We need to witness to lost souls abroad and on the home front. We should use our God-given talents to be an effective witness to those who live in darkness.

Meditate on Jesus' words in Matthew 25:34–38: "Then shall the King say unto them on his right hand, Come, ye blessed of my Father, inherit the kingdom prepared for you from the foundation of the world: For I was an hungred, and ye gave me meat, I was thirsty, and ye gave me drink: I was a stranger, and ye took me in: Naked, and ye clothed me: I was sick, and ye visited me: I was in prison, and ye came unto me." "He that is faithful in that which is least is faithful also in much" (Luke 16:10).

> **Bible Reading:** 1 John 3
> **One Year Bible Reading Plan:**
> Romans 15:22–33
> Psalms 107, 108

Amos Garber, Rosebush, MI

The rewards of witnessing are well worth the risks.

The Tale of the Goats

Christ also suffered for us, leaving us an example,
that ye should follow his steps.
1 Peter 2:21

A former missionary told the story of two rugged mountain goats which met on a narrow pathway. On the one side was a chasm one thousand feet deep. On the other side a steep cliff rose straight up. There was no room to turn around, and the goats could not back up without falling. Instead of fighting for the right to pass, one of the goats knelt down and became as flat as possible. The other goat then walked over him, and they both proceeded safely on.

In a sense, this is what Jesus Christ did for us when He left heaven's glory and came to this earth to die for our sins. He saw us trapped between our sins and God's righteousness with no way to help ourselves. He came in human likeness and took the form of a servant (Philippians 2:5–8). By dying for sinful mankind, He let us "walk over Him" so we could experience forgiveness and receive eternal life.

Peter pointed to Christ as our example of humility. When we are mistreated for Christ's sake, we must learn to be humble enough to let others "walk over us." This is not a sign of weakness, but of strength and true humility. Such a response, when done for Christ's sake, brings glory to God's name. "Seeing ye have purified your souls in obeying the truth through the Spirit unto unfeigned love of the brethren, see that ye love one another with a pure heart fervently" (1 Peter 1:22).

Bible Reading: 1 Peter 2:18–25
One Year Bible Reading Plan:
Romans 16
Psalms 109—111

Menno Yoder, Monticello, KY

Christ emptied Himself. Behold our pattern!

God Is What?

He that cometh to God must believe that he is.
Hebrews 11:6

The Bible tells us that God was in Christ Jesus reconciling the world to Himself. What does this mean? I personally believe it simply means this: God is Christ and Christ is God.

I worked and worked to be holy, humble, righteous, gentle, loving, and meek, but to no avail. The harder I worked, the worse it got. Then one day I came upon some books, and God began to speak to me in a new way. I cannot merit anything. All the works I do on my own do not mean anything to God. God notices our devotion to Christ. First Corinthians 1:30 says, "of him are ye in Christ." Not by me, by you, by someone else, or by our works; but by God are we in Christ.

We can talk, quote the Bible, preach, have devotions, or do other religious service, but if it is not by the Spirit and power of Christ, making Him the center of attraction, then it is dead works.

Our God is not capricious. He has spoken, and there is no authority under heaven or anywhere else that can change God's Word. He says, "He that cometh to God must believe that He is!" He is Christ. Christ to us is wisdom, righteousness, sanctification, and redemption. Let us orbit around Him, and we will not need to desire victory—we will have it. Of Him are ye in Christ Jesus.

Bible Reading: 1 Corinthians 1:12–31
One Year Bible Reading Plan:
1 Corinthians 1
Psalms 112—115

Danny Miller, Sarasota, FL

Anything outside of Christ is rebellion.

The Stowaway

A new commandment I give unto you, That ye love one another;
as I have loved you, that ye also love one another.
John 13:34

The ship was tilted at a strange angle. Everyone knew that it would soon depart for the depths of the sea. Only minutes before, the crew had discovered that only one of the small lifeboats was safe to use. They had quickly lowered it into the stormy sea, and now all but the captain were on it. The boat was already beyond its safe capacity, but there was room for one more. The captain was just ready to swing over the side when a dirty, tattered-looking boy came running up behind him—a stowaway! Quickly the captain helped him over the side. The boy slid down the rope and filled the last spot on the lifeboat. The crew tried to convince the captain to join them, but the captain refused, knowing that one more man would surely cause the boat to capsize. Finally, the men on the lifeboat pushed away. They watched as the ship went down, taking the captain to his watery grave.

Jesus commanded us to love each other as He loved us. He called it a new commandment. What is new about this commandment? Weren't God's people always supposed to love each other? Surely they were, but never before had God given such a clear example of how much to love. How did He love us? He loved us so much that He was willing to give His life for us, even when we were dirty, tattered stowaways.

Bible Reading: John 13:31–38;
15:1–17
One Year Bible Reading Plan:
1 Corinthians 2
Psalms 116—118

I may never have the opportunity to literally give my life for my brother as the captain did for the stowaway. I do, however, often have opportunities to give up my ideas, desires, comforts, finances, and many other things that are much less than my life.

Henry Yoder, Clarkson, KY

Love wasn't put into your heart to stay;
love isn't love until it's given away.

The Battle of the Will

Not my will, but thine, be done.
Luke 22:42

In His sovereignty, God chose to allow each of us to have a will. Webster's dictionary defines will as "desire; or something desired." We all have a will, and therefore we all have desires. This is a cause of great conflict in our lives. I have a will, but so does my wife and so do my children. Are all of our wills the same? Of course not! Each member of the local church also has a will. The bishop has a will as well as the newest member and everyone else from the youngest to the oldest. Is it any wonder that there are broken friendships, marriages, partnerships, and church splits?

Let us see how the prince of this world and the Prince of Peace handled their wills. Isaiah 14 shows us how Lucifer dealt with his will. Five times he said, "I will." Each time his will was in opposition to God's will. So much, in fact, that he was cast out of heaven.

Matthew 26 shows how Jesus dealt with His will in a time of great distress. In verse 42, He says, "Thy will be done."

Jesus humbled Himself and accepted God's will instead of clinging to His own will. Because He did this, God highly exalted Him and gave Him a name which is above every name (Philippians 2:9).

Lucifer chose his own will. Jesus chose the will of His Father. Since Jesus is our perfect example, let us perfectly follow His example, push aside our will, and accept God's will.

Terry Lester, Montezuma, GA

Bible Reading: Isaiah 14:12–15;
Matthew 26:36–46
One Year Bible Reading Plan:
1 Corinthians 3
Psalm 119:1–48

Where there is God's will there is the way!

Look for God in the Wilderness

*Fear thou not: for I am with thee: be not dismayed; for I am
thy God: I will strengthen thee; yea, I will help thee; yea,
I will uphold thee with the right hand of my righteousness.*
Isaiah 41:10

There he sat, under a juniper tree. He was the great prophet of
God who had won such a tremendous victory on Mt. Carmel just a
few days before. Oh, that had been so exciting—the many people,
the silence of Baal, the fire from heaven, and the drought-ending
rain. What a sense of victory the prophet had felt when he saw the
hand of God win back the hearts of the people!

Yet here he sat, discouraged, alone, and weary of living. A threat
from the evil queen of Israel had sent him fleeing into the wilderness, and the hope and confidence he had felt so recently had melted
away like snow in the summer sun. The future no longer looked
bright and promising, only dark and painful.

Sadly Elijah lay down, praying that he might die. But Elijah did
not die. Instead, he awoke to find God's presence in the wilderness
with him. In our Bible reading, he found nourishment (verse 5–8),
soft rebuke (verses 9 and 13), encouragement (verse 18), and a mission (verses 15–17). He was not consumed by the wind, the fire,
and the earthquake, but strengthened and directed by a still small
voice. Instead of finding death in the wilderness, Elijah found
strength to go on and to do greater and mightier works of God
than before.

Brother or sister, if you find yourself in the wilderness, do not
despair; God is there also. He wants to use your wilderness experience to purify and strengthen
you. Listen for His voice, not in
the loud and dramatic but in
the meek and quiet voice of the
Savior, and you too will find
hope and strength that will
make you a better soldier for
Christ.

Bible Reading: 1 Kings 19:1–18
One Year Bible Reading Plan:
1 Corinthians 4
Psalm 119:49–104

Samson Eicher, Butler, IN

The great Teacher can use even the wilderness for His classroom.

August 23

Children

Lo, children are an heritage of the Lord;
and the fruit of the womb is his reward.
Psalm 127:3

Psalms 127 and 128 could be called "Family Psalms." Here we have admonition for the family—God's eternal truth, which is for all time and all generations. Blessings are promised to those who walk in His ways with godly fear, having the Lord build their house. And we see God's mind concerning children: "Lo, children are an heritage of the Lord"—a reward, a gift, a blessing—not a burden. Children are gifts from God, but today many children are neglected abused, and not wanted. Often they are burdens to parents who live selfishly and do not see them as gifts from God.

Children are a large dimension of our lives. They are not just a consequence of marriage. Children help us realize our dependence on God. There are many lessons parents can learn from their children, such as patience, forgiveness, and love.

No life is complete that has not known the love of a child. The child need not be your own flesh and blood. If you have none of your own, love someone else's child. It is a worthwhile investment. As our children grow, we realize that they have gifts that we do not have and can do some things better than we can.

Today much is said about children's rights. The Scriptures tell us that children do have rights. They have the right to life, the right to the Kingdom of God, the right to obey, and the right to be persons. Children should be allowed their God-given rights and should never be abused, neglected, or oppressed. They should be brought up in the nurture and admonition of the Lord.

Bible Reading: Psalm 127, 128
One Year Bible Reading Plan:
1 Corinthans 5
Psalm 119:105—176

Edward Hochstetler, Hicksville, OH

Children's children are the crown of old men.

To Train a Child

_And, ye fathers, provoke not your children to wrath: but
bring them up in the nurture and admonition of the Lord._
Ephesians 6:4

God has called parents to take up the responsibility of training children. In Deuteronomy 6, He gives direction in that task to parents. They are to teach when they walk on the way, sit, talk, lie down, and when they rise up. Children tend to ask questions. Parents often get bored with hearing the same questions over and over. I am concerned about how some parents react to their children's questions.

God wants us to foster a friendly relationship with our children. This provides an ideal atmosphere to teach. We know what it is like to learn from an angry teacher.

Jesus, the perfect teacher, has these words for His apprentices, "Come unto me, all ye that labor and are heavy laden, and I will give you rest. Take my yoke upon you, and learn of me; for I am meek and lowly in heart: and ye shall find rest unto your souls. For my yoke is easy, and my burden is light" (Matthew 11:28-30).

Children should be seen as a people who are laboring and struggling to learn. God has given this precious assignment to parents. It is not His plan that it should be given to kindergarten centers, babysitters, or maids.

Someone said children are like wet cement. They are soft and teachable now but won't be later. Are we prepared to teach? By the grace of God we can.

Bible Reading: Deuteronomy
6:1–15
One Year Bible Reading Plan:
1 Corinthans 6
Psalms 120—123

Collins Okoth, Nakuru, Kenya

It is easier to build a boy than to mend a man.

Train Up a Child

Lo, children are an heritage of the Lord:
and the fruit of the womb is his reward.
Psalm 127:3

When I was working for a construction company, I was put in charge of pouring a pad of concrete. For the sake of time, we ordered the concrete before we were ready, hoping to be ready when it came. When it got there, we were not ready, so the trucks and drivers had to wait. By the time we were ready to pour, the concrete was getting hot and was starting to set up. We poured and leveled it and went to work troweling it. We worked desperately, but finally we quit with a less than ideal finish. That has been years ago, but I expect those trowel marks are still there today.

There are some similarities between our children and this pad of concrete. Before they even arrive, we need to be ready for these precious gifts with a diligently prepared, well-established, Bible-based home.

We need to take time to mold and shape them while they are still young, pliable, and teachable. Let us not wait until the last minute and then desperately try to correct their already set ways. We may still do some good, but we will wind up with a child with lifelong scars.

We should spend time with our children as they "cure." Let us strive for a smooth finish that will be satisfactory when the Owner drops by.

Bible Reading: Proverbs 22
One Year Bible Reading Plan:
1 Corinthians 7:1–24
Psalms 124—127

Wesley Yoder, Monticello, KY

The behavior of some children suggests that their parents
embarked on the sea of parenthood without a paddle.

Fathers and Children

For even hereunto were ye called: because Christ also suffered
for us, leaving us an example, that ye should follow his steps.
1 Peter 2:21

Do you realize what an influence you have on children? You do not have to be a father, as I am, but maybe a mother, uncle, aunt, older brother or sister. Fathers, especially, seem to be idolized by their younger children. They try to imitate Dad, and his word has authority to it.

Some time ago we had a snowstorm and received about sixteen inches of snow in one day. After a while some of the children and I went out to see what it was like. Walking out the driveway behind me, one of the children said, "Look, I'm following in Dad's footsteps."

This brought to me some sobering thoughts. Am I going where I want her to go? Is it safe for her to follow me? Do I allow things for myself that I do not want my children to have?

Recently I took my children to work with me. Two of the children were standing on the stepladder. The one who was old enough to read said, "This is all the higher we can go because on the next step it says, "Do not stand or sit." The one who could not read said, "Yeah, but did Dad say so?"

The writing did not mean much to him, but Dad's words did. We have much influence on our children. They know what is important to us. It is almost impossible to erase what is etched into their young minds. Whether they look to us as Dad or Mom, brother or sister, youth in church, or an acquaintance from elsewhere, we need to remember that they are following us. May we say with Paul, "Be ye followers of me, even as I also am of Christ" (1 Corinthians 11:1). Lord, help us to be positive influences on those who serve you following my example.

Freeman Miller, Auburn, KY

Bible Reading: 1 Peter 2
One Year Bible Reading Plan:
1 Corinthians 7:25–40
Psalms 128—131

No matter where He leads or what it costs,
the best thing we can do is follow Christ.

God's Plan—
Our Responsibility

*And he changeth the times and the seasons: he removeth kings,
and setteth up kings: he giveth wisdom unto the wise, and
knowledge to them that know understanding.*
Daniel 2:21

The word pictures in Isaiah 22 are so vivid. They begin with the judgment on Shebna. God would toss him like a ball into a far country. God was displeased with him for his correspondence with the Assyrians. Shebna thought he was secure in his office, but God removed him violently.

Eliakim, whose name means raised up by God, replaced Shebna as the treasurer under King Hezekiah. Isaiah gives us this word picture of Eliakim's life. He says he is like a nail or peg in a sure place. Vessels of all shapes and sizes would be hung upon him. He would have much responsibility in Israel. God would decide when and how much responsibility to place on Eliakim, and God would also decide when to remove Eliakim from the scene.

God also has a plan for your life. He wants you to accept the responsibility He desires to place on you. Remember, He will not place on you more than you can bear. You may be a nail that will need to bear only a few vessels. Fulfill your duties faithfully. God may place upon you many vessels of all sizes. Be faithful and hold in there until God decides it is time to remove some or all of your responsibilities.

Jesus Christ is a nail that is sure and strong. Remember, He said, "My yoke is easy, and my burden is light." When we face our responsibilities with Christ, we are following God's plan to be responsible.

Bible Reading: Isaiah 22:15–25
One Year Bible Reading Plan:
1 Corinthians 8
Psalms 132—135

Mark Webb, Aroda, VA

With God all things are possible.

The Blessedness of Forgiveness

*If we confess our sins, he is faithful and just to forgive
us our sins, and to cleanse us from all unrighteousness.*
1 John 1:9

Do we dare to accept forgiveness? In order to accept forgiveness we need to consider God's Word as the final authority. In it we find many precious promises of forgiveness to which the sin-weary soul may cling. In Psalm 103:13 we read, "Like as a father pitieth his children, so the Lord pitieth them that fear him." Isn't that a nice picture of mercy? One of the easiest things for parents to do is feel pity for a child's misdeeds and to forgive them even before they ask! We can be assured that God also wants us to accept His forgiveness.

The Psalmist says, "For he knoweth our frame; he remembereth that we are dust." That reminds us that God made us. It reminds us that He knows us better than we know ourselves. He knows how weak we really are, and He wants to forgive us before we have even asked Him. The Father sees us coming toward Him; when we are yet a great way off, He has compassion on us (Luke 15:20).

We should never attempt to make excuses for our sins! There are only two things that should be done about sin: confess and forsake it. To confess means to acknowledge our sins. If we confess our sin, God will cleanse us from all unrighteousness (1 John 1:9). We may count on Him to keep His word!

Sometimes we carry an unnecessary burden of guilt over past sins and failures. Even though we have confessed them, we find it difficult to believe that God has truly forgiven us. The Bible assures us that all confessed sins are instantly and eternally forgiven. Let us use God's Word to confirm the truth in our hearts.

Bible Reading: Psalm 103
One Year Bible Reading Plan:
1 Corinthians 9
Psalms 136—138

Marvin Gingrich, Meadville, PA

The truth shall make you free.

The Object of Love

And the peace of God, which passeth all understanding,
shall keep your hearts and minds through Christ Jesus.
Philippians 4:7

Arriving back in Ohio three weeks after moving to Michigan, we were eager to see our children and grandchildren again. We had returned to attend the wedding of one of our former employees. After the wedding dinner, I was standing outside on the lawn visiting, when I saw our two-year-old granddaughter, whom I had not met since our return. I was thrilled to see her come towards me, even though she was unaware of my presence.

Finally, when she was about thirty feet away, she looked in my direction. As our eyes met, she let out a shriek and came running towards me as fast as her short legs could carry her. She had her eyes fully focused on me, and would there have been any obstacles in her path, she would hardly have noticed them. Her desire was to be in the arms of the grandfather whom she loved, and little else mattered. I gathered her into my arms, and we had a wonderful reunion. Her sweet smile and sparkling eyes lit up her whole face in an expression of joy, as she lavished her love touches all over my face.

I, along with all other believers, am anticipating a glorious homecoming in heaven. I am eagerly looking forward to seeing Him whom I love. My heart throbs with love to see my Savior, the Lord Jesus. As we go home to the golden city we will be met by Jesus Himself with outstretched arms and a countenance of love, the likes of which we have never seen before. What are obstacles? What are hardships? They are mere flames that purify our love for Him. Let us focus on the Lord Jesus and not on the obstacles. May we press towards the mark for the prize of the high calling of God in Christ Jesus.

Bible Reading: Revelation 19;
Ephesians 3:14–21
One Year Bible Reading Plan:
1 Corinthians 10:1–13
Psalms 139—140

Ivan Mast, St. Jones, MI

We love Him because He first loved us.

Be True to Your Word

Let your communication be yea, yea; nay, nay:
for whatsoever is more than these cometh of evil.
Matthew 5:37

The Duke of Burgundy was presiding over the Cabinet Council of France. A proposal was made that would violate an existing treaty but secure important advantages for the country. Many "good" reasons were offered to justify this action. When all had spoken, the duke closed the conference without giving his approval to the proposal. Placing his hand on a copy of the original agreement, he said with firmness in his voice, "Gentlemen, we have a treaty."

Our life is to glorify God. To do so is to always be true to our word. In today's setting there is a strong temptation to think that keeping our word is not really important. After all, many people do not expect it of us. To lie, cheat, and misrepresent truth is common in our society.

As a brotherhood, we have an agreement on rules of conduct, but many feel free to violate these rules. If you are tempted by the world's ambitions and entertainment, remember you have a treaty. If you have made a commitment, keep it. If non-Christians can trust us in business, they will have more reason to believe us when we present the Gospel to them.

Today's Scripture reading gives priceless instruction for everyday living. But if we are not true to our word, all else is done in vain.

Bible Reading: Matthew 5:33–48
One Year Bible Reading Plan:
1 Corinthians 10:14–33
Psalms 141—143

Melvin Yoder, Gambier, OH

God always stands true to His Word. Do You?

The Call to Faithfulness

*For unto everyone that hath shall be given, and he shall
have abundance: but from him that hath not shall be
taken even that he hath.*
Matthew 25:29

The parable of the talents has made an impression on me for a
long time. What would God have us learn from this? I have
thought of some things that I will share:

1. Not everyone has the same amount of talents.
2. God only requires us to use what we have.
3. God is not in the comparing business.
4. We are not to use our talents selfishly.
5. God will require of us that which He has given us.
6. Our concept of God will determine how we use our talents.
7. Simple obedience to that which we know pleases God.
8. When we use what we have, God will give us more.
9. God desires that our lives are fruitful.
10. It is a grave sin to bury our talents.
11. Faithfulness is more important than doing great things.

God has given each one of us talents to use, although some of
us may not think so. Maybe we spend too much time dreaming
about things that we think would be worthwhile. God desires that
we do what we are able to do. This includes work we do in our
occupations, helping those in need, our work in the community
and church. Sometimes we are called to work behind the scenes,
where we are not noticed.

If we have not used our talents in the past, God is ready to
forgive us and give us another
chance. He will be patient with
us. Remember, even giving a
cup of cold water has its
reward. God is interested in the
small things as well as the more
noticeable duties.

**Bible Reading: Matthew
25:14–30**
One Year Bible Reading Plan:
1 Corinthians 11:1–16
Psalms 144, 145

Wayne Miller, Crossville, TN

---

*Let's not look for the great things until we
have learned faithfulness in smaller things.*

Micah and the Levite

I am the Lord: that is my name: and my glory will I
not give to another, neither my praise to graven images.
Isaiah 42:8

As I reflect on the deplorable condition in Israel described in Judges 17, it makes me sad. Meditate well on the situation. Without dedicated, godly leadership in Israel, the people resorted to doing what each thought right in his own eyes.

One result was the idol worship in Micah's house, who smugly concluded that God would now do him good because he had a Levite for his priest.

How naive! God cannot bless idolatrous worship even if it is performed by a thousand Levite priests.

We may think, "Oh, we would never do anything like that!" Yet, to fall down before a statue is not the only way to be an idol worshiper. Anything that comes between us and God can become an idol. What about well kept farms, new machinery, modern houses, late model vehicles, or even money?

The devil is ever present and witty to deprive us of pure worship of the one true God. Denominational or ancestral status does not make one a Christian. There must be a personal rebirth and an undivided devotion. After all, God will not allow His name to be polluted, and He will not give His glory to another (Isaiah 48:11). In judgment we will stand alone before God.

If a man as wise as Solomon could finally in his old age turn from the true God to worshipping idols, I greatly fear for myself.

Lord, keep us from idolatry.

Wilmer Beachy, Liberty, KY

Bible Reading: Judges 17
One Year Bible Reading Plan:
1 Corinthians 11:17–34
Psalms 146, 147

If anything comes between you and God,
that thing is closer to you than God is.

Lord, What Wilt Thou Have Me to Do?

*And he trembling and astonished said, Lord, what wilt thou
have me to do? And the Lord said unto him, Arise, and
go into the city, and it shall be told thee what thou must do.*
Acts 9:6

Many times we meet up with situations that cause us to wonder, "Lord, what should I do now?" or "Lord, which direction should I go now?" We may ask, "Lord, what do you want to tell me in this trial of faith that I am facing today?" How do you deal with uncertainties in life?

Our arm of flesh is often the first to suggest a remedy for the situation. The devil wants us to trust in our own wisdom and to make decisions from our standpoint, rather than falling on our knees and consulting God. We face bitter regret when we realize that God was not included. What a peaceful feeling to know that God was consulted, and we feel assured of our direction.

The life of Paul challenges us to prompt obedience once direction is received. His first question on the road to Damascus was, "Who art thou, Lord?" He responded, "What wilt thou have me to do?" Many times our attitude is, "Lord, what do I have to do?"

How willing are we to move on once God has revealed His will for us? Paul's conversion changed him from persecutor to preacher in a few days.

As we face decisions today, how will we respond? Are we willing to accept the direction God gives, or are we prejudiced in favor of our own desires? God's blessing can only rest on those who have fully committed their wills to God. May we never desire to knowingly walk outside of the will of God. God is always faithful to provide direction for us if we only ask Him with a resigned will. May God be near you today as you seek His direction for your life.

Dale Troyer, Linneus, MO

Bible Reading: Acts 9:1–22
One Year Bible Reading Plan:
1 Corinthians 12:1–19
Psalms 148—150

Lord, show me your way today.

A Lesson From Trees

Therefore we are buried with him by baptism into death: that like as Christ was raised up from the dead by the glory of the Father, even so we also should walk in newness of life.
Romans 6:4

I have noticed that while some trees lose their leaves and become bare skeletons in autumn, others retain some of their leaves all winter. The strong winds blow. The rain, sleet, and snow pelt those old leaves, but they continue to hang on. But as springtime and warm weather roll around, something marvelous begins to happen. The tree sap moves up the trunk and out into the branches, pushing the old leaves off. The forces of new life within are doing what the storms could not do from without.

We are somewhat like those trees. Before we give our life to Christ, old habits, thoughts, words, deeds, and motives hang on like those leaves. But when we allow Christ to come and dwell within our hearts, a new life comes forth. "Therefore if any man be in Christ, he is a new creature: old things are passed away; behold, all things are become new" (2 Corinthians 5:17). His life and work within continue to push off the old life. He desires to mold, shape, refine, purify, and renew us as we yield to His gentle promptings. When He convicts us of something, and we confess and forsake, we "put off the old man with his deeds, and put on the new man." We become more like Christ.

Bible Reading: Romans 8:1–17
One Year Bible Reading Plan:
1 Corinthians 12:20–31
Proverbs 1, 2

Floyd Yoder, Montgomery, IN

There is new life in Christ Jesus.

251

Is It a Matter of Prayer?

Hitherto have ye asked nothing in my name,
ask and ye shall receive that your joy may be full.
John 16:24

Several years ago we bought a piece of real estate with the building site back off the road a distance. The first thing we did was have a nice long driveway constructed, crowned with a thin layer of gravel. This worked very well except when the ground was muddy.

One weekend, shortly after a rain, a friend came to visit, and, of course, I wanted to show him our new building site. On the way back out to the main road, I became distracted for an instant, and, you guessed it, we slid off the main path and became hopelessly mired in mud. Finally, after fighting mud and borrowing a tractor, we got out.

Later that evening I asked my friend to lead in prayer, and he especially thanked the Lord for helping us get out of the mud. Immediately I felt ashamed; I thought we had gotten out easily, considering how hopeless it had looked. I had not even thought of making it a matter of prayer. Why is it that we often try to do things on our own?

We need to pray about the small things as well as the large. The more we pray about matters, the better we will see and understand God's answers. Praise God, we have a Lord who hears and answers prayer.

Bible Reading: Matthew 5:5–15
One Year Bible Reading Plan:
1 Corinthians 13
Proverbs 3, 4

Rudy Yutzy, Brookfield, MO

_____

Before you left your room this morning, did you think to pray?

Teaching

And thou shalt teach them diligently unto thy children, and shalt talk of them when thou sittest in thine house, and when thou walkest by the way, and when thou liest down, and when thou risest up.
Deuteronomy 6:7

"Teaching is an awesome responsibility." This phrase was often quoted by one of our former schoolteachers reflecting on her commitment to her calling and duty as a teacher. This high and noble responsibility rests upon each one of us. None of us is exempt, from the oldest to the youngest, because "somebody follows you."

As I went to the barn one morning, I saw our mama cat had just caught a rat. My curiosity was aroused as I watched her carry her prize back to her three small kittens. Eagerly I watched as I imagined she was going to give her kittens a good lesson in rat catching! I was disappointed! She deposited the very alive rat beside her three small kittens. Was her duty of teaching complete? She must have thought so! In perfect contentment she commenced to clean her paws and face and beautify herself. Does that sound like us? More concerned about ourselves than about our duties?

The small kittens, with their lack of training, pounced upon the rat in their own haphazard way of attack. With each bite the rat would whirl around and strike back. Disgusted, two of the kittens gave up. But one decided the course of success must be to stay as far as possible away from that rat's head. So the kitten grabbed the tip of the rat's trail! Away they went, the rat dashing away with the kitten sliding along behind!

Indeed, experience is a good teacher, but a good teacher is much better! May God give us wisdom to fulfill our awesome responsibility patterned after Deuteronomy 6:7.

Stephen Miller, Loyal, WI

Bible Reading: Proverbs 4
One Year Bible Reading Plan:
1 Corinthians 14:1–20
Proverbs 5, 6

---

*We plead the wisdom from our God through each and every day,
For courage, strength, and patience true to teach the godly way!*

A Lesson From the Nail

He must increase, but I must decrease.
John 3:30

Philip could have felt that his ministry was being elbowed aside and eclipsed when Peter and John came to the mission he had developed. They just seemed to brush aside recognition of his excellent beginning in planting the church. But he accepted it graciously and moved on to the next assignment the Spirit had for him! He did not seem to care who got the credit for what he did. Because of his faithfulness, his work was effective.

The nail may hold a few lessons for us. After the torturous manufacturing processes, it is driven into its place of service by blow after cruel blow of the hammer. Nothing is left to sight except the head.

The poor finish nail is not only driven to its niche in life like other nails, but the nail set comes along and drives its head well below the surface. As if that were not insult enough, putty fills the hole on top of the head, and paint permanently conceals the place where the nail does its work quietly and faithfully, unnoticed for its importance.

How important is the nail? Suppose all the nails in your house would suddenly go on strike and stop doing their jobs. That would bring chaos.

We, too, are called to silently and faithfully do our work, even if we are not noticed. We tend to think we should receive recognition for the "head-pounding" we endure to hold things together. But God notices all that pertains to His children's lives.

Our emotions are not made of steel like a nail, but of feelings and sensitivities. So we do need audible and tangible encouragement and compliments frequently. Today, your sincere compliment may be just what someone needs to encourage him to stick with it! Will you give one?

Elmer Schrock, Stuarts Draft, VA

Bible Reading: Acts 8:5–8, 14, 27–40
One Year Bible Reading Plan:
1 Corinthians 14:21–40
Proverbs 7, 8

It is amazing what God can do if we don't care who gets the credit.

Ask and Believe

*And all things, whatsoever ye shall ask
in prayer, believing, ye shall receive.*
Matthew 21:22

It was a cold, snowy night. I had my Sunday school class over for supper and an evening of fun. Now I was taking them home. At several places the road was nearly drifted shut. I was getting close to one of my student's homes. The road kept getting worse and worse. Finally, within half a mile of my destination, I got stuck.

After trying my best to get out, I knew I would need help. My brother and two of my students hurried on to enlist the help of a four-wheel drive truck. They were soon back.

We could not find a good place in the front of the car to fasten the strap, so we decided to attach the hitch and use it to pull out the car backwards. I got the hitch out of the trunk and put it on. Slamming the trunk shut I walked forward to start the car.

I was shocked to discover that the keys were no longer in my pocket. We had recently purchased the car and had only one set of keys. After vainly searching for the keys, I concluded that I had locked them in the trunk.

I decided to pray. Almost immediately, the thought popped into my head, "Check the snow around the hitch."

I grabbed a shovel and dug in. With the first shovel of snow, my friend exclaimed, "There they are!" Sure enough, there they lay. Soon we were out and back on our way.

What a great God we serve! He even cares about a lost set of car keys.

Jamin Yoder, Middlebury, IN

Bible Reading: Matthew 7:1–12
One Year Bible Reading Plan:
1 Corinthians 15:1–32
Proverbs 9, 10

---

*O how praying rests the weary!
Prayer will change the night to day;
So when life seems dark and dreary,
Don't forget to pray.*
—Mary Kidder (1820-1905)

*September 8*_____

Prayer

And it shall come to pass, that before they call, I will
answer; and while they are yet speaking, I will hear.
Isaiah 65:24

Prayer is communication between God and man. Being able to call on God is the greatest privilege any person can have. The Apostle Paul tells us in Galatians 4:6 that God has sent His Spirit into our hearts so now we may cry, "Abba, Father." That is a truly profound expression of God's grace toward us!

Prayer offered in faith is our most powerful resource, because Jesus Himself has said, "Ask, and it shall be given you, seek, and ye shall find, knock, and it shall be opened unto you." Then He goes on to say, "For everyone that asketh, receiveth, and he that seeketh findeth, and to him that knocketh, it shall be opened." If we continue to ask, seek, and knock, we shall be heard.

As Christians we need to recognize our needs. Jesus also said that the Father knows what things we have need of before we ask Him. We may ask, "Why do I need to pray if He already knows my needs?" God wants us to be specific about our needs to see if we are in tune with Him.

In Luke 11, one of the disciples asked Jesus to teach them to pray, so He taught them the Lord's Prayer. He also gave them a parable. He spoke of a person going to his friend at midnight and asking for three loaves of bread. The friend said, "Don't trouble me now, we are all in bed." But because of his urgent persistence, the friend rose and gave him as many loaves as he needed. The petitioner knew his friend had what he needed, so he kept on asking. God has what we need, so let us call upon Him in truth (Psalm 145:18).

Bible Reading: Luke 11:1–13
One Year Bible Reading Plan:
1 Corinthians 15:33–58
Proverbs 11, 12

Marvin Gingerich, Meadville, PA

Pray without ceasing.

Chased by Hornets

_Moreover the Lord thy God will send the hornet among them,
until they that are left, and hide themselves from thee, be destroyed._
Deuteronomy 7:20

I remember my first encounter with hornets. I was nine or ten years old. My brother and I discovered a hornets' nest high up in a tree in our front yard. We came up with the idea that we would like to hit it with something to see what would happen. As I remember, we tried all kinds of ammunition: balls, sticks, stones, arrows, and about anything we could lay our hands on.

One day we were successful, but not without casualty. One of us managed to strike the nest or at least the branch that it was on. As the hornets swarmed out, we raced for the house. I managed to get in the door in time, but my brother was not so fortunate. His eye swelled up until he could hardly see. We had more respect for hornets after this experience.

Recently I was reading in my Bible and came across the promise God gave to the Israelites that He would use hornets to drive out their enemies. My mind went right away to my childhood experience with hornets. I could just visualize the Amorites running away from the hornets, as we had run for the house. With God directing the hornets, it would be impossible to escape.

Joshua reminded the children of Israel of the fulfillment of this promise that God had given to their fathers. They were now in the land, and he did not want them to forget all that God had done for them.

When I consider the many things God uses to accomplish his plan, I marvel. It is encouraging to know that God still provides and delivers us today. The hornets are just one more reminder from His Word that God cares for His people.

Bible Reading: Joshua 24:1–25
One Year Bible Reading Plan:
1 Corinthians 16
Proverbs 13, 14

Mark Webb, Hicksville, OH

Hornets—a division of God's air force.

When God Is Silent

Unto thee will I cry, O Lord my rock; be not silent to me: lest,
if thou be silent to me, I become like them that go down into the pit.
Psalm 28:1

"God, where are you? Help!" . . . No answer. We seem to be in a canyon. The impenetrable walls seem so close and the darkness so thick. All we hear is our own pitiful cry for help ricocheting through the confining corridors of our experience. We beg God to speak. We plead for some sliver of enlightenment to explain our agony. We long for something concrete to grasp and understand. Yet God is silent.

Some of our darkest nights come after our brightest days. We rejoice in being able to understand, but in the darkness we tremble. In *My Utmost for His Highest,* Oswald Chambers states, "Whenever God gives a vision to a saint, He puts him, as it were, in the shadow of His hand, and the saint's duty is to be still and listen. There is a darkness which comes from excess of light, and then it is time to listen."

In the Garden of Gethsemane and on the cross, Jesus experienced great darkness and silence. Though He cried out, He was willing to go through the darkness because He was sure of the Light that had led Him there and of the Light that would follow.

Perhaps it is not so much that God is silent, but that He wants us to be silent. What we take as silence may often be God pleading, "Be still, and know Me."

Steven King, Aroda, VA

Bible Reading: Psalm 28
One Year Bible Reading Plan:
2 Corinthians 1
Proverbs 15, 16

When God's silence speaks, be still.

The Evidence of God

O LORD our Lord, how excellent is thy name in all the earth!
who hast set thy glory above the heavens.
Psalm 8:1

About 93 million miles from earth a blazing ball of energy hurdles through space at a speed of almost 12 miles per second. This ball of energy, the sun, has a diameter 110 times that of the earth, and a volume 1,300,000 times that of the earth. Its surface temperature is about 11,000 degrees Fahrenheit! Aren't you glad it is 93 million miles away? Fortunately, only about five ten-billionths of the energy of the sun reaches the surface of the earth. The sun's distance from the earth is just right to maintain life on earth. This right distance is just one of many conditions that are so unique that even evolutionary scientists are beginning to admit that the chances of having another planet that supports life are almost non-existent.

The first six verses of our Scripture reading speak about the powerful testimony of Himself that God has provided us in creation, especially in the vast and orderly arrangement of the universe. As verse three comments, this testimony is universal—all men can see God if they but look at His creation.

Then, in verse seven, the writer shifts our attention to the testimony of God that has been left for us in His Word. This Word is unique in its perfection. Its pages address the needs of all men, everywhere. Its testimonies point us not only to the Creator God, but also to the Redeemer God, the One whom men can know on a personal basis.

Praise God for leaving us these testimonies of Himself. May we appreciate the wonders of creation and the beauty of His Word! Truly they are marks of His love for humanity!

Samson Eicher, Butler, IN

Bible Reading: Psalm 19
One Year Bible Reading Plan:
2 Corinthians 2
Proverbs 17, 18

A truly blind man is a man who cannot see
God through Creation or His Word.

September 12

Faith—Our Means of Hope

And He [Jesus] said unto them, Why are ye so fearful?
how is it that ye have no faith?
Mark 4:40

Our key verse is taken from the very familiar account of Jesus calming the wind and the waves. This account is given briefly in just a few verses, but do we grasp the desperation of the disciples? Some of these men had years of experience with the dangers of the sea, but apparently they had never experienced a storm of such severity. The waves swept over them repeatedly until, in spite of their best efforts, they were "full of water" and feared for their lives. Yet the wind continued to howl, and the waves continued to beat upon them. Finally, in desperation, they looked to Jesus, their only means of deliverance.

This account contrasts the way we view life at times with the way our great God views it as He works all things together for good. God allows storms, perhaps severe storms, to come into our lives to test our faith and to draw us closer to Himself. Isn't it wonderful to have the promise that He will never leave us nor forsake us?

In our Scripture reading, we encounter many who faced trials and temptations which we can hardly comprehend. Some were miraculously delivered, others suffered and died, but they were victorious and obtained a good report. How? Through faith!

As we face storms such as sickness, pain, disappointment, discouragement, grief, depression, temptation, or even our daily cares and responsibilities, let us remember that faith is our link to the power which calmed the wind and the waves—God's power. With God, all things are possible. Let us "look unto Jesus the author and finisher of our faith; who for the joy that was set before Him endured the cross, despising the shame, and is set down at the right hand of the throne of God."

Bible Reading: Hebrews 11:23–40
One Year Bible Reading Plan:
2 Corinthians 3
Proverbs 19, 20

Anthony Martin, Greencastle, PA

Faith makes things possible, but not necessarily easy.

260

Our Infinite God

Thou knowest my downsitting and mine uprising,
thou understandest my thought afar off.
Psalm 139:2

Our God is all-present. Sometimes God seems far away, and we ask Him, "Where art thou?"

The answer comes back to us, "I am where you are. I am here. I am next to you. I am everywhere." God is infinite. Infinite is "immeasurable, boundless, limitless." We are quite the opposite. We are finite and measurable. Our minds can remember only so much. We have limits. Our body can only do so much, then it needs rest.

God is immeasurable. We read that the earth is His footstool. Try to imagine that this whole earth is only His footstool. We can somewhat imagine the immensity of God, yet our finite minds cannot grasp it. God has no limits. God is near to everything—He is everywhere at any given moment. God swallows up all space. We are totally surrounded by God. In Jeremiah we read, "Do not I fill the heaven and earth?" When you put a bucket into the ocean, the water surrounds it on all sides, and also fills the bucket. That is how God is. He surrounds us on all sides.

If God is so close at all times, why does He sometimes seem far away? Think of putting an angel and an ape together in the same room. They might be physically close together, but in reality they are far apart. That is why God sometimes seems far away. Man has sinned, and sin separates us from God. When we have sin in our life, we cannot communicate with God. Jesus came so we can get rid of the sin problem. Our sins can be washed away. When we have confessed our sins to God and man, we can communicate with God as we are totally surrounded by Him.

Bible Reading: Acts 17:22–31
One Year Bible Reading Plan:
2 Corinthians 4
Proverbs 21, 22

Jason Schlabach, Sugarcreek, OH

Our God knows everything about you and me.

Shake It Off and Step Up

I have fought a good fight, I have finished
my course, I have kept the faith.
2 Timothy 4:7

There is a story of a donkey that asked his grandpa, "How do I grow up to be like you?" Grandpa Donkey said, "I'll tell you a story. When I was young, I fell into an old, abandoned well. I began by braying and braying. Finally an old man heard and came by and saw me in the well. He looked and then left me in the well all night. The next morning he came back with a group of people. They looked down at me, and some even laughed at me. 'Well then,' the old man said, 'This well is no good, and the donkey's not worth saving. Let's fill it up with dirt.' I panicked, because I was being buried alive. After the first few shovelfuls of dirt came down, I realized every time dirt landed on my back, I could shake it off and step up. They kept shoveling, and I kept shaking it off and stepping up. 'Shake it off and step up; shake it off and step up,' I kept repeating to myself for encouragement. It wasn't long before I stepped out of the well, tired but victorious!"

Joseph is a good example of one who shook it off and stepped up. Though he was misused and sold by his brothers, he did not despair. God helped him shake off his misfortune, and soon he was given a step up in life. He was falsely accused and thrown into jail. Again, God was with him, and he shook it off and stepped up from jail. He eventually became second in command in Egypt. Only Pharaoh had more power. God's mercy and power are able and available as we believe in God and obey His revealed will. He will help us in those times of trials and despair to shake it off and step up like Joseph.

Bible Reading: Genesis
37:15–28; 39:1–6
One Year Bible Reading Plan:
2 Corinthians 5
Proverbs 23, 24

Tite Miller, Somerset, OH

Trials will make us or break us.

Where Is God Found?

And thine ears shall hear a word behind thee, saying,
This is the way, walk ye in it, when ye turn to the
right hand and when ye turn to the left.
Isaiah 30:21

Elijah found God on Mt. Carmel in a way that all Israel recognized. There was no disputing the fact. Now, in our Scripture reading, his life is threatened by Jezebel. He finds himself all alone.

Where is God now? Were all my efforts in vain? How could God allow such a victory to be spoiled by a vicious queen? Perhaps these and other questions plagued Elijah's mind. They were too much for him. He arose and fled for his life. But God followed him in mercy and helped him to understand where God is found. God very aptly illustrated an important truth about where to find Him.

The earthquake, wind, and fire, all vivid displays of power, failed to reveal the intimate presence of God. Only the still, small voice moved Elijah to the acknowledgment of God's presence.

God is often best found in the solitudes of life. Jesus understood that when he said to His disciples, "Come ye yourselves apart into a desert place, and rest a while." Surrounding ourselves with lots of commotion, people, and events hinders the still, small voice of God. Elijah did not realize that the frightening threat of Jezebel was the method God was using to get him out of the limelight and into the solitude of a desert experience. Moses needed the same thing. God caused certain events to move Moses out of Egypt to the back side of the desert where he learned who God was and who he himself was.

When the events of life force you out of active service into a desert place of solitude, sorrow, or suffering, do not despair. Look up in faith, and you will find God with all manner of strength and sustenance for you.

Bible Reading: 1 Kings 19:1–18
One Year Bible Reading Plan:
2 Corinthians 6
Proverbs 25—27

Delmar R. Eby, London, KY

When the outlook fails, try the up look.

The Cares of This World

And the cares of this world, and the deceitfulness of riches,
and the lusts of other things entering in, choke
the word, and it becometh unfruitful.
Mark 4:19

We are living in prosperous times. Many things enter into our lives and vie for our time. Our spiritual lives may become stunted because our work load is too great and does not allow time for study and meditation. We may at times need some relaxation and a few games, but with too much entertainment we may point some young person in the wrong direction. We have a responsibility to give guidance and point others in the right direction.

The young leaves of the Compass Plant always point north and south. The older leaves become jagged and frazzled, and, when covered with dew and dust, falter and point in all directions.

If we become weighted down with the cares of this life, and our character becomes sullied with worldliness and greed for material gain, we lose our sense of direction and can no longer point others to God.

Our lives must be clean and give distinct direction to those who follow us. We may at times feel that we are not important—no one cares or notices what we do and how we live. Yet all of us have role models. We have someone we appreciate and look up to.

Even in the darkest night one can trust the young leaves of the Compass Plant to give sure direction. In the same way, the life of the true child of God can be trusted to give direction even in the darkest times. Remember, someone follows you.

> **Bible Reading:** Mark 4:1–20
> **One Year Bible Reading Plan:**
> 2 Corinthians 7
> Proverbs 28, 29

Melvin L. Yoder, Gambier, OH

Keep out of your life all that keeps Christ out of your thoughts.

The Car With No Motor

And it shall come to pass, that before they call, I will
answer; and while they are yet speaking, I will hear.
Isaiah 65:24

The following is a true story which took place in Brazil. A Brazilian man was wonderfully saved from his life of sin. He began witnessing to his old drinking and gambling buddies, often inviting them to church. One day his buddies consented to go to church under one condition; he must take them to church in their car. That evening on his way to church, the Christian stopped by to pick up his old friends. They gave him the keys and sat in the back seat. When the Christian started the car, he noticed a sudden change in the three men. They fell deathly silent and did not talk through the whole trip. When he arrived at the church, they were sobbing. "What is wrong?" he asked them. "Get out and raise the hood," they answered. The Christian opened the hood and discovered there was no motor in the car. His friends had set this up for another occasion to mock him, but God had other plans. Through this incident, the three men were saved. God was faithful in answering the Christian's prayer. He is also faithful in answering our prayers.

Why is prayer so important? Without it we cannot grow spiritually. It lifts the petitioner to the realms of the heavenlies. It is a gateway to many blessings and brings fullness of joy. Through the prayer of faithful Christians, people are healed, and more people are added to God's kingdom.

God faithfully leads His children. When we pray, we need to ask in faith and not waver. God's will is always best for our life.

Bible Reading: Matthew 6:1–15
One Year Bible Reading Plan:
2 Corinthians 8
Proverbs 30, 31

Samuel Beachy, Belvidere, TN

Prayer will make a man cease from sin;
sin will make a man cease from prayer.

In Jesus' Name

To whom coming as unto a living stone disallowed
indeed of men, but chosen of God, and precious.
1 Peter 2:4

Prayer is a wonderful privilege. It gives us an audience with our Creator. Because we have often been quite neglectful and even heedless, we rightly feel mortification and shame in the presence of our infinite, thrice-holy God.

Unlike Isaiah, we need not enter His presence alone. Our Savior, the High Priest, goes with us into the presence of God. Like Isaiah, we will sense our need if we truly worship Him.

In our present human form, we cannot fully understand God, but that need not trouble us. In our earnest desire to know God we are blest. We need to thirst like a hunted deer (Psalm 42:1) and hunger like a newborn baby for the "sincere milk of the Word" (1 Peter 2:2). Such fervent desires bring us into favorable regard by our heavenly Father. With these words Jesus stresses the importance of being accompanied by Him as we enter God's presence: "No man cometh unto the Father but by me" (John 14:6). He further emphasizes this truth by referring to prayer's quest as occurring "in my name." This emphasis is provided in five repetitions (John 14:13, 14; 16:23, 24, 26).

What a glorious provision!

We are privileged to fellowship with God, and we are not out of our place to come to Him with confidence (Hebrews 4:16). Why not? Because we come in Jesus' name.

Why are we to come in Jesus' name? Because He was tempted as are we. He tasted death for us. He intercedes for us. We also give recognition to all these things when we come to God in Jesus' name.

Bible Reading: Isaiah 6
One Year Bible Reading Plan:
2 Corinthians 9
Ecclesiastes 1—3

Paul Miller, Partridge, KS

When we pray, we go with an authorized
Person into the presence of the King.

Spirit Fruit Expression

*Speaking to yourselves in psalms and hymns and spiritual songs,
singing and making melody in your heart to the Lord.*
Ephesians 5:19

In today's Bible reading we notice one of the most unusual military campaigns of all the battles ever fought on the face of this earth.

There are a number of parallels to that long ago day and our present experience. God's people were confronted by overwhelming odds; Christians today are still a minority. When facing a situation for which our resources are inadequate, paralyzed by fear, "neither know we what to do," we turn to God; they did too.

You may wonder how mere singing could ever win a battle, unless the decibel level was so high it burst the enemies' eardrums. No marvel though, their victory (and our success) is dependent on obedience. Remember, the battle is not ours, but God's.

Singing has been called the spiritual barometer of a society. This is why we have chosen to call it Spirit fruit expression. From the days of our martyr forefathers to the present, it is man's most beautiful form of adoration. It is the high note of praise causing earthquakes (by the hand of God) and bringing physical deliverance to Paul and Silas. How fitting that they in turn brought the message of spiritual deliverance to the Philippian jailor and his household.

Armed with this knowledge, how and what shall we sing? As I have already mentioned, it must convey our expression of the indwelling Spirit. Our songs will convey our experience. The melody is the vehicle or means by which the lyrics of a song are expressed. Therefore, it should be subordinate. Its role is to enhance or adorn the message of any given song.

One more aspect about singing—whether audible, in our hearts, from the lips of a child, or the purest strains of soprano, the Christian finds himself communing with the Creator in his spirit, soul, and body.

Bible Reading: 2 Chronicles 20:1–25
One Year Bible Reading Plan: 2 Corinthians 10
Ecclesiastes 4—6

Jerry Yoder, Auburn, KY

Take my voice and let me sing.

A Soft Answer

A soft answer turneth away wrath, but grievous words stir up anger.
Proverbs 15:1

I am a tree trimmer, and I once responded to a call in town, where the houses were adjacent to each other. The lawns were long and narrow. At the rear of the house was a fence with no gate. The only exit was a small one in the direction of the street.

I asked my potential customer if there would be a way to remove the brush, other than dragging it through that narrow opening. "Oh, you can back your truck into my neighbor's yard and toss the branches over the fence. He won't care," she replied.

I was the successful bidder. The day arrived to trim the trees and I backed up to the fence on her neighbor's property. Before we got started pruning, a man approached and, with an angry voice, asked, "Who gave you permission to back your truck into my yard?"

"The lady next door told me you would not mind," I answered.

"I have lived beside her for sixteen years, and she has been nothing but a problem to live with for all that time," he retorted. "And you had no right to do this without my permission."

"I'm sorry; I should have asked you. Could I still ask you? Or could I pay you something for this favor?" I replied softly.

"Oh, just go ahead. It will be fine," he added. Then he walked to the house.

Some people may say, "I would have given him a piece of my mind!" Haven't we all been tempted to do such a foolish thing? However, there is a better way. Proverbs 26:4 says, "Answer not a fool according to his folly, lest thou also be like unto him." Job 6:25 says "How forcible are right words."

May our prayer be that of the Psalmist, who prayed, "Set a watch, O Lord, before my mouth; keep the door of my lips."

Willis Halterman, Carlisle, PA

| Bible Reading: Proverbs 15:1–30 |
| **One Year Bible Reading Plan:** |
| 2 Corinthians 11:1–15 |
| Ecclesiastes 7—9 |

A soft heart with a soft answer is the key for a spiritual "locksmith."

A Word Fitly Spoken

A word fitly spoken is like apples of gold in pictures of silver.
Proverbs 25:11

David, fleeing from King Saul, found himself in need of food for his men. Hearing of Nabal, a wealthy sheep farmer, he humbly sent to ask him for some much-needed sustenance.

Nabal, foolish and churlish as he was, refused David's request. The refusal itself could not have been so bad, but the words he chose to use were not fit words. They were scornful and contemptuous. Through false accusation, he showed blatant disrespect to the future king. His pride and haughtiness spewed forth rudeness and unkindness. His words were "a maul, a sword, and a sharp arrow" to David's spirit (Proverbs 25:18). Though wrong, David's response was, "Gird ye on every man his sword."

Abigail, upon hearing of this interchange, acted without delay. She prepared heaps of good things and personally superintended their delivery. She humbly and graciously approached David as his handmaiden. With respectful words, she sought to reverse David's intentions. Her words were soothing even if they were a gentle reproof. They fell like a soft, cool breeze on David's inflamed spirit (see Proverbs 25:12, 15).

Our key verse now comes clearly into focus. David admits his hastiness as a mistake. He not only accepted her goods, but responded with, "Blessed be the Lord God, blessed be thy advice, and blessed be thou, I have accepted thy person."

The influence of fit words is inestimable. May we implore God daily for fit words, because unfit words are unacceptable to Him and to others. "Let the words of my mouth, and the meditation of my heart be acceptable in thy sight, O Lord, my strength, and my redeemer" (Psalm 19:14).

Bible Reading: 1 Samuel 25:1–35
One Year Bible Reading Plan:
2 Corinthians 11:16–33
Ecclesiastes 10—12

Delmar Eby, Manchester, KY

A soft answer turneth away wrath, but grievous words stir up anger.
—Proverbs 15:1

Justice or Mercy?

Not by works of righteousness which we have done, but according to his mercy he saved us, by the washing of regeneration, and renewing of the Holy Ghost.
Titus 3:5

Get what you deserve! The bold print blurted out across the top of an investment firm's advertisement. Really?

I pondered the merit of this statement and concluded that in the spiritual realm I definitely do not want what I deserve. Nor have I received it in the material. In both realms my testimony is, "Hitherto hath the Lord helped us." Consider the following:

Over 40 years ago, a family moved from norther Indiana to Georgia. They were friends of my parents; and sometime later, Dad decided we should visit them. Through this visit (I dare not call it a chance encounter) I met a young woman who has shared the joys and sorrows of life with me for nearly 39 years.

Life with her has been an unmixed blessing. I am reminded of the love Abraham Lincoln had for his wife, Mary Todd. In his proposal of marriage to her he wrote, "I could as soon stop breathing as to quench my love for you. There is but one thought that would restrain my request for your hand—I am not worthy."

Did I get what I deserved? Hardly.

In the course of time, financial reverses were visited on us. Through the aid of two brethren who cared, and the blessing of the Lord, those reverses became history. I learned firsthand the weight of the statement, "I know how to be abased and I know how to abound." But first I had to learn how to be abased.

Again, the question begs an answer. My experience in the spiritual realm is not so different from yours, my Christian friend. We, destitute spiritual paupers, have become heirs to wealth untold by our "acceptance into the beloved." We, who were of the wild olive tree, barren and unfruitful, were grafted contrary to nature, into a good olive tree, the writer to the Romans tells us.

Please, I do not want what I deserve.

Jerry Yoder, Auburn, KY

Bible Reading: Isaiah 61
One Year Bible Reading Plan:
2 Corinthians 12
Song of Solomon 1—3

Grace is everything for nothing, for those who don't deserve anything.

Mercy

The sacrifices of God are a broken spirit: a broken and
a contrite heart, O God, thou wilt not despise.
Psalm 51:17

The group came through the door slowly. The handcuffed prisoner between the two officers was noticeably shaken as he was led before the judge and the jury. The judge, seeing the stricken look on the prisoner's face said, "Son, you need not fear. This jury is not partial, but honest and always favors justice."

"Yes, your honor, but I do not want justice—I want mercy."

The Pharisee removed himself a distance from everyone else, until he was alone but not out of earshot, and he prayed, "God, I thank thee that I am not as other men are, extortioners, unjust, adulterers, or even as this publican." The publican could not believe his ears. A long accusing finger was pointed toward him and made him feel guilty. He felt wicked and condemned, and he realized his position before God. Without even lifting his eyes to heaven, he smote his breast saying, "God, be merciful to me a sinner!" (Luke 18:10-13).

The young malefactor grimaced as he endured the excruciating pain of crucifixion, but he could hear all the mockery heaped upon Jesus. Even his fellow malefactor taunted Him. Finally, he could stand it no longer and said, "Dost thou not fear God, seeing thou art in the same condemnation? We are getting justice as a reward for our deed, but this man has done nothing worthy of death." Then, addressing Jesus, he said, "Lord, remember me when thou comest into thy kingdom."

Jesus answered, "Today you shall be with me in paradise." Oh, what relief, hope, and mercy! God is always touched when a sinner truly repents and comes to Him for mercy, and He grants it so freely.

What about me? What about you? We cannot purchase mercy, and God is no respecter of persons. It is a gift He offers. Upon the broken and contrite heart He showers mercy.

Bible Reading: Psalm 51
One Year Bible Reading Plan:
2 Corinthians 13
Song of Solomon 4, 5

Wilmer Beachy, Liberty, KY

_____

God: undefinable.

Have a Good Day

This is the day which the Lord hath made;
we will rejoice and be glad in it.
Psalm 118:24

It was cold! The stars twinkled merrily down at me while the moon lay cradled in the splendor of light. I vividly remember how cold it was, for my nostrils wanted to stick together, and thinking how beautiful the snow was glimmering in the moonlight.

I also remember that dreary day when the sun refused to come out from behind all the dreariness. It never did get really light all day. Oh, that was a beautiful day too!

I was out making deliveries on another day that I will remember for a long time. It was really not fit for a person to be out that day. The snow refused to quit but came down in white splendor, accumulating happily on everything. Trees bowed gracefully under the weight, while every fence post stood proudly holding its sparkling crown. Fields and lawns were turned into works of art as knurled fences and hedge rows displayed their delight in illustrious creations. Driving was dangerous and tiresome that day. Yet it was a beautiful day!

This morning as I stepped outside, I realize that I had never seen a bad day. If God makes every day, then what is bad about it? Sometimes the sun shines upon us, and sometimes it does not. It is a fact that more people are depressed in the winter time when the days are shorter than at any other time. But will we allow that which is good to become evil for us? I love dreary days when the sun does not shine. I love sunny days when the sun is bright. I love the Creator God who designed these things to be. We do not see our days as much from the eye window, as we do from the heart. When the heart is cheerful, even a cloudy day becomes bright. Have a good day today!

Alvin Mast, Millersburg, OH

Bible Reading: Psalm 139:1–18
One Year Bible Reading Plan:
Galatians 1
Song of Solomon 6—8

Those who bring sunshine into the lives of others
cannot keep it from themselves.
—James Barrie (1860-1937)

Fret Not Thyself

Fret not thyself because of evildoers, neither be thou
envious against the workers of iniquity.
Psalm 37:1

At times life just does not seem fair. The ungodly seem to prosper more than the righteous.

In 1971 Jeffrey Borman was sentenced to prison for 92 years for a double murder. Jeffery's brothers were working for me at the time of the murders. He was released after serving only 21 years of that sentence. He will be on parole till 2052. Recently he purchased a lottery ticket and won 3.9 million dollars. No, it seems that life is not always fair.

Jesus spent his life doing good. He healed the sick, gave sight to the blind, cleansed the lepers, and preached the Gospel to the poor. He did all this without asking anything for Himself. Yet He was hated, scorned, and betrayed.

Today's Scripture reading reminds us that the Lord knows the days of the upright; and their inheritance shall be forever. The workers of iniquity shall soon be cut down like the grass and wither as the green herb. Surely we can delight ourselves in the Lord. We can know that our sins are washed away in the blood and that we have an eternal inheritance.

At times we wonder why God permits trials in the lives of His children, while the wicked seem to prosper. Those trials help to cleanse, purify, and prepare us for the rewards which God has prepared for us in heaven. Our hope is set on things above, and we long for the day when Christ will come for those who love His appearing.

Melvin Yoder, Gambier, OH

> **Bible Reading:** Psalm 37:1–18
> **One Year Bible Reading Plan:**
> Galatians 2
> Isaiah 1—3

If your labor for God seems unnoticed, remember,
the rewards are out of this world.

September 26_____

Capture the Vision

Where there is no vision, the people perish:
but he that keepeth the law, happy is he.
Proverbs 29:18

They call it wild carrot, a worthless weed. I call it Queen Anne's lace, a beautiful flower. They call it a weed patch; I call it my wild-life garden. It teems with busy bees, winsome wasps, beautiful birds, and rollicking rabbits. All kinds of insects abound in that "weed patch." The insects in those "worthless weeds" attract a great variety of birds. Those birds love the patch, which is so suitable for nests and food, and they respond in the most interesting way—they sing . . . and their songs enrich my life.

Okay, so you want me to cut that patch of weeds and meticulously trim around every tree and fence post. You want me to cut the grass down to a sociably acceptable, modern day, glossy, plastic look. You want to take away my birds that go "tweet," and the little insects that go "buzz." I am sorry, but I cannot do it. You see, I have a vision—for more weeds and trees and insects and birds and rabbits.

I wonder sometimes what we see when the holy assembly, the visible church, the saints of God, gather? Do we have the vision it takes to be what God really wants us to be? Most people are what they are because they are not overly concerned with what God thinks of them. They want to be saved, but not sanctified. They want security without commitment and to gain heaven without loss. If we want to see Jesus, we must see the bigger picture. Jesus is not just some sweet experience. He is also suffering and self-denial to us. Sounds strange to us modern, spoiled, bored people. Seems strange as weeds in a sterile world, does it not?

Alvin Mast, Millersburg, OH

> **Bible Reading:** 1 Peter 4
> **One Year Bible Reading Plan:**
> Galatians 3
> Isaiah 4—6

Do what you hope to become, and you will get there.

274

From Day to Day

Sing unto the Lord, bless his name;
shew forth his salvation from day to day.
Psalm 96:2

"One thing have I desired of the Lord, that will I seek after: that I may dwell in the house of the Lord all the days of my life, to behold the beauty of the Lord, and to inquire in his temple" (Psalm 27:4).

All the days of my life? "Day after day" often gets us down. The mundane things of life wear us out. How can we show forth His salvation day to day?

I often think of a man in a wheelchair, who told me the months and weeks fly, but the days drag by at times. This is when we often become weary, and we falter and faint. Paul writes, "And let us not be weary in well doing; for in due season we shall reap, if we faint not" (Galatians 6:9).

The evil one uses the nitty-gritty things of day by day living to wear us down. Unless we have a vibrant life in Christ on a daily basis, we soon lose out. Can we renew our covenant relation with God day by day? After all, His mercies are new every morning. We can have the work of the cross as a daily experience by faith in the living God.

I have been shocked by how many middle-aged and older people lose out in their walk with God.

May we live for God day by day and be ready when He calls us home!

Allan Miller, Sarcoxie, MO

Bible Reading: Psalm 96:2
One Year Bible Reading Plan:
Galatians 4
Isaiah 7—9

My heart is fixed, O God my heart is fixed;
I will sing and give praise.
—Psalm 57:7

The Need to Respond

But ye have not so learned Christ; if so be that ye have heard him,
and have been taught by him, as the truth is in Jesus.
Ephesians 4:20, 21

The skies were black and ominous with impending thunder-clouds from up the valley. As the storm rapidly approached, we dashed to the house. By the time the storm hit us, the creek which flows in front of our house was high and swollen already.

We watched in awe as logs and forest debris swept wildly past, for the creek had flooded its banks. Our quiet, peaceful creek had turned into a violent river.

As we moved the things which were standing in the yard fur-ther back from the raging current, my wife mentioned that the pic-nic table might also be washed away. Assuming that it was not in danger, I did not do anything about it.

When the torrents of rain quit, I went out to the barnyard to check how things were out there. While I was gone, the picnic table started to float. One of my daughters and my wife rushed out to rescue it. However, my daughter lost her footing and began to be swept out into the seething main current.

Seeing the danger, my wife grabbed her just in time. They both clung to a small tree till other help arrived, and they were brought safely to dry land again.

This near tragedy could have been avoided had I responded to another's observation. Our own understanding and judgment is not always sufficient. We need to submit ourselves to one another.

> **Bible Reading:** 1 Peter 5
> **One Year Bible Reading Plan:**
> Galatians 5
> Isaiah 10—12

Noah Yoder, Burkesville, KY

_____

Listen, think, and respond to fulfill the will of God.

He Put Out His Hand and Took It

Therefore said he, Take it up to thee.
And he put out his hand, and took it.
2 Kings 6:7

Took what? In this account from 2 Kings 6, the prophet received a direct, tangible gift from God. But before he could receive the gift, the prophet had to believe and respond with a conscious, deliberate action of his own.

I would like to suggest some applications to our experience with God.

When facing temptations, do we promptly utilize God's power to resist?

When we feel carnal passions welling up within, do we say, "Lord, control my spirit"?

When we sense that our spiritual temperature is low, do we reach out to God before discouragement overtakes us?

When led into the presence of a needy soul, do we immediately pray within, "Lord, please give me the words to speak"?

When the Lord lays a burden on our hearts to write or teach, do we saturate the topic before us with prayer?

When trying to find our way through important decisions, how long do we flounder about before we reach out, take God's hand, and allow Him to show us the way?

May we be spiritually minded enough to be constantly aware that God loves His children and desires to help them with every need.

Alan Priest, Burns Lake, BC

Bible Reading: 2 Kings 6:1–7; Matthew 6:25–34
One Year Bible Reading Plan:
Galatians 6
Isaiah 13—15

Faith is not belief without proof, but trust without reservation.

It Is I, Be Not Afraid

Come unto me, all ye that labour and are heavy laden, and I will give you rest. Take my yoke upon you, and learn of me; for I am meek and lowly in heart: and ye shall find rest unto your souls. For my yoke is easy, and my burden is light.
Matthew 11:28–30

My four-year-old son is afraid of thunderstorms. Recently, while we were getting ready for bed, we heard thunder off in the distance. He wanted to sleep in our bedroom on the floor. At 12:30 a.m., I awoke to a very bad thunderstorm. The wind was blowing. Bright lightning illuminated the sky, and thunder cracked like a horse whip. But Jaron slept through the entire storm. He appeared calm and relaxed, sprawled out on the floor.

Why? He knew that he was close to his daddy. I was left with a probing thought: "Do I trust my heavenly Father as Jaron trusts me?" What about when the checking account is low, and there is another doctor bill? Can I trust my children's future in His hands?

What can I do to make a difference? My own works and efforts are of little help as far as the future. Only God holds the key.

As Jaron trusted in me for reassurance when he was frightened, I need to trust my heavenly Father for physical and temporal things.

Bible Reading: Matthew 14:22–36
One Year Bible Reading Plan: Ephesians 1
Isaiah 16—18

Aaron Mast, Caneyville, KY

Worry is like a rocking chair; it gives you something to do, but you never get anywhere.

God's Possession

The earth is the Lord's, and the fulness thereof;
the world, and they that dwell therein.
Psalm 24:1

Although God put us on the earth, the earth still belongs to Him. He only intends for us to live, work, and fulfill His will for our lives while we are here.

As we meditate on the key verse, we think of the many possessions God has. The mineral, oil, and gas deposits beneath. All the beasts of the forest and the cattle on a thousand hills. We see the beautiful landscape, hills, mountains, valleys, running streams, trees of all kinds, flowers, and birds of their different colors and songs. Our different houses and all the improvements that are made on this earth by the skill and industry of man are His.

In the kingdom of grace, these are emptiness. They mean nothing to the soul, but it should be a comfort to us to know that all the earth is the Lord's. Everything is under His eye; all are in His hand. Wherever a child of God goes, he may comfort himself with the thought that he does not leave his Father's ground. Our share of the earth and its goods are only lent to us; they are the Lord's.

The last part of Psalm 24:1 speaks of they that dwell on earth. That includes you and me. He is the Creator of our bodies. Even our tongue is not our own. It is to be at His service. It is the Lord's.

As we travel through this life as strangers and pilgrims, we enjoy God's possessions and are blessed. We are comforted, knowing that God the Father has given Jesus power over all flesh, that He should give eternal life to as many as the Father has given Him (John 17:2).

Bert Raber, Chuckey, TN

Bible Reading: Psalm 104:1–25
One Year Bible Reading Plan:
Ephesians 2
Isaiah 19—21

Our walk on earth is sweet, but sweeter
far the ending, to rest at Jesus' feet.

100% Heaven Raiser

And whatsoever ye do, do it heartily, as to the Lord, and not unto men.
Colossians 3:23

While at work one day, I saw a truck drive by with the words painted on it: "100% Hell raiser." I wondered if the driver comprehended the seriousness of the motto on the door of his pickup. Probably not, since he drove the truck through the middle of town, where everyone could see it. Many people today are bound to the ruler of this world. They serve him without reserve. It seems that the wickedness of society is ever increasing.

Before we accept Jesus Christ as our Savior, we are servants of sin. Romans 3:23 tells us that all of us have sinned. This means every human being. One hundred percent of humanity has come short of the glory of God. Let us thank God that He provided a means for us to quit serving sin! First John 1:9 proclaims that if we confess our sins, Jesus will cleanse us from all unrighteousness. Not just some sins will be cleansed, but one hundred percent of our sins will be washed away. There are no sins we can secretly hide from the Lord and still expect to experience His grace. We must totally surrender ourselves to His will to find rest for our souls.

After our conversion experience, we should serve the Lord one hundred percent of the time. Give God the praise and glory He deserves! The Lord provided us a pardon for our sins. We can find time to do many things in life. Let us also find the time to meditate on His word, not only fifty percent of the time, but one hundred percent of the time.

Mike Janecek, New Bethlehem, PA

Bible Reading: John 8:31–47
One Year Bible Reading Plan:
Ephesians 3
Isaiah 22, 23

Let's be 100 percent on fire for the Lord.

Thanks for the Pain!

Now faith is the substance of things hoped for,
the evidence of things not seen.
Hebrews 11:1

What is faith? George Mueller once said, "Faith does not operate in the realm of the possible. There is no glory for God in that which is humanly possible. Faith begins where man's power ends." We see many examples of that in the Bible. In Matthew 8:5–13 we see the centurion's faith; and in Matthew 9:1, 2, the faith of the sick.

Two-year-old David was diagnosed with leukemia. His mother, Deborah, took him to a hospital in Boston, Massachusetts to see Dr. Truman. The doctor's prognosis was devastating: "He has a 50-50 chance." Through the countless clinic visits, blood tests, intravenous drugs, fear, and pain, the mother's ordeal was almost as bad as the child's. She stood by, unable to bear the pain herself. David never cried in the waiting room, and although his friends in the clinic had to hurt him and stick needles in him, he hustled in ahead of his mother with a smile, sure of the welcome he always got. When he was three, David had to have a spinal tap—a painful procedure at any age. It was explained to him that, because he was sick, Dr. Truman had to do something to make him better. "If it hurts, remember it is because he loves you," Deborah said. The procedure was horrendous. It took three nurses to hold David still, while he yelled and sobbed and struggled. When it was almost over, the tiny boy, soaked in sweat and tears, looked up at the doctor and gasped, "Thank you, Dr. Tooman, for my hurting."

Do we thank God for the hurts, the trials that come into our lives? George Mueller once said, "God delights to increase the faith of His children." Trials, difficulties, and sometimes defeat are the very food of faith. We should take them from His hands as evidences of His love and care for us in developing more and more that faith which He is seeking to strengthen in us.

Jason Knepp, Kenora, ON

Bible Reading: Hebrews 11:1–23
One Year Bible Reading Plan:
Ephesians 4
Isaiah 24—26

Faith is to believe what we do not see, and
the reward of faith is to see what we believe.

From Everlasting to Everlasting, Thou Art God

And I say also unto thee, That thou art Peter, and upon this rock I will build my church; and the gates of hell shall not prevail against it.
Matthew 16:18

The snow-covered mountain peaks rose in beautiful splendor on that Sunday morning in Romania. This was our first service in the newly repaired church building—a building that had stood silent and empty for forty-six years.

When we first saw the old building, it was in a sad state of disrepair. The floor was completely rotted out, the windows were broken, and the doors unusable. However, the heavy masonry walls were still standing rigid and strong, and the red clay tile roof still protected the building from the elements. Finally the last crumbling plaster was patched, the last window pane replaced, and the interior walls shone, gleaming white with their new coat of paint.

On that special Sunday morning, the sun shone brightly through the clear glass onto the clean, white walls. It seemed that God was giving a special confirmation of His presence. The building was well filled, and there were smiles on our faces as we rejoiced together in the beauty of the moment.

Old Brother Titos sat on the front bench with tears streaming down his wrinkled, weather-beaten cheeks. You see, in 1953, this church had been closed down by the communists. Old Brother Titos was the only man left of the original church. It was such a blessing to see him and such a confirmation of his faith to once more join in worship in this place. The atheistic communist government was history, and the church was as alive as ever!

I chose this text from Matthew 16:18 for the sermon that morning. In this very village where a pastor had been cruelly beaten and the church doors locked for forty-six long years, the voices of worshipers rose again to the throne of our eternal God.

Joe A. Miller, Seymour, MO

Bible Reading: Matthew 16:13–28
One Year Bible Reading Plan:
Ephesians 5
Isaiah 27, 28

The church must either "send" or "end."

Originals or Duplicates?

There is one glory of the sun, and another glory of the moon,
and another glory of the stars: for one star
differeth from another star in glory.
1 Corinthians 15:41

Originals: made according to the deliberate design of an originator.

Duplicates: mere imitations of originals, lacking individual
expression.

Have you ever stopped to consider that God made no duplicates, only originals? God does not operate a mass production
assembly line or a copy machine, turning out so many thousand
identicals a day. He created you and me and Asia's billions by deliberate design, with an express purpose—a purpose that can only be
fulfilled by that individual whom God created to fulfill it. I cannot
fill your place, and you cannot fill mine.

Even nature speaks to us of the one, supreme Originator God,
who gives a different design to each snowflake that whitens the
landscape. He sees each sparrow that falls to the ground. He calls
by name each one of the starry hosts, which man admits are innumerable. He even knows the number of the hairs on our heads!
This God knows and cares about you! He made you with unique
talents, abilities, insights, and feelings.

He knows our downsitting and uprising, our thoughts, and all
our ways. He knows our weaknesses, He remembers that we are
dust. How could He forget? He made us!

Regardless who you are or where you came from, be yourself.
Remember, God has a plan for you. Ask Him to reveal it to you,
then keep your eyes fixed upon it. Set your heart to fulfill the purpose He has for you, not His purpose for someone else. And even if
His assignment places you in
some lonely, lowly corner
somewhere, do it with dignity
because you are still in the
King's service. Even two mites
are great in His eyes, when
given out of love for Him!

Bible Reading: Matthew 6:25–33;
Isaiah 40:21–31
One Year Bible Reading Plan:
Ephesians 6
Isaiah 29, 30

David Keeney, Waynesboro, VA

_____

God made people, not puppets.

*October 6*_____

Zaccheaus, Come Down

For whosoever exalteth himself shall be abased;
and he that humbleth himself shall be exalted.
Luke 14:11

Zaccheaus in the sycamore tree—how well we know the story. We quickly recite the facts. He was short, "little of stature," the Word tells us. He was rich. He was a publican and therefore a sinner. But before we stifle a yawn and allow our minds to wonder, "Is that all?" Breathe the prayer of the psalmist: "Open thou mine eyes that I may behold wondrous things out of thy law."

This man, in at least one sense, was a model or prototype of many of us who desire to see the Savior. We somehow have the idea that we must go up. But Jesus said, "Come down."

Let us suppose that Zaccheaus would have refused to come down. While he dawdled to consider his options, his mind went back to a conversation he had with a friend a few days earlier. "Friend," he said, "I am a man with wealth and power. I have a fine family, but somehow—and I do not understand how this can be—somehow, I am not satisfied."

His friend replied, "There is a man called Jesus; He speaks of an abundant life, an everlasting kingdom. He is constantly inviting people to come to Him for rest. He is going through Jericho soon. You may want to meet Him."

For Zaccheaus, the moment of truth had arrived.

Jesus said, "Make haste and come down," and Zaccheaus obeyed. It was his first step on the way to salvation. "The way up is down," as someone has said.

Today, Jesus is still asking men to "come down." Come down from your sycamore tree of position, pride, and power. Come down from your sycamore tree of self-interest—business, job, things, whatever it might be.

Unless and until we do, we will miss out on the most fulfilling experience in all of life: "Today I must abide at thy house."

Jerry Yoder, Auburn, KY

Bible Reading: Luke 19:1–15
One Year Bible Reading Plan:
Philippians 1
Isaiah 31—33

In thy presence is fullness of joy.
—Psalm 16:11

284

What Love!

For God so loved the world, that he gave his only begotten Son, that whosoever believeth in him should not perish, but have everlasting life.
John 3:16

Have you ever stopped to think how much Christ suffered during His trial and crucifixion? Think of all the pain He must have gone through when they placed the crown of thorns on His head, hit Him with a reed, had Him scourged, and when the nails pierced His hands and feet. The pain must have been nearly unbearable. Not only did He face physical pain but also the fact that He was alone. The perfect Son of God died the cruelest death, the death of the most wicked criminal with the sins of the whole world on his shoulders.

While He was hanging on the cross, the thieves who were being crucified with Him mocked Him. But after watching and listening to Jesus for a while and noticing how He loved His persecutors, one thief repented of his past life. Notice how Jesus, though ridiculed earlier, forgave the man and promised him eternal life.

The love of Christ amazes me. What can I do to possess this kind of love? Imagine asking God to forgive those who are tormenting you. Though we know we should have this kind of love, it seems so often it is easier to hold a grudge against our enemies. Do not! Love like Christ did while He was suffering.

Just before He died, Jesus said, "It is finished!" I do not think He meant only that His life was finished, but also, now the plan of salvation was complete. Through His death He had made it possible that we could be saved.

Praise God that Jesus did not remain dead! Within a few days He arose, the glorious conqueror of death. Jesus is still alive today, and I praise Him with my whole heart. He conquered death and has shown me how to be victorious through loving as He has loved me.

Bible Reading: Luke 23:34–47; Matthew 28:1–6
One Year Bible Reading Plan:
Philippians 2
Isaiah 34—36

Marlin Coblentz, Hicksville, OH

Christ has done so much for me, the least I can do is live for Him.

Never to Return

*And he shall dwell in that city, . . . until the death of
the high priest that shall be in these days . . .*
Joshua 20:6

Crossing his weary legs, Talmon seated himself atop the thick wall surrounding Hebron. Looking into the Judean mountains and letting his gaze wander up to their highest peaks, his mind drifted to home. At the same time, he realized that he would probably not be alive if it were not for this very city and the purpose it served.

Shuddering, he recalled the event that had led him here. He and his neighbor Arah, an obstinate, hot-headed fellow, had taken their axes into the forest near their small town of Aijalon. They were hauling out timber for a new house Arah was building. To his absolute horror, Talmon miscalculated the fall of a towering oak. Trying in vain to warn Arah, he watched, terrified, as the merciless giant crushed its unsuspecting victim. Unsure of what might happen, but knowing all too well the incredible wrath of Arah's younger brothers, Talmon ran for home to tell his family what had happened and to bid them farewell. Then he turned southeast through the foothills toward Hebron. He had to hurry!

He had been acquitted of intentional murder, but according to Moses' law, he must stay here until the death of the high priest. Only then would it be safe for him to return home.

We, also, are pursued by judgment. Unlike Talmon, we have been found guilty at God's bar of justice. But God in His mercy has also provided a refuge for us.

Jesus is not only our "city of refuge," He also became the Lamb of God in sacrificial death to take away our sins. But it does not stop even there! He is also the eternal High Priest. Because He never dies, we must dwell in Him forever. Never again may we return to our old life!

> **Bible Reading:** Joshua 20
> **One Year Bible Reading Plan:**
> Philippians 3
> Isaiah 37, 38

Steven King, Aroda, VA

To experience Christ and then turn away is gravest folly.

Don't Hang Onto Sin

*Blessed is the man unto whom the Lord imputeth
not iniquity, and in whose spirit there is no guile.*
Psalm 32:2

A story is told of a man who was very tired and decided to rest in the branches of a tree. He found a nice place and had a good rest. He slept so comfortably that he forgot that he was on a branch. The hour was late, and darkness had arrived when he awoke with a jolt. Forgetting that he was on a branch, he began to fall. On his way down, his outstretched hand caught a branch, and he held it tightly. Hanging there, he heard a voice telling him, "Release the branch," but because it was very dark, he did not dare to let go. He hung on till morning only to discover that he was but a few inches from the ground. He hung in the tree all night experiencing extreme pain and weariness, when he could have safely dropped to the ground.

We sometimes hang onto sin. We get tired and pressed down for a long time, yet we are only a "few inches" from forgiveness and experiencing peace with God. Let us today live in peace by confessing our sin and repenting of it. We should not let the shame of confessing take the place of peace of mind and the joy of being forgiven. May God help us to deal with sin immediately.

Timothy Senerwa, Nakuru, Kenya

Bible Reading: 2 Samuel 11; Psalm 32:1–4
One Year Bible Reading Plan:
Philippians 4
Isaiah 39, 40

To sin is human; to persist in it is folly.

287

October 10

God's Provision

Which of you by taking thought can add one cubit unto his stature?
Matthew 6:27

I heard a preacher talk of a fish in the vast Pacific Ocean that was afraid that it would run out of water. What a foolish thought for that fish!

Often we get carried away with worries. All we see and feel is trouble. Recently I read these words from a book: "People worry a lot in fear of the future. Yet there is no guarantee that these things will even come to pass. Worry for the past doesn't in any way alter or erase it."

There is only one worry that a person should consider: "Am I right with God?" That settles it all. Nothing is more important than that. Having all your past forgiven by the blood of Christ is imperative. Then you can look forward to the future with confidence.

"For whatsoever is born of God overcometh the world: and this is the victory that overcometh the world, even our faith" (1 John 5:4). This is faith anchored in the fully furnished treasures of God. Look around. Before we ever felt cold, He began storing up oil, gas, and coal to warm us. Before we could see, He created the beautiful moon, stars, and sun. Before we got hungry, He provided fertile fields and numerous lakes and oceans filled with all kinds of fish. He gave us enough air to breathe and many places to go. Today, whatever the pressing worries that hang heavily on your heart, come to Jesus with all your needs. Remember, you do not need to worry, like the fish in the water, that your needs will empty the stores of God.

Collins Okoth, Nakuru, Kenya

Bible Reading: Matthew 6:19–34
One Year Bible Reading Plan:
Colossians 1
Isaiah 41, 42

Worldly worries cause spiritual death.

Can Gifts Be a Snare?

For this cause I bow my knees unto
the Father of our Lord Jesus Christ.
Ephesians 3:14

A story is told of a Greek who had spent many years working in a foreign country. Before he returned home, he used all his fortune to purchase a diamond. He was traveling home by ship to spend his last years with his family. After some time of rest in his room, he decided to go up on deck to see what was happening. He discovered interesting games taking place. He felt he could also put on a show. Quickly he decided to get his diamond. He started throwing this gem up into the air. He was a talented juggler, and he would catch the diamond just before it hit the deck. The onlookers cheered. He did this several times and successfully had it land into his hands. But the game ended poorly. For some unknown reason, the sea waves drew the ship slightly off course. He vainly struggled to catch the diamond, but down into the sea it disappeared. What a sorrowful man he was!

What caused this man to act this way? Today's Scripture passage tells of a mortal standing in the place meant for God alone, and there is an inner urge in each of us to impress others. Thoughts and actions arising from self glorify the creature rather than the Creator. Often I have caught myself in this kind of snare: trying to show the best of myself in the way I say or do things. Only God deserves honor and glory for what I am. I have since surrendered to God all He has given to me. I have asked Jesus' blood to cleanse me of this impurity. I have fully made up my mind not to allow any gift to honor myself but God alone.

Collins Okoth, Nakuru, Kenya

> **Bible Reading:**
> 2 Thessalonians 2
> **One Year Bible Reading Plan:**
> Colossians 2
> Isaiah 43, 44

Jesus calls us to a life of humility.

October 12

Response or Reaction?

And the Lord turned the captivity of Job,
when he prayed for his friends.
Job 42:10a

How do we cope with the trials and afflictions of life? Some trials may be the result of our own doings. We then need to confess, accept God's forgiveness, and go on our way rejoicing. At other times, trials may be the results of that over which we have no control, such as an illness, an accident, or a death. In such circumstances, we can accept them as something the Lord has allowed for our good, or for the good of those around us. We may *react*, act in opposition to—which will result in a miserable life. Or we may humbly accept our lot and profit, learn, and grow thereby.

Unless we are motivated by the divine nature, the root of which is love, it is almost impossible to respond to trials in a way that is pleasing to God and brings satisfaction in life.

Job is a good example of a man who stood the test of loss and affliction. He had many questions. He lost everything but his trust in God. Faith in God was enough to see him through.

There is still unlimited grace and strength for those who thank and praise the Lord when it is the hardest to do so (Isaiah 50:10).

Why not praise the Lord?

Bible Reading: Job 1, 2:9, 10
One Year Bible Reading Plan:
Colossians 3
Isaiah 45—47

Kore Yoder, Belleville, PA

God is still on the throne, and He will remember His own.

What's the Message of Your Countenance?

Iron sharpeneth iron: so a man sharpeneth
the countenance of his friend.
Proverbs 27:17

Have you ever wondered about the message your facial expressions send? As a youngster, I noticed the ministers' faces as they sat facing the congregation Sunday after Sunday. They looked very sober and heavyhearted! I wondered where the joy of the Lord was. The face of another man I knew was always twisted with anxiety as he drove down the road. As he leaned over the wheel, his face was drawn into wrinkles and frowns. Was there fear in his heart? Stress? A severe struggle?

We dare not evaluate others on the basis of their facial expressions, but David mentions twice, "the health of the countenance." Facial expressions may be friendly, serious, fickle, sad, or joyful. A Belizean brother Mark Meighn told me that during Hurricane Mitch people looked as though they did not believe that God is in control.

What is the remedy for an unhealthy countenance? David relates it to trust! "Why art thou cast down, O my soul? And why art thou disquieted within me? Hope thou in God: for I shall yet praise him, who is the health of my countenance, and my God." Shouldn't hope in God bring a healthy countenance? A heart that is neither fickle nor gloomy, but stable because it trusts in God will bring a healthy countenance. With that enhancement in the heart, how can we help but have a healthy countenance?

Bible Reading: Psalm 42
One Year Bible Reading Plan:
Colossians 4
Isaiah 48, 49

Elmer Schrock, Stuarts Draft, VA

A spiritually healthy heart eliminates
the need for a pasted-on countenance.

*October 14*_____

Photographing Shoes

Not by works of righteousness which we have done, but
according to his mercy he saved us, by the washing
of regeneration, and renewing of the Holy Ghost.
Titus 3:5

"I should have photographed your shoes before I started." So said a shoe shine man at the Washington National Airport. I had hurriedly left home on church work and had neglected to clean my shoes. While at the airport, I asked about a shoe shine. The man was not sure he wanted to tackle such an awesome job, but with an agreement to pay a little more, he consented.

He made that comment after he had done a very nice job. He was obviously pleased with his efforts. I had to agree, the shoes had been improved 100%.

I wonder, has my life improved 100% since the day Jesus came into my heart and cleansed my soul? I look back at my unsaved, ugly, sin-stained life. The stains were more noticeable than the ones on my shoes. The deliverance and regeneration reaches to this day. How I rejoice at the remembrance of that experience with God and the difference it made in my mind, my heart, and my life.

Am I allowing God to keep me pure and spotless? Am I careful to maintain good works? Have I praised God for doing the "shoe shine" on my heart? It is too awful to consider what would have been my lot, had God not provided a plan for my soul. I shudder to think of the calamity that would have befallen me, had I not responded to His call. When I consider the many failures I have made because of being in this body, I lift my voice in praise to my God.

Why be high-minded, as though we are something, when it is God who has changed us? I would be embarrassed if God had photographed my life before I became His child. But He has cast my sins into the sea of forgetfulness.

Bible Reading: Titus 3
One Year Bible Reading Plan:
1 Thessalonians 1
Isaiah 50—52

Allan Miller, Sarcoxie, MO

Jesus cleanses and makes men holy.

God Sees!

The eyes of the Lord are in every place, beholding the evil and the good.
Proverbs 15:3

An early morning phone call brought the news that our friend's house was on fire! We rushed to the scene. What a devastating sight greeted us on arrival! Fire trucks, hoses, and firemen were all over the place. Smoke and flames poured from every window! Furniture, clothes, photo albums, and many irreplaceable items perished in the flames. The family huddled together in the cold, weeping as they watched their belongings go up in smoke.

Through the smoke, I noticed the gospel sign in the front yard: "The eyes of the Lord are in every place."

What a blessed, comforting thought! Our great God is watching His children. He saw to it that no one was hurt by the fire. He saw the family's tears, disappointments, dashed hopes and dreams, and He felt their sorrow.

We would not plan things the way they happen many times, but when we face adversity, let us remember that we have a God who has a plan for every step of our life. He understands and knows what we need most. In His great love, He sometimes allows possessions to be taken away from us. In His love, He sometimes allows temptations to come our way, to make us stronger. And because of the trials we face, we are better equipped to help others face similar struggles.

It is important that we respond in the proper way to the trials we face. We must have a heart that truly desires the center of God's will. Through the aid of the Holy Spirit, we can trust God to bring forth the very best in our lives.

Bible Reading: Psalm 139
One Year Bible Reading Plan:
1 Thessalonians 2
Isaiah 53—55

Vernon Miller, Masaya, Nicaragua

We don't know what the future holds,
but we can trust Him who holds the future!

No Man's Land

. . . Choose you this day whom ye will serve . . .
Joshua 24:15

While crossing the border between Kenya and Uganda, we passed through a strip of barren land. It is a desolate place, lacking houses, crops, or cattle. The only activity I saw was a few folks walking from one border to the other. Neither of the two countries bordering this real estate claim sovereignty over it.

The spiritual parallel of this brings some thought-provoking questions. Today we see people who wish to dwell in such a state. They deny being citizens of the kingdom of darkness, but neither can they be identified as citizens of the kingdom of light. At times we refer to them as marginal Christians, not being able to point out specific sins in their lives. Still, we question their claims of being sincere believers.

But with God, who knows the hearts of all men, there is no question. Jesus says in John 10:14, "I know my sheep and am known of mine." To Him the distinction is clear. Either we are inside or outside. Jesus Christ is the Door, the entrance to eternal life. If you are staying in "no man's land," hanging in indecision, God is calling you to state your intentions. "Choose you this day whom you will serve," was Joshua's challenge to the people. They clearly answered, "We will serve the Lord!" Sadly, the resolve of the congregation did not last. According to Judges 2:7–13, after the faithful leaders passed on, the people fell away. We need more than an initial commitment; we need to continue in the way of truth. Where am I today: on the solid Rock, in the valley of indecision, or back in the miry pit? Wherever we find ourselves, let us renew our covenant with our God, starting today!

Bible Reading: Joshua 24:14–28
One Year Bible Reading Plan:
1 Thessalonians 3
Isaiah 56—58

Raymond Fisher, Nakuru, Kenya

Who will leave the world's side?
Who is on the Lord's side?
—Frances Havergal, 1877

Where Are Your Hands?

_Hear the voice of my supplications, when I cry unto thee,
when I lift up my hands toward thy holy oracle._
Psalm 28:2

I was handing out tracts on the street and met one young man whose response was, "No, thank you, my hands are in my pockets." He was not interested enough to make the least effort to obtain what I offered him.

How often do we reveal our values by what we do with our hands? Consider the hundreds of references in the Scripture that pertain to the hands and their use.

As we refer to a few, we notice the varied possibilities open to our hands.

• Proverbs 6:10-11 warns the sluggard that folding his hands in a little more sleep will lead him to poverty.

• Proverbs 31:13-24 tells of the virtuous woman, whose hands are ever busy taking care of her household and meeting the needs of the poor around her.

• Ephesians 4:28 commands those who formerly stole to steal no more but to work with their hands things that are good.

• 1 Timothy 2:8 exhorts us to lift up holy hands.

• Hebrews 12:12 asks us to lift up the hands that hang down.

The Pharisees tried to be cleansed by washing their hands often. Pilate tried to clear his guilty conscience by washing his hands.

Bible Reading: Ephesians
4:17–32
One Year Bible Reading Plan:
1 Thessalonians 4
Isaiah 59—61

Where are your hands? Are they lifted up to God in holy consecration and service? Are they busy doing good? Are they extended toward the needs about you? Or are they hanging down deep in the pockets of selfishness, indifference, and despair?

Willis Martin, Wellsboro, PA

Whatsoever you do, do it heartily, as to the Lord.

Humble Availability

Also I heard the voice of the Lord, saying, Whom shall I send,
and who will go for us? Then said I, Here am I; send me.
Isaiah 6:8

One of the biggest hurdles many men face is the fear of public speaking.

I remember an incident from my boyhood years that made a deep impression upon me. In each Sunday evening service one of the men was responsible for the devotional period. It also was his duty to ask someone to conduct the next Sunday evening devotional. The plan was a good one. If everyone did their part, it was an interesting asset to the church service.

But there seemed to be so many Moseses and Jeremiahs who had heavy tongues or were too young. Out of the whole church, there were only a handful of Christian men who would say with Isaiah, "Here am I, send me."

We little boys would always stay with our fathers after the meeting was over. On one particular Sunday evening, I remember following my father as he went from one brother to another, looking for someone willing to take their part the next Sunday evening. He suffered the same predicament that Ezekiel did when "he sought for a man among them that should make up the hedge, and stand in the gap before me . . . but he found none" (Ezekiel 22:30).

Finally, in desperation, he asked one of the men known to accept the responsibility. The man paused a moment and then said, "If you pray for me, I will." What a blessed saint of God! That evening he became a hero in my life. May his tribe increase.

| Bible Reading: Exodus 4:1–20 |
| One Year Bible Reading Plan: |
| 1 Thessalonians 5 |
| Isaiah 62—64 |

Stephen Miller, Loyal, WI

It is a great deal easier to do that which God gives us to do
than to face the accountablity of not doing it.

Acceptance

To the praise of the glory of his grace,
wherein he has made us accepted in the beloved.
Ephesians 1:6

"Woof! Woof!" Bonnie, our Norwegian Elkhound, was barking in a high excited voice. Then I heard the raucous growling of a raccoon. There came a mixture of both, accompanied by the snapping of twigs as I made my way through the early morning darkness to get the cows. Shep, our cattle dog, was helping me round them up.

Now Shep does not have the nerve to kill raccoons like Bonnie, his counterpart. Nevertheless, he dearly loves to be praised and to make an impression on his master. After the cows were rounded up, Shep saw his opportunity. He met the smaller dog carrying the dead coon. With his eyes gleaming, he showed his teeth threateningly and growled maliciously.

As soon as she dropped it, he grabbed the coon and came straight toward the barn where I had begun my other chores. His head was high in the air, and his short bob tail was wagging vigorously. He dropped it right at my feet, stood a little to the side, and waited expectantly for the praise he felt he would get.

I do not remember what I told him. But before we condemn Shep too harshly, let us consider ourselves. If I am honest with myself, I have to admit I have the same desire for praise that Shep has. I have to acknowledge that I have been guilty of saying and doing things that I thought would impress other people. I thought if I could get other people to like me, I would be happy. But I was not. I thought if I hinted something to lift me up a few inches in the sight of my neighbor, I would be happy.

But praise God, He showed me differently. He pointed out to me that as long as I am pleasing to Him, that is all that counts. He showed me that He has made me accepted in His Beloved, and I am a vessel to the praise of His glory. Furthermore, He told me that I am pleasing to Him and a sweet savor since He has forgiven all my sins.

Wonderful Jesus!

Edward Lambright, Campbell Hill, IL

Bible Reading: Ephesians 1
One Year Bible Reading Plan:
2 Thessalonians 1
Isaiah 65, 66

*Except for **accept**, we'd be lost.*

*October 20*_____

Immediately

And whatsoever ye do, do it heartily,
as to the Lord, and not unto men.
Colossians 3:23

In our schoolroom, we had a large poster of a lazy polar bear lying on the snow up in the Arctic, somewhere. Underneath were the words, "If I get the urge to work, I hold still till the urge goes away."

That principle works when it comes to writing to a friend or to a shut-in. Even when I get an inspiration or thought for *Beside the Still Waters,* and if I do not do anything about it, it soon leaves, and I forget it.

But that is not the way the disciples responded when Jesus called them. They straightway (immediately) left their nets and followed Him. Look what a wonderful blessing they received. They received first hand knowledge of Jesus' teachings and works. I do not think they would have obtained such blessings if they would have dawdled or answered, "Yes, we'll come soon."

Let us not be like the polar bear. When the alarm goes, get up. When our children or wife ask us a question, let us answer them immediately. When there is a need for somebody, let us respond right away.

If we train ourselves to respond immediately in life's daily challenges, we will be more prone to hear when Christ calls us to follow Him.

Atlee Miller, Hillsboro, WI

> **Bible Reading:** Matthew 4:18–25;
>   Mark 1:16–22
> **One Year Bible Reading Plan:**
>   2 Thessalonians 2
>   Jeremiah 1, 2

Procrastination is the thief of time.

Learn of Me

Behold the Lamb of God, which taketh away the sin of the world.
John 1:29b

John's exclamation regarding Jesus presented here is of paramount importance; for Jesus is the door by which we enter the realms of the saved.

The Lord said, "He that sees me hath seen the Father." So how shall I, a mortal man, "see" the Holy One of Israel? In fear and trembling. The Christians' glimpse of God brings a twofold experience. When confronted with the sheer majesty of His divine presence, we, unable to bear the sight of such incredible beauty and holiness, must avert our gaze. It is then that we realize our imperfect mortality. For a fleeting moment I see myself as God in His Word has described me.

We tend to emphasize the "rest" Christ brings to our souls. However, before we find this rest in full, we must learn of Him.

It is through Christ's meekness that we see true greatness. This quality is abundantly illustrated in Jesus' life.

To the 5000, He was the satisfaction of hunger. To the woman at the well, He was the thirst-quenching water of life. To the disciples, He was the stiller of the storm. To the 10 lepers, He was the Great Physician, curing the "incurable." To the Pharisees, He was "the friend of sinners." "To him that overcometh," He is the One who presents us with "a white stone and in the stone a new name [is] written" (Revelation 2:17).

Bible Reading: Matthew 11:28–30; Isaiah 53
One Year Bible Reading Plan:
2 Thessalonians 3
Jeremiah 3, 4

Jerry Yoder, Auburn, KY

I am the way, the truth, and the life.
—John 14:6b

Tomatoes or Grass

For if we have been planted together in the likeness of his death,
we shall be also in the likeness of his resurrection.
Romans 6:5

Day after day the drought continues. The grass has long since turned brown, and the newly planted trees are dying. Shall we continue to water these trees, or shall we root them up?

The tomatoes are watered by a drip system irrigation with a deep pond for the water supply. They withstand the test of the drought and continue to yield fruit.

Now let us take a look at ourselves. Are we like the shallow rooted grass and the newly planted trees? Are we dying spiritually from the heat of the times? Or are we like the tomatoes, planted in God's life-giving water of grace? "Blessed is the man that trusteth in the Lord and whose hope the Lord is. For he shall be as a tree planted by the waters and that spreadeth out her roots by the river, and shall not see when heat cometh, but her leaf shall be green: and shall not be careful in the year of drought neither shall cease from yielding fruit" (Jeremiah 17:7, 8). If we trust in the Lord's grace, and by faith derive strength from Him, we shall not cease from yielding fruit during the drought of the times.

If we trust in our own righteousness and think we can do well enough without the grace of God, we can neither produce the fruit of acceptable service to God nor reap the fruit of blessing from Him. "But he answered and said, every plant which my heavenly Father hath not planted shall be rooted up" (Matthew 15:13).

May we all be transplanted in the Lord's vineyard and partake of His life-giving water so we can yield fruit, even during times of severe heat and drought.

Bible Reading: Psalm 1; 92
One Year Bible Reading Plan:
1 Timothy 1
Jeremiah 5, 6

Lester Gingerich, Holton, MI

_____

God's love does not exempt us from trials,
but sees us through our trials.

The Great Invitation

Let the wicked forsake his way and the unrighteous man his thoughts:
and let him return unto the Lord, and he will have mercy upon him;
and to our God, for He will abundantly pardon.
Isaiah 55:7

We all have an invitation. "Come unto me, all ye that labour and are heavy laden, and I will give you rest. Take my yoke upon you and learn of me; for I am meek and lowly in heart: and ye shall find rest unto your souls. For my yoke is easy, and my burden is light." These are Jesus' own words in Matthew 11:28–30. This invitation is to all mankind. No matter who you are or what upbringing you have had, you are invited. We are invited to take that provision which the grace of God has given us through the perfect sacrifice of Jesus on the cross. It is free.

What is the qualification? We must have a thirst for the righteousness of God. Jesus cannot use those who are self-sufficient and satisfied with the world. We must first see our need of the Savior, and that we cannot go on of our own selves. This is what the Scriptures mean when they speak of repentance.

There are two things involved in repentance: to ask God for forgiveness, and to forsake sin. It involves a complete turn around as Saul experienced on the way to Damascus. When we come to God for forgiveness, He removes our transgressions from us as far as the east is from the west.

We must take God's example and forgive those who have wronged us. Peter asked Jesus, "How many times shall I forgive?" Jesus answered him, "Not only seven times, but seventy times seven."

There is no excuse not to accept Christ's invitation. Let us fall on our knees and accept the salvation God has given us through Jesus Christ our Lord.

Jason Schlabach, Sugarcreek, OH

Bible Reading: Isaiah 55
One Year Bible Reading Plan:
1 Timothy 2
Jeremiah 7, 8

Do not refuse this great invitation!

Caught in the Enemy's Net

Watch ye therefore and pray always.
Luke 21:36a

One warm summer evening I was standing on the porch at my son's house, and a small creature flew past me. It was a lightning bug. My eyes followed the blinking light, but suddenly the bug stopped.

Examining the reason for the abrupt halt, I discovered that it had been caught in a spider's web. It was a victim of an enemy's tactic. In a short time, the tiny creature was so tightly wrapped with strands of fiber that it was pathetic. It had become the prisoner of a superior power who had subtly ensnared it. All it could do was flash.

Seeing the utter despair and hopelessness of that tiny lightning bug, I put out my hand, and with compassion of heart, freed it from its bondage. In a moment, it spread its wings and flew away in freedom.

The incident reminds me that we need to be on guard continually, lest we also get caught in the enemy's net. The devil, who is our adversary, has a multitude of snares ready to capture us.

Let us beware of the trap of materialism, which has caught many a traveler. "They that will be rich fall into temptation and a snare, and into many foolish and hurtful lusts which drown men in destruction and perdition."

The Internet is also a snare. The devil may have been unsuccessful in his attempt to trap many believers with TV, but now he is using another method. Some, maybe more than we know, are falling into this one. Will you? Will I?

We may say in our hearts, "I realize that others have lost out spiritually, but I am strong." Can we hear the words of Peter who said to Jesus, "Though all men forsake thee, yet will not I"?

Let us watch and pray.

Willis Halteman, Carlisle, PA

Bible Reading: Psalm 142;
2 Timothy 2:15–26
One Year Bible Reading Plan:
1 Timothy 3
Jeremiah 9, 10

With God all things are possible.

Angels

*For I say unto you, That in heaven their angels do always
behold the face of my Father which is in heaven.*
Matthew 18:10

About sixty years ago, the feed man came to my uncle's place
to deliver feed. He unloaded the feed and got into the truck to leave.
He turned the key and pushed the starter button, but the truck
would not start. He tried again, but the engine just would not start.
He said, "This is strange." He got out of the truck and walked up
front to open the hood. There, in front of the truck, sat my little
cousin. He picked her up and set her safely to the side. He got back
into the truck, and the truck started right up. He did not see the
angel, but we know that "the angel of the Lord encampeth round
about them that fear him, and delivereth them" (Psalm 34:7).

There are many angels. When Jacob was returning to the promised land, "the angels of God met him." When Jacob saw them, he
said, "This is God's host" (Genesis 32:1, 2). When Elisha's servant
was afraid of the mighty host of Syria, Elisha said, "Fear not, for
they that be with us are more than they that be with them." Then
Elisha prayed that God would open the eyes of his servant, "and he
saw: and behold, the mountain was full of horses and chariots of
fire round about Elisha" (2 Kings 6:16, 17). In today's Scripture reading, we have a view of heaven where "ten thousand times ten thousand and thousands of thousands" of angels are praising the Lamb
of God.

Bible Reading: Revelation 5
One Year Bible Reading Plan:
1 Timothy 4
Jeremiah 11—13

Usually, we do not see
angels, yet they are "ministering
spirits, sent forth to minister for
them who shall be heirs of salvation" (Hebrews 1:14). Thank
the Lord for His wonderful,
unseen ministers!

Enos Schrock, Rochelle, VA

He shall give His angels charge over thee.
—Psalm 91:11

The Ministry of Angels

For he shall give his angels charge over thee,
to keep thee in all thy ways.
Psalm 91:11

A British express train with Queen Victoria on board cruised through the night toward London. Suddenly, in the fog, its beam shone upon a ghostlike figure in a dark cloak standing on the track waving its arms. The engineer brought the train to a grinding halt. He got down from the train, but the figure had disappeared. On a hunch, he walked a short distance into the fog ahead of the train.

Suddenly he stopped, and in stricken horror saw that the bridge just ahead of the train had been washed out by a swollen stream. While the bridge was being repaired, they continued their search for the mysterious flagman, but to no avail.

Later, when the train reached London, the engineer noticed a moth at the base of the headlamp. On impulse he picked it up, wetted it and stuck it on the headlamp. He turned the headlamp on, and there was the ghostlike flagman! God had, through the ministry of His angels, placed the moth there at the precise time it was needed, saving the train and its passengers from a horrible fate.

Have you considered that there are angels, sent from God, continually watching every step you take? Whether on the highway or in the office, angels are by our side, keeping us in all our ways. Thank God right now for His angels, and thank Him for the times when you were kept from danger.

Bible Reading: Psalm 91
One Year Bible Reading Plan:
1 Timothy 5
Jeremiah 14—16

Joel Gingerich, Kensington, OH

The angel of the Lord encampeth round about them
that fear him, and delivereth them.
—Psalm 34:7

Priceless Provisions

Ho, everyone that thirsteth, come ye to the waters . . . yea,
come, buy wine and milk without money and without price.
Isaiah 55:1

When we are in the market for certain items, we are usually attracted to things that carry a high price tag, thinking they are probably of great value. We are also attracted to things which have a low price tag because we are inclined to buy as cheaply as we can. The Lord has something to offer us that costs no money and does not have a price tag on it. When something free is offered to us, we question what the reason might be. I once owned a litter of mixed breed puppies and wanted to give them away. So I placed a sign along the road offering free puppies. Our neighbor said, "You can't give puppies away. People will think they are no good." So I put a price on them of $15.00 each and sold every one.

The priceless provisions of our Lord appear to some people to be worthless, because they see no price tag to reveal the value of them.

How do we come and buy if they cost no money and are without price? I find that when I lay down my life to Him, He is pleased to share with me these priceless provisions. We sometimes say it costs our all. As true as this may be, I find that I have nothing to offer. Yet the Lord is pleased to accept this as payment—my willingness to pay if I could.

Alvin Coblentz, Carrolton, OH

Bible Reading: Isaiah 55
One Year Bible Reading Plan:
1 Timothy 6
Jeremiah 17—19

Grace is God's riches at Christ's expense.

Directed By God

In all thy ways acknowledge him, and he shall direct thy paths.
Proverbs 3:6

Have you ever carried a lantern on a dark road at night? You cannot see more than one step ahead of you. But as you take that one step, the lamp moves forward and another step is made plain. The amazing thing is that you reach your destination safely without once walking in darkness. You have light the entire way, even though it is one step at a time.

What a beautiful example of how the Lord guides His children through life! Many Christians who have walked with the Lord for a long time can say from personal experience that this is the way He has led them and assured them of reaching their destination. Nevertheless, the dark curtain of the unknown veils the Christian pilgrim's pathway.

The prospect of lurking dangers, pitfalls, and tragic missteps often upsets some weary travelers. They lose the peace and confidence that the Lord intended for them to enjoy. But as they refuse to worry about tomorrow and trust Him for today, they find grace and guidance for each step of the way. The writer of Proverbs said, "Trust in the Lord with all thine heart. . . . In all thy ways acknowledge him and he shall direct thy paths." And David recorded this promise, "I will instruct thee and teach thee in the way which thou shalt go: I will guide thee with mine eye" (Psalm 32:8).

We do not have to see beyond what God shows us today. When we simply follow His leading, we have enough light for each step of the way. Isn't it wonderful to be directed by Him?

Bible Reading: Proverbs 3:1–20
One Year Bible Reading Plan:
2 Timothy 1
Jeremiah 20—22

If we could see, if we could know—we often say,
But God in love a veil doth throw across our way;
We cannot see what lies before, and so we cling to Him the more,
He leads us till this life is o'er—trust and obey.

William Miller, Middlebury, IN

Hold firm the lantern of truth, and it will guide you aright.

Weight on Us

*Looking unto Jesus the author and finisher of our faith; who for the joy
that was set before him endured the cross, despising the shame,
and is set down at the right hand of the throne of God.*
Hebrews 12:2

It was a warm summer day. My friends were back from fur-
lough, and it was my privilege to help move them back into an
Indian village where they were missionaries. My job was to carry
their young son on my back for the one and a half hour hike. It was
a beautiful trail over steep, rocky hills and winding paths through
rich, green jungle; but gradually the thirty-some pounds got heavy.
Surely the village lay just around the next bend, well no, but maybe
just over that hill . . . With each disappointment, the load grew
heavier until it was all I could think about. In due time, we came
over a knoll, and there before us lay the village. Suddenly I did not
feel my burden. The goal was in view!

Then I realized how much the hike was like our earthly pilgrimage. With the vigor we join the race before us. We enjoy the
challenge and lay hold of God's provisions for us. But gradually
life becomes burdensome. We need to consider Him, who for the
joy set before Him endured the cross. Let us drink long and deeply
of His love, for it casts out fear—
the enemy of faith. It will be
worth it all when we see Jesus.

Are you feeling worn? Look
ahead, brother! Do you see what
I see? It is not far now. We are
almost home.

Bible Reading: Hebrews 12
One Year Bible Reading Plan:
2 Timothy 2
Jeremiah 23, 24

Verton Miller, Strawberry, AR

When in heaviness through manifold temptations, consider Him!

God—My Refuge

I will say of the Lord, He is my refuge and
my fortress; My God; in him will I trust.
Psalm 91:2

Consider the security of those who abide in the secret place of the most high God. The one who dwells in the secret place will say of the Lord, "He is my refuge, a hiding place from danger, and my fortress, a defender against my enemies."

A refuge is a safe retreat from a pursuing enemy. A fortress is a tower of defense, standing firm to meet the attacks of the enemy. We have no power or might of our own to resist the temptations and trials that come our way. They are too strong for us. But in our safe place of refuge, there is safety.

The picture of a mother hen gathering her chicks under her wings illustrates the truth. During a storm or when a hawk flies over, the hen quickly gathers her chicks under her sheltering wings. Under God's wings are security, stability, and safety for us.

He has promised those dwelling in the secret place complete deliverance. He shall deliver you. He will protect you from every danger. He will cover you with His feathers. He will free you from every fear. You shall not be afraid. He will keep you from harm. No evil will befall you. No plague will come near you. God's promise to those abiding in Him is that He will deliver them, set them on high, answer them, be with them, honor them, and satisfy them.

> **Bible Reading:** Psalm 91
> **One Year Bible Reading Plan:**
> 2 Timothy 3
> Jeremiah 25, 26

Andy J. Mast, Holmesville, OH

_____

This God is my God, in Him will I trust.

Imitate the Original

*That ye be not slothful, but followers of them who
through faith and patience inherit the promises.*
Hebrews 6:12

The Apostle Paul set before the Ephesians an astonishing, yet reasonable, demand—to be Godlike in all words, works, and ways. As a child watches his or her father and unconsciously becomes like him in habits and nature, so God sets the example for His redeemed children to follow. As He does, so are we to do. The word "followers" in Ephesians 5:1 is in the Greek *mimetes* (mim-ay-tāc) which means "imitators." "Therefore be imitators of God as beloved children."

We need to understand that by ourselves we cannot follow the divine example. God not only presents Himself for our imitation, He gives us the grace and power whereby we can exhibit His divine virtues. Christ is within us, enabling us to walk as He walked. He is our "original," and by His indwelling Spirit He helps us to imitate Him. Our peace depends on imitating Him.

From today's Scripture reading we see that one characteristic of Christ recommended for our imitation is God's love. As His dear children, we are to walk in love. Too often we are poor imitators of the original when it comes to loving as He loves. We need daily to ask for grace and power to outwardly display Godlikeness in a godless world.

Bible Reading: Ephesians
5:1–21
One Year Bible Reading Plan:
2 Timothy 4
Jeremiah 27, 28

Benuel S. Stoltzfus, Parkesburg, PA

Be ye followers of me, even as I also am of Christ.

November 1

The Effects of Sin

And sin when it is finished, bringeth forth death.
James 1:15

Last summer my renter planted a field of soybeans. We had plenty of rain, so the beans soon started to grow heartily. But something happened; gradually I saw less of the beans and more Johnson grass (a weed). Soon you could not tell it was a bean field. Instead, it looked like a Johnson grass field.

I figured that it would not be salvageable, but he sprayed the field. The beans again began to thrive, and the Johnson grass was all killed, except for one little spot he missed. In some parts of the field, the beans were thinner because of the damage the weeds had done, thus hurting the yield.

I had to think how much sin is like this; it can be in one's life and cause destruction, as this weed did. Do we see sin as serious? Do we acknowledge that sin will destroy us if we do not apply repentance in our lives? Do we secretly feel that somehow God will shower His blessings on us, and we can hide our sins?

The beautiful application of repentance will cleanse sin like the spray did the field. Do we give up on a person because he is too vile as I gave up on the field? Are we convinced that God's cleansing power can make a vile person clean? Do we witness to those who need cleansing?

If we have one area in our life that we do not repent of, then sin will still keep us from being clean; and the consequence will be eternal destruction. Sin leaves scars, even though we are made clean. We will reap what we sow (Galatians 6:7).

Bible Reading: Matthew 13:18–50
One Year Bible Reading Plan: Titus 1
Jeremiah 29, 30

Wayne Miller, Salem, IN

Your sins have withholden good things from you.
—Jeremiah 5:25b

Spiritual Fitness

*For bodily exercise profiteth little: but godliness is profitable
unto all things, having promise of the life that now is,
and of that which is to come.*
1 Timothy 4:8

I could not believe what I was reading. I had been scanning the "Speak Out" column in our local newspaper, in which people write to express their opinions. They occasionally write to commend someone, but more often than not, they air a complaint against something or someone. The complaint that had caught my eye was very unusual. It simply said: "I'm fat, fat, fat! I'm so ugly and fat, fat, fat!" I surmised that some poor soul had failed on perhaps their 26th diet, and had given way to panic.

The diet/fitness craze of today has reached gigantic proportions. Fitness centers have sprung up everywhere, and the diet section dominates a sizeable portion of every bookstore and library. It is obvious that people are very much concerned about their physical health and vitality.

Are we equally concerned about our spiritual health and stamina? Are we eating right? We must feast on God's Word in order to build lean, sinewy, spiritual muscle. Then we will not fail in the most grueling fight against Satan's forces. Are we getting proper exercise? We must exercise our spiritual man on the treadmill of obedience to God's commands. We should be straining every nerve to be a brighter witness, a more faithful warrior, and a more willing servant. Are we getting adequate rest? We can experience sweet rest by trusting in the promises of God. Relaxation is ours when we surrender our wills to God and allow Him to work out the details of our lives.

Bible Reading: 1 Timothy 4
One Year Bible Reading Plan:
Titus 2
Jeremiah 31, 32

If we follow this simple fitness plan, we can avoid the frustration and despair that comes with spiritual defeat.

Titus Hofer, LaCrete, AB

I can do all things through Christ which strengtheneth me.

Obedience or Sacrifice

Behold, to obey is better than sacrifice,
and to hearken than the fat of rams.
1 Samuel 15:22b

The prophet Samuel was deeply grieved over Saul's actions. After a troubled night, he rose early and went to meet the deviant king. Verse 12 of our Bible reading gives a brief preview of the condition of Saul's heart. The "place" he set up seems to have been a monument in his own honor. His own honor and position were his primary concerns.

Samuel warned Saul clearly of the condemnation God had pronounced on him. He identified Saul's actions as sins of arrogance and disobedience.

Although Saul winced at God's rejection, he fell short of true repentance. He offered lip service to God, shifted the blame, and promised sacrifices; but his heart was still set on his own honor.

Today we fill Saul's shoes. Will we make the choices he made? God cannot be honored by my life if my own ambitions, position, or reputation are most important to me. God made us, and He owns us. We are His, not our own. Obedience is the real proof that we accept God's ownership. The sacrifices that God rejects are the attempts to buy the ownership of our own lives. God will not exchange His ownership rights for some temporal object. Besides, all we have to offer is already God's and He has made us stewards of these things.

God is calling us to His service. He offers training, boundless resources, and an eternal reward. Let us respond as Isaiah did in Isaiah 6: "Here am I, send me!"

Bible Reading: 1 Samuel 15
One Year Bible Reading Plan:
Titus 3
Jeremiah 33—35

Samuel Bauman, New Ringgold, PA

No truth of God stored in the mind, will ever meet our needs
until that truth gives birth to faith, and faith gives birth to deeds.

Our Country

My kingdom is not of this world.
John 18:36a

The bumper sticker accused me, "Our country is in its present condition because good people like you don't vote!" Would going to polls and voting for a politician who seems more conservative help our country return to God? That sounds like a simple solution. Let us pause and ponder before we register and rush to the polls.

Wouldn't it be safer and wiser to look at the example of Jesus? He kept His country's laws and refused to be made an earthly king (John 6:15). He recognized it was right to pay taxes (Mark 12:17) and He paid them (Matthew 17:24–27). He recognized His responsibility to His country (Matthew 13:54; 10:6). He spoke frankly to its leaders of their hypocrisy and wickedness (Matthew 23:1–35). He warned His countrymen of the coming judgment (Matthew 23:36–39). He wept over His countrymen's sins (Luke 19:41–44).

Jesus was a model citizen, but He refused to become involved politically! In the New Testament age, the roles of church and state have been separated. It is not the state's responsibility to be the standard bearer of truth. Neither is it the church's responsibility to wield God's sword of vengeance. God, in the New Testament age, has given the church the awesome responsibility of being His standard bearer of truth. God has given the state the responsibility of being a "revenger to execute wrath" (Romans 13:4).

The church which dabbles in politics becomes a confusing "hybrid." Does God need our vote? Do we agree God is sovereign and raises up rulers (Daniel 2:37; 4:17, 25, 35)? Do we conclude we voted against God if the candidate we voted for was not elected?

Bible Reading: Romans 13
One Year Bible Reading Plan:
Philemon
Jeremiah 36, 37

As eye catching as the bumper sticker was, I feel a responsibility to modify it. "Our country is in its present condition because many good people do not follow Christ's example."

Jim Yoder, Clarkson, KY

Hearken unto me, my people; and give ear unto me, O my nation.
—Isaiah 51:4

A Good Deal

But was in all points tempted like as we are, yet without sin.
Hebrews 4:15b

We all like good deals and go different places to find them. But in our spiritual life we face "deals" too. The devil comes to us from time to time and tries to make deals with us to serve him. He has a substitute for peace, and he offers us things that on the surface look good.

If we turn down one deal, he comes back and offers us another and says, "It's all right." But we know better than to yield to him.

The devil has been making deals for a long time. Way back when he came to Eve, he offered her a deal, and she ate the forbidden fruit. She found that the devil's peace was short lived.

When Jesus was in the wilderness fasting forty days, the devil came to him. Jesus was, of course, hungry; and the devil asked Him to turn the stones to bread. Then he offered Jesus another deal. He took Him to the pinnacle of the temple. He even used some Scripture. He also took Him onto a high mountain, offering Him the kingdoms of the world. Jesus was tempted in all points as we are, yet without sin.

The devil is still trying to make deals with you and me. He tries at our weakest points. Jesus made one deal; it never changes. He went to the cross and shed His blood so we can have life and have it more abundantly. He gives us eternal life in heaven. He gives us everlasting peace. Now that's a good deal! Let us accept it.

Dan Hostetler, Mena, AR

Bible Reading: Matthew 4:1–16
One Year Bible Reading Plan:
Hebrews 1
Jeremiah 38, 39

He that believeth on the Son hath everlasting life.
—John 3:36

Unannounced Inspection

And they were judged every man according to their works.
Revelation 20:13b

One Wednesday evening, we were just ready to leave the nursing home when some visitors walked in. These visitors turned out to be the state inspectors. They had arrived for their annual inspection. We knew that it was getting close to the time that they would come, but we did not know the day or the hour.

As they made their exit on the third day, they reminded us of the purpose of their visit. They are committed to helping us provide quality care for the elderly. They informed us that they had gone through our records carefully. They told us they had opened any door and drawer that they wanted to, and sorted through whatever they chose to. They had some suggestions for us, but nothing serious enough to give us a deficiency.

As I pondered on this, my mind thought about how we say our lives are open to the brotherhood. I wondered how we would respond to an unannounced inspection of our homes. Suppose your church leaders would show up some evening to go through your house and records. The purpose of their visit would be to be assured that you are living a quality Christian life.

We all know the Lord is returning to hold an unannounced inspection. We know He is coming. We just do not know when. He will examine every aspect of our lives. He knows the thoughts and intents of our hearts. The Bible says that all things are naked and open before His eyes. Are we ready for such an inspection?

Bible Reading: Luke 17:20–37
One Year Bible Reading Plan:
Hebrews 2
Jeremiah 40—42

We have the opportunity today to correct and remove from our lives the clutter that does not belong there. Lord, help us welcome an unannounced inspection!

Mark Webb, Aroda, VA

Search me, O God!

November 7

Be Thou Faithful

Be thou faithful until death, and I will give thee a crown of life.
Revelation 2:10b

Recently we had the opportunity to visit Yellowstone National Park as a family. While we were observing the many different geysers in one area of the park, a first time viewer from one of the southeastern states asked which one of these geysers is what they call "Old Faithful." There are more than 200 active geysers in the park, but of these, there is only one that over the years, by consistently erupting at regular intervals, has merited the name "Old Faithful."

What a challenge to us, as we face decisions every hour of the day at home, in church and business life. In an evil society that is ever changing, where seducers wax worse and worse, the call for faithfulness becomes more urgent.

Faithfulness is a virtue attainable by the child of God. Otherwise, the command would not be in the Scriptures. Jesus, our great high priest, suffered and was tempted, yet remained faithful unto death. Because of this and His resurrection, we have the power to be faithful. There is absolutely no excuse for unfaithfulness.

Are we faithful to God? Are we faithful to our calling as a husband, father, wife, mother, youth, minister, lay brother, prayer warrior, soul winner, steward of God's possessions, or provider for the needs of others?

By God's grace, may those around you and the rising generation call you faithful. When the King of all kings, in the time of all times rises from His throne to judge the world, will He say, "Well done, thou good and faithful servant"?

Bible Reading: Luke 12:41–48; 16:1–13
One Year Bible Reading Plan:
Hebrews 3
Jeremiah 43—45

Joseph Miller, Lamar, MO

The faithfulness of Abraham still speaks today.

Go for Help

The righteous cry, and the Lord heareth,
and delivereth them out of all their troubles.
Psalm 34:17

Life is a vast expanse of experiences. These experiences lift us up when they bring us success, but when trouble is our portion, our spirits become discouraged. Problems have a tendency to compound and rob us of our sense of control, which can bring feelings of fear and rejection.

In 1 Kings 19, the account is given of Elijah's experience after winning a great victory over the prophets of Baal. Queen Jezebel vowed to kill Elijah, and Elijah fled to the mountains alone. Elijah felt afraid and rejected. He tried to find a safe place by hiding in a cave. God's ultimate question was, "What doest thou here?" God explained to Elijah that there were yet seven thousand in Israel who had not bowed their knees to the image of Baal. There were yet seven thousand safe places for Elijah to go. It was not necessary for him to hide alone and in despair of life.

Rather, God commissioned others to enter into the situation so that Israel's problems could be addressed. Hazael was to be king of Syria; Jehu was to be king of Israel, and Elisha was to take over for Elijah. The message for us is do not withdraw into a shell and become a cocoon, nor put on a bold, aggressive front, keeping people at a distance. The message is go for help. God alone knows the answers to the problems of man's heart, but many times God uses others to bring solutions and hope into a desperate situation.

Bible Reading: 1 Kings 19:9–21
One Year Bible Reading Plan:
Hebrews 4
Jeremiah 46—48

Edgar Bauman, Listowel, ON

The Lord helps those who acknowledge their need of help.

The Fires of Hell

Seeing then that all these things shall be dissolved, what manner of persons ought ye to be in all holy conversation and godliness?
2 Peter 3:11

Have you ever burned yourself with hot grease or by striking a match? How terribly that does hurt! You could cry and cry.

Sometimes, when my wife is baking bread, she asks me to shift the bread in the oven. When I open the door, I feel the heat coming from inside.

My mind goes easily to the words of Peter, who said that this earth and all the works that are in it will be burned up with fervent heat. All the skyscrapers, massive buildings, and the sinful works of men will be destroyed. But, beloved, we can rejoice because our names are written in the Lamb's book of life!

Jesus said, "Behold I come quickly and my reward is with me. Behold I stand at the door and knock: if any man hear my voice, and open the door, I will come in to him, and will sup with him, and he with me." Try Him, and you will see.

Only those who do not trust Him and do His will, will hear His voice saying, "Depart from me, I know you not."

Today you have a choice. You may live with Him forever. Friend, hell is an awful place. Be prepared, for His coming is closer than we think.

| Bible Reading: 2 Peter 3 |
| One Year Bible Reading Plan: |
| Hebrews 5 |
| Jeremiah 49, 50 |

Mark Meighn, Belize City, Belize

Let's live to reign with Him!

Ribbon of Thoughts

The thoughts of the wicked are an abomination to the Lord:
but the words of the pure are pleasant words.
Proverbs 15:26

Our thoughts are the results of past experiences. How we organize our thoughts and relate to situations today is heavily dependent on the things we have observed and meditated upon in the past. Habitually avoiding bad company, evil places, and corrupt literature in the present will give us the opportunity to lay a foundation for pure thoughts in the future. When we lust, we record data in our memories that will keep flashing out as we go through life.

Recently, a friend of mine bought a used typewriter and a partially used ribbon. All the words that the former owner had typed with this ribbon were on record. Reading the words on the ribbon revealed this person's walk of life.

God is also recording all our thoughts, words, and actions. Evil surmising, covetousness, corruption, and impure thoughts may be hidden from our fellowman, but not from God. If your closest earthly friend would take a tape recording of all your thoughts and sit beside you reading the miles of ribbon to you, what would your response be? How would your tape read? Would not your eyes drop with shame at the beginning?

As your friend read, again and again your eyes would drop with shame. Your friend would keep pulling out the ribbon. On and on he would read. Suddenly, your eyes would light up as you realize that more and more pure thoughts are replacing the bad ones. As he came to the end, you could rejoice. The thoughts have become more and more pure and Christ-like. This is the way our lives should be. Progress should be visible. After we become accustomed to disciplining ourselves to avoid sin, our thoughts will become purer.

Harvey D. Yoder, Marion, MI

Bible Reading: Psalm 139
One Year Bible Reading Plan:
Hebrews 6
Jeremiah 51, 52

Bring to nought every evil thought.

Zero Percent Unemployment

Son, go work today in my vineyard.
Matthew 21:28

What is that, I wondered? As I sat reading my Bible one morning, my eye caught a movement on the floor. At first glance it looked like a piece of chocolate cake moving sporadically across the tiles. Immediately I suspected the propellent of the crumb. I was right; an early rising, industrious little ant was struggling valiantly under the strain of towing an object twice its size. At times it seemed he lost his direction, but as I continued watching, I could see that this little fellow knew where he was headed. Although he paused periodically to rest, he never gave up, but continued steadily on. The last I saw of him, he was still holding a southwesterly course, slowly but surely proceeding toward his destination.

What a lesson! What an example! Here in Kenya, idleness is a serious problem. In America spiritual laziness is increasingly evident. Everywhere the Christian needs to be encouraged to be about the Father's business.

Here are some questions to ponder. Have you ever seen an idle ant? Have you ever heard of one taking a vacation? Have you ever observed ants feuding and fighting about who gets the honor for a certain project? In spite of the smallness and seeming insignificance of the ant, God uses them to teach us some powerful and important principles. In the work of the kingdom there is always much to do. God always has an opening for the willing worker. Training and skills are not of primary interest to Him, but rather a yielded heart that says "amen" to His will. Let us take a cue from the ant and faithfully labor in our Master's vineyard wherever He calls us until our final transfer to our eternal home.

Raymond, Fisher, Nakuru, Kenya

Bible Reading: Proverbs 6:6–11; 24:30–34
One Year Bible Reading Plan:
Hebrews 7
Lamentations 1, 2

In God's economy, unemployment is nonexistent.

Prepare for the Unexpected

Be ye followers of me, even as I also am of Christ.
1 Corinthians 11:1

One day several years ago while working in my shop, I saw a police car pull into my driveway. Two policemen stepped out. They informed me that they had a warrant for my arrest.

Since I could not think of a legitimate reason why they would want to arrest me, I just casually responded, "Well, here I am."

It turned out they really did not have a warrant but were there to ask me a few questions about repairing a motor in their car.

What if they would have been there to arrest me, or to question me about my faith? This scene is very real for many fellow Christians in recent times. Without time for farewells, they are taken from their families to be imprisoned for months or years, sometimes never to return. This they endure for the sake of their faith in Jesus Christ.

As I pondered this incident, I wondered if I would have been prepared to go with them? I wondered how my family would have been prepared physically; but even more, I wondered if I had provided for their spiritual needs. If I were to be taken away suddenly and without warning, would I have taken sufficient time to teach, instruct, and to live an example of faith so my family would desire to continue on, even in my absence? What if I would not have been allowed one more opportunity to speak to them?

May we not neglect today to provide for the spiritual welfare of our families, friends, and neighbors.

Willie Borntrager, Monticello, KY

Bible Reading: Acts 4:1–31
One Year Bible Reading Plan:
 Hebrews 8
 Lamentations 3—5

Hold them near while they're here. Don't wait for tomorrow.

No Detours

And an highway shall be there, and a way,
and it shall be called The way of holiness.
Isaiah 35:8a

"Save a 25 minute delay, Exit Now!" The sign flashed along the interstate on which we were traveling. In the few seconds that we had to make a decision, we decided to exit. You know time is important when you're traveling. However, it did not take long to realize we had made a mistake. The detour we took caused us a loss of an hour and took us on some very rough roads.

We are faced each day with these kinds of choices. "Sign up today and save!" "You deserve this break!" "Last chance to win big!" "This may be your last catalog!" "This price is good only for today!" Most of the decisions that we make on impulse end up causing us grief.

Does this not remind you of our spiritual pilgrimage? The devil offers all kinds of allurements, trying to get us to exit the highway of holiness. His desire is to get us to detour and never again get on the right way. Satan's detours cause us to lose so much. Many have lost their purity of mind and body. Even those who have by the grace of God made it back onto the highway of holiness have encountered some very rough going.

God has a plan mapped out for our lives. How often we fail to take the route that He has prescribed! Our desire should be to stay so close to God through His Word, His Spirit, and His people, that we remain in His will. Press on! Keep your eyes on Jesus. This is the only way to obtain heaven, our final destination.

Bible Reading: James 1
One Year Bible Reading Plan:
Hebrews 9
Ezekiel 1—3

Mark Webb, Aroda, VA

Walk in the Light!

Problems? Seek Help!

*And call upon me in the day of trouble: I will
deliver thee, and thou shalt glorify me.*
Psalm 50:15

At times while on the job, a piece of equipment gives me some trouble. I can waste a lot of time getting frustrated trying to get it going. Often I end up asking somebody who knows more about it for help. At times the solution is quite simple; other times it is a complicated job to get it working again.

So it is in spiritual life also. We run into a problem, a decision we need to make, and it looks ever so complicated. But praise the Lord, we have One who knows all about it! He knows the solution, and He will help us through. Sometimes the answer may be simple, other times it may be more complicated, as the Lord has something to teach us. "But God is faithful, who will not suffer you to be tempted above that ye are able; but will with the temptation also make a way to escape that ye may be able to bear it" (1 Corinthians 10:13).

We read accounts in the Bible of the Israelites facing great armies. When they trusted in the Lord, they gained victory. At times, they did not even need to fight, but simply stood back and let the Lord fight for them. Through this the Lord was glorified, and Israel's enemies feared the Lord (2 Chronicles 20). When they trusted in their own strength, or in that of other nations, they were defeated miserably (1 Samuel 4). "Stand back and see the salvation of the Lord!"

Philip Cross, Leitchfield, KY

Bible Reading: Psalms 46, 47
One Year Bible Reading Plan:
Hebrews 10:1–23
Ezekiel 4—6

*But thanks be to God, which giveth us
the victory through our Lord Jesus Christ.*

Faith

And the apostles said unto the Lord, Increase our faith.
Luke 17:5

We have heard it mentioned countless times and defined from all angles. But, oh, to grasp its significance! How could faith make king David God's friend in spite of serious failures, while lack of faith made the Pharisees arch enemies of Jesus regardless of their legal righteousness?

What is the real issue with faith? It is so winsome with God and yet so difficult for men to attain! Faith is a response of acceptance and cooperation toward God.

Romans 10:17 gives us the first step toward attaining the life-changing faith of Hebrews 11. Faith is a response to God's message. The core of His message to man is in the Bible. We must expose ourselves to God's message and its evidence.

God does not expect a blind faith that accepts His message without evidence. The evidence God gives is a necessary foundation for faith. He offers evidence that is universal, irrefutable, and threefold: the evidence of the Word, the evidence of Creation, and the evidence of the Spirit's voice in our hearts.

Unbelieving man rejects God's evidence, though he cannot refute it. Faith accepts God, not only as Creator, but also as Owner. Faith accepts and cooperates with all God's claims on our lives today, and continues to accept as He continues to reveal His will. Faith is convinced that God's way is best. Faith puts me completely at God's disposal and brings me under His blessing. "But without faith it is impossible to please him: for he that cometh to God must believe that he is, and that he is a rewarder of them that diligently seek him."

Bible Reading: Hebrews 11
One Year Bible Reading Plan:
Hebrews 10:24–39
Ezekiel 7—9

Samuel Bauman, New Ringgold, PA

Faith is the link that connects our weakness to God's strength.

In Heaven for a Hundred Years

And I saw no temple therein: for the Lord God Almighty
and the Lamb are the temple of it.
Revelation 21:22

A minister from my home community had witnessed to his milkman and talked to him about heaven.

One day the milkman said, "Enos, what are you going to do after a hundred years in heaven?" After a few days this minister began to wonder, "Well, what are we going to do after a hundred years?" He finally concluded that if life here is pleasant when everything goes well, then it must be very pleasant in heaven, where all goes well all the time.

It will take eternity to learn all that God is and to praise Him for all He has done. However, to be with Him is what matters; we will desire nothing more. God is our Creator, Redeemer, and Lord. We, who are saved by the power of Jesus' blood and overcome will worship Him face to face. God delights in our worship.

One of the blessings of heaven is there will be no curse. The enmity between the woman's seed and Satan will not be there. The curse of sorrow, sweat, thorns, thistles, and death will not be there.

My mind cannot fathom what kind of place that will be! And a hundred years? No, we will not go by years, but it will be on and on and on! Eternity! As the song goes, "No wishing for elsewhere to be." The chief end of man is to worship God and to enjoy Him forever.

Bible Reading: Revelation
21:1–5; 22:1–6
One Year Bible Reading Plan:
Hebrews 11:1–19
Ezekiel 10—12

Allan Miller, Sarcoxie, MO

Heaven does not go by time.

Let Us Not Be Deceived

If any man among you seemeth to be wise in this world,
let him become a fool, that he may be wise.
1 Corinthians 3:18b

Our first parents were deceived into disobeying God's Word when they ate of the forbidden fruit. Because of their sin, we all inherited a sinful nature. The sinful nature makes man gullible, causing many to believe almost anything without first searching out the truth.

We read in Matthew 24 that the disciples asked Jesus to tell them when the things Jesus predicted would happen, and what would be the sign of His coming and the end of the world. Jesus said, "Take heed that no man deceive you." We need to take warning lest we be deceived. Satan is very sly. If he can get you to believe those who distort the truth, he will have you deceived.

The Lord Jesus may return soon. We see the signs of the last times. May we be watching and waiting so we will not be caught unawares. When the Lord returns, let us not be found slumbering or sleeping. We want to be prepared to join Him in that great marriage supper. We do not know when to expect Him. It may be morning, noon, or midnight.

In Matthew 25 we read of ten virgins who went to meet their bridegroom. Five of them were wise, and five were foolish. At midnight there was a cry, "Behold, the bridegroom cometh! Go ye out to meet Him." The foolish virgins did not have enough oil with them; their lamps went out. The wise virgins had plenty of oil. Their walk with the Lord was reflected as they helped others by giving the thirsty a drink, giving the hungry meat, giving the stranger lodging, visiting those who were sick and in prison, or by clothing those who were naked. The foolish virgins were deceived into thinking they had plenty of time.

Bible Reading: Genesis 3
One Year Bible Reading Plan:
Hebrews 11:20–40
Ezekiel 13—15

Amos Garber, Rosebush, MI

Beware of the half-truth—
you may have gotten the wrong half.

Character Counts

Let this mind be in you, which was also in Christ Jesus.
Philippians 2:5

Character is "the real me"—what I really am in my heart. When the chips are down, the props are taken away, and the veneer of reputation is removed, we arrive at our inner sanctum—character.

Someone has said that a true Christian is like an onion. You peel all the outer layers away, and when you come to the heart, you still have an onion. What you see is what you get.

Character, of course, is a neutral word; it may denote something good or bad. The burden of responsibility for good character qualities, in one sense, has been lifted from me. A marvelous transaction took place one day, wherein I presented my emptiness to my Savior and Lord, and He provided a tremendous filling of that void. When we subject ourselves to His lordship, we avail ourselves of the admirable attributes of Christ. Before I found the Lord, the virtues I longed for always seemed to be just beyond my grasp. It is true, there were times when, ever so briefly, the quiet satisfaction of knowing patience, obedience and kindness was mine. But the truth is, we must follow God's order; anything less is a counterfeit. It seemed as if God was asking, "So, you desire that attractive personality? Good. But this is how it must be done." And He introduced the Savior.

For me, it was like the songwriter's experience: "Joy of heaven to earth come down." I came to realize what all Christians must surely know: Genuine Christian character will manifest itself only if it has no rival, or merit of man.

Jerry Yoder, Auburn, KY

Bible Reading: Ephesians 4:1–24
One Year Bible Reading Plan:
Hebrews 12
Ezekiel 16

Reputation comes from without. Character comes from within.

*November 19*_____

The Realm of Life

What is man, that thou art mindful of him?
and the son of man, that thou visitest him?
Psalm 8:4

In the beginning God made the heaven and the earth. With awe we look about us at the works of His fingers. We see the spectacular mountains, the green growth that the earth regenerates in spring and summer. As the rays of sunshine slant down on the ground, things that lie still and dormant suddenly spring to life. Birds twitter and tweet. When dusk arrives, the frogs and katydids mingle their songs, giving us sweet natural music. We see the marvelous, tiny insects. In the shadows of the night we lift our faces toward the heavens and see the planets, constellations, and the lesser light that rules the night. These fit together like the internal parts of a clock and are always on time.

As we mature, we are apt to think, "What is my purpose in life? How do I fit in to complete the puzzle?" We see that even the works of nataure are beneficial. Bees pollinate the flowers, and lady bugs keep destructive scales in check. But what about me?

When God created man, He made him for a special purpose. He needed caretakers to maintain His handiwork. Not only did He need caretakers, but He wanted someone to love and to fellowship with. Shouldn't you feel unique and special that God chose you to be part of His circle of love?

Since the dawn of history, many men have trod the way we are traveling now. Death brought their mortal bodies to a halt. All returned to dust and the majority have long been forgotten, but they had a bearing on how the world is today. Either they extended God's loving care throughout the world, or they frustrated it. Let us be ministers of His love.

Bible Reading: Genesis 1:26–29; Psalm 8
One Year Bible Reading Plan:
Hebrews 13
Ezekiel 17—19

Harvey D. Yoder, Marion, MI

Conclusion—Fear God and keep His commandments.

Thankfulness

*Giving thanks always for all things unto God and
the Father in the name of our Lord Jesus Christ.*
Ephesians 5:20

Have we found ourselves grumbling and complaining about our lot in life? We are surrounded by troubles. Many people are going through trials. But we should be thankful, even if circumstances would cause us to be otherwise.

Here are three reasons we should be happy.

1. We owe it to God. "Know ye that the Lord he is God; it is he that hath made us, and not we ourselves, we are his people, and the sheep of his pasture. Enter into his gates with thanksgiving" (Psalm 100: 3, 4). We owe God thanks for these temporary blessings of strength, food, water, shelter, blood, and breath. But most of all, we should thank God for being our Redeemer.

2. We should thank God because acknowledging His goodness enables us to see Him as He is. When we are thankful, we can see God's love and goodness; our eyes are open, and we are receptive to His will. Unthankfulness blinds our eyes. We cannot ignore God's lovingkindness without losing touch with Him on Whom our very life depends.

3. We should be thankful because all of life's circumstances are in God's hands, and thankfulness enables us to handle trials. We need to be thankful in all things and recognize the hand of God in sorrow as well as in joy. Times of tears will come. We cannot escape trials. But we can thank and trust Him in all things. Recognizing that God controls all events, even the painful ones, helps us accept difficulty with confidence.

Can we look up and thank Him every day? David, in Psalm 119:164 says, "Seven times a day do I praise thee." Some of the most thankful people are the ones that have the least. They are thankful because they live in the sunshine of God's care.

Bible Reading: Ephesians
5:1–21
One Year Bible Reading Plan:
James 1
Ezekiel 20, 21

Eli Yoder, Stuarts Draft, VA

He enjoys much who is thankful for a little.

November 21 _____

Giving Thanks

O praise the Lord, all ye nations: praise him, all ye people.
Psalm 117:1

When did you last take time out to really thank God for the many wonderful things He has done for you? Wives, do you really thank God for your husband, or do you take him for granted? Stop and think what a blessed wife you are. You and your husband are Christians.

What a blessing that you can rest assured of your husband's whereabouts. You can tell others where he is, and he goes where he says he will go.

More than that, you have someone you can look up to. Always remember to pray for your husband. It is always a comfort to me whenever I get home from work and I hear my wife say, "I prayed for you today."

Husbands, have you thanked God for your wife lately, even today? Sometimes we take them for granted. Do not forget that she is not your slave, but your wife. Ask yourself what you would amount to if it were not for your wife. Really, what kind of man would you be? Brethren, God gave them to us. Let us be thankful for God's blessings and really appreciate them.

Parents, when was the last time you stopped to thank God for your children? The Bible says that children are a heritage from the Lord. Children are really fun to have around. But sometimes we find ourselves sighing over them. Why is he or she like this? Why can't they be like so and so's children? Let us not allow these evil thoughts into our minds but instead give God thanks and praise for our children. Pray earnestly for them. Let us be godly role models for them.

Bible Reading: Colossians 3
One Year Bible Reading Plan:
James 2
Ezekiel 22, 23

Mark Meighn, Belize City, Belize

Let us live lives of thankfulness.

Thank God for Your Home

_And ye fathers, provoke not your children to wrath, but
bring them up in the nurture and admonition of the Lord._
Ephesians 6:4

Nineteen-year-old Jason stormed out of the house in a fit of rage.
Dad had made him mad again. Couldn't his parents ever get along
with each other? He had had enough. He was going to get back at his
parents for the way they had treated him. "The next time you hear of
me, it'll be in the headlines," he called over his shoulder angrily.

He drove off in the car and picked up his friends, Pat and
Freddie. They left their home state of South Carolina and drove to
Atlanta, Georgia. There they decided to rob a bank or steal a vehicle. After searching awhile at a mall for a chance to do this, Freddie
left his two friends and caught a bus back home. The other two
boys continued north and happened to end up in our small town.
They decided to steal a vehicle. One day, our local newspaper ran
the sad story of an elderly couple murdered in their own house.
Their pickup truck and about $300 were stolen. The two boys were
eventually linked to the murder and arrested.

Last week our local newspaper bore the headline that one of
the boys, Jason, was convicted and received two life sentences plus
ten years in prison. A sad story it is, and yet so typical of the world
about us. Children end up doing things they never imagined in
reaction against their parents' treatment. Neither parents nor children can be blamed for the other's mistakes, and yet parents have a
great responsibility to influence their children for the right.

Have you thanked God today for your godly parents? Do it
now. If you do not have godly parents, have you thanked God for
your salvation, that you can teach your children what is right? Do
it now. If your father made mistakes and did not treat you right,
have you forgiven him? Do it now. If there is bitterness in your
heart toward your home life, have you rid yourself of it? Do it
now. Life is too short and eter-
nity is too serious to hold a
grudge. Purpose now to be the
kind of person that you would
wants others to be to you!

Bible Reading: Ephesians
5:25—6:9
One Year Bible Reading Plan:
James 3
Ezekiel 24—26

Tim Mast, Crossville, TN

A happy family is but an earlier heaven.
—Sr. John Bowring

331

Giving Thanks Is Better
Than Casting Blame

*Now when Daniel knew that the writing was signed, he went
into his house . . . ; he kneeled upon his knees three times a day.*
Daniel 6:10a

Beep, beep, beep! "Why is that vehicle in front of us rolling
backwards while we wait on the red light?" questioned the driver
we were traveling with. The eighty-year-old man did not realize
that he was to blame, for it was his vehicle that kept easing forward
until it almost made contact with the car ahead of us. My wife and
I were witnesses from the back seat of his car.

How often the Lord sees our misdeeds, while we blame another.
In the Scripture reading today, Daniel was put to the test. He would
have had plenty of reasons to blame others. Yet not one accusation
escaped his lips. Daniel was aware that the prohibition against
prayer had been signed by the king, but it did not make him stop
praying to his God. He trusted God and blamed no one. He did not
even blame the king for signing such a decree. Because of Daniel's
fervency in prayer, his life was spared.

This is my prayer today. Lord, help me to see myself as You see
me. Help me to see that I cause
myself more problems than anyone else has ever caused me.
Help me to realize as I focus on
You and surrender my talent,
time, and abilities for You, I will
be more and more like You.

Bible Reading: Daniel 6
One Year Bible Reading Plan:
   James 4
   Ezekiel 27, 28

William Troyer, Huntland, TN

Overlook the faults of others, and look into your own.

Stability Amidst Winds of Doctrine

Carried about with every wind of doctrine, by the sleight of men,
and cunning craftiness, whereby they lie in wait to deceive.
Ephesians 4:14

Someone has said, "Wherever God builds a castle, Satan builds one too." He knows by confusion people will begin to doubt and fall into deception. Deception is Satan's device. Confusion paves the way to deception. Confusion often comes when we want to please everybody and are not willing to take a stand for what is right.

May we not be as the man and his son in one of Aesop's fables. The man and his son were leading a donkey. One man they met told them they were foolish to walk when the donkey had no load. They decided the boy would ride. The next man criticized them for letting the boy ride while the father walked. They decided the father should ride instead of the boy. Soon another person was encountered who complained because the boy was walking. They decided that both would ride. The next man reproved them for their cruelty to the animal because they both rode. They got off, tied the donkey's legs, put a pole between them, and carried the donkey. For this they were laughed at until they started to put the donkey down. The donkey began to kick and rolled into a river and drowned.

Bible Reading: Ephesians
4:1–16
One Year Bible Reading Plan:
James 5
Ezekiel 29—31

We may listen to advice, but when we act, our actions must be based on the truth. Having taken a stand, stand steadfastly.

Andrew L. Miller, Greensberg, KY

Building according to every man's advice
will produce a crooked house.

Tangling With Failure

Yea, though I walk through the valley of the shadow of death, I will fear no evil: for thou art with me; thy rod and thy staff they comfort me.
Psalm 23:4

"Marcus, would you be willing to start a song in the program?" my teacher asked me. Instantly fear laid its tormenting grip on my heart. After contemplating, I agreed to start the parting song. I was in the seventh grade, twelve years old, and my voice was changing. Starting songs scared me.

The time arrived when we were practicing the year-end program and were ready to start the parting song. Fear gripped my heart tightly and caused me to lock up. Fear of failure had me in its grip. Had I only been clothed with humility and the truth, I would never have experienced this torture.

It was more important to me that others thought well of me and accepted me,, than for me to lovingly contribute to the program. If the whole schoolroom would have erupted in outright mockery of my off-key singing, I could still be comforted by the truth that God loves me. This truth would have sustained me through the mockery. Jesus said in Luke 9:24 that if we seek to save our souls, we will lose our lives. But if we give up ourselves and move out with a passion to love, we will find the liberated and only worthwhile life.

David says that even in the valley of the shadow of death, or let us say the valley of mistakes, he will fear no evil. Truly, it is a blessing to fail at starting a song, if that leads us through the death of pride. Let us be humble enough to risk failure, for success is failure turned inside out.

Bible Reading: Psalm 25
One Year Bible Reading Plan:
1 Peter 1
Ezekiel 32, 33

Marcus Troyer, Belle Center, OH

Negative emotions in failure are the gauge of our load of baggage.

A Thankful Heart

*Be careful for nothing; but in everything by prayer and supplication
with thanksgiving let your requests be made known unto God.*
Philippians 4:6

Look at the setting of our Bible reading in Luke 17. There were
ten lepers. Lepers were outcasts of society. They were alienated
from their families, the synagogue, and the community. Their lives
were lonely, full of rejection and physical suffering. They had very
little hope for the future because leprosy was an incurable disease,
which usually resulted in an early death.

Imagine these ten lepers walking along, knowing their future
was hopeless. They saw Jesus far off and cried out to Him for
healing. When Jesus saw them, He had compassion on them and
told them to go show themselves to the priests. When they obeyed,
they were healed.

What a tremendous experience to be healed of leprosy! But
only one out of the ten lepers remembered his awful disease. He
turned back and fell at Jesus' feet thanking Jesus for healing him.

I have to ask myself, "Am I thankful from the depths of my
heart for what God has done for me and is still doing for me day
after day?"

Sometimes someone does me a favor. Later I remember that I
forgot to thank the person, and I have to wonder why I forgot. I
have come to the conclusion that too often I am so occupied with
what I am doing and with my schedule that I forget the acts of
kindness of others on my behalf.

Am I that way with God? Am I so involved with tangible things
and difficulties along the way that I become unthankful because
my thoughts and focus are on
the wrong object? My desire is
to remember God's goodness
and mercy He has shown me
and to have a thankful heart.

Abe Gingerich, Free Union, VA

Bible Reading: Luke 17:11–19
One Year Bible Reading Plan:
1 Peter 2
Ezekiel 34, 35

True worship springs from a thankful heart.

Treasures

And wisdom and knowledge shall be the stability of thy times,
and strength of salvation: the fear of the Lord is his treasure.
Isaiah 33:6

Recently our family went to Missouri to visit family and friends. During our vacation, we visited a museum in Kansas City called Steamboat *Arabia*. The museum held the treasures of a pre-Civil War era steamboat, *Arabia*. This steamboat was carrying a load of goods for settlers in the west when she hit a snag and sank in the Missouri River. Over a period of time she was completely covered with mud and silt.

In 1988, five men decided to dig up the steamboat (now some 130 years old) to see if she held any treasures. One of the men was at the museum to give a presentation. He shared some of his personal experiences during the excavation of the steamboat. One of the first things they found was a barrel full of perfectly kept china. He found a beautiful vase that he claimed for his own. He said he would share everything else, but this was his.

He took the vase home and proudly displayed it on his fireplace mantle. But he began to worry that someone might knock it off or drop it while admiring its beauty, so he put it in a box under his bed. But then he started to worry that someone might steal it, so he decided to put his vase in a safe.

Then he made an interesting statement. "I began to realize that a treasure is worthless unless it is shared with others." He put his beautiful vase in the museum with the other treasures to be enjoyed by hundreds of thousands of people.

If this is true concerning treasures that will some day perish and be forgotten, is it not much more important that we share our priceless treasure which will endure through all eternity?

Bible Reading: Luke 8:26–40
One Year Bible Reading Plan:
1 Peter 3
Ezekiel 36, 37

Melvin Troyer, Clarkson, KY

Publish it abroad, Jesus saves to the uttermost.

Hammer Control

The heart is deceitful above all things,
and desperately wicked: who can know it?
Jeremiah 17:9

Recently our local newspaper ran an article about an incident that happened at a convenience store in town. Two men got into a heated argument. One man reached into his truck, pulled out a hammer, and struck the other man several times, sending him to the hospital.

Some people might think it is time to consider legislation to control hammers. Can you imagine the lengthy arguments in Congress as they try to figure out which hammers should be outlawed—the brick hammer or the claw hammer (surely a rubber mallet would be legal). Should there be an age limit, 18 or 21, before one may purchase a hammer (of course, with a three-day waiting period in order to have a background check)?

Ever since Adam and Eve sinned in the garden, man has been trying to lay the blame for his actions on someone or something else.

People murder others, then blame gun manufacturers for making the guns. People develop lung cancer from years of smoking, then sue the tobacco companies for making cigarettes. Alcoholism is passed off as a disease.

We blame our parents, church situations, or a brother who wronged us. Granted, there are people that mistreat us or situations that severely test us, but still we are responsible for our actions and how we respond to others.

In Luke 15:18, the prodigal son spoke the three hardest words for the flesh to acknowledge: "I have sinned." I am here in the pigpen because of my own selfish choices. But the good news is if we are willing to humble ourselves and go to the Father, and whomever else we have wronged, and tell them, "I have sinned," He is ready to forgive us and give us heaven's best.

Bible Reading: Jeremiah 17:9
One Year Bible Reading Plan:
1 Peter 4
Ezekiel 38, 39

Melvin Troyer, Clarkson, KY

The heart of the matter is the heart.

*November 29*_____

Broken Cisterns

*For my people have committed two evils; they have forsaken
me the fountain of living waters, and hewed them out
cisterns, broken cisterns, that can hold no water.*
Jeremiah 2:13

We have a very slow well at our home. It measures in gallons
per day, not gallons per minute. After living here several years and
running out of water every day in the summer and fall, I decided to
put in a cistern to catch and hold rainwater for use in the dry times.
I contacted a man who builds concrete tanks. He assured me his
tanks were watertight. I bought three 1,000 gallon tanks, hired a
backhoe, and put them in. They were made of a top and bottom
half with a seal between. I paid extra for a special sealing tape on
the outside to be sure they would not leak. The rain came, but the
tanks did not fill up! They leaked at the joint. The builder said,
"You need to bury them and pack dirt around to seal them." I hired
a backhoe and buried them and packed dirt around them. Again
the rain came, but the tanks still did not fill up. They were broken
cisterns. What I needed was new cisterns.

I think we are sometimes the same way in our Christian lives.
We are to be cisterns holding the living water of God, but we too
are broken and leak. We try to pack our lives instead of dying to
self, being born again, and becoming a new cistern. God's fountain
of goodness and mercy flows into us; but if we are broken cisterns,
we cannot hold it. No matter how much teaching we sit under or
how many books we read, if we do not have a new cistern to hold
it, we can never be filled with God's love—filled with the Holy Spirit.
We must also guard that we do not fill up and then think we do not
need the source. When my cisterns are full, I do not think about rain
as much as when they are empty.

We can keep trying to patch and pack the leaks in our old cistern, or we can die to self and
become a new cistern, a fit vessel to hold the abundance of the
fountain of living water God has
for us.

David Schroeder, Bradford, TN

Bible Reading: Jeremiah 2:1–19
One Year Bible Reading Plan:
1 Peter 5
Ezekiel 40

_____

Is your cistern broken or new?

The Rock

_Hear my cry, O God; attend unto my prayer. From the end of
the earth will I cry unto thee, when my heart is
overwhelmed: lead me to the rock that is higher than I._
Psalm 61:1, 2

Imagine yourself on a boat approaching the western end of the Mediterranean Sea on a calm summer morning. At first you see only the waves undulating lazily before you. But then your straining eyes make out a projection that looms on the far horizon. When you are quite close, you are struck with awe at the sheer enormity of the great rock that leaps up from the sea to peak at over 1,000 feet in the blue sky above. You realize that this must be the famous "Rock of Gibraltar."

For thousands of years the Mediterranean waves have spent their force on the rock's gray limestone sides. But the rock is still there. For thousands of years the hot sun has beat down on the rock's craggy crown. But the rock has not moved. As the wheels of time have turned, great men and great kingdoms have risen and fallen, but the rock has stood firm. When sailors first began to navigate the seas in their fragile crafts, they too must have been impressed with this great fortress and must have spoken of it on their voyages. Today the Rock of Gibraltar has become a household word. Whether you speak of someone's convictions or of the ice cream you are trying to dip, when you say something is "as solid as the Rock of Gibraltar," people immediately visualize something very solid and unyielding.

Friends, there is a Rock we can depend on as well. A Rock that will help us never to be moved by any wind of opposition or fire of trial. A Rock that is far more unchanging and far more steadfast than any earthly rock.

In his farewell song, Moses pointed his people to this Rock. In His mountaintop sermon, Jesus reminded His followers of their need to build their lives on this Rock. In today's uncertain world, we also can have perfect confidence in this Rock. There is no safer place on which to build our marriages, our homes, our relationships, or our entire lives. Are you building on the Rock?

Bible Reading: Deuteronomy
32:1-14; Matthew 7:21–27
One Year Bible Reading Plan:
2 Peter 1
Ezekiel 41, 42

Titus Hofer, LaCrete, AB

Neither is there any rock like our God.

December 1 _____

Influence

Ye are the light of the world. A city
that is set on an hill cannot be hid.
Matthew 5:14

The Bible contains many figures of influence. Leaven is one, picturing the gradual fermenting of influence into a whole mass, for good (Matthw 13:33) or for evil (Luke 12:1). A canker is used in 2 Timothy 2:17, a sore in the flesh which is fatal unless stopped. Tares are another influence, choking the good wheat (Matthew 13:24–30). In John 12, when Mary anointed the feet of Jesus with spikenard, the house was filled with the odor of the ointment. It did not just stay on Jesus' feet.

In our Scripture reading, Jesus uses two figures, salt and light, to teach us that our lives spread influence. They speak either of godliness, influencing for truth and righteousness, or that of darkness, and that which will be cast out and destroyed. "Let your light so shine before men that they may see your good works and glorify your Father which is in heaven" (Matthew 5:16).

When there is light, one can see. Light is life! Without it we perish. Christians are to let their light shine so others can see God. Paul told the Corinthians, "Ye are our epistles written in our hearts, known and read of all men" (2 Corinthians 3:2).

My life, whether godly or otherwise, speaks. It does not stay only with me, but it also influences others. Christians are the salt of the earth. The power of influence is mighty!

Edward Hochstetler, Hicksville, OH

Bible Reading: Matthew 5:1–16
One Year Bible Reading Plan:
2 Peter 2
Ezekiel 43, 44

A little leaven leaveneth the whole lump.

Commitment

Commit thy way unto the Lord, trust also
in him, and he shall bring it to pass.
Psalm 37:5

To commit myself to someone brings accountability and responsibility. It means to bind oneself: I am obligated to; I have pledged. Are we willing to commit our lives, ways, plans, and future to God? How about a commitment to the brotherhood? Is it possible that Satan has succeeded in blinding our minds to the blessing commitment can bring to our lives? Perhaps the most important commitment is being totally honest with God and man. If we have not learned that, we will find it very difficult to be committed in other areas as well. An older man once said that because of his upbringing he could say, "I would rather die than lie."

The story of a Spanish explorer, Cortez, who landed at Vera Cruz in 1519, can teach us a lesson about commitment. He began his conquest of Mexico with a small force of 700 men. Upon landing, he set fire to his fleet of eleven ships. His men on the shore watched their only means of retreat sink to the bottom of the Gulf of Mexico. There was now only one direction to move—forward into the Mexican interior to meet whatever might come their way.

We too must purposely destroy all avenues of retreat as Christ's disciples. We must resolve that whatever price is required to be His follower, we will pay it.

Daniel B. Miller, Middlebury, IN

Bible Reading: 1 Peter 2
One Year Bible Reading Plan:
2 Peter 3
Ezekiel 45, 46

It is better to not promise, than to promise and not keep it.

Attentiveness

That ye be mindful of the words which
were spoken before by the holy prophets.
2 Peter 3:2

When Henry Nelson of Wilmington, Delaware, arrived home one evening, he discovered that his apartment complex was being fumigated with hydrogen-cyanide. He removed the sign, tore down the barricade, and went in. Neighbors tried to warn him and called the authorities. But by the time help arrived, it was too late. Henry Nelson was dead.

Mount St. Helens in the Cascade Mountains of Washington state was dormant for several hundred years. However, a few years ago, authorities discovered that there was activity and reason to believe there might be a serious eruption. People were evacuated from the area. But Harry Truman, who had grown up on those beautiful slopes, refused to leave. When the eruption was over, Harry and his home were buried under tons of volcanic ash.

Both men disregarded both written and verbal warnings, and it cost them their lives. If they had learned to be attentive, they would not have died.

When we ignore the instructions of the written Word, we show the highest disregard for God.

"My son, hear the instructions of thy father, and forsake not the law of thy mother. For they shall be an ornament of grace unto thy head, and chains about thy neck" (Proverbs 1:8, 9).

Bible Reading: 2 Peter 3:1–14
One Year Bible Reading Plan:
1 John 1
Ezekiel 47, 48

Melvin L. Yoder, Gambier, OH

_____

Give ear, and live!

The Sunset

For to me to live is Christ, and to die is gain.
Philippians 1:21

Traveling home from the distant town of Jinotega late one afternoon, we were all tired. The road was bad, the vehicle was crowded, and it was one of those times when it would have felt really good to have been at home NOW instead of traveling another two or three hours. Jinotega is situated in a valley, among the beautiful rugged mountains of Nicaragua. Naturally, the road is a genuine mountain road, winding through the hills and hollows. As we rounded a curve, to our right unfolded one of the most beautiful sunsets one could ever hope to see. Out across a valley, behind a distant mountain, the sun was setting in full grandeur, like a golden ball of fire. Being from the western plains, we viewed the awesome scene with something like a holy emotion.

We say the elderly are in the sunset of life, but in reality, none of us, whether middle aged or young, know just where our "sun" is positioned on the horizon. The apostle Paul said in Philippians 1:20 whether by life or death his desire was to magnify Christ.

There is a feeling akin to a holy awe that comes over us when we take a tiny infant into our arms for the first time. The miracle of life is awesome. Is it any less awesome to stand by the still form of a loved one who has won the battle and gone to meet his Maker and his Savior? There is rejoicing in heaven over one soul that is saved, but what must take place when one saved soul returns to the God who gave it, having magnified the name of Christ first by his life, and then again by death?

Bible Reading: Philippians 1
One Year Bible Reading Plan:
1 John 2
Daniel 1, 2

Ivan Petre, Masaya, Nicaragua

To die is but to live—for eternity.

Honesty

For with what judgment ye judge, ye shall be judged; and with
what measure ye mete, it shall be measured to you again.
Matthew 7:2

Honesty is a fruit of a Spirit-filled life. Loving our neighbor as ourself prohibits our being dishonest with him.

The story is told of a farmer who delivered a pound of butter to the baker each week. In turn, he would purchase a loaf of bread from the baker. The baker noticed that the pound of butter seemed to be getting smaller and smaller. One day he confronted the farmer about the apparent problem.

"Don't you have scales to weigh your butter?" he asked.

"No," the farmer replied.

"Well," asked the baker, "how do you know you are giving me a pound of butter if you have no scales?"

The farmer answered, "I always use your loaf of bread, which is labeled one pound, as a balance."

Verse 12 of our Scripture reading teaches us to do to others as we would have them do to us. Verses 18–20 remind us that a good tree cannot bring forth evil fruit. Our daily conduct should reflect an attitude of putting others first. Let us always be sure to be honest in all our dealings.

Bible Reading: Matthew 7
One Year Bible Reading Plan:
1 John 3
Daniel 3, 4

Melvin L. Yoder, Gambier, OH

The best way to teach the Word is to live it.

The Comfort of God

I will not leave you comfortless; I will come to you.
John 14:18

Life seems cruel at times. A harsh word from someone you love and trust can bring pain and tears. We know that God has said, I will never leave you comfortless, but when death claims a loved one, we struggle, our hearts bleed, and we cry and reach out for someone to cling to. God asks us to love each other because He knows how frail we are.

A small Indian village had a rite of passage when a boy came to manhood. At sundown he was led deep into the forest to spend the night alone, without his knife, bow and arrow, or tomahawk for protection. This experience was intended to teach him to face fears, loneliness, and anxieties alone with no one to aid him. He sat alone in the chill of night, with the sounds of wildlife around him. Suddenly there arose the shrill, blood-curdling death shriek of a dying rabbit. Too slow to escape, he became the evening meal for a hungry prowler. The boy's hair stood on end. How he longed for the safety of home and his father's protective presence.

The boy was unaware that not many yards away his father stood guard behind a large tree, bow in hand, ready to kill any animal that might bother his son.

When death stalks the neighborhood and claims a loved one; when billows of doubt begin to roll, and uncertainty threatens; when fears and anxieties want to reign, and comfort seems far away; remember, our loving Father is stationed nearby, ready to help us in our time of need.

Bible Reading: John 14:25–29
One Year Bible Reading Plan:
1 John 4
Daniel 5, 6

Melvin L. Yoder, Gambier, OH

Trust is the conqueror of difficulties and fears.

Submission

It is good for a man that he bear the yoke in his youth.
Lamentations 3:27

Youth is a beautiful and challenging time of life. The Bible speaks of the strength of youth, but Solomon pleads with youth to remember their Creator. Jeremiah, in our text in Lamentations, tells us that we should bear the yoke in our youth. Why should a man bear the yoke in his youth?

When children are still very young, they must first learn obedience and submission to their parents. When they become young men and women, they will find it easier to surrender their wills and lives to Christ. They will recognize that they have not yet learned the hardest lessons of life and be willing to listen and quietly do what is required of them. As they quietly observe the lives of faithful men and women who weather the storms of life, it will help them find direction in later years, when they become more responsible and face more difficult decisions and problems.

We read in Lamentations 3:31 that God will not cast off forever; He will have compassion, and later we will realize the blessings of faith in Christ. Difficulties in our youth serve to create a solid foundation that will help us weather the storms of life.

| Bible Reading: Lamentations 3:22–36; Ecclesiastes 12 |
| One Year Bible Reading Plan: 1 John 5 / Daniel 7, 8 |

Paul Jantzi, Milverton, Ontario

The crown is not won in the beginning or middle of the race, but by he who endures to the end.

Hungry?

Blessed are they that do hunger and thirst
after righteousness: for they shall be filled.
Matthew 5:6

What makes you head toward the kitchen to look for something to eat? "Well," you say, "it is because I'm hungry." Okay, are you really hungry, or just bored? Sounds like Mom, right? We all know it is necessary to eat to have the energy we need to work. We often think we need three meals a day as well as some snacks. However, how much emphasis should we put on eating?

Job says, "I have esteemed the words of his mouth more than my necessary food." Job hungered more for God's Word than for natural food. Jesus expressed the same thought when He said His meat was to do the will of God.

When does food taste the best? When we are really hungry. Going to God's Word out of duty and not because of a real hunger for what He has for us is like going to the kitchen because we are bored. Reading God's Word, hearing the Word preached, praying, and fellowshiping with other believers are all ways we can be nourished in our spiritual lives.

When we sit down at the table to eat, we bow our heads and thank the Lord for the food before us. We ask Him to give us strength and nourishment from the food we are about to eat. We should do the same as we sit down to partake of the Word of God. Asking God to bless His Word to our lives will make victorious Christian living possible.

Bible Reading: Psalm 19:1–14
One Year Bible Reading Plan:
2 and 3 John
Daniel 9, 10

Mark Webb, Aroda, VA

_____

God is great, and God is good,
and we thank Him for our food.

The Rock Higher Than I

What time I am afraid, I will trust in thee.
Psalm 56:3

This psalm is a Michtam of David, which some believe means "jewel" or "golden," that is to say, a poem of brilliant thoughts, worthy to be engraved in permanent records.

This prayer was raised to heaven while 1 Samuel 21:10–15 was happening. David faced some very difficult situations. He prayed to God for mercy. His life was hanging on a thread, and he was often at death's door. But his faith was as strong as a rock, because he trusted in his "strong Rock," in God, . . . the strength of his heart (Psalm 73:26). He asked, "Lead me to the rock that is higher than I" (Psalm 61:2).

Of what was David afraid? He had enemies distorting his words; their thoughts were against him for evil; they gathered themselves together; they hid themselves; they marked his steps; they even waited for the poor psalmist's soul. How would you feel if many would hide, not only looking closely at your steps, but also waiting for your soul? No doubt you, too, as the psalmist, would confess: "Thou tellest my wandering." You would also pray, ". . . put thou my tears in thy bottle: are they not in thy book?"

But even so, the psalmist's testimony was tremendous, ". . . this I know; for God is for me." Let us remember, "If God is for us, who can be against us?" "I will not fear what man can do unto me." "When I cry unto thee, then shall my enemies turn back." "Shall they escape by iniquity? In thine anger cast down the people, O God." What a demonstration of God's power! David only had to cry unto Him! Do you know how everything is going to end up? (Read verses 10–13.) Psalm 34 is David's song of thanksgiving for this freedom.

We, too, when facing distress, can apply all of our resources. But let us not forget that the most important thing is to pray and trust God for the results.

Richard del Cristo, Bonao,
Dominican Republic

Bible Reading: Psalm 56
One Year Bible Reading Plan:
Jude
Daniel 11, 12

Fear God, and you will have nothing else to fear.

Peace Be Unto Us

In whom we have redemption through his blood,
the forgiveness of sins, according to the riches of his grace.
Ephesians 1:7

The Apostle Paul starts most of his letters with the salutation, "Grace be unto you and peace from God the Father and from our Lord Jesus Christ." It is important to notice that peace is a result of understanding and experiencing grace. How do we experience grace? "For by grace are ye saved through faith . . ." (Ephesians 2:8). We can see that faith is the channel, grace is the source, and peace is the result.

Paul gives us a clear picture of God's gift of salvation by grace in Ephesians 2:4–7. In this passage the apostle tells us that the purpose of salvation is to bring man into a relationship with God in which God can demonstrate the surpassing riches of His grace to all believers in Christ forever more. The blessings of grace are seen in the unconditional love of God (v. 4), in the believer's new life and position in Christ (vv. 5, 6), and in his inheritance of the riches of God's limitless grace (v. 2).

It is necessary to realize first of all that grace does not originate with man but with God. God is an infinite being. He is without limits, extending beyond measure or comprehension, without beginning or end. Everything coming from God is the same, including His gift of grace. Since the gift of grace is manifested in God's giving His only begotten Son (John 3:16), the motivation for grace can be nothing less than the infinite love and goodness of God. Grace is infinite love expressing itself in infinite goodness.

Bible Reading: Ephesians 2
One Year Bible Reading Plan:
Revelation 1
Hosea 1—4

Marvin Gingerich, Meadville, PA

Not by works lest any man should boast.

Everything Goes Wrong

For Christ also hath once suffered for sins, the
just for the unjust, that he might bring us to God.
1 Peter 3:18a

The hay lies dry and brittle in the noonday sun. It is indeed time to get it baled. The sun shines with full force on the pair out in the hay field. The baler bangs and clatters, the tractor chugs, and the wagon lurches along behind. The boy grabs another heavy bale and throws it to the top of the load. A shower of chaff sticks on his arms and face, which are pouring out perspiration. As the boy grabs another heavy bale, the twine bursts in midair. The bale explodes in all directions. The bales keep coming, but the baler has stopped knotting on the right side. The bales spill out onto the wagon. The boy yells with all his might. The half-asleep tractor driver jerks awake and stomps on the brakes. The jerk is too hard. The precariously stacked bales slowly tip to the ground despite the boy who desperately tries to hold them back but is knocked flat. The sun keeps shining, hotter than ever. The load is tipped, the baler does not work, and feelings are aroused.

How do we respond to our loved ones when everything goes wrong? So often we snap and growl irritably or put a scowl on our faces and do not say a word, but inside we are boiling over. How did our Savior react when everything went wrong? All His friends forsook Him, and He was falsely accused and badly mistreated. He kept right on loving them with compassion and never lashed out with angry words.

A jar of honey and a jar of vinegar stand side by side. Their true contents are not revealed until they are upset. We, too, are revealed when we are upset. Are we sweet or sour?

Bible Reading: 1 Peter 3:8–22
One Year Bible Reading Plan:
Revelation 2
Hosea 5—8

Edward Lambright, Campbell Hill, IL

_____

The true test of your character is when everything goes wrong.

With Wings As Eagles

God is our refuge and strength, a very present help in trouble.
Psalm 46:1

"Be still and know that I am God; I will be exalted among the heathen, I will be exalted in the earth" (Psalm 46:10). This is a key to receiving strength from the Lord. We have to "be still" and realize who God is. Everything that we know is created of God. He is the Master of the universe. If we do not recognize God as such, then we will try to draw strength from the wrong source.

We must also realize that we are nothing of ourselves. If we depend on our own strength, we will soon fail because we are human. God does not make mistakes; what surer source of strength can we have? "What shall we then say to these things? If God be for us, who can be against us?" (Romans 8:31).

God is often referred to as "The Rock." Jesus is referred to as the chief cornerstone. In Psalm 18:2, David talks about the Lord being his "rock." "The Lord is my rock, and my fortress, and my deliverer, my God, my strength, in whom I will trust; my buckler, and the horn of my salvation, and my high tower." When we build a house, we put the foundation on a solid base. If we did not, it would only be a matter of time before the house would fall apart. Likewise, if we do not base our faith on the Lord Jesus Christ, it is just a matter of time before our spiritual lives will crumble and fall apart.

Bible Reading: Psalm 46
One Year Bible Reading Plan:
Revelation 3
Hosea 9—11

The Bible makes it very plain that the Lord is the only true source of strength (Isaiah 40:31; Psalm 27:1). Let us live our lives in such a way that there is no question that true strength comes only from God.

Lael B. Miller, Sugarcreek, OH

Give me, O God, this day, a strong and
vivid sense that Thou art by my side.

A Learning Process

Look not every man on his own things,
but every man also on the things of others.
Philippians 2:4

For nine years we had only one child. We were able to give him all our attention. To us he was special. After we received our daughter by adoption, our relationship with our son had to alter a bit. No longer were we able to give him all our attention. At first it was a bit difficult both for him and for us.

Now we have two unique children. There is sufficient love and attention for both, but there needed to be a learning process. Having a sister takes away some of the loneliness of being an only child. But there is also some give and take involved. There are things to learn from each other.

Our interests tend to be turned inward. We are selfish by nature. Changing that is a learning process. As we rub shoulders with others, we broaden our horizons a bit.

Each one of us is unique in our own way, but we need to give up the idea of being special, or expecting to be privileged above others. We are not above or below any other.

When we receive Jesus as Lord and Savior of our life, we learn how selfish we really are. As we learn from Jesus, our desires and interests begin to change. Little by little the Holy Spirit points out these needs to us. Becoming like Jesus is a learning process.

Wayne Miller, Crossville, TN

Bible Reading: Philippians 2:1–24
One Year Bible Reading Plan:
Revelation 4
Hosea 12—14

When we take an interest in the things of
God and others, we become less selfish.

How Does Your Countenance Read?

For thou hast made him most blessed for ever: thou hast made him exceeding glad with thy countenance.
Psalm 21:6

We notice in today's Bible reading that if we sing praises to the Lord with a glad and joyful countenance, we can be blessed of the Lord. It is our desire to be blessed of the Lord and also to be a blessing to others. We can be a blessing to a brother or sister if we meet them with a smile or with a glad and joyful countenance. We may uplift another's spirit if he is troubled or downcast for any reason. It is a real ministry to have a joyful or cheerful attitude.

We need to be sure that we do not act out of pretense. In Psalm 43:5 David asked this question: "Why art thou cast down, O my soul? and why art thou disquieted within me? hope in God: for I shall yet praise him, who is the health of my countenance, and my God." The Lord God gives a healthy countenance. Only in Him can we experience joy and gladness.

Let us reflect the peace and joy of our Lord Jesus as we mingle with the world so they will desire the same thing. Let us encourage one another to good works and to strive to have a closer walk with God. May it be our desire to follow Jesus' teachings more and to bring forth more fruit for His glory.

"Thou hast made known to me the ways of life; thou shalt make me full of joy with thy countenance" (Acts 2:28).

Amos Garber, Rosebush, MI

Bible Reading: Psalm 21
One Year Bible Reading Plan:
Revelation 5
Joel

The light of God's Son in your heart will put His sunshine on your face.

Life or Death

Let no corrupt communication proceed out of your mouth,
but that which is good to the use of edifying,
that it may minister grace unto the hearers.
Ephesians 4:29

Do you realize the power we have to help or harm others? In Proverbs 18:21 we read that death and life are in the power of the tongue.

These life-words might be called encouragement. Every Christian, regardless of gift or training, is called upon to encourage his brothers and sisters (Hebrews 10:24).

God instructs us to encourage one another whenever we come together. There are many ways to encourage one another by kind deeds, but the capacity of words to do serious damage or great good makes verbal encouragement an especially important subject to consider.

It is interesting and a bit distressing to notice how often our polite greetings like "Good to see you," or "How are you?" are only gracefully disguised ways of saying, "Keep your distance; I'm just being polite." I suppose we must accept that everyday life will include many situations where words are superficial, but it should not be that way among believers.

We must no longer be content with shallow words that mean little. We must set out with a clear awareness that words can both tear down and build up. Words are like a sharp knife—in the hands of a surgeon a knife can heal, but in the hands of a careless child it can harm.

Words can encourage, discourage, or do nothing. Shallow words accomplish little, death-words discourage, and life-words encourage. We must learn to speak sincerely, using our words to help other Christians pursue the pathway of obedience more zealously.

| Bible Reading: Ephesians 4:11–29 |
| One Year Bible Reading Plan: Revelation 6, Amos 1—3 |

Leon Jay Hershberger, Mio, MI

Many people seem to live in utter disregard
of the effect of their words on others.

Bear One Another's Burdens

Bear ye one another's burdens, and so fulfil the law of Christ.
Galatians 6:2

A few years ago while touring Grand Canyon National Park, my wife and I were hiking down the trail with its twists, turns, and steep declines. We noticed various people coming up the trail. Some were climbing vigorously, while others with heavy burdens on their backs were climbing more slowly. We especially noticed an elderly couple with heavy bags advancing slowly up the mountain.

Upon returning back up the trail, we observed this elderly couple once more. They had not progressed much farther, and the wife had a bloody wound on her forehead. We asked them what happened. They explained that she had stumbled because of the weight she was carrying. She fell, hitting her head against a rock. We offered to carry her pack up the mountain, which she accepted.

Because we had not taken anything along to eat, we were also soon tired. Another couple took notice and gave us some of their trail mix, which refreshed us and gave us new strength to proceed.

I had to think how much this is like our Christian life. If we take notice of people, we may see a brother or sister struggling when their going grows tough. We can lighten their load by giving them a word of encouragement, visiting with them, and telling them we care.

In the same way, if we share our burdens with a friend, we become refreshed and can all help each other proceed up the mountain of life.

Friends, let's help someone carry their burden. They may lighten yours someday.

Bible Reading: Galatians 6
One Year Bible Reading Plan:
Revelation 7
Amos 4—6

Steven Hershberger, Millersburg, OH

_____

To bear is to care.

December 17

Saving the Shipwrecked

Finally, be ye all of one mind, having compassion one of another, love as brethren, be pitiful, be courteous.
1 Peter 3:8

A parable I learned about has come to mean a lot to me. It compares the church with a lifesaving station. It has challenged me to put my profession into action. Our churches should be reaching out to the lost and ministering to needs whether those needs are in our church or "out there."

There is a danger of our churches becoming a "club," just a social place for our own benefit. When this happens, we become overly concerned with the size and condition of our church buildings. We become critical and judgmental of those who are being rescued, not sure if we want them in our church. We find it harder and harder to actually brave the sea, looking for and rescuing the lost. We are content to let others, who have dedicated themselves to doing it full time, do the "unpleasant task."

There is a danger that my life will become out of touch with the heart of the Father, so I will not be concerned with those outside of my small circle. Material pursuits, focusing on myself, pride, sin in my life, being too busy with good things, not spending time alone with God, and many other things may drown out the call to reach out to those around me.

What about my life, my church? Am I active in saving shipwrecked souls? Shipwrecks are occurring all around us. Many are perishing each day. Do I really care? If so, how much?

"Lord, forgive me for my apathy. Forgive me for my lack of compassion, without which I lose the motivation to action! Father, draw me close to you today; help me walk, listening to Your Spirit, so that when you prompt me, I will do whatever You ask. Then Your work will be accomplished, and Your name will be glorified."

Bible Reading: Matthew 25:34–46
One Year Bible Reading Plan:
Revelation 8
Amos 7—9

Michael Webb, Hoagland, IN

Take an inward look so that you can reach out.

No Fault

Then said these men, We shall not find any occasion against this Daniel,
except we find it against him concerning the law of his God.
Daniel 6:5

The story of Daniel in the lion's den is often told to children with outstanding exclamations about God sending an angel to shut the lions' mouths. But I would like to focus on Daniel's worship of God and the testimony of the other two presidents and the 220 princes concerning Daniel.

These men said, "We shall not find any occasion against this Daniel, except we find it against him concerning the law of his God." If someone was watching to try to "frame" us, would they come to the same conclusion that these men had about Daniel?

They could find no fault with Daniel's life. "Forasmuch as he was faithful, neither was there any error or fault found in him" (Daniel 6:4).

They tried to find mistakes he had made, but they could not find anything of which to accuse him. So they concluded that they must find something concerning the law of his God. The king was sorry that he had allowed his vanity to get him into a corner, and he tried hard to find a way to deliver Daniel. But because the law of the Medes and Persians could not be altered, he commanded Daniel to be cast into the lions' den.

Look at what he said: "Thy God whom thou servest continually, he will deliver thee." What a testimony!

Do our neighbors, co-workers, or even our enemies say this about us? I recall an ungodly boss saying about one of the brethren who was his employee that he would build the world on his word.

May we seek to live so that no fault can be found in us, other than concerning the law of our God.

Allan Miller, Sarcoxie, MO

Bible Reading: Daniel 6
One Year Bible Reading Plan:
  Revelation 9
  Obadiah

God, thee only will I serve.

December 19

Sowing and Reaping

*Be not deceived; God is not mocked: for
whatsoever a man soweth, that shall he also reap.*
Galatians 6:7

While Jesus spoke with the woman at the well, the disciples
went into the city to buy food. Upon their return, He said, "I say
unto you, lift up your eyes and look on the fields; for they are white
already to harvest" (John 4:35). We are sowing seed every day,
whether it is good seed or bad. Let us examine ourselves to be sure
it is good seed and will reap life everlasting. Let us not give the
world reason to doubt our faith and our walk with Jesus.

In John 4:31–34 we read, "In the mean time his disciples prayed
him, saying, Master, eat. But he said unto them, I have meat to eat
which ye know not of. . . . My meat is to do the will of him that sent
me, and to finish his work." We do not have any indication of Jesus
eating or drinking anything while He was at this place. It seems as
if Jesus was more concerned about the harvest than about His hunger. Shouldn't we also be more concerned about lost souls than
about hunger and quenching our thirst? Let us take the many opportunities that come our way to witness to a lost and dying world.

Do I let my light shine so the unregenerated in heart may be
convinced that there is more to life than just living for self and for
pleasure? The harvest is today; it will not wait. Many souls are passing on to their reward—some to eternal bliss, others to eternal doom!
Let us be zealous in the Lord's work. "And let us not be weary in
well doing: for in due season we shall reap, if we faint not" (Galatians 6:9). Someone who faints is oblivious to his surroundings; he
is of no assistance to anyone. Let us follow Paul's admonition to be
urgent in serving the Lord in every area of our Christian life. "Therefore, my beloved brethren, be ye
steadfast, unmoveable, always
abounding in the work of the
Lord, forasmuch as ye know that
your labor is not in vain in the
Lord" (1 Corinthians 15:58).

> **Bible Reading:** Galatians 6
> **One Year Bible Reading Plan:**
>   Revelation 10
>   Jonah

Amos Garber, Rosebush, MI

Sow good seed along your pathway. It will bring forth good fruit.

God's Word Is Alive

Being born again, not of corruptible seed, but of incorruptible,
by the word of God, which liveth and abideth forever.
1 Peter 1:23

I have often marveled at the tremendous potential hidden in a tiny seed. If a seed is given the right conditions, it can blossom into a productive plant or tree. In a similar way, God's Word can transform a spiritually dead person into a fruitful Christian.

At a young age I started working for my uncle because there was not enough work for all of us at home. Since I always loved to read, I would spend my evenings reading my uncle's new Bible story books. The Bible stories were interesting, but they also made a deep impression in my heart.

A number of years went by as I worked for several other farmers. I finally reached the age when I became accountable for my sins. I began searching for an answer to the need I felt in my heart. I read any religious literature that I could get my hands on. The final result of this search was that God found His way into my heart. The peace and joy within was wonderful beyond words!

When I look back over those years, I conclude that some good seed was planted in my heart through those wonderful Bible stories. The Bible tells us that the rain and snow are sent from heaven to water the earth that man might have bread. "So shall my word be that goeth forth out of my mouth: it shall not return unto me void, but it shall accomplish that which I please, and it shall prosper in the thing whereto I send it" (Isaiah 55:11).

Bible Reading: Isaiah 55; Jeremiah 23:29
One Year Bible Reading Plan:
Revelation 11
Micah 1—4:8

As parents, we should not neglect to plant the precious seed into our children's hearts. God honors His Word and will perform a miracle in their hearts years later.

Raymond Martin, Lewistown, PA

The entrance of thy words giveth light;
it giveth understanding unto the simple.
—Psalm 119:130

359

Why Me?

For ye are bought with a price: therefore glorify God in
your body, and in your spirit, which are God's.
1 Corinthians 6:20

I am sure you have heard this question before. It can be asked in desperation, mockery, disbelief, or thankfulness. I would like to propose that this is a question that we should ask ourselves daily. See how many of these apply to you. "Why was I born in North America instead of some Third World country?" "Why was I permitted to hear the Gospel and come to the saving knowledge of Jesus Christ when over 2 billion people have yet to hear the Gospel once?" "Why should I enjoy having God's written Word so freely when 80 percent of the world has never owned a Bible?" "Why do I live in financial luxury when 40,000 people are dying daily because of starvation or malnutrition-related diseases?" "Why me?"

Although we may never know the answers to these and other questions, I think we can attempt some answers. God has been speaking to me about the responsibility I have to the rest of the world, to both unbelievers and Christians. There are opportunities all around us today. Today, Christians in democratic nations have more financial means and more advantages such as advanced communication, easier travel, and better education than ever before. Surely God has not blessed us with all this only to have us heap it upon ourselves, satisfying only our own desires.

"Lord, help me to really understand my situation as compared to the rest of the world. Help me to first give You praise and adoration for Your blessings. Help me to understand that everything I have belongs to You. Lord, I dedicate my all to You for Your work, Your service, Your church, and Your world. I give my money, time, talents, abilities, reputation, and everything that I am or have. Lord, I am bought with a price— I am yours. Do with me as You please."

Michael Webb, Woodburn, IN

Bible Reading: 2 Corinthians 9
One Year Bible Reading Plan:
Revelation 12
Micah 4:9—7

Help me, Lord, to answer the question, "Why me?"

Moldy Cheese and Hairy Bread

_But seek ye first the kingdom of God and his righteousness:
and all these things shall be added unto you._
Matthew 6:33

Oley Severson was born in Sweden and grew up in a family of fishermen. Due to hard times, Oley decided to cross over to the "promised land" of America. He was poor, but after several years of scrounging he saved enough to buy the ticket. He decided to save on his fare by taking some food along. He bought a large slab of good country cheese and seven loaves of dark rye bread.

The departure day came, and he was on his way with his food and a small sea chest. Day after day, Oley ate cheese and rye bread, but thoughts of his future outweighed the inconvenience.

But alas, storms swept across the ocean, slowing the ship considerably and adding to the days of travel. Oley was tired of the now musty cheese and blue-green hairy-edged bread. How good was the smell from the kitchen above! Finally, he gathered courage and decided to visit the area from which this good smell of food came. He wandered up the two flights of stairs, being careful to stay out of the waiters' way. Suddenly a ship's officer noticed him and berated him for being a potential stumbling block. Oley, being desperate, blurted out to the officer (with the limited English he knew) of his present food predicament. The officer could hardly believe his ears! "Hey, you know what? When you bought your tickets, your meals were included. And you have been eating only moldy bread and cheese!" Soon word swept over the ship and people flocked to the dining room door to get a look at this young man. But Oley did not care. He had two more days of travel left and not a moment to lose. He hunched down and started eating the delicious food before him.

My friend, since you have accepted Christ as your Savior, what food have you been eating? This world has nothing to offer but moldy cheese and hairy bread! The price has been paid in full at Calvary. Let us not be foolish and lose out on the faithful promises of God!

Bible Reading: Matthew 6:19–34
One Year Bible Reading Plan:
Revelation 13
Nahum

Wayne E. Miller, Rushsylvania, OH

Blessed are they which do hunger and thirst after righteousness: for they shall be filled.
—Matthew 5:6

December 23

New Leaves

For as he thinketh in his heart, so is he.
Proverbs 23:7a

"I would sure like to have one of those," I thought as I admired a flourishing banana plant in a friend's classroom. To my delight, I was later able to obtain two of them. With enthusiasm, I planted them in the backyard, giving them plenty of water. And grow—did they ever grow! Fresh new leaves unfurled one after the other from the center of the plant. It reinforced over and over this law of God: life results in growth.

I saw it clearly in my thriving banana plants. It can be seen as well in the lives of those who are grafted into the vine—Jesus Christ. The presence of this new life through Jesus always results in new growth.

As Christians, it is reassuring to notice this growth in our spiritual lives. However, we sometimes wonder (especially at the end of the year), "Have I really grown this past year?"

How can we tell? Where in our lives can we place a spiritual growth and temperature gauge?

Can we place this gauge on our words? Although this is a helpful place to observe, it is not a foolproof area to place our gauge. It is quite possible for us to learn a "Christian's" vocabulary and become very adept at using it properly in our prayers and testimonies, and yet have no real leaves of growth unfurling in our lives.

How about placing the gauge on our actions? This is more reliable than our words. But, again, basically any good deed we do can be cleverly done with a wrong motive behind the deed. What appears to others as new leaves of growth in our lives, may be done selfishly and proudly reducing them to dead foliage of little value to God.

An old Puritan writer has wisely observed the most reliable area to place our spiritual temperature gauge. Put it on your heart. Check the desires of your heart. What do you want, and what do you long for? This gives a most accurate reading because the things I desire cannot be counterfeited. In all reality, I am what I want.

Joshua Yoder, Clarkson, KY

Bible Reading: John 15:1–17
One Year Bible Reading Plan:
Revelation 14
Habakkuk

Check for new leaves today.

Jesus Signed My Pardon

And if Christ be in you, the body is dead because of sin;
but the Spirit is life because of righteousness.
Romans 8:10

In 1830, a man named George Wilson was arrested for mail theft for which death was the penalty. After a time, President Andrew Jackson gave Wilson a pardon, but Wilson refused to accept it! The authorities were puzzled. Should Wilson be freed or put to death?

They consulted Chief Justice John Marshall, who handed down this decision: "A pardon is a slip of paper, the value of which is determined by the acceptance of the person to be pardoned. If it is refused, it is no pardon. George Wilson must be put to death."

We, too, are sentenced to death because of our sinful nature, since Adam and Eve fell into sin in the Garden of Eden. Jesus Christ pardoned us from our sins by dying for us on the cross.

"Let the wicked forsake his way, and the unrighteous man his thoughts: and let him return unto the Lord, and he will have mercy upon him; and to our God, for he will abundantly pardon" (Isaiah 55:7). Now it is our choice if we are going to accept that pardon through faith in Jesus Christ. Through faith He sends us His Holy Spirit to guide us into all truth.

Bible Reading: Romans 8:1–18
One Year Bible Reading Plan:
Revelation 15
Zephaniah

If you have never accepted God's pardon, now is the time to believe and be saved.

Elmer Stoltzfus, New Holland, PA

Greater love hath no man than this, that a
man lay down his life for his friends.
—John 15:13

The Birth of a Savior

*Let us now go even unto Bethlehem, and see this thing which
is come to pass, which the Lord hath made known unto us.*
Luke 2:15b

Do you find this story dry and boring? Have you heard it so often that it has lost its beauty? The story of Christ's birth, like all of the Bible, should never grow old for us. If we have a vibrant relationship with the Man whose birth is told here, then the story will hold great depths of meaning for us.

Two thousand years ago Jesus left the splendor of heaven to come to this sin-cursed earth to live a hard life and to suffer a horrible death. He did not have to do it. Why should the Creator suffer for the created? In His position, I probably would have said, "It is their own fault. They are just getting what they deserve. Why did they have to go and sin in the first place? It is not my problem. Why should I die for them?" But His love for you and me was so great that He willingly came to earth in such an humble manner.

Pause for a moment and consider what the Son of God had to give up to come and provide a way of salvation for us. Isn't it amazing? Doesn't it thrill your heart with joy? Doesn't it make you want to love Him who loved us so greatly?

Many have heard the good tidings of the birth of Christ like the shepherds did, but few have taken the spiritual journey to Bethlehem to "see this thing which is come to pass." Many are celebrating Christmas, but few know the Christ of Christmas.

May we make Christmas a day of remembering what Christ has done for us.

Henry Yoder, Clarkson, KY

Bible Reading: Luke 2:1–20
One Year Bible Reading Plan:
Revelation 16
Haggai

---

*The birth of Christ brought God to man, but it took
the cross of Christ to bring man to God.*

Our Great God

The heavens declare the glory of God;
and the firmament sheweth his handywork.
Psalm 19:1

As I took a little stroll in the woods, I noticed many things going on in nature. A deer bounded gracefully out of sight, squirrels chattered and played in the leaves, and birds sang their sweetest notes. There were hardy plants of all kinds growing. The bigger plants stood tall where I could see them plainly. The smaller flowers and ferns were not so easy to see, but each was in the place where God had put it and was growing hardily.

We often refer to this as nature, but it is more than nature. There is a great God controlling all of this.

"Nevertheless he left not himself without witness, in that he did good, and gave us rain from heaven, and fruitful seasons, filling our hearts with food and gladness" (Acts 14:17).

God causes the rain to water these things. He gives the sunshine to make them grow. Often when there is a thunderstorm with lightning flashing and thunder cracking loudly, we almost cringe under the greatness of God. But do we also see God's greatness when we look at nature and the peaceful quiet things on this earth?

"Before the mountains were brought forth, or ever thou hadst formed the earth and the world, even from everlasting to everlasting, thou art God" (Psalm 90:2). Do we believe this? God is from everlasting to everlasting. The God our forefathers and the patriarchs served is still the same God today. Truly we serve a wonderful God!

Steven Farmwald, Albany, KY

Bible Reading: Psalms 97, 98
One Year Bible Reading Plan:
Revelation 17
Zechariah 1—3

God is great, therefore He will be sought;
God is good, therefore He will be found.

December 27

Setting Goals

I press toward the mark for the prize of the high calling of God in Christ Jesus.
Philippians 3:14

In school we emphasize the importance of setting goals. We teach the children not only to set goals, but also to do their very best to attain those goals. We set goals regarding our finances. We have goals for our future. We set goals to lose weight or get more exercise. We have goals to spend more time with our families. It is important to set worthwhile goals and work hard to obtain them.

The Apostle Paul had a goal to be all that he could be for God. This goal is the most essential goal of our Christian lives. How do you know what God wants you to be? God has a race for you to run. He does not show us the entire course, but He has told us what the final prize will be. Listen for the call of God on our life, and move forward. Put your best into every situation and opportunity God brings your way. Be the best you can be for God.

In setting spiritual goals, we must focus on knowing Christ. We must be willing to forget or leave those other trophies we may have achieved. If we are weighted down by hanging onto our past accomplishments, we may lose the final prize. Paul says, "Follow me, as I follow Christ." Knowing Christ is more than knowing about Christ. It is being a part of His sufferings, death, and resurrection. May God help us to set goals that we also may encourage others to follow!

Mark Webb, Aroda, VA

Bible Reading: Philippians 3
One Year Bible Reading Plan:
Revelation 18
Zechariah 4—6

If you aim for nothing, you are sure to hit it. Aim high!

Lift Up Your Eyes

For I know that my redeemer liveth, and that he shall stand
at the latter day upon the earth: And though after my skin
worms destroy this body, yet in my flesh shall I see God.
Job 19:25, 26

If there is one identifying characteristic among those we call "great," it would have to be the sense of purpose found in a goal.

David was surely aware of this. His son at a later date posted the warning, "Where there is no vision, the people perish."

"Lift up your eyes," David wrote. Look beyond the humdrum of the here and now and set some goals. The spark of life, after all, is found in the expectancy of anticipation. A goal tends to pull us out of the run of complacency; it energizes us and gives a reason for doing what we are doing, beyond the mere need of completing the task at hand.

Goals are not limited to any particular individual but are available to everyone, regardless of age, race, or color.

Goals. For some, the word has a rather stern, demanding sound. They speak of discipline and commitment. This is true. But in practice they are the perfect antidote to that abiding human tendency—laziness. Unspoken or spelled out, they keep us on track. Call it a target or a destination, they not only keep our focus on the future, but provide a sure sense of where we have been.

There are many valid goals for us to strive for. Then again you may be satisfied with the ultimate goal, the one overshadowing desire, the guiding principle for every word and action. D. L. Moody called it, "my Coronation Day." In that day we discover that the Bible is indeed true. That which we presently call death will usher us into the realms of eternal life. It will be a marvelous goal attained. Truly a grand finale!

Bible Reading: Psalms 121, 122
One Year Bible Reading Plan:
Revelation 19
Zechariah 7—9

Jerry Yoder, Auburn, KY

Direction determines destiny.

The Second Advent

*For as the lightning cometh out of the east, and shineth even
unto the west; so shall also the coming of the Son of man be.*
Matthew 24:27

The moment that you are reading this, the second advent has
not yet come. Yet it is closer than when you started reading the
title. Around two thousand years have passed since His first coming. The second millennium has come and gone. The signs of spring
can be seen, proclaiming that the time is fast approaching. Since
the ascension of Jesus, men have awaited the day of His return with
anticipation, but many dawns have come, the sun has set, and still
He has not come.

Each one of us will someday come face to face with Him. We
have no other choice. But we do have a choice how we will meet
Him. If we know Him, we have nothing to fear; but if we do not
know Him, we have need to be concerned. Jesus will come like a
flash of lightning out of the sky with power and great glory to require
the salvation that He provided the first time He walked among
men. He will meet us as we are at the time. All things will lay open
and unhidden before Him in the
day of judgment. John the Baptist and Jesus both proclaimed
that we need to repent, for the
kingdom of heaven is at hand.
Let us patiently await His arrival
with expectation!

> **Bible Reading:** Matthew 24
> **One Year Bible Reading Plan:**
>   Revelation 20
>   Zechariah 10—12

Harvey D. Yoder, Marion, MI

Waiting denotes readiness.

Me and God and a Cave

_. . . And after the fire a still small voice. And it was so, when Elijah
heard it, that he wrapped his face in his mantle, and went out,
and stood in the entering in of the cave._
1 Kings 19:12, 13

I sat at the mouth of a cave that my brother and his friends had
discovered about thirty-five years ago. I marveled at the quietness
that so delicately touched this secluded place. Here there was no
roar of traffic or the tiresome babbles of busy life. There was just
God-induced silence. Isn't it remarkable how loud God is in silence?
He spoke to me there in His beautiful way, as I intently listened to
His every word.

God and I communed there in the cave for quite some time.
One thing that I love God for is that not once did He condemn me
for past sins. The quiet presence of God moved upon me and caused
me to gather my thoughts and bring them to the obedience of Christ.
Praise overwhelmed me, and I worshiped God. I felt that even the
trees would clap their hands (Isaiah 55:12).

When it is just you and a cave, the silence screams harshly at
you. If it is you, God, and a cave, the silence is kind as He tenderly
whispers to you. Do you want a blessing today? Find a cave and
listen. If you don't have a cave, then find a closet, a barn, a bedroom, or any place that is quiet. Maybe you do not have time for a
cave? Maybe you do not have
time for silence? Maybe you do
not have time for God? If you
want to find a cave, you can find
one. But if you wait too long, you
might eventually not want one
(Hebrews 3:7, 8).

Bible Reading: Psalm 1
One Year Bible Reading Plan:
Revelation 21
Zechariah 13, 14

Alvin Mast, Millersburg, OH

Be still and know that I am God.
—Psalm 46:10

Get Rid of Your Burdens

Casting all your care upon him; for he careth for you.
1 Peter 5:7

A man was driving along a road with his horse and wagon when he came upon a man walking. The pedestrian had a heavy bag over his shoulder. The driver stopped and offered the other a ride, which he gladly accepted. As they were traveling on, he noticed that the man still had his bundle on his shoulder. The driver asked the traveler why he did not set the bundle on the wagon and relax as they were driving. The man replied, "It is very kind of you to take me along, but I don't want you to have to carry my bundle also."

Some people want to take their burden to the Lord, and then bring it home again to worry and fret over. The song writer says, "Take your burden to the Lord and leave it there."

In Matthew 11:28, 29, Jesus said, "Come unto me, all ye that labour and are heavy laden, and I will give you rest. Take my yoke upon you and learn of me; for I am meek, and lowly in heart: and ye shall find rest unto your souls." This rest speaks of eternal rest for the soul.

The dictionary defines "yoke" as that which joins together or closely unites. If we are joined together and closely united with Jesus, He will carry our burdens. If you are heavy laden and weary, cast your burden at Jesus' feet, at the foot of the cross. Then you can experience the peace and joy that is possible only in Christ Jesus.

Bible Reading: 1 Peter 5
One Year Bible Reading Plan:
Revelation 22
Malachi

Elmer Stoltzfus, Dundee, NY

If you trust, you don't worry; if you worry, you don't trust.

Contributors Index

T

Troyer, Andrew 6/18
Troyer, Ben.................................... 1/8, 2/13
Troyer, Dale 4/1, 9/2
Troyer, Jesse 4/4
Troyer, Marcus 3/7, 3/8, 11/25
Troyer, Melvin 11/27, 11/28
Troyer, Vernon 8/10
Troyer, William 11/23

W

Wagler, Stephen 8/2
Webb, Mark 2/14, 2/25, 1/24, 3/31,
     5/20, 6/14, 6/24, 8/5, 8/27, 9/9, 11/6,
     11/13, 12/8, 12/27
Webb, Michael 1/10, 12/17, 12/21

Y

Yoder, David Lee 5/8, 6/25
Yoder, Eli 5/27, 6/22, 11/20
Yoder, Ervin 4/5, 4/26
Yoder, Floyd 9/3
Yoder, Harvey 1/28, 5/26, 11/10,
     11/19, 12/29

Yoder, Henry 2/23, 8/20, 12/25
Yoder, Jadon 3/25
Yoder, Jamin 9/7
Yoder, Jerry 1/18, 3/9, 3/30, 7/5, 9/19,
     9/22, 10/6, 10/21, 11/18, 12/28
Yoder, Jim 5/11, 5/25, 11/4
Yoder, Joshua 4/30, 8/14, 8/15, 12/23
Yoder, Kore 10/12
Yoder, Leland 3/28
Yoder, Leon 1/27, 5/5
Yoder, Melvin 2/6, 3/5, 5/31, 6/23,
     7/7, 8/30, 9/16, 9/25, 12/3, 12/5, 12/6
Yoder, Menno 8/18
Yoder, Nelson 7/21
Yoder, Noah 9/28
Yoder, Tim 2/27
Yoder, Timothy 2/24
Yoder, Timothy 1/25
Yoder, Wesley 8/25
Yutzy , Rudy 9/4

Z

Zehr, Lester 3/14, 7/1

373

Scripture Index

Dates in bold type identify the daily key verses

380

Subject Index

385

386

You Can Find Our Books at These Stores:

CALIFORNIA
Squaw Valley
 Sequoia Christian Books
 559/332-2606

COLORADO
Fruita
 Grand Valley Dry Goods
 970/858-1268

FLORIDA
Orlando
 Borders Books and Music
 407/826-8912
Miami
 Alpha and Omega
 305/273-1263

GEORGIA
Glennville
 Vision Bookstore
 912/654-4086
Montezuma
 The Family Book Shop
 478/472-5166

ILLINOIS
Arthur
 Clearview Fabrics and Books
 217/543-9091
Ava
 Pineview Books
 584 Bollman Road

INDIANA
Grabill
 Graber's Bookstore
 260/627-2882
LaGrange
 Pathway Bookstore
 2580 North 250 West
Middlebury
 F and L Country Store
 574/825-7513

 Laura's Fabrics
 55140 County Road 43
Nappanee
 Little Nook Bookstore
 574/642-1347
Odon
 Dutch Pantry
 812/636-7922

 Schrock's Kountry Korner
 812/636-7842
Shipshewana
 E and S Sales
 260/768-4736
Wakarusa
 Maranatha Christian Bookstore
 574/862-4332

IOWA
Carson
 Refining Fires Books
 712/484-2214

KANSAS
Hutchinson
 Gospel Book Store
 620/662-2875
Moundridge
 Gospel Publishers
 620/345-2532

KENTUCKY
Harrodsburg
 Family Bookstore
 859/865-4545
Manchester
 Lighthouse Ministries
 606/599-0607

LOUISIANA
Belle Chasse
 Good News Bookstore
 504/394-3087

**Our books may also be found on many
Choice Books bookracks and Lantern Books bookracks**

MARYLAND
Grantsville
Shady Grove Market and Fabrics
301/895-5660
Hagerstown
J. Millers Gospel Store
240/675-0383
Landover
Integrity Church Bookstore
301/322-3311
Oakland
Countryside Books and More
301/334-3318
Silver Spring
Potomac Adventist Bookstore
301/572-0700
Union Bridge
Hege's Catalog Store
410/775-7643

MICHIGAN
Burr Oak
Chupp's Erbs and Fabric
269/659-3950
Clare
Colonville Country Store
989/386-8686
Holton
Country Cottage Bookstore
231/821-0261
Snover
Country View Store
989/635-3764

MINNESOTA
Harmony
Austin's Mohair
507/886-6731

MISSOURI
Advance
Troyer's Grocery
573/722-3406
Rutledge
Zimmerman's Store
660/883-5766

St. Louis
The Home School Sampler
314/835-0863
Seymour
Byler Supply & Country Store
417/935-4522
Shelbyville
Windmill Ridge Bulk Foods
4100 Highway T
Versailles
Excelsior Bookstore
573/378-1925
Weatherby
Country Variety Store
816/449-2932
Windsor
Rural Windsor Books and Variety
660/647-2705

NEW MEXICO
Farmington
Lamp and Light Publishers
505/632-3521

NEW YORK
Dunkirk
The Book Knook
716/366-0685
Seneca Falls
Sauder's Store
315/568-2673

NORTH CAROLINA
Greensboro
Borders Books and Music
336/218-0662
Raleigh
Borders Books and Music #365
919/755-9424

NORTH DAKOTA
Mylo
Lighthouse Bookstore
701/656-3331

**Our books may also be found on many
Choice Books bookracks and Lantern Books bookracks**

OKLAHOMA
Miami
Eicher's Country Store
918/540-1871

OHIO
Berlin
Gospel Book Store
330/893-3847

Christian Aid Ministries
330/893-2428

Brinkhaven
Little Cottage Books
740/824-4849

Carbon Hill
Messiah Bible School
740/753-3571

Dalton
Little Country Store
330/828-8411

Fredricksburg
Faith-View Books
330/674-4129

Fruita
Grand Valley Dry Goods
970/858-1268

Mesopotamia
Eli Miller's Leather Shop
440/693-4448

Middlefield
S & E Country Store
440/548-2347

Millersburg
Country Furniture & Bookstore
330/893-4455

Plain City
Deeper Life Bookstore
614/873-1199

Sugarcreek
The Gospel Shop
330/852-4223

Troyer's Bargain Store
2101 County Road 70

OREGON
Estacada
Bechtel Books
530/630-4606

Halsey
Ketch's Variety
541/369-2369

PENNSYLVANIA
Amberson
Scroll Publishing Co.
717/349-7033

Belleville
Yoder's Gospel Book Store
717/483-6697

Chambersburg
Burkholder Fabrics
717/369-3155

Pearson's Pasttimes
717/267-1415

Denver
Weaver's Store
717/445-6791

Ephrata
Clay Book Store
717/733-7253

Conestoga Bookstore
717/354-0475

Home Messenger Library &
Bookstore
717/866-7605

Ken's Educational Joys
717/351-8347

Gordonville
Ridgeview Bookstore
717/768-7484

Greencastle
Country Dry Goods
717/593-9661

Guys Mills
Christian Learning Resource
814/789-4769

**Our books may also be found on many
Choice Books bookracks and Lantern Books bookracks**

Leola
  Conestoga Valley Books Bindery
  717/656-8824
Lewisburg
  Crossroads Gift and Bookstore
  570/522-0536
McVeytown
  Penn Valley Christian Retreat
  717/899-5000
Meadville
  Gingerich Books and Notions
  814/425-2835
Millersburg
  Brookside Bookstore
  717/692-4759

  Country Furniture and Bookstore
  330/893-4455
Mount Joy
  Mummau's Christian Bookstore
  717/653-6112
Myerstown
  Witmer's Clothing
  717/866-6845
Newville
  Corner Store
  717/776-4336

  Rocky View Bookstore
  717/776-7987
Parkesburg
  Brookside Bookstore
  717/692-4759
Quarryville
  Countryside Bargains
  717/528-2360
Shippensburg
  Mt. Rock Bookstore
  717/530-5726
Springboro
  Chupp's Country Cupboard
  814/587-3678

SOUTH CAROLINA
Barnwell
  The General Store
  803/541-6109
North Charleston
  World Harvest Ministries
  843/554-7960
Summerville
  Manna Christian Bookstore
  843/873-4221
Sumter
  Anointed Word Christian
    Bookstore
  803/494-9894

TENNESSEE
Crossville
  MZL English Book Ministry
  931/277-3686

  Troyer's Country Cupboard
  931/277-5886
Deer Lodge
  Mt. Zion Literature Ministry
  931/863-8183
Sparta
  Valley View Country Store
  931/738-5465

TEXAS
Kemp
  Heritage Market and Bakery
  903/498-3366

VERMONT
Bennington
  Christian Book Store
  802-447-0198

VIRGINIA
Bristow
  Son Recording
  10100 Piper Lane
Dayton
  Books of Merit
  540/879-5013

**Our books may also be found on many
Choice Books bookracks and Lantern Books bookracks**

Mole Hill Books & More
540/867-5928

Rocky Cedars Enterprises
540/879-9714

Harrisonburg
Christian Light Publications
540/434-0768

McDowell
Sugar Tree Country Store
540/396-3469

Woodbridge
Mennonite Maidens
703/622-3018

WASHINGTON
North Bonneville
Moore Foundation
800/891-5255

WEST VIRGINIA
Renick
Yoder's Select Books
304/497-3990

WISCONSIN
Dalton
Mishler's Country Store
West 5115 Barry Road
Loyal
Homesewn Garments
715/255-8059

CANADA

ALBERTA
Cleardale
Cleardale Christian Bookstore
780/685-2582

BRITISH COLUMBIA
Burns Lake
Wildwood Bibles and Books
250/698-7451

MANITOBA
Arborg
Sunshine Christian Books
204/364-3135

ONTARIO
Aylmer
Mennomex
519/773-2002
Brunner
Country Cousins
519/595-4277

Lighthouse Books
519/656-3058
Floradale
Hillcrest Home Baking and Dry
Goods
519/669-1381
Linwood
Living Waters Christian Book-
store
519/698-1198
Mount Forest
Shady Lawn Books
519/323-2830
Newton
Canadian Family Resources
519/595-7585

**Our books may also be found on many
Choice Books bookracks and Lantern Books bookracks**

Lord, please calm this child's fears, and give me wisdom in what to do. I'm just as fright-ened as he seems.

She stood, legs aching, and Travis also tottered to his feet. On tiptoes, she pushed on the door above her. It wouldn't budge. Travis watched for an instant then scooted to the opposite side of the center bench. There, he climbed the bench's middle support like a ladder, guiding his head out through the wide window and scrambling out of the coach. With little effort, he lifted the door open, and kneeling on it, he beckoned her up.

Hannah gathered her bag and his small pack, handed them up to him, and then planted her foot atop the bench's center support. One hand gripping the door frame, the other clasping Travis's, she climbed up and popped her head outside the coach. Body aching, she crawled out and sat, her legs dangling inside.

All was deathly still. She swept the scene with a measured glance, her hand straying to cover her mouth as she did. The coach's wheels were splintered beyond repair. The driv-er's seat and tongue were sheered off, as was the metal rail that once sat atop the coach. Near the twisted railing lay Mr. McCaffrey. Hannah gulped a breath, scanning more of the wreckage.

For a good ways up the steep incline, a wide swath of earth was churned up like a farmer's field ready for planting. Trees were snapped off or uprooted where the coach had plowed over them. Scattered along the path were the still forms of five of the draft horses. The sixth one was still upright, fighting to loose itself from the harness now entangled in a downed tree. Also dotting the slope, Mr. Racklin's and Mrs. Jamison's forms.

Hannah swung her legs over the side and jumped down. Her feet under her, she hiked her skirts and ran toward Mr. McCaffrey.

"Oh, Father. . .please don't let them all be dead."

◆ ◆ ◆

Finn lay as still as possible, breath coming in sharp gasps. Nausea swept him in waves. Pain coursed like lightning through his body, concentrated along his left side. He squinted at the bright sky but quickly snapped his eyelids shut to block the sun's blinding rays.

Footsteps approached and skidded to a halt nearby. A shadow covered his head, and he blinked at the shadow's source.

"Mr. McCaffrey? Can you hear me?" Miss Stockton dropped to her knees, and the light blinded him once again.

Jaw clenched, he nodded once.

"Oh, thank God. I thought. . . ." The woman gulped a breath. "I thought you and the others were dead."

The others. Bob, Mrs. Jamison, and the boy. Gingerly, he turned his head but saw only trees, rocks, and broken stagecoach parts. "Are they?"

"Travis has a nasty cut on his head. I haven't checked on Mrs. Jamison or Mr. Racklin yet."

Finn attempted to push himself up on his elbow, but fire blazed through his side.

"Please don't move." Miss Stockton planted a firm hand against his shoulder. "Your left leg appears to be broken, and I should check for other injuries."

"No. . ." He ground out the word between clenched teeth. Finn stole a glance toward the high mountain path they'd traveled, then shut his eyes tight.

It was a miracle anyone had survived. That cliff was treacherous. Their saving grace was that the drop wasn't as sheer on this side of the mountain.

"Help me up." He pleaded with his eyes, reaching for her arm. "Have to check. . .on the others. . ."

"No, sir. I'll check on them."

Finn bit back a curse. "I'm the jehu. Passengers' safety. . .is *my* job." A job at which he'd failed miserably.

"You're not going anywhere until we splint that leg and check you for other injuries."

He balled a fist as another wave of pain coursed through him. "Then go. Check them. . .please."

The woman's disheveled red hair tumbled from its pins as she nodded. She beckoned to someone, and Travis appeared.

"Travis, stay with Mr. McCaffrey. Understand?" She motioned and pantomimed, the boy looking confused. She put both hands out, palms toward him. "Stay here."

His eyes lit with understanding, and the kid sat near him. The woman nodded then hurried away.

Finn fought to lift his head and look himself over. The movement sent sparks sizzling through his body. Instead, he brought the heel of his right palm to his forehead to ease the steady pounding between his temples.

What in tarnation happened? He was an experienced driver. Never lost a coach, though he'd had to nurse a few to the next station when a wheel went bad or a horse lame. He'd been driving stagecoaches too long, and he knew that span of road too well.

Beside him, Travis's eyes grew wide, and he scrambled onto his knees. The boy tugged Finn's duster coat open and touched his side. A blaze of pain ricocheted through Finn's midsection, and he batted the boy's hand away. Undaunted, Travis held up his palm, now covered in bright red blood.

He, too, touched his side, fingers finding a large wet patch. Fire roared through his torso and dizziness rocked him.

The boy lunged to his feet, eyes trailing up the slope in Miss Stockton's direction. His face contorted with concern, and he waved his arms wildly. He paused, signaled again. The boy glanced Finn's way, an apology in his eyes.

"It's all right, kid. Just. . .sit dow—"

Travis bolted. Finn grabbed for his leg and missed. The sudden movement reignited the lightning bolts, and his world went dark.

Chapter Four

H annah laid the last rock in place over the joint grave of Edwina Jamison and Bob Racklin then arched her back to loosen the knots. She glanced heavenward, her lower lids burning with hot tears. "Lord, please receive their spirits into Your hands and help us get out of this predicament. I—we—need You more than ever, Father."

As she'd assessed their situation earlier, her initial thought had been to wait, perhaps climb up to the narrow mountain path above. After studying the incline, she ruled that out. It was far too steep, especially with an injured man in tow.

She'd thought that another stage would come, or the next station would send a search party when they didn't arrive. Those thoughts had dissolved when she saw the claw marks that marred the only surviving horse's neck and shoulder. Despite being unfamiliar with most mountain wildlife, she could identify the marks of a bear easily enough. It was autumn. Bears were foraging far and wide, preparing for hibernation. What better feast than the carcasses of the five draft horses she couldn't bury?

For all these reasons, she'd decided they couldn't stay put, though how she was to move Mr. McCaffrey was a perplexing dilemma. Even if the wounded jehu were able to sit astride a horse, the huge animal was far too large to ride for any distance like a saddle horse. Since she'd finished burying the dead, she could focus on that task.

She gathered the pile of supplies she'd collected—the sawed-off shotgun and a rifle she'd found among the wreckage, a bag with ammunition, the knives she'd taken from Bob Racklin's belt, and the matches she'd found in his pocket. She wrapped the items inside the petticoats she'd taken from Mrs. Jamison's body before burying her, then headed down the mountainside toward Travis, Mr. McCaffrey, and the skittish horse.

At her approach, Travis touched Mr. McCaffrey's shoulder, though the man didn't stir. Travis frowned. The poor child had been scared senseless at his earlier discovery of the jagged gash that wrapped around Mr. McCaffrey's rib cage. He'd only calmed after she'd stanched the bleeding and bandaged the wound. Since the man had passed out, she'd set and splinted his leg. It appeared he'd not yet regained consciousness.

Hannah laid aside the supplies and checked Mr. McCaffrey's pulse. A little fast, but strong considering his injuries. What concerned her more was the warmth of his skin. Fever could easily set in, though it hadn't yet. The sooner she found water to clean his and Travis's wounds, the better. All the more reason they needed to move fast.

She smiled at Travis. "You've done well." She signed the compliment, though she didn't expect him to understand. To convey her happiness, she gave his shoulder a gentle squeeze. He smiled, the grin wobbling.

"Lord, would You show me how I'm to move Mr. McCaffrey? We need water, food, and shelter—and quickly."

Her mind churned as she rose and surveyed the scene again. She ambled toward the stagecoach to peruse the contents of the rear boot, if any. To her surprise, the leather cover was still buckled closed. On tiptoes, she unfastened the sturdy flap but was disappointed to find only Travis's small trunk, splintered beyond repair, and a disheveled stack of blankets. She gathered the blankets and Travis's warmest clothes. Otherwise, there was little of value.

Before stepping away, Hannah felt the corner of the heavy leather cover, an idea forming. If she could remove the boot cover from the coach, perhaps she could tie it between two sturdy branches to form a travois to transport Mr. McCaffrey.

It was worth a try.

◆　◆　◆

All around him, his world swayed, bumping in unusual fashion. With every jostle, pain stabbed his left leg, stealing his breath. He pried one eye open with some effort, the other following suit. Above him, the sky was streaked in shades of orange, red, and purple. Beneath his head—or very near it—the heavy footfalls of a horse. He twisted to see what lay over his shoulder but caught only a glimpse of a chestnut horse's rump before pain sliced his ribs.

A small hand touched his shoulder, and Finn twisted around. Fire lit his left side, and he stifled a cry. The hand disappeared, and soon the jostling ceased.

"Mr. McCaffrey?"

Both Miss Stockton and Travis appeared, the boy with a bandage wrapped around his head.

"Thank God, you're awake." She touched his forehead. "How are you feeling?"

"Cold." Finn's voice rasped, and his hand strayed to his side to find his shirt unbuttoned, torso bandaged. He tugged the shirt in place to ward off the chills.

"You're feverish."

He glanced around, trying to place his surroundings. Nothing was familiar. "Where. . .are we?"

"Somewhere in the mountains." Her voice quavered.

He squinted, and his brain spun, trying to understand.

"Do you remember? The stagecoach crashed."

"Crashed?" The memories jogged loose. He'd been driving the mountain pass, Bob Racklin jawin' while he fought to concentrate on Sam's news. A black bear—

The hair-raising ride flashed through his mind, even while his thoughts raced to Sam and Ezra receiving the news of an accident. "Oh, God. . .no." He closed his eyes to block the images. "The others?"

Silence. He forced his eyes open.

Miss Stockton's face had gone ashen. "They didn't make it." She looked away, her chin trembling. "I buried them."

"They're dead?" *God, no. Why would You let them die? Why didn't You save them?*

A single choking sob bubbled out of Miss Stockton, and she clamped a hand over her mouth. After a few deep breaths, she wiped her eyes and looked at him once more.

"I'm sorry. We need to keep moving." She blinked furiously, her voice pinched. "I've searched for a stream all afternoon. I can hear water flowing nearby, but the sun's nearly gone, so we must hurry."

Once again, he looked at his surroundings. No stagecoach. No mountain road. Nothing familiar. "You left the stage?"

She nodded. "I thought it was best."

"No. Shoulda stayed." Finn ground out the words, glaring despite the throbbing of his skull. "They'll. . .look for us."

Eyes wide, she rose. "I'm well aware, sir." She glared back. "However, I thought the stench of five rotting horse carcasses might attract predators. Besides, we're without food and water. Unless you'd rather I let you die, I must have water to tend your injuries." She gulped a breath. "Excuse me. I'm losing the light."

Miss Stockton stalked off, Travis trailing behind her. The swaying began again, and with it, the jolting pains.

Stupid. He could barely string together a sentence, much less muster the strength to attend to his own needs. Miss Stockton had buried the dead and hauled him out with only the help of a scared deaf boy. She was doing her best. Her reasoning for abandoning the scene was sound. It wouldn't have been *his* choice, but he was in the uncomfortable situation of not being in control.

Finn blinked at the sky as the red hues succumbed to the purple shades. Moments ticked by, and finally the movement stopped as the chuckling of water filled his ears. The sound drove home the realization that his mouth was dry as cotton.

Silence stretched for an eternity. Had she left? Who could blame her if she had? She and Travis could make faster time without him. Finally, the contraption he was on jostled, rose up, and at the same time, the thud of hoofbeats sounded. Finn grunted at the awkward shift then relaxed as he was lowered to the ground.

Miss Stockton appeared. "Mr. McCaffrey?"

"Hmm?"

"I'm sure you're thirsty. The canteen was crushed in the accident, so you'll have to squeeze some water from this." She placed a sopping cloth in his hand. "I'll help you sit up some."

She looped an arm under his head and gingerly lifted him. The movement sent stabbing pains through him, and he sagged against her.

"Please stay with me." Her words oozed concern and fatigue.

He gulped. "I'm still here." With uncoordinated fingers, he squeezed the cool liquid into his mouth, though much of it ran down his chest. Tiring quickly, he shook his head against her shoulder. "Let me go."

She lowered him down as Travis approached with firewood. He dropped the pile, and she rose to meet him.

"Well done. Thank you." She patted the boy's cheek. "Please stay with Mr. McCaffrey while I build a fire." She guided the boy to his side and patted the ground beside him. The kid sat.

Miss Stockton inhaled deeply and sighed. In the last vestiges of light, her shoulders slumped. She looked durn near ready to drop herself.

He caught the hem of her skirt. "Ma'am?"

She knelt. "Did you need something?"

"You should rest." She was, after all, the only thing standing between the boy and him living or dying out there.

"I appreciate your concern, but there's still so much to be done. Perhaps sometime before sunup." She rose and stalked off.

Finn balled a fist and struck the ground. He ought to be helping her, not adding to her load.

Chapter Five

Hannah roused from slumber, rolled in a cocoon of woolen blankets. Every muscle ached, both from sleeping on the ground and from the battering she'd taken during the crash. Not to mention all the other things she'd done—burying the dead, building the travois, wrestling Mr. McCaffrey onto it. She tested her limbs to see where the worst of the pain was located. Her thighs ached as if bruised, probably from being trapped under the bench. One elbow was stiff and swollen. Nothing life-threatening, thank God. Not like Mr. Racklin and Mrs. Jamison. She bit her lip and prayed again for the deceased.

It had been late by the time she'd crawled into the blankets. Her body cried for more rest, but instead, she sat up, drawing the wool tight around her shoulders. She glanced around the camp she'd hastily thrown together. The horse foraged nearby, not too troubled by the claw marks marring its neck and shoulder. Travis stood at the edge of the stream, head still bandaged. He held a sturdy branch, a knife tied firmly to one end. His attention focused on the water, he tracked something then lunged, thrusting the makeshift spear into the stream. A spray of water glinted in the morning sun, and Travis jerked straight up, as if startled, and wiped his face on his sleeve.

Behind her, a weak chuckle drew her attention. From his crude bed, Mr. McCaffrey watched Travis, right arm propped under his head. He grinned. "The boy's hungry."

She knew that sensation well. Her stomach had protested much of the night. "I suspect we all are. Unfortunately, I'm not sure what luck he'll have catching breakfast that way." She knelt beside him and touched his forehead. The fever lingered, though perhaps not as high.

"That boy"—his blue eyes held hers—"is a survivor."

Her heart pounded. Even dulled by pain and rimmed with dark circles, the man's eyes captivated her. The intensity of his halting statement kept her from responding with anything other than a nod. She broke the gaze, her cheeks warming furiously.

What was she thinking? How easily she could forget the overheard conversation between him and the young woman carrying his child. Perhaps that woman had also been charmed by his very blue eyes.

Hannah shoved aside all thought of his eyes and loosened the bandages around his rib cage.

"How are you feeling today, Mr. McCaffrey?"

He caught her wrist. "Call me Finn. Please."

A lump formed in her throat. She was hardly ready to call any man by his given name, and particularly not this one. She'd promised herself that wouldn't happen again. Not after. . .

She was being ridiculous. Mr. McCaffrey was offering it solely for simplicity's sake. Wasn't he? Given names were far more practical in their present circumstances.

Hannah Rose, forget all your silly notions, and focus on getting out of these mountains.

She touched her chest. "You may call me Hannah Rose."

A startled gasp escaped her. She'd offered the man her *middle* name—her papa's pet name? It had to be pure exhaustion. "Or just Hannah."

He wobbled a grin at her. "Which one?"

She looked to the bandages. "Just Hannah."

"All right, Just Hannah." He closed his eyes, a hint of a smile on his lips.

Once he quit distracting her, she cleaned the wound without interruption. To her surprise, it didn't appear as infected as she'd feared. Red, angry, hot to the touch, but better than it had looked last evening.

Lord, thank You that it isn't worse. With no supplies, no tools, we're in a bad way out here. Please continue to guide us, and let us be found. Soon.

She applied fresh bandages torn from Mrs. Jamison's petticoats then looked at the splint on his leg. Another splash, followed by a triumphant laugh, sounded. Beside the stream, Travis hoisted a good-sized fish from the water, spear through its body as he stabilized it with a hand around its wriggling tail. He headed in her direction, a huge smile brightening his face.

"Told you." Finn grinned at her. "A survivor."

◆　　◆　　◆

Finn gritted his teeth and clung to Hannah, arm looped around her neck as she helped him back onto the travois. His body trembled. If only she'd been strong enough to lift the contraption into place over the horse's back while he was still on it, like she'd lifted it down the previous night.

"Easy. You're almost there." She panted the words in his ear, her breath fanning his sweaty skin.

His backside touched the travois, and he went limp, pulling her down with him. She braced a hand against the travois frame, her nose nearly touching his.

Hannah tensed.

Finn didn't move as he stared at the golden flecks in her huge hazel eyes.

"Let me go, Mr. McCaffrey." Urgency filled her words.

Lord, Hannah's real pretty. . . .

"Mr. McCaffrey!" Her panicked tone registered, and he released her. She righted herself, tugged her dress bodice into place, and patted her hair, which suddenly tumbled loose from its pins.

Waves of dizziness swept him. His whole body sagged, and he gulped air like the golden trout Travis had caught a couple of hours earlier. Durn it. Hardly right, a man should feel so weak. . .so useless.

She turned her back and shook the rest of her hair loose. Finn's pulse quickened as she brushed the auburn curls, and he rubbed his fingertips together, imagining their softness.

Finn balled his fists and turned his face away. He had no business thinking such thoughts about Hannah Rose Stockton.

"Hannah." He squeezed his eyes shut. "Just Hannah, you fool." The combination of pain, exhaustion, and fever must have addled his brain. He'd do well to focus on escaping these mountains and returning to Ezra and Sam, rather than woolgathering about running his fingers through Hannah's hair.

Moments later, footsteps rustled nearer, and he turned. She tied off a thick braid with a torn strip of fabric and, with a quick flip, she tossed the braid over her shoulder, though it slid to the front and thumped against his elbow as she stooped beside him.

"I thought you'd be asleep by now." She settled a soft hand against his forehead then slid it around to his cheek. Her touch was a comfort, and not just for the warmth against the chill of his fever. Truth be known, he liked having her so near.

Finn shook his head. "Leg hurts." There'd be no comfort unless they found a bottle of whiskey to dull the pain. God forbid that should happen. Strong drink might loosen his tongue, and he'd tell her just how pretty she was.

Keep your fool mouth shut, you idiot. What woman would have use for a weak, helpless man like him?

She nodded. "I'm sorry. I suspect it'll be worse once we start moving, but I'll take the smoothest path I can find. I plan to follow the stream. Maybe we'll run into a miner or someone living up here who might help us. Does that sound like a good plan?" Her hazel eyes were full of uncertainty and questions.

He rolled a glance skyward. "Reckon so." If she knew how confused his thoughts were, how utterly inadequate he was in this current state, she wouldn't ask. Travis would give better advice.

Hand still against his stubbly cheek, she rolled his head toward her. "Try to rest. I'll do everything I can to get us out of this mess."

Finn caught her hand as she withdrew it. Her eyes widened.

"I'm sorry," he whispered.

"For what?"

"Causing such trouble." Iffen he'd seen the bear, none of this would've happened. They'd be somewhere between Strawberry and Placerville about now.

"You've nothing to apologize for."

Travis appeared, toting a couple of blankets. Hannah wiggled her hand out of Finn's grasp and took them, draping them over Finn and tucking them under his shoulders. "Try to rest."

She stood and settled a hand on Travis's shoulder. The boy looked up, eyes full of expectation.

"Help me with the horse." She signed the statement and beckoned him to follow. They disappeared, and a moment later, the jarring sway of the travois began.

Finn gritted his teeth to ward off the spikes of pain. Within moments, his head swam, and he gulped down air in a vain attempt to settle himself. To no avail.

God in heaven, please help me.

Chapter Six

Hannah plodded, every muscle screaming. The late afternoon sun slanted across the rugged terrain and glinted on the stream's surface. She gauged the sun's position against the peaks around her. Wouldn't be long before the sun sank behind them and darkness descended. Time to make camp.

At the sound of a distressed cry, Hannah stopped the horse and scurried to Finn McCaffrey's side, Travis on her heels. The jehu slept as he had most of the day, though his blond hair was damp with sweat. He must've done battle with the blankets. The rumpled covers lay diagonally across his body, binding one arm and the opposite leg.

"Has your fever finally broken?" she asked, despite the man being asleep. She touched his forehead but quickly pulled back. His skin was unexpectedly fiery. She touched his stubbly cheek.

He flinched, drew a sharp breath. "Don't touch her." He batted her arm away.

Travis startled at the unexpected movement.

Hannah held up a cautioning hand. "It's all right. He's dreaming."

The boy's brown eyes clouded with concern.

"Mr. McCaffrey." Hannah patted his cheek. "Wake up."

He panted, fighting to extract his left arm from the woolen blankets.

She gripped his shoulders and gave him a mild shake. "Mr. McCaffrey!"

His blue eyes snapped open, wild and distant, and his right hand shot to her throat. Yelping, Hannah drew back, though he held her fast. Her own hands circled his wrist while his fingers tightened, digging into her flesh. She struggled to draw a breath.

"Stop!" Travis screeched and clawed Mr. McCaffrey's hand. Unsuccessful, the boy grabbed the travois frame and tilted it sideways.

The pressure on her windpipe loosened, and she collapsed, sputtering and coughing as the travois dragged past, the horse walking on without them.

Travis bent low beside her. "He hurt you?"

One hand braced against the ground, she sucked down several breaths, cleared her throat, and coughed again. She willed her heart to slow its thundering staccato. When she finally glanced sideways, Travis's big brown eyes brimmed with tears.

Scared her, but he hadn't hurt her. Not badly, anyway. Hannah shook her head.

The boy stared as if assessing the truth.

Her eyes strayed toward the horse, still pulling the travois. She pointed. "Stop the horse."

With a firm set to his jaw, he scrambled after the big animal.

Clearing her throat again, Hannah looked heavenward, her own eyes stinging with tears. "Lord, how long must we keep wandering out here? Mr. McCaffrey is growing worse. Please, help us."

"You tried to kill her!" Travis stood over Mr. McCaffrey, both fists clenched as if ready to pounce.

Muscles leaden and clumsy, Hannah stumbled up, caught her balance, and ran toward the pair. As she reached Travis, she spun him to face her. "Don't hurt him." She signed and spoke the words.

Travis's eyebrows crinkled in confusion.

"He has a fever." Again, she signed, then settled the boy's palm against Mr. McCaffrey's forehead.

He jerked his hand away, darting a glance between them. "He's dying?"

Not if she had anything to say about it. Hannah shook her head. "He's very sick."

Silent, the boy backed off, frowning.

Hannah turned to her patient. "Mr. McCaffrey?" She peeled the blankets away from his torso and loosened the bandages binding his ribs.

"I'm sorry." His voice was unsteady, eyes glassy. "Didn't mean it. I'm so sorry."

"It's all right. It was a nightmare." A product of the fever, no doubt. "Who were you trying to save?"

"What?"

"Just before I woke you, you called out, 'Don't touch her.' It sounded like you were trying to save someone."

His breath caught, and he rolled his head to the side.

Dumb question, Hannah Rose. Don't remind him of the nightmare.

She peeled back the dressing and bit her lip. The gash had grown worse since she'd last cleaned it. She must get the infection under control or he *might* die. Hannah laid the dressing back in place. "You rest. I'll be back soon to tend that wound."

Hannah and Travis unpacked, setting the bags on the ground near the travois. It took both of them to unstrap the contraption and lift it from the horse's back. Afterward, she sent him to gather firewood, and while she waited, she dipped the cloth into the icy stream and returned again to Mr. McCaffrey's side.

"Drink, Mr. McCaffrey." She lifted his head and squeezed the water into his open mouth. Several times, he opened his mouth for more. When he shook his head, she laid the cloth aside and looked again at the wound tracing his ribs. If she had a way to heat water—a pot or tin cup—cleaning his wound would be far more effective. She rose and extracted a linen handkerchief from her bag and dunked it in the stream.

"Ma'am?"

Hannah met his eyes as she eased back to the ground beside him.

"You mind. . .talking to me? Keeps my mind. . .off the pain."

How could she refuse him? He hadn't complained once since the crash. "Of course. What would you like me to talk about?"

He closed his eyes and shrugged. "Anything. Where you're from?"

She inspected his wound, dabbing at it. "I left Illinois two years ago to move to San Francisco."

"Why'd you. . .come west?"

"My aunt and uncle came out during the gold rush to open a boardinghouse. About three years ago, they heard of a small town needing a schoolteacher. I thought it would be an adventure, so I applied, and they accepted, even though it would take me months to arrive."

He peeled one eye open to look at her. "The deaf school?"

A lump knotted around her heart. "No. I'm not a teacher at the deaf school, just a lowly assistant."

"Why'd you quit teaching. . .to become. . .an assistant?" He closed his eyes.

Hannah rolled a glance heavenward. *Lord, of all the things we could talk about, why did he choose this?* "It was a bit of a misunderstanding. I. . .didn't actually get the job."

He squinted at her. "A misunderstanding?"

She sighed. "You're obviously hurting. Rest now, Mr. McCaffrey."

"Asked you. . .to call me Finn."

Mute, she nodded.

"Why didn't they. . .hire you?"

Blast that nosey man for pressing her. "Unlike so many others, this town required its teacher to be married." She focused on his wound so he wouldn't see the depth of her hurt.

"They didn't. . .tell you. . .before you came?"

"They didn't tell me that fact since my letter stated I was to be married a month after I wrote them." She sat up straight and craned her neck, looking anywhere but in his blue eyes. "It didn't occur to me to share the news that my groom called off our wedding in order to marry my sister."

He grunted. Before he could question her more, she climbed to her feet.

"Where is that boy? He should've been here with the wood by now." Even to her own ears, her voice sounded pinched. Hannah laid aside the handkerchief, avoiding the certain pity she'd find in Mr. McCaffrey's eyes. "I'll be back in a moment." She scurried off after Travis.

Hannah gulped back the tears threatening to spill down her cheeks, and clenched her teeth. *Lord, please be kind and let Mr. McCaffrey pass out before I return—and make him forget that whole conversation. Please?*

The fast-moving stream cut between two steep, rocky hillsides, dense patches of brush and a scattering of trees dotting each. She walked along the stream bank, searching the hills and watching for movement. It would hardly do to call Travis's name. Lord willing, he would be somewhere out in the open.

Ahead, the space between the hills narrowed where a rocky outcropping jutted toward the stream. Several huge stones formed a natural path across the water, and a wet shoe print marred one's surface. She teetered across the stepping-stones to the far bank, reached the narrowest point between the hills, and skirted past the rocks.

Beyond them, Hannah stalled. The area opened into a wide plain where the ground pitched gently downward. The stream picked up speed, running toward a cliff some thirty feet beyond. Not far from the stepping-stones, a sizeable pile of firewood lay abandoned. Beyond it, Travis stood with his back to her as he picked dark clumps of fruit from a thick stand of chokecherry bushes.

"Hungry again." She grinned.

On the far side of the dense thicket, the brush rustled and shook. Grunting and snuffling sounds caught her attention. Every hair on her body stood at attention. What-ever was there was *big*. She turned toward Travis, and her mouth went dry.

Oblivious.

A black bear crashed through the thicket and swept the scene with a glance. Travis turned, wide-eyed, his face going deathly pale.

The bear took a lumbering step toward Travis. The boy matched the movement, shuf-fling backward into the bush. He sidestepped, backed up another step, and another.

Hannah flicked a glance toward the cliff some fifteen feet beyond, then to the bear.

"Hey!" She forced the word out, though it was a mere squeak. She stomped her feet, stumbling on a rock. Knees weak, she went to all fours. "Hey, bear!" Hannah scooped the stone as she pushed back to her unsteady legs. "Leave him alone!" She flung the rock, just as her father had taught her as a girl. It struck with a thud.

The beast turned. Hannah hiked her skirts and ran.

◆　◆　◆

Finn covered his eyes. He owed the woman a better explanation. His fingers had been around her throat, for pity's sake. If Travis hadn't called out, the outcome could've been far worse.

He could let her believe some fever-induced nightmare made him do it, but this nightmare had haunted him throughout his life, the images always the same.

Little hands carrying a platter mounded with food to the table. Tripping on a chair leg, platter overturning on the dirt floor. Heart pounding as Pa turns that drunken stare his way.

"Stupid kid!" Pa's fearsome backhand landing hard across his cheekbone. *"That was the best we were gonna eat all month."*

Ma scooping his frail body into her arms, cradling his head against her shoulder. Whispered words soothing his broken spirit. Pa cursing, dragging Ma up by her hair, shaking her.

"Told you before, Bess. I'm sick of you turning that boy into a chicken-hearted little coward."

Small hands balling into fists. Undernourished body lunging up off the floor. *"Don't touch her!"*

Alcohol-drenched breath laughing in his face. *"You really saying that to me, boy?"*

Little limbs trembling. Squeaky voice vanishing.

Pa's face twisting into an ugly mask. *"That's what I thought. Get lost, you little coward."*

Backhand striking him again. Lights exploding in his head. Body slamming into the hearth. Can't breathe.

Ma struggling to free herself. *"Leave him be, Jonas. He's a child."*

"Someone's gotta toughen that brat up." Pa's big hand circling Ma's throat, squeezing. Ma fighting, eventually going limp. Him tossing her aside. The sickening crack of her head hitting the edge of the hearth.

Finn lurched onto his right elbow before the image of her lifeless eyes lodged again in his brain. He gulped air, fighting the pain that sliced through him from ribs to toes. As dizziness swept him, Finn sagged onto the travois, lying partially on his right side, head lolling heavily against his upstretched arm.

"God, help me." He panted the desperate prayer. *It's been twenty-seven years, and the fear is still as real as the day it happened. Lord, I don't want to keep dreaming this dream. I don't want to be like Pa. I don't want the fear of being like him to rule me anymore.*

He waited for his head to stop swimming and some strength to return to his limbs, though the prayer kept replaying in his mind. "God, help. *Please.*"

"Finn?" Hannah's frantic cry split the stillness. "There's a bear!"

The words made little sense, but her tone tugged him to action. He struggled onto his elbow again and craned his neck in time to see her racing toward camp, a bear gaining on her.

"Bear!" Again, Hannah's panicked scream pierced his thoughts.

Feet from him lay his Model 1853 Sharps rifle and bag of ammunition. Teeth gritted, Finn rolled onto his belly. Pain ripped through his side and pulsed into his leg, but he dragged the gun and bag near. Head swimming, he fumbled to produce caps and paper bullets from the pouch, somehow loaded the gun, and fired.

The rifle roared, concussion echoing between the hills as darkness claimed him.

Chapter Seven

The gunshot, aimed at the far hill, thundered in Hannah's ears. Several frantic glances behind her showed that the lumbering black form was speeding up and over the rise. She slowed, eyes pinned on the peak. When the animal didn't reappear, she slowed more. Her muscles rebelled, locking tight, and she collapsed. Lungs burning and body trembling, she huddled on the ground, whimpering.

Hannah lay still for several long moments, scanning her surroundings. When she did move, she struggled to sit up and face the direction she'd come from. At the sight of Travis watching her from beside the stepping-stones, sobs boiled out of her.

Thank You, Lord. He's safe.

She fought to her knees but couldn't muster the strength to stand. Pounding footsteps drummed into her consciousness, and she looked up to see Travis approach. He skidded to a halt and latched on to her. She clung to him, collapsing once more to a seated position. He gripped her just as fiercely, his thin frame shaking.

When they both pulled themselves together, Travis hung his head. "I'm real sorry. Am I in trouble?"

Fresh tears stung her eyes, though she choked them back with a rough chuckle. She held the boy's face between her hands and shook her head. "No."

His eyebrows nearly disappeared under the bandage covering his forehead. "I'm not?"

"No." She again shook her head then kissed his hair.

He crinkled his nose and swiped at the locks as if to remove the kiss, though a lopsided grin stole across his face when he thought she wasn't looking.

Legs like warm butter, Hannah rose and staggered a few steps before Travis looped an arm around her waist. She hugged him again before heading toward the stepping-stones.

Lord, Travis is so hungry for attention and eager to please. Thank You for letting him speak to me. It's a breakthrough.

As they passed by, her gaze fell across the camp on the far bank, Mr. McCaffrey lying facedown in the grass. Her heart lurched. Despite her shaky legs, she hurried on, Travis keeping pace with her.

Once they reached the stepping-stone path, Hannah and Travis split the pile of kindling he'd gathered and ferried the wood across, though her arms shook with the weight. On the other bank, Travis stalled, eyes pinned on something. He nodded to the charred remnants of a stone fireplace and two partial walls.

Hannah stared at the burned remains then back toward the camp. The sun was dipping lower every minute. She needed to check on Mr. McCaff—on Finn—to be sure he hadn't reinjured himself, but there could be something usable within the rubble.

Something to hold and heat water. She shook her head.

"First, check on Finn. Once you know he's all right, you can search the ruins."

But what if the bear returned?

The unbidden thought shuddered through her. She touched Travis's arm, starting again toward camp. He trotted along beside her.

At the camp, Hannah dumped the wood and knelt beside Finn. She lifted his shirt to find blood oozing from his wound. She pressed the soiled dressing against it and gauged the daylight. Too much to do. She must get Finn settled, start a fire, search the burned cabin, tend Finn's wounds—hopefully with warm water—and find some way to feed Travis. What else was she missing? The temperature was dropping quickly. She should build some kind of a shelter for them. Fatigue stole through her.

"One thing at a time, Hannah Rose." She caught Travis's attention with a wave and offered him the matches she'd pilfered from Bob Racklin's pocket. "Start a fire, please." She gestured toward the piles of wood.

He looked at the wood and snatched the matches. No need to explain further.

Hannah wrestled Finn onto his back, her muscles quivering. Once he was settled, he blinked distant eyes.

"Mr. McCaffr—" She caught herself. "Finn?"

The jehu looked toward her. "Huh?"

"Are you in pain? Worse pain, I mean?"

His eyes slid shut, as visible chills swept his body. Perhaps he hadn't truly been awake. She focused on stanching the bleeding.

"The bear?" Finn's unexpected words startled her, and she sat straighter.

"The gunshot scared it off. Thank you."

His eyelids fluttered halfway open. "You. . .hurt?"

"No." She drew a shaky breath. "Travis found a thicket of chokecherry bushes, but he couldn't hear the bear foraging on the far side of it. The beast turned on him, so I. . ." She shuddered, her throat constricting.

"You. . .drew it. . .away."

She bit her bottom lip and nodded.

A weak smile sprouted on his chapped lips. "Brave."

A sound between a snort and a sob burst out of her. Terrified, more like.

He caught her hand and pinned her with an intense gaze. "Bravest woman. . .I ever met."

Certainly not. "That has to be the fever talking."

"Me and Travis. . .can thank you. . .getting us outta here."

"I haven't gotten us out of anywhere yet. For all I know, we're deeper in the mountains than when we started."

Another deep shudder gripped him, and he sucked in a sharp breath, his teeth chattering audibly.

Hannah pulled her fingers from his grip and pressed his palm to the soiled dressing. "Hold this."

Once he took over, she draped two blankets over him, tucking them around his right side before folding them back to expose the wound. He was quiet but for the clacking of his teeth. She set to work.

"Chokecherries?" he asked after some time.

"Yes. Why?"

"The bark. . .good for fevers. Roots. . .good. . .for wounds. Bleeding, too."

Her chest constricted at the thought of returning to the bushes.

"Take. . .my Sharps." He attempted to sit up.

"Stay still." Hannah settled a firm hand against his shoulder.

She loaded the gun and stuffed extra ammunition in her skirt pocket. Taking one of Mr. Racklin's knives to cut branches and dig roots, she gestured for Travis to stay with Finn, then set off.

There was little time to search the ruins and gather what she needed from the choke-cherry bushes. She must hurry, or she'd lose the light completely. Legs still too wobbly to run, she chose a purposeful walk, heart pounding the whole way.

Lord, I've had my fill of bears. Please protect me. And if You'd be so kind, we need something with which to carry and heat water.

She turned toward the burned-out structure, stomping her feet and rattling the brush as she picked her way toward it. At the edge of the remains, she stepped up to the soot-blackened fireplace and scanned the dusky area. What had once been the floor was now a tumbled-down pile of rubble. If there were time, she'd dig through the debris. Why hadn't she discovered this place sooner?

Lord, please hold the light just a few minutes.

She hurried to the back side of the ruins. There, the trees were thicker, the shadows deeper. A light-colored tarpaulin flapped in the chill breeze, drawing her attention. She crossed to it and lifted a corner. Logs, chopped and split, as if waiting for her. Without hesitation, she pulled the tarp down and reached for several pieces. As she did, something fell with a metallic clang.

Hannah peered over the woodpile, craning to see. Hidden behind the firewood sat an ax, a pickax, and a miner's gold pan. She grabbed the pan.

She shot a glance heavenward. *This is perfect. Thank You.*

With urgency, she tossed the pan and a couple of armloads of wood onto the tarp, grabbed the rifle, and dragging the tarp by its corners, headed toward the stepping-stones. The load slid over the carpet of dead leaves and pine needles easily but hung up on a large rock in the path. She stalled to free it, and in the process, kicked something buried in the leaves. The *tink* of glass carried to her ears.

Dropping to a knee, Hannah patted the ground. Where was it—whatever *it* was? She widened the search until she laid hold of cool glass and extracted a brown bottle, empty but for the dirt that had worked its way inside. Once cleaned, it could serve as a canteen of sorts.

Her chest easing with the timely finds, she tugged the tarpaulin free and hurried to her next task.

The chokecherry patch.

◆ ◆ ◆

A frigid gust of air woke Finn. He lay still, sorting through the sounds. Crackling fire. Someone snoring softly to his left. Where was he? He inhaled deeply, and pain roared through his side. With it, memories of the crash flooded him.

He pried heavy eyelids open. Above him stood a rudimentary lean-to made of sticks and stretched tight with a wool blanket. To his left, Travis slept in a woolen cocoon. To his right, a fire blazed, heat warming the air inside the shelter. Beyond that, the sky was a hazy shade of gray, the sun trying to peek through above the hills. Tendrils of steam rose from the water's surface, and frost covered the grass.

Finn tugged the pile of blankets around his shoulders and looked again at the lean-to. When on earth had Hannah built it? He'd been vaguely aware when she returned from the chokecherry patch the night before. He had no recollection of it then. He'd half-awakened a few times during the night when she'd fussed with his bandages, but he'd quickly dropped back to sleep.

"Hannah?" His voice thick, so he cleared his throat and tried again. "Hannah?"

From somewhere beyond the lean-to, a sharp intake of air broke the stillness. Footsteps crunched on the frost-laden grass. Wrapped tight in several blankets, Hannah appeared, her face drawn and eyelids drooping as if she'd just awakened. Her soft smile was genuine, a welcome sight. "You're awake."

He mustered a smile of his own. "Sorry to disturb you."

"That's all right. It's time I have another look at your wound." She tugged a glove from her right hand. "The chokecherry tea seemed to help your fever. Unfortunately, darkness fell before I could dig up any roots." She laid her hand on his forehead.

Finn jerked back from her icy touch. "Good night, woman. You're freezing." He wrapped her small hand between his larger ones, liking the fit of them. Alternately, he blew into his fists and rubbed the warmth into her frigid fingers. When he clasped her open palm against his bare chest to rub the back of her hand, it warmed him as much as he meant to warm her.

Hannah's cheeks flamed, and she pulled free of his grasp. "That's enough, thank you." A shudder gripped her as she turned toward the crackling fire. "I'll prepare more tea before I head back to the chokecherry patch to gather the roots."

He tucked his arms back under the blankets and watched her. Her normally graceful movements were stiff, whether from cold or something else, he couldn't determine. She dipped a wide, shallow bowl into the stream then squatted on the far side of the fire, every movement seeming pained. She held the bowl over the edge of the flame.

After a moment, her eyelids dipped, and she fought them open. A second time, they slid shut, and the big bowl faltered, spilling water into the fire. A sizzling cloud of steam rose, and her eyes grew wide. She jerked the bowl upright.

"You're exhausted. How long since you slept?"

Sighing, she returned to the stream to refill the bowl.

"How long, Hannah?"

She squatted beside the fire, stirred the flames with a sturdy stick, and held the bowl over the heat.

"Hannah!"

She glared in his direction. "I don't know. I've rested as I could, but someone had to stay awake and make sure the bear didn't return—tend to your needs, and Travis."

Finn's chest constricted. Durn it all, but he should be the one taking care of her—soothing her fears and helping to shoulder the burdens, rather than being one. He should be helping her with Travis. Who better than him? His life had mirrored Travis's in many ways. Travis's ma was dead like his. The boy's pa was a good-for-nothing drunk like his. If the kid's bony frame was any indication, he'd experienced true hunger like Finn had all those years ago.

Lord, Travis needs a family. You were real good to let Ezra take me in after Ma's murder. I was fortunate to have him and Sam. Now Travis needs a pa, and I'm volunteering for the job, and to be Hannah's husband, too, iffen she'll have me.

The prayer tumbled from his mind so suddenly, it startled him.

Get a hold of yourself, you fool. You've known them for a matter of days. Hardly your best days, at that. Keep in mind, your pa murdered his own wife. He roughed a hand over his stubbly jaw and tried to corral his thoughts before they rabbit-trailed too far. "We're beholden to you, but you gotta rest, too."

With her free hand, she pulled the blanket tighter around her shoulders, tugging it closed in front. "There's too much to be done, and I need to do it. Look what happened when I sent Travis off alone last night."

"Nothing's that pressing. My fever's down. I'm feeling stronger. Travis is sawin' logs next to me. Rest awhile."

Hannah shook her head. "What about getting us out of here? We'll freeze if it gets any colder."

Finn tried to judge the time despite the thick gray clouds. "What is it? Couple hours past dawn? Rest awhile. We'll still have the bulk of the day for traveling."

"What abou—"

"Do you just like to argue?" He shook his head. "Quit being so durned bullheaded and admit you need to rest."

Her eyes grew wide, and she drew back as if struck. In an instant, her expression shifted, hazel eyes sparking fire. She laid the bowl aside, shrugged out of the blanket, and stood. "If you think *this* is bullheaded, you have much to learn." She stepped out of sight, and when she returned, she carried his Sharps. "If you need anything, wake Travis."

His stomach knotted. "Where are you going?"

"For a walk." She stalked away.

"When you expectin' to be back?" He craned his neck to watch her departure.

"When it suits."

Chapter Eight

*B*ullheaded. Why was that the first word men used to describe her? Her fiancé, Andrew, had bandied the term during some of their more heated discussions. The memories struck the still-raw nerve, and she squeezed the rifle tighter and quickened her pace.

"Lord, I'm not, *am I?*" She loved imparting knowledge and could hold her own in debates on various topics. From childhood, she'd displayed an uncommon determination when she set her mind to something. Having never married, she'd learned to be independent. Did those qualities make her contrary? Not to her way of thinking. Not when balanced with her nurturing heart, her caring nature, and her sense of humor—despite the fact that the latter might have abandoned her. So why did men jump to such an assessment so quickly?

"Why do I care what that man thinks? Once we leave these mountains, it's not likely I'll see him again." They'd go about their respective lives, letting this nightmare fade into their memories.

So why did that idea of forgetting all of this—of forgetting *him*—leave her empty?

"You must be tired if your thoughts are straying there, Hannah Rose." A fierce shake of her head dislodged the silly thought. "Lest you forget, he has a woman with a child on the way."

She marched toward the stepping-stones, though as soon as her foot alighted on the path, she paused. *The knife.* She'd left it at camp. Without it, she'd be unable to dig up chokecherry roots. For a moment, she stood, rubbing her arms to dislodge the bone-jarring chill that had settled over her. She had no desire to return to the camp and face Finn's badgering. The man was right—she was exhausted—but he had no right to call her names. Not when she'd done all this to save his life.

"Stop it. You're letting him under your skin." After Andrew's betrayal, she had vowed no man would have that chance again.

Hannah glanced toward the burned-out cabin, recalling the ax and pickax beside the woodpile. They would do. She hurried to the back of the burned structure, gathered the rusted tools, and walked to the front of the ruins as the gray clouds split momentarily, allowing beams of sunlight through. The view from what must have been the front door caught her. The stream dominated the foreground, flowing down the gentle grade toward a cliff. Beyond the cliff, a panoramic view of other peaks, layer upon layer. Absolutely breathtaking. No wonder the cabin's owner built in that spot.

Still rubbing warmth into her arms, she drank in the view before heading across the stream. After scouting for bears, she approached the chokecherry patch and stared at the nearest bush. Hopefully the roots wouldn't be buried too deep. With her muscles already aching from the crash and constant overuse, she lacked stamina for digging deep to gather the roots Finn's wound would require.

Starting with the pickax, she probed the ground and found a root. She made room by removing a few low branches with the ax then cleared the soil from around the root. With it exposed, she chopped the root free and dug out two more for good measure. She bundled the roots and branches in a handkerchief, gathered the tools and gun, but paused. Thoughts still churning over Finn's hurtful remark, she wasn't ready to return to camp.

Hannah paced to the cliff's edge. The sound of rushing water filled her ears as the view caught her all over again. "Lord, Your handiwork never ceases to amaze me." She faced the stream, craning her neck to view the waterfall as it crashed over the edge of the cliff onto the rocks below. A hazy mist rose as it cascaded over those rocks and fell even farther. Her smile widened. How majestic the sight must be from below.

With her eyes closed, she pictured the view, though something niggled in her thoughts. She tried to push it away, but the troubling feeling wouldn't leave. She looked around. All was still. Only her footprints marred the frosty ground. Nothing appeared out of the ordinary. Was something wrong at the camp?

She turned toward the stepping-stones and peered at the camp. The fire still blazed. Other than Travis emerging from the lean-to, nothing stirred. The big draft horse stood at ease, seemingly unconcerned. Yet the sensation wouldn't leave. Something was wrong.

"What am I missing, Lord?" Hannah turned a slow circle, sweeping her surroundings with a gaze, her eyes settling on the stream as it flowed toward the cliff. It struck her then, and her stomach churned.

"No!" She clamped a hand over her mouth and turned moist eyes toward the overcast sky. "Lord, no. Why didn't I realize this before?" And what on earth was she to do about it?

◆　◆　◆

Rapid footsteps alerted Finn to Hannah's return. Gingerly, he craned his neck, but she came into his view only as she reached the fire and stormed past.

"Hannah, I'm sorry." He tried to track her movements, but she stepped out of view behind the lean-to. He scrubbed a hand over his stubbly jaw. "You still upset with me?"

The footsteps stilled. Silence. From his spot beside the fire, Travis darted a look between them.

"Hannah?"

"I'm upset with myself." Her voice quavered.

Concern threaded through him. "Why?"

Silence loomed again.

The lean-to frame blocked his view, frustrating him. "Would you stand where I can see you, please?"

She appeared, Sharps in one hand, bundle of sticks in the other, and heaved a sigh. Her shoulders slumped.

"What's wrong?"

Hannah's face contorted. "I've been following the water downstream, thinking it would lead us out of the mountains."

"Smart thinking."

"It isn't. The stream runs over a cliff up ahead. There's no way we can follow it. We came all this way, and—" Before he could speak, she sunk to the ground beside him, skirt billowing around her. "We're lost, Finn. If we'd stayed at the crash site—"

"You did what you thought was right. We'll find our way."

"I don't know where to go from here."

Somehow, he couldn't force himself to feel the fear and frustration eating at her. "Right now, I'm more concerned about you. You need sleep. I can durn near promise you a solution will come iffen you'll rest."

She stared at him, a war raging in her eyes. When she drew a breath to speak, Finn silenced her with a hand.

"You've taken real good care of me and Travis. Let us repay the favor. He can tend the fire. I'll keep watch for trouble. Once you wake, we'll figure the rest out. All right?"

Face buried in her hands and slender frame shaking, she finally nodded.

Thank You, God. She was showing some sense. "C'mere." He pulled Travis's blankets from beside him.

She drew closer and wrapped the woolen blankets around her shoulders. Gritting his teeth against the pain, Finn inched farther into the shelter, making room. At her hesitation, he patted the space beside him.

"It's warmer in here than out there, and my intentions are nothing but pure."

Hesitating, she scooted under the covering and curled onto her side, tucked one arm under her head, and blinked at him, seeming uncomfortable.

He stared up at the shelter above. "Rest well, Hannah." Finn closed his eyes.

"Thank you."

Within minutes, her breathing slowed, and she shifted, her elbow touching his shoulder. He looked her way again. The worry that had etched her face moments before had disappeared. Long lashes rested against her lightly freckled cheeks. Perfect lips parted slightly as she exhaled. His heart pounding a little faster, Finn looked away and focused on a pinhole in the blanket above.

Shoot, Lord, she's even prettier up close.

A glance toward Travis sent his thoughts ricocheting over the crazy prayer he'd prayed earlier. He'd spent much of his adult life avoiding women, for fear he'd make a lousy husband like his own father. He'd been avoiding home as much as he could ever since Ezra fell ill, it being too hard to watch him decline. The job with the stage company had provided a perfect distraction to help him dodge the difficult parts of his life.

Sam would need help caring for Ezra and her baby. Despite hardly knowing either of them, he felt drawn to both Hannah and Travis. The idea of them not being around left a knot in his belly. Maybe it was time to settle down, make some attempt at a real life. But doing what?

Lord, am I thinking crazy? They're practically strangers. I don't even know if I got what it takes to make a good husband and father.

Finn squeezed his eyes shut. Better not to dwell on it. His thoughts were probably still pain-and-fever addled. That's all. He tried shifting his thoughts to safer topics, but within moments, his eyes strayed again to her pert nose and the dotting of freckles sprinkled over her features. Easing his position, he shifted slightly, and she did also, settling her cheek against his shoulder.

Her warm breath stirred against his cheek and neck, sending shivers through him. He closed his eyes, warring inside about whether to draw her closer or pull himself back.

No, he wouldn't break his vow. He'd be nothing less than a gentleman, though her softness burrowed so close was tempting. He laced his fingers over his chest, turned his face away, and closed his eyes.

Lord, help me.

For what seemed an hour, he tried to keep his mind occupied with anything other than the beautiful woman beside him. At some point, he must have dozed off for Travis was suddenly at the opening of the lean-to shaking them both. Hannah stirred, huddled nearer, and slept on. Finn glanced heavenward to find the sun high in the sky. He squinted at the boy.

The kid glanced back and pointed. "Riders coming."

The sound of distant hoofbeats stole into his consciousness, slowing as they neared.

"Hellooo," a familiar voice called. "Finn McCaffrey—you in there?"

Chapter Nine

Strawberry, California

Hannah woke, vaguely aware of a foreign sound in her otherwise silent surroundings. She opened her eyes. Bright sunlight flooded the room, and scents of fresh-baked bread and cooking meat wafted up from downstairs. She stretched and swung her stocking feet over the edge of the bed. Only then did she realize Margie Gouldrie was peeking through the door at her.

"Didn't mean to wake you, dear. Go back to sleep." The gray-haired woman smiled. "I was delivering your clean clothes." She pointed to a pile of both her and Travis's folded garments on a nearby chair.

After all she'd been through, Hannah would have welcomed the mundaneness of ironing, but in the three days since the rescue, Margie hadn't let her lift a finger. The dear woman had taken charge of her and Travis, insisting both rest.

"Thank you, but I've slept enough. I hope Travis hasn't been pestering you." She stood and fluffed her dress into place, slid her feet into her shoes, and bent to fasten them.

"The scamp's been fine. He's visited the horses at the corral, and now he's playing checkers with Finn."

At the mention of the jehu's name, Hannah's hands faltered, though she recovered quickly. "He's awake, then?"

Between the infection, the fever, the copious amount of whiskey the rescuers poured down his throat before moving him, and the morphine the doctor dosed him with after, Finn hadn't been conscious in two days. After concentrating so much of her attention on his care, she'd found herself at loose ends knocking around the inn with nothing to do. Yet she couldn't bring herself to return to San Francisco until she knew he'd turned the corner.

"He's awake, hungry, and itching to be outta bed. Thankfully, Travis has kept him distracted this afternoon."

"That's good news." She stood and smoothed her skirt again.

Outside, the rumble of an approaching stage split the stillness, and the hostlers' muffled voices rose over the din. Margie smiled. "I best get downstairs. They've got a half hour to feed the passengers before they head to Placerville." She turned down the hall, and the staircase creaked. "By the way," she called, "Finn's been asking after you. Since you're not gonna sleep, you'd make him a happy man if you went by for a visit."

Her cheeks warmed at the idea, and Hannah castigated herself. To squelch the anticipation, she forced herself to unbraid and brush her hair then take her time pinning it up. Finally, she meandered down the long hall, finding Finn's door open.

His gaze met hers as she stepped into view. Travis, seated cross-legged beside Finn on the big bed, turned when Finn's attention shifted. The boy waved then twisted back to the checkerboard and moved a piece.

"Howdy, Hannah." Finn smiled. His features were etched with pain, eyes rimmed with dark circles, but he was upright, reclining against a pile of pillows. The bandage about his bare midriff accentuated his slim waist and broad shoulders.

Goodness, when had the hall grown so warm? She dipped her chin, averting her eyes, and resisted the urge to tug at her neckline. "How are you feeling?"

"Some better."

At Travis's urging, Finn considered the board and moved a checker. In turn, the boy made multiple jumps, ending the game.

Finn grunted and rolled his eyes, sending Travis into gales of laughter. "Lost count how many games this kid's won."

Her chest swelled. "He's got a sharp mind. I'm anxious to get him to the school so he can start learning in earnest."

His expression clouded. "When will you go?"

"I'm not sure. Soon." She resisted telling him she'd waited for him to improve.

When Travis motioned to the reset checkerboard, Finn shook his head. "Not right now."

Without complaint, Travis moved to the far corner of the bed and balanced the board on his lap, playing against himself.

Finn pointed to the chair next to the bed. "Would you sit awhile so we can talk?"

Concern threading through her, she took the offered seat. "Is everything all right?"

Intense blue eyes met hers before he turned to stare at his lap. "Need to tell you some things. They ain't easy to talk about." Seconds ticked by before he began. "In the mountains, you asked who I was trying to save."

She shook her head. "Finn, you don't have to expla—"

He held up a hand. "I need to say this."

Hannah pursed her lips and nodded.

"I didn't have the best start in life. My ma was real kind, a lot like you with the tender way you cared for me, your patience with Travis."

Her stomach fluttered, though she chided herself for so easily falling for his charms.

"Pa was a different sort—mean on his best days, vile and abusive when he was drunk, which was most of the time. When I was eight, he got angry, lit into Ma over a mistake I made. I tried to protect her, but he knocked me across the room then went after her again."

His eyes slid shut, and he clenched his teeth, his voice a mere whisper. "He put his hands around her throat. Killed her right in front of me."

"Oh, Finn." Tears welling, she clasped his hand as memories of that moment in the mountains returned. "I'm so sorry."

When he opened his eyes, they were distant. "I ran away after that. Spent some time on my own. Did all right until winter. Then I about starved to death."

Silence stretched between them.

Hannah swallowed, trying to bury her threatening tears. "What happened?"

Finn glanced at her. "Snuck into a house, tried to steal food and warm clothes." A faint smile crossed his lips. "The man that lived there caught me in the act. Coulda turned me over to the law. He took me in instead, raised me like his own."

"God provided for you." She squeezed his fingers.

"Eventually." Finn looked at her. "I overheard some of your discussions about Travis the day we left. He hasn't had it easy, either."

Hannah glanced Travis's way, liking that he'd entertained himself while they talked. "No. His mother is deceased, and his father is neglectful."

"Me and him got more in common than either of us would care to admit."

Throat knotting, she nodded.

"So what'll happen to him now?"

She shrugged. "I'll take him back to San Francisco, and he'll be enrolled in the school."

"What about a home, a family? Will he live with you, or—"

"Many students reside at the school. Travis can stay in the attic room at my aunt's boardinghouse until he gets comfortable with the changes he's facing."

Finn shook his head. "He needs more than that, Hannah. He needs a real home, not some institution. Travis needs a family—a ma and a pa."

Her brows knitted in confusion. Of course, he needed a family, but God hadn't allowed that, and there was little she could do to remedy the circumstance. While Travis's father had signed the boy into her care, it was temporary. She had no expectation that she, a spinster, would get to keep and raise the young man.

He twined his fingers between hers. "I'm real fond of you, Hannah. I was hoping I could come calling soon. I'd like to court you, think about marriage, giving Travis a real home."

Blood draining from her face so quickly she felt almost dizzy, Hannah pulled free of his grasp and stood. Courting. . .and marriage? She'd promised herself no man would get near enough to speak of such things again. Especially *this man*. Not when another young woman carried his child.

"I don't think that would be wise, Mr. McCaffrey."

Confusion etched his face. "Mr. McCaff—"

She turned toward the door, stopping to drag Travis from the bed. Checkerboard and checkers scattered in all directions.

"Hannah, wait," he called as she pulled Travis through the door and down the hall. "Please talk to me!"

Travis tried to jerk free, but she tightened her grasp. She hurried into her room and shut the door, bracing her back against it. Gulping air like a fish out of water, she fought back tears.

"Lord, this wasn't supposed to happen."

Travis watched her, wide-eyed. Only after her breathing slowed did she beckon him nearer. He hesitantly moved toward her.

"I'm sorry if I hurt you." She signed the words with trembling hands, though she had little hope he'd understand.

The boy shook his head. "What's wrong? You angry?"

"No." Hannah shook her head and tried to smile.

"Sick?"

Heartsick, maybe. Again, she shook her head. "No."

She paced to the window. The stage stood ready for departure. How much of the thirty minutes was left until they pulled out? Perhaps half—enough time, if she hurried.

Hannah grabbed her bag from the corner and threw the clothes Margie had delivered into it. Motioning for Travis to stay, she hurried to his room and collected his few belongings. Shoving them into the bag, she hurried back to him.

"It's time for us to go." She signed the words, took his hand, and started toward the door.

Travis resisted. "Go? We're leaving?"

She nodded. Slipping her arm about his shoulders, she led him into the hall. At the staircase, Travis glanced back toward Finn's room, though he didn't resist Hannah's direction. She led him downstairs and turned toward the front door.

A crowd of about six people had gathered in the small lobby, though the group went outside when someone announced the stage would be loading momentarily. She approached the counter where Margie stood.

The older woman looked up, eyes widening as her gaze fell on Hannah's bag. "You're not leaving, are you?"

"Is there room on today's stage?"

Margie hesitated then nodded. "There's room, but are you sure you're ready?"

"It's time. Travis needs to be in school, and I'm eager to see my aunt and uncle. They won't stop fretting until they see I'm all right."

Appearing almost rattled, Margie nodded. "Of course. The stage will be loading shortly."

As Hannah thanked her for her kindness and hugged her farewell, the front door burst open. They all turned to see the brown-haired young woman from the Virginia City station. The young woman's eyes strayed to Margie.

"I'm Samantha Foster. I'm looking for Finn McCaffrey."

Margie's focus shifted, and Hannah led Travis outside, her stomach knotting uncomfortably.

Yes, indeed. Time to move on.

◆　◆　◆

Finn stared into the hallway, chest tightening. Blast his stupid leg. If he were able to get up, he'd chase Hannah down and hold her until that panicked look left her eyes. Let her know he didn't expect anything other than to get to know her under better circumstances. *Then*, iffen things worked like he hoped, they could consider marrying and adopting Travis.

"Lord, I really mucked this up, and I'm helpless to fix it." He scrubbed a hand over his face. How was he to chase Hannah down when he couldn't even dress himself? According to the doctor, he'd be hobbling on crutches for weeks to come, useless for work or much else. Finn glared at the ceiling. "You know I hate this, right?"

He plucked a checker from the quilt and flung it vehemently toward the door. It hit the door frame and ricocheted across the floor.

Quick footsteps clicked down the hall, and hope sprouted in his chest. Perhaps she'd returned. He pinned his gaze on the doorway, and soon a womanly form stepped into view. Only it wasn't Hannah.

Sam.

She attempted a smile, but it crumpled, and she clamped a hand over her mouth to stifle a sob. Without waiting for an invitation, she bolted into the room and fell into his arms.

Finn held her, murmuring comforting words as she clung to him, her hot tears wetting his shoulder. When she finally collected herself, she sat back.

"I saw the crash on my way here. Did you have to pick the most treacherous spot on the trail?"

He hung his head. "I'm sorry. I didn't mean to worry you."

"Well, you did, you big galoot. Now what's wrong? The telegram I got said you're hurt."

"Nothing that won't mend. Leg's busted. Laid my side open pretty good."

She glanced at the bandage then shook her head. "If you weren't already such a mess, I'd make a mess of you, Finn McCaffrey."

He grinned but sobered quickly. "Sam, where's Ezra? You didn't bring him all this way, did you?" *Lord, please tell me she didn't.* The man was too old and brittle to handle such a trip.

She also turned serious but made no response.

"Did you?"

She wiped away another tear. "He collapsed again. He's taken a bad turn. Doc doesn't think he'll last more than a couple weeks."

His jaw went slack. "Then what're you doing here? You should be with him. Did you leave him home alone?"

"He's with Doc while I came to bring you home. He's asking for you." Sam slid back into his arms and rested her cheek against his shoulder. "How soon can you travel?"

The thought of going anywhere in his present state set his teeth on edge. He'd had enough jostling and pain to last a few lifetimes. Yet Ezra was asking.

He'd known the time was coming ever since the man had collapsed two years ago. Once the immediate crisis was done, Finn had taken the job with the stage company so he wouldn't be around as much to watch Ezra's decline. Yet, right then, there was nothing he wanted more than to be with the man who'd become his father nearly thirty years ago.

"I don't know about traveling. My leg's still paining me pretty fierce. Margie would know when the doctor's supposed to look in on me."

Sam sat up. "I can fetch her."

"Yeah. Ask her to come up here. Oh, iffen you see a pretty redheaded gal a little older than you, that's Hannah. Ask her to come up, too. Got a few things to discuss with her, as well." He shot a prayer heavenward that Sam or Margie could convince Hannah to return.

Sam's brows arched. "I'm not sure if she's the same one, but a red-haired woman and a boy—looked to be about ten—were preparing to leave when I came in."

His gut clenched. "Preparing to leave?"

Chapter Ten

San Francisco
Late January 1863

H er cloak over her arm, Hannah checked the rooms lining the main hall of the school. All were neat and tidy, ready for the next day's activities. She stepped back into the hall in time to see several darting forms burst past the front windows. A smile curved Hannah's lips as she hurried to watch the children running and chasing one another after a long day of study. A muffled giggle punctuated the happy scene.

Across the yard, Travis trotted after eleven-year-old Millie Gordon. *Lord, help us all. That boy is hopelessly smitten.* He could do far worse. Millie was a sweet girl, and she seemed as taken with Travis as he was with her. Hannah had been expecting the infatuation to wane, but after three months, it hadn't happened.

Pulling on her cloak, Hannah stepped onto the stoop and watched the children play. After a moment, Millie approached Mr. Crandall, the teacher. Her brow creased with worry, she signed furiously, pointing toward the gate. Hannah caught enough of the statement to understand the girl was speaking about Travis, who'd disappeared.

At her approach, Millie repeated herself.

Travis jumped the fence to talk to a strange man.

The crisp breeze carried the excited sound of Travis's voice, though she couldn't distinguish the words.

"Thank you. I'll get him." She signed the words, both for Millie's benefit and Mr. Crandall's, who was deaf himself. Heart pounding, she hurried toward the gate.

Who on earth was he talking to? Travis had come out of his shell among the students and school staff. He was comfortable talking with the boardinghouse residents if she translated for him. Yet he wasn't overly confident with strangers. This was someone familiar to him. She raced through the gate, an unfamiliar man's back coming into view as she neared.

A chill slid down her spine. Could it be his father, come to reclaim him—or some more distant relative she knew nothing about? Seeing how Travis had thrived at the school, she'd fight to keep him.

"Pardon me, sir. Can I help you?"

Leaning on a gnarled wooden cane, the man turned and pushed his hat back. The late-afternoon sun glinted on piercing blue eyes. "Howdy, Hannah."

Her breath caught, and warmth flooded through her at Finn McCaffrey's rich voice. Her heart kicked into a thunderous gallop.

Travis bolted toward her, chattering so fast she couldn't keep up. She silenced him with a sign. At his crestfallen expression, she pulled him to her side and smiled at him.

Only then did she look again at Finn, warning herself not to let him see the effect he'd had on her.

"Mr. McCaffrey." She smiled politely. "What a surprise. You're looking well."

"So are you. Real pretty, in fact."

Heat flooded her cheeks. She could only hope he wouldn't notice her blush. "I didn't expect to see you again. What brings you to San Francisco?"

He shrugged his shoulders. "Gave up my job with the stage company and moved out this way about a month ago."

"You gave up your job?"

Finn nodded. "Some things changed. I needed to change with 'em."

Her gaze strayed to the cane. "Your leg. Shouldn't it have healed by now?"

"It's healed. Still pains me when I'm on it too much." He shrugged, looking uncomfortable. "I bought a livery stable a few blocks from here. Been trying to work up the gumption to come see you. We never got to finish our conversation."

Her lungs constricted. "I believe we did. You asked to come calling, and I answered."

His expression faltered, and she looked away. *Lord, I don't want to hurt him.*

"Can I ask why you said no? Is it because of what your intended did to you, or something else?"

Hannah's jaw went slack, and she glanced heavenward. *Didn't I ask You to make him forget that conversation, Lord?* How on earth had he remembered it, as much pain as he was in?

A pair of women walked by, nodding hello as they passed. Finn greeted them, touching his hat brim. Travis mimicked his gesture.

When Finn's attention returned to her, she motioned toward the gate. "I'd prefer not to have this conversation on the street. We can use one of the schoolrooms, if you'd like."

At his nod, Hannah herded Travis back into the schoolyard. She explained to Mr. Crandall that Finn was a friend and they needed a moment to talk, then asked Travis to wait outside. She led Finn inside to the main classroom, lit the lamp on the teacher's desk, and closed the door partway.

"So did you turn me down because of what he did? If so, you need to know that I'm not him. I wouldn't do that to you."

The man didn't waste time. She'd barely regained her bearings from his surprise appearance, and he was pressing the issue.

Hannah folded her arms. "I wish I could believe that, but I don't."

"Why?" He hobbled toward her. "Hannah, what am I fighting here? Are you resisting me because of something I did, or have his actions colored all men as traitors in your mind?"

Her eyes stung. Any man interested in her would have to overcome her fears after Andrew's betrayal, but that should hardly concern Finn McCaffrey. "I overheard the young woman in Virginia City tell you she was with child."

He considered the statement then cocked his head. "That's why you left?"

She nodded.

"Because you think the baby's mine."

"What should I think? I heard your response. The impression I got was the baby wasn't expected, nor was the news well received."

A wry smile broke across his face. "You're right on both points, but that's not because I got Sam Foster in the family way. That's her scoundrel husband's doing." He paused. "Hannah, Sam's my *sister*. She came to tell me the news of her condition before I rolled outta town."

His sister? Once the words registered, her legs grew so shaky she leaned heavily on the nearest desk. "Oh."

He settled his hands on her shoulders. "You all right there?"

Mortified, Hannah buried her face in her hands. "I'm such a fool. I owe you an apology."

"Well, in your defense, you didn't know either of us, and I herded her outside when I saw where the conversation was going. Easy mistake to make."

She risked a look at him. Dancing blue eyes peered back. "You're too kind. I assumed terrible things about you both. How can you dismiss that?"

"You don't understand, Hannah Rose."

Her breath caught at his use of her papa's pet name, and she hung on his next words.

"You and Travis have been echoing in my mind and heart ever since we left those mountains. There ain't been a day I haven't thought about or prayed for you both. I've begged God for another chance to get to know you. If dismissing a silly misunderstanding gives me that chance, I'll take it. I'm asking you again, Hannah Rose. Can I come callin'?"

Her belly fluttered so furiously she pressed her hands to it. She'd lain awake every night praying for him, trying to tell herself the concern was due to his injuries. Such lies. Loneliness for him had nearly suffocated her at times. It had made little sense, given they barely knew each other, but when Travis began begging to take the stagecoach to see him, she'd known there was more to both their feelings than she cared to admit. He'd echoed in their hearts and minds also.

"Well?"

She closed her eyes, swallowed hard, and gave a hesitant nod. "Yes."

A work-roughened hand cupped her cheek and tipped her head back. Warm lips pressed hers, gently at first then with more intensity. Hannah's heart pounded as she fought the conflicting urges to pull away and to press in.

Loud footsteps intruded on their moment, and they broke the kiss as Travis slammed into them, wrapping his arms around their waists. She and Finn burst into laughter at his beaming grin.

"Are you two getting married?"

Finn looked at him then shifted his gaze to her. "Tell him. . .iffen I have my way, the answer's yes. Real soon."

Epilogue

Early June 1863

Finn paced the front porch, hands shoved in his pockets. Travis watched his movements from the chair nearby. Another torturous scream emanated from inside the house, and Finn stalled, chills racing along his spine. He held his breath until the unnerving sound ended.

Lord, please be merciful. How long is this gonna take?

He leaned against the railing, staring in the direction of McCaffrey's Livery next door. He was losing a day of work, but he didn't mind. How could he when the baby was coming?

When the next scream started, Finn gripped the porch railing and puffed out his cheeks as he waited for it to end. The cry crescendoed then dropped off suddenly, replaced with joyful, if muffled, laughter. Hope flooded his thoughts. Unable to resist, he climbed onto the railing and peeked over the porch roof toward the second-story window.

"Hannah?" He hollered her name, not caring who heard. "Hannah Rose!"

The window slid open, and his bride of one week leaned out, grinning. From inside, a thin wail rose. "Congratulations. You're an uncle. Mama and baby are both fine."

Tension drained from his body. "That's good."

"Once they're both cleaned up, you and Travis can come in. It shouldn't be long." She ducked back in the window.

"Wait. Boy or girl?"

Too late. The window closed.

Finn glanced heavenward. "Thank You, Lord."

He ducked under the porch roof and stepped down. Travis stared wide-eyed, trepidation etching his features.

"The baby's here." Finn signed the statement.

Travis bolted to his feet. "Is it a boy?" At Finn's shrug, he spun toward the door. "Let's find out."

Finn clamped a hand on his shoulder and signed, "Hold on there, kid. We have to wait."

With a roll of his eyes, Travis slumped into the chair again. "More waiting?"

Finn couldn't help but laugh at the boy he'd come to think of as a son. In two weeks, they'd see the judge to make his adoption legal. The days couldn't go fast enough.

"A little wait." He held his fingers close together to indicate *small*.

"Why'd we send the other kids home if all we're gonna do is sit around for hours?"

He hadn't wanted to return the deaf students to the school before their riding lessons were complete. Teaching the children to become competent horsemen had become one of the highlights of his week, and they all seemed to love it, as well. "Because I needed to focus on Aunt Sam having her baby."

Finally, the midwife invited them in, though she warned they could stay only a moment before Sam would need to feed the baby. They raced upstairs to Sam's room, slowing themselves half a step before reaching the door. Finn looped an arm around Travis's shoulders and pushed the door open.

Sam smiled, her hair matted with sweat and fatigue lining her face. By the window, Hannah cradled the new babe. Travis beat a path to see his new cousin, but Finn stood a moment, drinking in the scene before heading to Sam's side. Pushing her hair back, he kissed her forehead. "How you doing, sis?"

"I'm good."

"What'd you have?"

"A girl. Charlotte Anne."

His gaze strayed toward Hannah as Travis craned to see the baby. "Named her for your ma, huh?"

Sam nodded. "She's so pretty, Finn. You gotta see her."

She didn't need to ask twice. He hurried toward his bride.

Sunlight fell across Hannah's shoulders, making her red locks glow. As he approached, she glanced up, pure contentment on her face. He eased an arm around her waist, and Hannah smoothed the blanket away from Charlotte's face. The wee girl turned toward the touch, her lips working.

"You're right. She's beautiful, sis."

"Can I hold her?" Travis asked.

The midwife cleared her throat.

Finn looked at Travis. "Later, Squirt. Aunt Sam needs time with the baby." He stumbled through the signs then herded the boy out the door, Travis grumbling about *more waiting*.

Hannah handed the baby over and slipped out, grinning as she joined him. "She truly is beautiful."

"Reckon so, but I was having a hard time focusing."

"Why on earth?"

He drew her to a halt as Travis headed downstairs. "Didn't I tell you? I had a dream the other night."

Worry creased her features. "About your father?"

Finn shook his head. "I haven't dreamed about him since that day in the mountains."

"Then what?"

Pulling her to him, he settled his mouth near her ear. "That we had a baby of our own. Seeing you holding Charlotte got me to woolgathering about the day that might come true."

She pulled back, her cheeks flushing. "I hope it's soon."

"Well, iffen I have my way—" He claimed her lips.

Author's Note

Dear Reader,

When I began brainstorming this story and realized I wanted to include a deaf child as a main character, I researched historic deaf schools in the western states and territories. I was pleasantly surprised to discover the California Institution for the Instruction of the Deaf and Dumb and Blind in San Francisco.

The school opened in 1860 due to the efforts of twenty-three influential ladies who wanted to ensure that deaf and blind children of California were not left to sleep and beg on the streets. Instead, these children were given a healthy environment in which to live and learn.

The day the school opened, they had three students—two deaf and one blind. Within months, their numbers grew to double digits. By 1865, the school building and property had become cramped, and they searched for a new, larger location. It took until 1869 before they opened a new facility in Berkeley, California, where the school continued to grow. In the early 1900s, they separated the school into two—one for the deaf and one for the blind. Both schools live on today. They are now known as the California School for the Deaf and the California School for the Blind.

I hope you enjoyed the story as much as I did! Thanks for reading.

Jennifer Uhlarik

Jennifer Uhlarik discovered the western genre as a preteen, when she swiped the only "horse" book she found on her older brother's bookshelf. A new love was born. Across the next ten years, she devoured Louis L'Amour westerns and fell in love with the genre. In college at the University of Tampa, she began penning her own story of the Old West. Armed with a BA in writing, she has won five writing competitions and was a finalist in two others. In addition to writing, she has held jobs as a private business owner, a schoolteacher, a marketing director, and her favorite—a full-time homemaker. Jennifer is active in American Christian Fiction Writers and is a lifetime member of the Florida Writers Association. She lives near Tampa, Florida, with her husband, teenage son, and four fur children.

Letters from Lucy

by Jenness Walker

Chapter One

Texas

Lucy Frederick had lived in western Texas for a whole month and hadn't caught sight of a single rattlesnake, much less a robbery, saloon fight, or range war. Aunt Margret's town of Ripple saw less action than a sewing circle.

The dime novels lied. Novelists must be failed journalists—writers who came west at the promise of adventure and instead landed in a sleepy town. With nothing noteworthy to write about, they had to use their skills somehow. So they lied. Thus the beginning of the dime novel.

Lucy was certain that was the way it happened, because her life was following that same wretched path.

With a sigh, she swept up the envelope holding her latest imagined news article and flounced down the stairs of her aunt's boardinghouse. She'd send the letter back home to her friend Amelia and try not to be bitter at her father. Newspaper mogul Henry Frederick had either been deceived the same as Lucy, or, after the fire fiasco, he'd finally found a way to keep his inquisitive daughter out of trouble.

Father was never deceived.

Since Lucy hadn't yet developed his instincts, when he'd proposed the trip—or banishment—from Boston to Texas, she'd been gullible once again. Maybe Father was right: she wasn't cut out to be a journalist.

Outside on the boardwalk, she strolled toward the mercantile, giving her high collar a discreet tug as she skimmed through her fake article again.

On Tuesday, just outside this particular Texas town, the clouds blew in a hint of rain. However, the welcome overcast skies failed to dampen the spirits of an unnamed resident. A fight over a mere trifle sent him out into the hills on the wild ride of a lifetime. Said resident and his lady had words over burnt beans, and his horse lit out with all the fury of a woman's wrath licking at its hooves.

Then the front hoof sank into a prairie dog hole, and though the horse survived the incident with only a swollen knee, the owner's life and fortunes changed in a serendipitous moment.

For through the unlikely event of burnt beans, a fight with the cook, an escape to sulk, an industrious rodent, an ill-timed step, a sudden downpour, and a need for cover, this unnamed resident discovered a stash of stolen gold.

◆　◆　◆

"Mornin', Miss Lucy."

She caught the scent of pipe tobacco, gun powder, and magnolias. "Good morning,

Sheriff," she answered, flipping through the rest of the pages without looking up. Her feet knew this path to the post office very well, and she wanted to read the part about the heroic cowboy Sam Brazos once again.

"Aunt Margret is in her garden," Lucy said after a moment. "But if you're still set on courting her, I'd suggest tossing the bouquet and offering peaches instead."

"Aw shucks." Groaning, he fell in beside her, his steps almost as heavy as his jowls. "Is she still offended at my coon dog eating her pie while y'all were at church Sunday?"

"Yes, sir. And the cake, too."

"Now, now, the cake wasn't Rufus."

"Same size paw prints in the flour. The scent of skunk lingered the entire day, and everyone knows Rufus tangled with one."

"Well, now, Miss Lucy. You need to come work for me!" The sheriff clapped her on the back.

As she lurched forward, she felt fit for the journalism world after all. Never mind the fact that she hadn't noticed the clues until *after* she'd witnessed the four-legged culprit's escape.

"Next time I have a murder investigation, I'll come callin'."

Lucy's ears perked up as she searched out his face for the first time. "When was your last one?"

He scratched his head. "I don't rightly know. Four years ago? Naw, I was back in Kentucky. Tell the truth, we haven't seen a single murder here since I came to town. Would you believe it?"

"Yes, Sheriff." Her shoulders sagged as she folded her letter and tucked it inside the envelope. "Yes, I would."

The sheriff tipped his hat and retraced his steps as Lucy stopped in front of the entrance to the post office—a small booth partitioned off the mercantile. What she wouldn't give for something interesting to happen in this insufferably dull town. For an outlaw to come bursting out of this very building, or—

The heavy door creaked open, and a tall, lean cowboy stepped through, his smoky-blue eyes smoldering below the rim of his black Stetson.

"Miss Lucy." The man held the door wide, his demeanor aloof as always.

Sam Brazos—the genuine but still oh-so-swoon-worthy version—was the one redeeming factor of her father shipping her off to her aunt's. Lucy was sure the boarding-house guest had a million stories to tell, but around her his lips were sealed, the expression on his clean-shaven face impossible to read.

So she dreamed up the stories and sent them to Amelia. And then she dreamed of him.

Reaching into her hidden pocket, Lucy clutched her lucky pen and breezed by Sam, trying not to be the bother he seemed to believe she was. Then he leaned closer, and she caught a whiff of leather and the woods and the strong, sweet smell of grape, which was pretty remarkable, considering there were no vineyards in the area. There were, however, Texas mountain laurels, and they'd covered the Rocking R Ranch last time she'd been out there.

What business did Sam Brazos have at the Rocking R?

"Something wrong with Gus?" he asked quietly, stopping Lucy in her tracks.

She forced her gaze away from the stubble darkening his strong jaw and glanced toward the postmaster. Gus cast anxious looks out the window while attending Mrs. Thorp and Widow Aurilla.

"What time is it?" Lucy asked.

"Half past noon."

Relaxing, she answered, "Polly delivers his lunch on Thursdays. She must be late."

Sam's brow furrowed, and Lucy filed away the confused expression for use in her next article. Or, just because.

"Everyone knows Gus Wiley turns into an ogre when he's hungry," she explained. "Usually I avoid him during the dinner hour, but I ran late."

Sam nodded toward the letter. "Working on that?"

"A little article I'm sending back to Boston." She hid the envelope from view.

He didn't need to know it was a pointless exercise—only something she penned for her friend's amusement and to keep her writing skills intact. And he definitely didn't need to know that, since he'd galloped into town a week after her own woefully uneventful arrival, most of the articles revolved around him.

Sam tipped his hat lower, but she still felt his intense scrutiny. If he didn't stop staring, she was going to start babbling. In fact, her lips were already moving. . . "How is Jerusha today? Did Doc Smith go out to see her yet? I've been so worried—" She broke off when she saw the thunderstorm clouding Sam's eyes as he loomed over her.

"Have you been following me?" he asked through clenched teeth.

"What? No!" A blush heated her cheeks, and she averted her eyes, remembering she'd considered that exact course of action on several occasions for reasons both personal and writing-related. But she'd never actually done it.

Which was probably why she failed at the journalism thing.

"How did you know I went to Rockin'—"

"Why, Lucy Frederick!" Widow Aurilla called from the desk. "We was just talking about you."

Sam drew back, his narrowed gaze skimming over her. "You'll be at dinner?"

For once in her life, Lucy couldn't find her voice. She bobbed her head.

He nodded back, parted his lips as if to say more, then spun on his heel and strode across the dusty street.

"Is Sam Brazos going sweet on you?" Mrs. Thorp's wide face dimpled as she reached Lucy's side. "Inviting you to sit with him at dinner? Ain't that precious."

Lucy opened her mouth to protest, but Widow Aurilla piped up first.

"Them weren't Cupid's arrows shooting from his eyes, Hester."

"Well, I shore felt some heat." Mrs. Thorp fanned broad hands in front of her face as Widow Aurilla rolled her eyes.

"You be careful, Lucy girl. Mark my words, that boy needs watched."

Mrs. Thorp guffawed. "Oh, he's being watched, ain't he, love?"

"Hester!"

A smirk stole over Lucy's face even as Mrs. Thorp's surprisingly sharp elbow nudged her ribs, because Sam Brazos was indeed impossible to miss. Even now he drew her eye like words on a page as his confident stride ate up the distance between him and his destination, other pedestrians making way for him. Sam Brazos was a force to be reckoned with.

And she'd drawn his ire.

"Have a care, Lucy," the widow cautioned. "There's trouble a-brewing, and it blew in around the time of his arrival."

Lucy dragged her gaze from the tall cowboy. "What kind of trouble?"

"Oh, I've heard rumblings. A bit of this and a touch of that. But mark my words. . . whatever's going on, that dark-haired stranger is in the thick of it."

"I think he's a Pinkerton agent." Mrs. Thorp wiggled her eyebrows.

"I think he's a rustler." Widow Aurilla drew herself up and placed a firm hand on her friend's not-so-firm arm. "But enough gossip. Just be cautious, dear. If any shenanigans occur, we need you and yer purty handwriting to let the world know what happened here."

Lucy blinked, and Mrs. Thorp snorted. "Don't listen to her, Lucy. If I were you—shucks, if I were *me* without my mister, I'd be using that purty handwriting on fancy love letters to the boy."

With that, they paraded down the boardwalk, with Mrs. Thorp's boisterous laughter floating behind them.

A smile teased Lucy's lips as she stared at the saloon doors Sam had pushed through. A rustler? A Pinkerton agent? She doubted both tales, but behind every bit of gossip, there was usually a kernel of truth. Whether or not the two older ladies were on the right track suspecting the handsome newcomer, Lucy held hope that trouble was on the way.

Trouble meant a story. A *real* one. One of these days she'd prove her father wrong. She could find a good lead, and she could do it justice.

She only needed the chance to try.

The saloon doors sprang back open, and Sam stomped out, his frustration visible from where Lucy's feet had anchored themselves to the boardwalk.

Maybe today would be that day.

Chapter Two

Sam studied the street before him and caught a glimpse of Lucy Frederick standing near the mercantile. No one got under Sam's skin quite like the redheaded writer. Most days he wanted to strangle the woman, with her wide, inquisitive eyes, endless questions, and overall nosiness.

He beat the dust out of his hat, watching careful-like as Lucy moseyed along, all grace and fire wrapped in the latest fashion.

He wouldn't strangle her, of course. That was a mite harsh. Gagging her, on the other hand, with the occasional hog-tying session to keep her cute turned-up nose out of trouble—*that* he'd strongly consider. These were dangerous parts. He'd be doing it for her own good. If she'd trailed him out to Rockin' R Ranch, he doubted she'd had the good sense to take anyone with her.

Maybe he should teach her to shoot. A reluctant smile twisted his lips as he made his way toward the livery stable. As if that fancy pen she always carried around wasn't dangerous enough.

Checking on Stinkeye was a good excuse to question the stable boy. The blacksmith's son was usually a fount of information, which Sam needed after the saloon keeper had shut down his latest lead to clear his name. But Sam wasn't going to question the boy about the contents of saddlebags or a certain choice snack or suspicious money. No, he had something else in mind.

"Miss Lucy ain't been on a horse since last Friday," Dusty answered as he bit into the piece of licorice Sam offered. "She fancies takin' Dellarosa on jaunts here and yonder, but since the boardinghouse has a few extra guests now, she's been helping there."

Sam remembered seeing her elbow-deep in flour, pounding the life out of her aunt's bread dough. The image of her freckled cheeks adorned with a dusting of white would carry him through the tough chewing to come later.

"You're absolutely sure?"

"Been here all day, mister." Dusty's wide mouth opened in a full-blown grin, displaying his crooked teeth and a hint of the black candy Sam knew to be his favorite. "A boy don't rightly forget Miss Lucy."

He had a point. But if she hadn't followed him, how did she know about Rockin' R? Sam glanced down, saw the mud splatters. Had she seen his boots and guessed he'd crossed the river to head to the ranch? Was it as simple as that? As simple as knowing about the postmaster's lunchtime habits?

"She saved my mouser the other day, you know."

Sam looked up from his absentminded inspection of Stinkeye's hooves. "I didn't."

"Yessiree, I told her Checkers went missin', and next thing I know, she tells me where to find his new hiding place. All because she saw a dead mouse and a few pieces of yarn."

It truly was the mud, then. Sam shook his head in amazement. The lady drove him crazy, but she could be exactly what he needed to clear his name. That is, if she'd give him a chance.

On the other hand, she could turn around and use him to *make* her name. Was that a risk he was willing to take?

He had dinner tonight to figure that out.

That evening, six sweaty gents gathered around the plank table in the boardinghouse dining room. Casting furtive glances in Sam's direction, Lucy passed a basket of sliced bread while her aunt ladled stew. The meat looked like rabbit, but with the feud between Margret and the sheriff's coon dog, Sam couldn't be sure.

The seat beside him remained empty. Come to think of it, half the town had started avoiding him the past two days, going so far as to duck around corners when they saw him passing their way. The saloon keeper had clammed up something fierce—claiming he was no rat, and that's all he'd say to the likes of Sam.

Why? Because the man was guilty? Or because he'd learned Sam's secret?

If Sam didn't know better, he might come to the conclusion that all of Ripple, Texas, was in on some sinister scheme.

But then there was the other half of town. . .

Lucy slid onto the bench beside him, managing the bustle of her dress like the lady she was, all while interrupting Sam's train of thought and her aunt's long-winded blessing. When the prayer ended, Lucy took a dainty bite and cast him a sidelong look, no doubt determining which of her endless questions to ask first.

Tonight he had some of his own.

"I was told some interesting things about you today, Mr. Brazos," Lucy said before he could start.

"Really?" A muscle jumped in his jaw. "I was about to say the same."

Her eyes widened. "I'm an open book."

"Are you?" He'd seen how she hid her mail from him.

"Mostly." Her cheeks turned a becoming shade of pink. "Everyone has secrets."

"That's the truth." Her secrets might not be as damaging as his, but she had them nonetheless. "As a journalist, how do you feel about exposing and exploiting those secrets?"

This time all color fled from her face, accentuating her delicate freckles.

"Well, I never, Mr. Brazos," Margret scolded. "Is that any way to talk to a lady?"

"She's right, Sam, my boy." Jasper Groth pointed a fork at him. "If you're going to win a fine young lady like Miss Lucy, you need to handle her with care. Flattery, poetry, trinkets—that's the ticket. None of these taxing questions."

Sam smothered a laugh behind his hand as Lucy's cheeks flushed once again, her eyes narrowing into slits as the arrogant former actor offered sample compliments for Sam to use at his discretion.

Lucy's nostrils flared, and she took in a fortifying breath to set Jasper to rights, no doubt. Which would probably end in Jasper's confusion and Lucy storming off to her room before Sam could ask for her assistance.

"Jerusha's fine, by the way," Sam blurted, surprising even himself.

Lucy focused back on him. "Truly? I was afraid to hope."

"The snake must not have been poisonous." Sam smiled at a memory of the six-year-old, curly-haired blond tucking a purple flower—one she'd stolen from a mason jar on her mother's table—into his leather hatband.

A flower that probably remained there for Lucy to see at the mercantile. One that he could still smell now, come to think of it. Of course. Between the laurel, the mud, and Lucy's ever-observant eye, his earlier destination had been obvious.

Yet he'd snapped at her.

"It seems I owe you an apology." Sam's delivery was stiff, but it seemed to be enough.

Lucy's face softened, making her a mite prettier, if that could be believed. "You're forgiven. . .in exchange for an interview."

His spine stiffened. "For what purpose?"

She shrugged. "I'm a journalist, and you're an interesting subject."

He couldn't help hoping a small part of her meant that personal-like. As he considered, Sam shoveled into his lukewarm stew, pushing away the image of the coon dog. He'd intended to tell Lucy his story anyway, but not for print. He needed use of her other skills—her observations, the information she was able to gather through conversations unavailable to him. But why should she agree when she would gain nothing in return?

There had to be some solution. He needed her.

Wrestling with his bread, he tore off a small piece to spare his teeth.

And they *all* needed her out of Margret's kitchen.

◆　◆　◆

After the kitchen had been put back to rights—with the help of a certain gentlemanly cowboy hauling in water and dirty dishes—Lucy closed the door to her room and immediately crossed to the window.

Sam had spoken to her. Not much, but more than his usual monosyllable answers. His voice had rumbled through her, gruff yet gentle, with an accent she couldn't completely place, but his words articulate all the same.

She'd intended to learn more about him, yet he'd refused her interview request, and the words he did speak only added to the mystery that surrounded him as surely as the night did now.

Lucy leaned closer to the glass for a better view of Sam crossing the street. He paused on the boardwalk as if to listen. When he faded into the shadows, Lucy swept up a wrap and flew barefoot down the stairs and into the night.

As she tracked Sam's progress across the town, she couldn't help noticing that so many more stars graced the sky. She could almost learn to like it in Ripple, if only life wasn't so predictable. Following Sam was a good way to fall in love fast. With Texas, of course. Not the cowboy. She hardly knew him.

But, if she had anything to say about it, that was about to change.

Moving as silently as her skirts permitted, Lucy tiptoed into the livery and past Admiral's stall, on to Dellarosa's. The sweet mare nickered at the sight of Lucy, who reached out to stroke the horse's muzzle.

Before she could see if Sam Brazos's mustang was still present, a strong hand gripped her arm. Lucy whirled with a gasp. Sam released her, but her skin still burned hot as he folded his arms across his broad chest. His sharp-eyed appraisal missed nothing of her hurried attire.

"Do you often rendezvous with boardinghouse men after dark?"

"How dare you! I never—"

"Truly?" He wore a smirk as he stepped into the circle of lantern light. "Then what are you doing?"

Lucy bit her lip against the impulse to defend herself. He knew she wasn't that kind of woman. "I lost something," she finally answered. Her Boston home. Her hope of a future in the newspaper business, or of ever making her father proud. Her head whenever she was around Sam.

Those eyes, though. As stormy and ever-changing as the ocean back home, deep-set in his handsome face, hooded by the barn's thick shadows. His confident stance and muscular frame convinced her he could handle the world. Protect her, if she ever needed protecting. Which she didn't.

Except maybe from ruffians like him. Because, after all, those eyes. . .

"How about you let me assist you?"

The mock concern in his voice brought Lucy crashing back to the present. "Better yet, why not allow me to interview you?"

"Here? I don't figure it's proper. If you promise to return to the boardinghouse real prompt-like, I reckon I'll answer one question." He turned his turbulent gaze to the street, giving her more opportunity to study him.

Something that was quickly becoming a favorite pastime, all in the name of research, of course.

With only one question, Lucy blurted out the thing foremost on her mind. "Why are you here?" He had no family in the area. No job that she knew of. This town had nothing special to recommend it.

Sam met her searching look, his eyes glinting in the dim light. His answer came then. Low, accompanied by an ironic smile. "I lost something."

If she had her reticule, she'd hit him with it. "That's no answer."

"No?" He shifted, his gaze falling to her lips. His voice softened. "It's late. Go home, Miss Frederick."

"You have no idea how much I wish I could."

Yet, at that moment, staring at Sam's far-too-attractive mouth as he stared at hers, Lucy wasn't sure there was anywhere else she'd rather be.

Chapter Three

If it had been anyone else on his trail, Sam would've left them trussed up and sleeping with Stinkeye. But the lantern light flickering over Lucy's delicate features made Sam forget she was only out for a story and didn't care who she had to hang to get it.

Why did she have to be so blamed pretty?

He was perilously close to kissing her, but then the Texas Rangers wouldn't be the only ones after his hide, and frankly, Margret and the rest of the Fredericks might be the deadlier of the two forces.

It wasn't until Lucy's lemonade-scented breath fanned his face that Sam realized he had indeed leaned close, his body proceeding while his brain took a detour.

He jerked upright and motioned toward the door. "Allow me to see you safely back."

With a huff, she clasped the shawl tightly and said, "Have it your way."

Sam surely imagined her haughty words were breathier than normal, but he followed her with wobbly knees just the same. She walked briskly, her skirts swishing in the quiet of the evening. They shouldn't be seen together—she had her reputation to think of. But he couldn't allow her to risk the walk alone. Especially when he caught the briefest glimpse of bare feet as she moved forward.

Shaking his head in consternation, Sam kept his distance with a wary eye on the empty boardwalks. They were almost in the clear when the saloon doors swung open a few paces away. Lunging, Sam caught Lucy's arm. He hauled her to the side of the building, out of sight as upbeat piano music spilled into the stillness.

"What—"

Sam clamped a hand over her mouth, noticing the softness of her lips seconds before the sharpness of her white teeth. "Did you really—"

"I did." She shook free. "Now hush." Turning, she craned her ear toward the sound of voices.

Sam couldn't decide whether to swear or leave her to her own devices, but he swallowed both instincts, rubbed his damp hand against his chest, and leaned with her to listen to the half-drunk whispers.

"Jasper bought hisself a shovel today."

Sam recognized the voice but couldn't place it.

"You dragged me out here to tell me that?"

A thump and an annoyed "Ow."

"Wait. You said Jasper? Lazy, gad-about Jasper?"

Sam inched closer, his shoulder brushing Lucy's. She didn't appear to notice. He couldn't say the same.

"The very one."

"Whyever for?"

The blacksmith. That's who the second man was. Sam nodded in satisfaction. Someone he'd marked off the list, but the first voice. . .

"Gold," that voice said. "He's looking for gold."

Sam flinched. Lucy barely spared him a glance as she moved closer, her nose grazing the edge of their cover.

"Yessir. Hidden treasure, I tell ya."

"What the henhouse Hatty does Jasper know about treasure?"

"He ain't told me how he come to find out. But I 'spect he has a map."

A cowhand from Rockin' R. Sam was sure of it. He chanced a peek around the corner and determined him to be too small of stature to remain on his suspect list. Another one gone.

The man's tale was going into fiction now, the way rumors grew and speculation became fact. But there was truth way back in that first nugget: gold.

Jasper probably heard it from Lucy's aunt. . .who doubtlessly heard it from Lucy herself.

Sam gritted his teeth. If Lucy already knew about the gold, why did she need an interview with him? Was she trying to wrangle a confession?

As the men's voices faded away, Lucy whirled. "I have to go."

"What about that interview?"

Her full lips twisted into a scowl. "We had it. I'm still stinging with the disappointment. Good night, Mr. Brazos. Best wishes with your. . .search."

At that, her eyes sharpened, as if connecting dots to the rumored gold. She reached to detain him, but Sam wasn't about to be caught in her trap.

"Good night, Miss Frederick." Tipping his hat, he spun on his heel and stalked toward the livery stable, because he'd rather bunk with Stinkeye himself than spend another moment in the company of that conniving, beautiful, annoying, captivating, and otherwise confusing woman.

◆　◆　◆

Lucy blamed her sleepless night on impatience. It had been far too late to pound on Jasper's door last night to ask what he knew of lost treasure, so she planned a breakfast interrogation after assuring he received the largest portion of Aunt's flapjacks.

Her first real lead in a month didn't stand a chance of resisting her, and *that* was the reason her heart pounded so furiously when she'd returned to her room last night. The circles under her eyes and the fanciful dreams she'd weathered in the brief moments of respite. . .they were all due to postponing her questioning of Jasper Groth.

Surely that was all.

Aunt flipped the bacon a final time. "Fetch the basket, throw the biscuits inside, and we'll be ready."

Lucy moved to obey while sipping black coffee in hopes of jolting herself awake.

"I have half a mind to lock you in your room today," Aunt said, peering down her long nose. "There've been some strange goings-on. I've heard rumblings."

"Like what?" Lucy kept her tone nonchalant, but she took extra time prying biscuits loose.

"The mercantile is completely out of shovels and picks. Something about a scavenger hunt with a big prize at the end, but no one seems to know who's putting it on. And I wasn't invited. An oversight for sure."

"I'm sure, Aunt."

"No matter. I've no time for silly games. With your fondness for nosing things out, I'd send you in my place. . .but for the second fact."

Lucy grew concerned as Aunt's face turned stern and a touch fearful. "What's wrong?"

"I don't know the exact way of it, but I've heard from both Polly and Ruthie James. Cattle missing from the Rockin' R, and no one's ridden in from Cantwell's place. I wouldn't be surprised if the story's the same there. . .unless the old man is up to something, because you know he's always coveted Ernest's watering hole."

Lucy hadn't known that. The one time she'd met Mr. Cantwell, he'd seemed perfectly content with beans and salt pork. Someone with those simple tastes couldn't be overly ambitious, could they?

"Mark my words, girl, there's going to be trouble."

"Are you talking range war?"

"Why, no, I'm sure it won't come to that. This is Ripple, after all. Frank—er, the sheriff would step up." Aunt considered the matter then gave a decisive shake of her head. "No, it won't come to that. But I declare, times are changin'."

Did she ever hope so. "Of course, Aunt." Lucy dried her hands on her apron. "Do you need me for anything else?"

"You run along. Eat up, and be careful, you hear me?"

"Always, Aunt." She gave the bony woman a hug and turned toward the dining room. She had an interview to conduct.

◆ ◆ ◆

"You just missed Miss Lucy," Dusty said around a mouthful of apple.

Sam frowned. "Where's she headed?"

"The Rockin' R, I 'spect. Talked about checkin' on Jerusha."

More likely, she was after word on the missing cattle everyone had been discussing at breakfast when Sam had popped in for biscuits. "She rode by herself?"

"Not entirely." The boy crunched another bite, spitting out a seed that missed Sam's boot by too narrow a margin.

"Then. . . ?" Sam prompted, maneuvering so a hay bale provided some cover.

"Right. She took Rufus along."

"Rufus?" Stomach churning, Sam tried to place the name, mentally ticking off those who he'd cleared of committing the crimes in Fort Worth. Was Lucy in danger?

"Sheriff's coon dog. Packed 'im right in her saddlebag." Another crunch. "Why? You seein' green, mister?"

"Absolutely not." Those bats fluttering around his innards were from concerns for her safety, not jealousy. With practiced movements, he hefted his saddle onto his horse.

"There's a shortcut to the Rockin' R."

Sam glared over Stinkeye's back. "Who said that's where I'm headed?"

Dusty shrugged. "Just sayin'."

Sam gave in. "Where?"

Wearing a broken-toothed smile, the boy gave him directions. Sam cinched the saddle and mounted up. To save a damsel-in-distress or spy on her, he wasn't certain. Whatever the case, he found himself urging Stinkeye to go a mite faster.

He'd crossed the river and reached the end of Dusty's shortcut when he heard barking. Skirting the edge of the path, Sam searched the terrain for danger. Off the main trail, Lucy held her seat like a queen, back straight, prim in the sidesaddle, her green riding habit draping the wide hindquarters of the dark bay mare. The dog's front paws were planted on the saddle horn as it faced off with another rider.

Sam couldn't see the man's face, but the horse had a princely head and a coat of gleaming black. There could be only one stallion like that in all of Ripple, and it belonged to Jasper Groth.

Sam's eyes narrowed. Though he'd never cared for Groth, Sam hadn't considered the man a danger. But what if the bumbling persona was all an act? The man had told of once having a name on the stage. Spreading gossip about hidden gold—that could be in preparation to ward off suspicions and enable Groth to start spending his own stolen goods.

If that theory proved true, why was he meeting Miss Lucy secret-like? More importantly. . .why was Lucy meeting him?

The bats came alive inside again, and Sam grimaced as he nudged Stinkeye into a walk.

Rufus turned, redirecting his baying as Sam approached.

"Oh, there you are, Mr. Brazos," Lucy called, a fixed smile on her face as she pushed Rufus from her ear. "I was afraid you wouldn't catch up!"

Anger began a slow simmer as he guessed at the reason for her playacting. "My apologies. Next time we'll be more prompt-like."

"Is Stinkeye's hoof all right?"

"Perfectly. Thank you. Howdy, Jasper."

The stocky man tipped his hat. "Brazos. Good day to you, Miss Lucy." He spurred the black into a trot as Sam reached Lucy.

Concerned, he gave her a quick appraisal. Her color was high, but she appeared untouched. "What was that about?"

"The insufferable man. This morning after you left the breakfast table, I asked him about the rumored treasure. He refused any information unless I met him in private. Not trusting his intentions, I rebuffed him. Somehow we crossed paths, and he believes I came searching for him. Playing 'hard to get,' he accused." She practically spit out the words. "If it hadn't been for Rufus and your timely approach, I'm quite certain he would have forced a kiss."

"Is that such an easy task with you?" The question was unfair, but he couldn't stop it. Was Lucy the kind of girl who chased bad men for the thrill of danger? Did she ever stoop to using her womanly wiles to win a story?

Lucy's eyes flashed. "How dare you!"

Why else would she have looked at him the way she had last night—through those thick lashes, her lips full and parted, her cheeks flushed as if she fancied him? Had she looked at Jasper that way during their conversation at breakfast?

"I reckon that's not an answer," he said.

"I had thought you a knight of the range, riding to my rescue. And here you are as black-hearted as they come."

He bit back the apology on the tip of his tongue. "My, my, Miss Lucy. Do you reckon you're being a bit too...poetic?"

Her delicate chin rose. "Words are my calling. It cannot be helped."

"And you'll do anything for a story. Why is that?" He studied her, calming his anger and, yes, a smidge of jealousy as he took in the depths of her green eyes, trying to find the motivation behind her searching. "Why are you here, Miss Frederick? You asked me. Now I reckon I get to ask you."

"You failed to give a real answer."

He knew part of the story. Something along the lines of an irresistible tip, a clandestine carriage ride to an exhibition hall, a fire, and a misunderstanding. Carefully framed questions put to Margret Frederick had awarded him that much. In an ironic and possibly naive twist, Lucy had been shipped out West for her own safety.

Sam softened. "It's true I'm in search of something. I didn't lie to you."

"The gold?"

"No." Not directly. "I can't tell you more."

"Cannot or will not?"

The urge to confess once again took him by surprise.

Lucy drew herself up straight. "What if I start the conversation? Would that make it easier? I'm here because my father no longer wanted responsibility for me...and I would very much like to prove he can be proud of me after all." She focused on the dog, stroking his silky ears. "Your turn."

He shoved his hat tighter on his head. "My trouble is my own. I'm sorry." Truly.

She seemed undaunted. "Then you at least admit you are in trouble."

He growled. Rufus growled back.

Lucy surprised him with a laugh, light and contagious. "You'll tell me. I know it. Now...were you headed to check on Jerusha?"

"Among others."

She fluttered thick lashes at him. "You're spying on me. Admit it."

Those blasted bats danced again. "I'm looking out for you," he corrected.

"Whatever the reason, I'm grateful for your appearance." Wearing a bright smile, she held out a hand.

He bent low over it, keeping a wary eye on the coon dog. A rumbling in Rufus's throat backed Sam and Stinkeye up too soon, and Sam lost his grip on Lucy's ink-stained fingers. He cleared his throat and nodded to the trail. "Shall we?"

With practiced ease, she turned Dellarosa and fell in beside him. "Now, where were we? I believe you were fixing to tell me about where you lived last, what your family's like, and what you do on these mysterious rides of yours."

Sam shook his head and laughed.

Chapter Four

Lucy watched Sam over the rim of her chipped Staffordshire teacup. He exuded masculinity, with his muscular arms, broad chest, and worn but tidy clothing hinting at adventures lived. Still, he didn't appear out of place as he balanced Jerusha on one knee and the little girl's doll on the other.

Lucy pushed aside a sudden longing and focused on the matter at hand. The one *always* at hand—finding a newsworthy story.

"Yes, she seems to be fine as a fiddle," Lillie Jo answered Sam. "The bite scared her more than it hurt, I believe, but my girl is Texan through and through. She's made of sterner stuff than the girls you may have been acquainted with back East."

"I can see that," Sam said.

Biting back a terse response to the veiled insult, Lucy instead tucked away the fact that Sam had, at some point, been back East.

"You don't know the half of it," Lillie Jo said. "Tell them, Ernest."

The gruff rancher stopped drumming his fingers against the table and drew in a grumbly breath. Lucy studied him carefully. He appeared anxious to get back in the heat, not thrilled about Lillie Jo coercing him to attend unexpected guests after his lunch.

Because he had fences to mend, missing cattle to round up? Or did he fear a slip of the tongue that would alert Lucy to a darker plot afoot?

Frankly, it was easier for her to believe ill of Ernest than Old Man Cantwell. The young rancher's eyes were shifty, his lips pressed in a firm line beneath his uneven beard. Perspiration dotted his brow, soaked his shirt in a V across his chest and circling under his arms. From hard work? Or nerves?

The more he talked, telling the story of Jerusha falling into the river. . .or off a donkey—Lucy wasn't sure which with the way Ernest mumbled—the more she became convinced he was hiding something.

"That happened when?" Sam asked. The jut of his jaw indicated Lucy wasn't the only one on a mission here.

"Last May," Ernest said. "Had to ride clear to Possum Hollow to find a doc to look 'er over, since Doc Dillehay was missin', and not for the first time."

"Doc Smith wasn't around these parts last spring?"

"Naw. He didn't show till mid-June. Since Dillehay up and disappeared a week or two earlier—probably got hisself lost in his cups again and fell into trouble—we needed Smith, sure as shootin'."

The rancher grew agitated again. If Lucy allowed Sam to direct any more of the conversation, she wouldn't get the scoop on the cattle.

Sending her cowboy a sharp look, Lucy spoke up. "Well, it's a good thing he stuck around. You have no time to do any nursing these days, I'm sure, what with all your cattle trouble."

Ernest went still. "What d'ya mean, cattle trouble?"

Lucy cleared her throat. "I heard a rumor that some cows went missing."

The rancher met his wife's questioning gaze and gave his shaggy head a quick shake. "Someone's got you barkin' at a knot, Miss Lucy. Ever'thin's fine at the Rockin' R."

Giving a tight smile and noncommittal nod, Lucy allowed the conversation to veer off the course she'd set it on. But one thing she knew—everything was *not* fine at the Rocking R Ranch.

◆   ◆   ◆

Sam kept a wary eye on Rufus all the way back to Ripple, and the dog returned the favor. Lucy was quiet most of the way, probably mulling over what she'd learned, same as Sam.

Which wasn't much.

They passed the doctor's home, and before Main Street, the coon dog jumped free, paws skittering over a pile of hulls.

Lucy spoke in a grumpy voice. "Besides making sure the sweet girl was recovering from her trauma. . .well, that was a waste of a beautiful morning."

"It wasn't wasted," Sam said.

The sun danced off fiery strands of Lucy's hair as she glanced over at him. "No cattle rustling after all, unless he's hiding it for some reason. The ranch isn't doing well, I hear, and with his carpentry skills—"

Suppressing a smile, Sam shook his head while Lucy ran through her theories. She'd probably gotten that particular bee in her bonnet from spying sawdust on the rancher's boots and a train schedule, or some such. She really was a marvel.

"I imagine he's selling out and didn't want Lillie Jo to know yet," Lucy continued as the horses entered the livery stable. "Which isn't newsworthy, and it's none of my business."

Most of what she wrote probably wasn't any of her business, but Sam didn't feel up to reminding her of that fact.

"But it seems *you* whittled out some information you needed, for whatever reason."

"I reckon I did." Sam swung down from the saddle and moved to assist her. "Thank you for giving me the excuse for a visit." His hands found her waist, let go sooner than he would have liked.

Lucy smoothed her skirts. "I'm glad *some*one got something out of it."

"Again, it wasn't time wasted."

"For *you*."

"For you, as well. Think, Lucy. Did anything strike you as interesting?"

"I already said—he's hiding something."

"Besides that?"

"Jerusha has more lives than the stable boy's cat?"

Sam laughed then sobered, and Lucy tilted her head. "What is it?"

"Maybe I imagined it, but there's something about Doc Dillehay's story that stuck in my craw."

Whatever the case, now Sam knew Ernest was still a suspect, as he'd been missing for enough time in May to travel to Fort Worth. Whether he'd been gone long enough to do what Sam had been framed for. . .well, he'd have to check on his story. Also, he could add both doctors to the list, as neither were yet accounted for during the pertinent dates.

Would the search never end? He'd felt close enough to smell the murderer's foul breath, but then he took three steps backward. One thing was sure as shootin'—he was ready to hang up the fiddle on watching over his shoulder and weighing each word he allowed to escape his lips.

"Doc Dillehay?" Lucy repeated. "Why?"

"I can't rightly say."

This was the West. People disappeared for countless reasons. Dillehay could have made a run for the border. His horse could have run away, leaving him injured. Outlaws could have cornered him. He could have gotten a hankering to return east—

Lucy interrupted his thoughts, raising one thin eyebrow. "I have a feeling you're not who you say you are, Sam Brazos."

His heart stopped then stuttered on. "Who do you think I am?"

"I'm not sure, but I do believe there's a good chance a newspaperman lives under that cowboy disguise of yours."

Sam forced his breathing to return to normal. "Is that a compliment, Miss Frederick?"

"I'm afraid so." A smile lit her face, crinkling her nose.

He'd dodged a bullet, but Lucy was mighty smart. She already suspected him of hiding something. She'd realize the truth about him soon enough.

Then what? Wouldn't it be better to tell her, to convince her he stood in the right? To ask for her assistance, even?

"Miss Lucy"—Sam held out his arm to escort her to the boardinghouse—"might I request a few more moments of your time? I reckon I could use your help. That is, if you're willing."

"I'm intrigued." She didn't seem to mind his use of her given name. Or didn't notice. Except, Lucy noticed everything. "Do tell."

Before he could begin, Jasper strode by whistling, a shovel propped on his shoulder. Sam ushered Lucy toward her aunt's garden, only to be blocked by Old Man Cantwell, who jabbed a stubby finger into Sam's chest.

Sam tugged Lucy behind him and faced off with the weathered rancher as he tried to understand the accusations flying his way.

"I don't give a rotten fig if you *are* a high-falutin' Pinkerton agent! Whatever Ernest told you, it ain't true, and you ain't gonna arrest me. I ain't left this town for nigh on twenty years. Stay on my own property most times, all peaceful-like. Want no trouble from no one. So there!" The man's chest rose and fell at the exertion, and the veins on his neck throbbed.

"I'm not sure what—"

"See here, you no-account—"

Lucy stepped out from behind Sam, pushing away his protective arm. "Mr. Cantwell, are you concerned about the rustling charges?"

The blustering began again. Warily eyeing the man's gun hand, Sam tried to force

Lucy out of harm's way once more. She refused to go, holding out a calming hand and smiling.

"No need for this, Mr. Cantwell. The Rockin' R seems to know nothing about missing cattle. Mr. Brazos is not hunting you...." Lucy arched her eyebrows at Sam. "Are you, Mr. Brazos?"

If Cantwell truly hadn't left town in twenty years—and Sam's information so far confirmed that—Lucy was right. "I'm not a Pinkerton agent, Cantwell. You're safe on that front."

"You're not?" he asked.

"I'm not," Sam said.

"You're sure?" Lucy asked, a smile playing around her full lips.

"I figure I would know."

"Huh." Cantwell squinted at Lucy. "I reckon that's what they have to tell people."

She shrugged. "I reckon."

"Well then. My cattle are my own. That's all I have to say. Evening, ma'am." He tipped his hat, squinted his eyes at Sam as if searching out telltale signs of Pinkertonism, then ambled away.

Lucy turned to Sam. "You were saying?"

"Yes." He cleared his throat, searching for the train of thought so thoroughly derailed. "There's something in my past you should—"

"Lucy!" At the sound of Margret's strident call, Sam clammed up, sliding a hand over his raspy jaw.

"I'm sorry." Lucy appeared as frustrated as he felt. "I must go."

"Will you be at supper?"

"You ask this question of me two days in a row, Mr. Brazos?"

"Sam. Call me Sam."

She bit her lower lip as the corners of her mouth curved. "All right. Sam. As I do have a habit of eating three times a day whenever possible—yes. I'll be at supper."

"Until then."

"Be sure to hold off on any arrests if I'm not present."

"I am not a Pinker—"

"You heard Cantwell. That's what they all say." She flounced away, her laughter floating over her shoulder.

Chapter Five

Curiosity kept Lucy on edge all through folding linens, helping prepare stew for the boarders, and setting the table. Was Sam looking for someone and needed her help tracking down clues?

If he was a Pinkerton agent, he should be an expert in that area.

Maybe he needed Lucy to accompany him to question a woman he couldn't for propriety's sake? Lillie Jo, perhaps, in connection to the missing/not missing cattle.

Or he could be seeking a newspaper job and wanted her to put a recommendation to her father. A lot of good that would do.

Whatever the case, she was dying to hear his story. When she finally slid onto the bench across from Sam, those riveting eyes caught hers. Her bright smile faltered when his stare slipped away, not acknowledging any connection.

Right. He would want to keep their conversation private. A secret. She could play along. She picked up her spoon.

"Miss Lucy," one of the boarders said, pointing to the waspish man next to him, "Lasso Larry here was expounding on the fact that there's an outlaw hiding in these very parts. Any guesses who it might be?"

"Yes, Miss Lucy," Sam asked, his casual tone not matching the ice in his eyes. "What do you know about an outlaw hiding in our very midst?"

Lucy's forehead wrinkled at his tone, but she turned her attention back to the gentleman. "I can hardly imagine anyone in Ripple being dangerous." Unless they counted the peril Sam presented to her emotions. She chanced a quick look in his direction, noting his hand fisted around his fork. "No one I've come to know, at least. But the reverend's wife did mention the other day that a few articles of clothing were missing from her clothesline. Perhaps the outlaw has stowed away in a barn or a cave near the church building."

Aunt Margret gave a thoughtful nod. "That could explain the hand pies Mrs. Thorp claimed disappeared from her windowsill."

"Perhaps," Lucy said, fairly certain the dear lady had managed to make the hand pies vanish all by herself.

Still, there might be a story with this latest rumor. She'd have to track it down to its source. But not until Sam finally told her what was on his mind.

Wishing supper would end, Lucy took another bite and kept watch on the mysterious cowboy for the signal he was ready to speak to her. But when she returned from clearing the table, Sam was long gone.

◆ ◆ ◆

At first opportunity, Sam hightailed it to the livery. Dusty was taking excellent care of Stinkeye, but he checked on the horse anyway as he couldn't handle more conversation now. Not with anyone hankering to share the latest gossip, and *absolutely not* with the one he suspected started it all.

In the midst of brushing the mustang's coat too vigorously and waging a silent debate over cutting his losses or sticking it out, Sam heard someone behind him.

"Mr. Brazos?"

He didn't need Dusty's openmouthed grin to tell him who the sweet, slightly husky voice belonged to. A muscle jumped in his jaw. Sam composed his expression, set aside the brush, and turned to greet Lucy Frederick.

"It's Sam."

She stood with hands on her slim hips. "Are you always this way?"

Sam gave himself a once-over then met her eyes and rested his arms on the edge of the stall. "I'm a lowly cowboy. Dirty, a mite rough around the edges, with only the great outdoors to call home and a worn-out horse to take me there."

Lucy rolled her eyes. "Must you try your hand at waxing poetic? Not everyone is skilled in that area."

His hand clutched at his heart as Dusty chortled. "You wound me, Miss Lucy."

"I doubt that very much."

She was beautiful when she was sassy—which was most of the time, come to think of it.

"You know very well I'm not talking about your appearance, which is. . .passable. Even pleasing to some. Mrs. Thorp, for example."

Sam elbowed the snickering Dusty, sending him away with a glare.

Lucy continued without batting any of her thick, curly lashes. "Though I want to revisit the topic of you, in fact, being a cowboy, at this moment what concerns me is twice now you've begun telling me something vitally important—so much so that you were actually requesting my aid. And then you pull a vanishing act."

"I'm a cowboy, Miss Lucy, not a magician, or at least not a very good one. Here—" He spread his arms wide. "You've found me."

"I believe you're trying too hard to convince me of the drifting cowboy act."

Shifting uncomfortably, Sam maintained his poker face. "What else do you believe?"

"That you *do* need my help, but you're too proud to ask a woman for anything."

Quirking an eyebrow, Sam leaned against a stall. "Why, Miss Frederick, I asked you for a second biscuit this very morning."

Her cheeks reddened, and if she weren't so much a lady, Sam was certain his own would be stinging. Well deserved, but he couldn't help tweaking her tail. Besides, if she were mad at him, he was less likely to succumb to the temptation to kiss her.

Maybe.

"Mock me if you will, but I'll find the truth about you, Sam Brazos. You can forget obtaining my assistance, though I would have willingly offered it because—"

She looked away, and suddenly Sam was desperate to know her thoughts. "Because what?"

She refused to meet his gaze.

"Miss Lucy," he said, softer now. "I want to know."

She peered through lowered lashes, though flames leaped in the jade depths of her eyes. "Then I guess you have your own mystery to solve, and let's hope you're better at that than poetry. Good evening, Mr. Brazos."

She whirled, her skirts a frothy cloud of blue, a honey-scented breeze floating in her wake.

Dusty poked his head out of Admiral's stall. "Gummy! That there be some woman, mister."

"I reckon you're right," Sam murmured.

"You made her awful mad."

"That I did."

He shouldn't have antagonized her. He needed her on his side. What's more, he *wanted* her there, more than was probably healthy, all things considered. He lived in search of a killer. She, in search of a story.

One he could give her.

Sam scratched the back of his neck. Now if this wasn't a pickle, he didn't know what was.

◆ ◆ ◆

Wrapped in a shawl the next day, Lucy bent over her paper, writing furiously. Ink stained her fingers, and her words scrawled around black spots, evidence of her agitation while refilling her Waterman's Ideal Fountain Pen.

All fault belonged at the feet of the most infuriating, obnoxious, mysterious, arrogant, frustrating, handsome, secretive, and frustrating Pinkerton agent/drifter/cowboy she'd ever had the privilege and misfortune of meeting.

Catching herself before she could hurl her treasured pen across the room. . .again, Lucy grumbled under her breath and focused on the last section she'd written.

The passenger knew the stagecoach was doomed as shots rang out through the humid morning air. She'd just tucked her treasured locket into her right boot when the door flung open and a masked man peered inside. Determining not to swoon, the passenger stared him in the face, unwilling to show herself a shrinking violet before a common thief. Instead of ordering her down or snatching her reticule, he stared back, his eyes a stormy blue. Declaring her to be in danger from the outlaw gang he rode with undercover as a Pinkerton agent, the gunman and his noble steed escorted her to the safety of a nearby ranch.

The cad. Even the fictitious version of Sam Brazos had the ability to charm her into making him a hero. But *not* to win her forgiveness. He'd insulted her. He'd hurt her. Worse, he'd made her think he was going to kiss her, and she hadn't been able to stop thinking about the notion ever since.

Was he toying with her emotions on purpose? Or was there something about her that repelled him every time she let down her guard? Father had warned no man would want a lady journalist, that chasing stories would lead her to surrender good manners and breeding, that if she didn't want to become a bitter old spinster, she'd best leave the news to men.

Marriage or her stories: that was the choice. She hadn't listened to Father at the time. She wanted—*believed* she could have both. The lack of any viable marriage proposals should have been her first clue if she truly was so good at putting together the facts. Brushing it off as a sign God hadn't sent along the right match may have been naive.

Anger faded, taking her energy with it. Lucy lined up the corners and folded the stained pages, tucked them into an envelope already addressed to Amelia, and informed her aunt she was going out.

At the post office, she responded as briefly as possible to Mrs. Thorp and Widow Aurilla, who persisted in telling her about a possible sighting of Butch Cassidy.

The amateur journalist in her itched to take notes, and she wrapped her fingers around her lucky pen. . .but didn't pull it free of its hiding place. A week ago, she would have, even traveled to the site and nosed around for clues to corroborate their words. Maybe she still should, since she was well on the way to spinsterhood. But the way those two sweet biddies gossiped, the story probably began as a lost prairie dog emerging among the potatoes in Polly's root cellar.

She was learning.

When Gus noticed her, he stretched his lips in a toothy grin. "I declare, Miss Lucy. Two letters this week?"

"What can I say? Things are getting more interesting."

Gus's catlike eyes gleamed. "They shore are."

"So you'll take care of that for me?"

He nodded, his Adam's apple bobbing as he swallowed a sip of lemonade Polly must have delivered. "I'll treat it like my own. Like always."

"Thanks." Lucy offered a weak smile and turned to go, barreling into the chest of the man she least wanted to see at the moment.

"Miss Lucy." Sam tipped his hat, a devilish glint in his eye.

"Mr. Brazos." Lucy kept her voice cool, hoping he didn't catch the slight waver at the end. She pushed by him and out into the harsh sunlight, lamenting the fact that the spots she saw as her eyes adjusted took on the shape of Sam's chiseled silhouette.

She half-expected him to follow. Squaring her shoulders, she braced for it—to go through the whole teasing, infuriating routine again. But no footsteps sounded behind her, and the only voice to hail her belonged to Doc Smith.

"Afternoon, Miss Frederick. Where're you headed?"

Though she didn't know him well, the doctor reminded her of a cross between St. Nicholas and a boxer. His dimpled smile was jolly, his dark eyes on the shifty side.

"Back to the boardinghouse, Doctor. And you?"

"I've been at the sheriff's office." He fell into step beside her, offering her a pecan before popping a handful into his mouth. "Voicing some concerns."

"What seems to be troubling you, Doctor?" she asked, hoping she hid her curiosity with her casual tone. She didn't want to come across too terribly nosy.

He cast her a sidelong look and gave the nuts another crunch. "You seem to be very astute. With your background growing up in the home of a newspaperman, your eyes are probably more open to the state of Texas and even the nation. Maybe you could share your thoughts with the sheriff as well. Maybe you could make a difference."

A trickle of warmth soothed her wounded ego. "I'm listening."

"When I came to Ripple a year or so ago, the small, safe community drew me in. I settled here and haven't had any regrets. . .until the past month." He stopped, seeming to struggle with his next words.

"Yes?"

"The gold fever. The scuttlebutt about murderers and cattle rustlers and kidnappings. . ."

Lucy's brow creased. She hadn't heard that last one as of yet.

"I'm considering pulling up stakes."

"Where would you go?"

"I don't know. I do not wish to leave. I'm comfortable here. But when the time comes that I feel I should rummage through the wanted posters to make sure I know the truth of the patients I treat, well. . .that's not the life I was hoping to find here in the sleepiest town in Texas."

Wanted posters? Now there would be some fodder for article ideas. Why hadn't she thought to look at those?

Her father was right. But again. . .she was learning.

"I wouldn't leave yet," she said, forcing herself to return to the conversation. "The town needs a good doctor. I'm sure the storm will blow over soon and everything will go back to normal."

"You may be right, young lady. I hope you are. Once that Sam Brazos leaves town, I'm sure it'll calm right down."

"Sam?" She coughed into her hand to cover her surprise. "Er, Mr. Brazos? What role do you believe he plays?"

The doctor looked at her steadily. "All of them." Nodding his farewell, he added, "I'll think on what you've said. Be careful, Miss Frederick. Maybe this town will get a newspaper someday, and they'd be fortunate to have someone with your class involved in the running of it."

Lucy watched him walk away, his shoulders droopier than his mustache. Interesting character, if a bit on the melancholy side. Would he consent to an interview—life as a doctor in the Wild West? Not that Ripple was wild.

Or was it?

Passing the sheriff's office, she paused. Now that the idea had been planted in her mind, she was itching to see those posters, but she needed something besides a bat of the eyelashes to convince the sheriff to allow it. Without extra persuasion, the sheriff wouldn't permit the niece of his lady love to look on such evil—she could almost hear him utter those very words.

She needed something to distract him.

She needed Aunt Margret.

Chapter Six

A brisk ride outside town relaxed Sam. He'd explored along the river to the north last week. The hills to the east the week before. Allowing Stinkeye to choose the path, Sam left the trail leading south and began memorizing the landscape, to keep the image of Lucy's face from haunting his thoughts. The hurt and confusion swirling in her sea-green eyes yesterday—he'd put them there. That was on him.

But if she had suspicions about him, why couldn't she come out and ask? Why dance around it, all coy-like? Why spread lies and suspicions behind his back? That didn't seem to fit who she was.

Who he wanted her to be.

Stinkeye's ears twitched. Sam placed a hand near his gun and eased the stallion to a walk, at the ready for whatever was around the corner. As they cleared the brush, the postmaster whirled, brandishing a shovel.

Sam eased away from his weapon. "Just me, Gus."

"Aw, shucks, Brazos." The shovel hit the ground, and the scrawny man leaned against it. "Scared the ever-livin' out of me."

"Out for an evening ride. You're about to lose the light, though. Find anything yet?"

"Who says I'm lookin' for somethin'?"

Sam gestured to the shovel. Shrugged.

"Right." Gus looked down. "I figger you've heard the rumor, then."

"About hidden gold? Yes."

"Well, it's more'n a rumor, and I'm gonna be the one to find it, shore as shootin'. If you're figgerin' on searchin', you'll have to find another spot."

"Just riding," he repeated.

"All right, then." Gus continued to eye him suspiciously.

Sam edged Stinkeye past then halted as Gus's words clicked. Sam half-turned in the saddle and said, "How do you know it's not a rumor?" If the postmaster knew about the gold, maybe he also had a clue to the killer's whereabouts.

Those yellowish eyes narrowed a mite. "Same way I know about the killer hidin' about these parts. Same way I know about the rustlin' and the train robbers. Same way I know about you."

Sam startled. "And how's that?"

"Miss Frederick's articles, of course."

Sam felt pretty certain Stinkeye had trampled his innards. Clearing his throat, he said, "She mentioned me?"

"Are you accusin' me of—?"

"I'm not accusing anyone of anything. Only making sure I understood. You've seen the articles?"

"Several of them. Yup."

"She wrote about me?"

"I seen your name, shore enough. Sam Brazos—right there in black and white, clear as day."

Sam had heard enough. Thumping his heels against Stinkeye's sides, he raced back toward town, stewing over what he'd learned. Lucy had written about him, which he'd suspected—but not that she'd named him outright! Although the gold must not have been attached to his name, not if Gus had tried to hide the fact from him at first.

So what had she accused him of? Had her father's paper run the story yet? Had she sent the articles anywhere else?

His location was blown. He'd have to act fast.

And do what? He didn't feel any closer to clearing his name than when he'd seen the first wanted poster.

But Lucy Frederick was toying with him, and he didn't appreciate it. Not one bit.

◆ ◆ ◆

All it took to win Aunt Margret's cooperation was hinting at espionage. The poor sheriff didn't know what caused Aunt's apparent change of heart, but he'd had eyes only for the older woman and her peach pie since they set foot in his office. After waving a hand toward the wanted posters, he didn't glance Lucy's way again.

Aunt played it for all she was worth—batting her eyelashes and even offering Rufus a pat on the head, though she did kick at the dog when it dared raise its nose to test the peach-scented air.

The stack of papers resting on a broken armchair was haphazard and dusty. Forgotten. Was the town so sleepy Sheriff Frank had let down his guard? Lucy flipped through the posters, trying to disturb them as little as possible.

The Cisco kid. John Wesley Hardin. There were train robbers. Murderers. Gang members. Wanted dead or alive, with hefty rewards offered for some. So many names and so many crimes. She skimmed the descriptions and studied the drawings one by one.

"Why, Sheriff, you go too far!"

Lucy cut her eyes to the older couple. Aunt Margret stood, hands balled at her sides, crumbs around her mouth and slimy peaches on the floor by her feet.

"I can feed my own self perfectly fine, thank you. If you try a stunt like that again, you're liable to wake up one morning without a head! Not that you'd miss the brain portion."

"Now see here, Margret. Settle yourself! I was just—"

As they continued to argue, Lucy refocused on the task at hand. By the tone of her voice, Aunt's patience was dangerously near its limit. Lucy flipped quickly through the next three posters. Then the world began to spin.

A crude sketch stared up at her, $800 REWARD emblazoned above it. Simple as it was, with a tidy beard and mustache drawn in, she knew that face. Even if she didn't, he hadn't bothered to change his name.

Sam Brazos. Wanted for stealing from and killing his partner.

Her Sam.

Lucy shot to her feet, scattering posters across the floor.

Aunt Margret took that as her cue. "You can keep the pie, Sheriff. You can even feed it to that mangy mutt of yours. Yes, I *will* insult your dog because he smells like death warmed over with a side of sauerkraut."

Lucy frantically scooped together the papers, tucking that particular one in her pocket next to her lucky pen.

"There's no call for—"

Air. She needed air. Rushing outside, Lucy breathed in a lungful of dust. Choking, she hurried down the boardwalk, not bothering to wait for Aunt Margret.

Sam. A wanted man. There could be no mistake he was an outlaw. The description had read like the man who galloped across the pages of her articles. Blue eyes. Five feet eleven inches. His build, his hair color, his weight. Even the fact that he was considered handsome.

She stopped dead in her tracks as Sam swung down from Stinkeye's sweaty back and stormed into the livery.

Handsome? Yes. Yes, he was. But. . .a murderer? A thief?

Forcing her feet onward, she passed Doc Smith, Mr. Thorp, and Widow Aurilla in quick succession, paying no heed to their greetings.

"Lucy?" Aunt called. The older woman's shoes clattered against the boards as she hurried to catch up. "What is it, dear? Did you get your story?"

Lucy's stomach churned. She'd found a story all right.

But it was one she desperately did not want to write.

◆　◆　◆

Back in his room, Sam threw his few belongings into his saddlebags, stopping only to grip his Colt as hurried footsteps approached. When they passed without more than a slight hesitation, he rose and crossed to the window.

No posse waited outside. Maybe they weren't coming. Maybe Lucy hadn't informed the sheriff about all her suspicions, preferring to keep Sam around to provide more story fodder.

But he couldn't risk it. Sam refused to hang for something he didn't do. Worse, he refused to let George Keene's killer ride free.

He had to see Lucy once more, had to look into her eyes and ask why. Then he would go. Hide in the hills maybe, wait until things had died down and hope he could pick up the trail of George's murderer again.

Or maybe it was inevitable. Maybe he was destined for life on the dodge and should hit the trail south to the border. Live the life of the outlaw she believed him to be.

Snapping himself out of it, Sam crept to the door and listened. When the hall proved quiet once again, he swiftly moved down the hall to Lucy's room. Too close to Jasper for his liking, but if anyone disturbed her, she'd have the rest of the house leaping to her defense.

She was safe.

Too bad Sam was not.

"Miss Frederick?" When he knocked on her door, it creaked open slowly, revealing a tidy room, but no Lucy. The desk proved to be the only exception to the neatness, with fancy papers and writing materials strewn about, almost as if she'd pushed aside a pile in frustration. Did one of those papers mention him? Was she composing another imagined crime to pin on the infamous Sam Brazos?

He was halfway across the room before he could reconsider. The papers on the desk were blank, except for one, half hidden near the bottom of the pile. He tugged it free then nearly dropped it as if burned.

A wanted poster. For him.

In Lucy's room.

The irritating, nosy, beautiful, endearing redhead who'd half-stolen his heart—she'd been playing him. He'd suspected all along, hadn't wanted to believe it. But here—here was proof in black and white. His likeness stared up at him on a paper declaring him dangerous, wanted, worth an $800 reward if captured.

Lucy hadn't needed the money—just that blasted story.

And he'd let her close enough to get one.

Chapter Seven

"If you boil that spinach any longer, we're gonna be drinkin' it."

Lucy jerked to attention. The water had turned green, and she pulled the pan from the heat.

"Gonna tell me what's troublin' you?" Aunt Margret asked, not for the first time.

"No, Aunt." Not until she decided what to do. She'd hidden the poster in her room, unwilling to have it burn a hole of guilt and grief through her pocket. The sheriff hadn't seen it, Lucy was certain. Should she show it to him? Confront Sam first?

But that would give him time to escape. . .and the chance to add another notch to his gun, unless that was only a dime novel thing. Regardless, the headlines would be humiliating. Something about a novice reporter's first brush with a real story proving fatal?

Father would grieve. . .but he would run that article. She had no doubt.

"Slice a boiled egg atop that spinach," Aunt ordered. "Mind it's a boiled egg you crack open. I don't want scrambled spinach, and that's a fact."

The eggshells chipped off in tiny pieces, taking bits of the tender egg with it. Broken. Mangled. Like her heart.

Lucy tried to pull herself together, but it was a hopeless case. Sam couldn't have committed the crimes the poster accused him of. Not the man she was coming to know. The one with the strong, honest jaw, the helpful hand, the quick compliment, the clear blue eyes that caused her insides to smolder.

Not her Sam. They were mistaken.

They had to be.

But his spot remained empty at the dinner table. Her aunt cast concerned looks Lucy's direction, and Jasper talked more loudly to try to cajole her into joining the conversation. More talk of gold fever. More rumors that may not be rumors after all.

She should take notes. Instead, she played with her food, pushing the salty ham around her plate, jumping up to assist Aunt and escape to the kitchen for a few moments to herself. And helping to clean up when Sheriff Frank and Rufus made an unwelcome visit.

All the while, Lucy kept her mouth closed in a firm line, preventing her from blurting out what she'd learned or asking her aunt for advice on what to do.

Sam had saved her from unwanted attentions. He'd played the gallant, albeit sarcastic, escort. He'd been a welcome addition to this new place she was to call home.

She wouldn't turn on him until he'd had a chance to explain himself. Until she'd looked into his eyes and searched out the truth.

Once the sheriff had gone and the guests had been seen to, Aunt finally grabbed

Lucy's arm, work-worn fingers holding her in an iron grip. "Look at me, girl. Tell me what's got you all in a tizzy."

Tears welled. Lucy blinked hard then widened her eyes, trying to keep the moisture from escaping.

"Did that boy go and break your heart? I always figured him for a good man—you can tell by his ears. But if he hurt you—"

"His ears?" Lucy sputtered out a laugh, teardrops falling at the same time.

"Why, yes, didn't your daddy teach you anything? When a man's ears are—"

As Aunt continued her explanation, Sam crossed the street outside, his hat shadowing his face. Headed toward the livery stable, no doubt. To go where? To rob some unsuspecting traveler? To rustle steers from Rockin' R? To practice his gunslinging skills so he could outdraw anyone standing in the way of what he wanted?

What about her? Did he want her?

Or was she in his way?

"Excuse me, Aunt." Gathering her skirts, Lucy rushed to her room to collect the poster before escaping outdoors. Casting one quick glance behind her, she slowed her pace to a ladylike stroll while her heart fairly burst within her. The folded paper burned through the skin of her hand until she felt the whole town could see it glowing like a scarlet letter.

Sam Brazos. Guilty of murder and thievery.

Lucy Frederick. Guilty of being gullible, of hoping against hope, of betraying her journalist ambition, of protecting an outlaw.

The livery seemed deserted when she entered. Stinkeye stood in his stall, glaring in her general direction.

"Don't look at me like that," she hissed.

"Feeling guilty?"

Whirling, she spotted Sam lounging on a bale of hay, his back against the wall. His hands were loose, but his gun hung in its holster, strapped to his lean waist.

"Why should you say that?"

"Stinkeye looks at everyone like that. Hence the name. So if he's offending you, I reckon it indicates you feel guilty-like."

Of all the nerve. Lucy refrained from whipping out the poster, but she did stomp her foot a little. "I assume you're dying for a confession?"

"I'd like to hear it. Yes."

"You—" She sputtered and fumed and threw out all the mean names she could think of as he slowly pushed to his feet and moved closer. When she stopped for breath, she saw something in his eyes. Not the amused condescension she'd expected. A hint of anger, yes. But something deeper. Something. . .sad. Vulnerable, even.

He was going to leave.

Her heart caught in her throat. That's not what she wanted. Not at all. She wanted him to tell her it was a misunderstanding. That everything would be okay. She wanted him to sweep her into his arms and—

Then he did. Leaned over her, tipped up her chin with gentle fingers, ran his thumb lightly over her lower lip, lowered his mouth to hers.

Lucy was pretty sure she should be yelling for help, but her mouth was quite occupied.

Or maybe beating his chest—the hard planes of which her hands were currently caressing as they slid upward of their own accord. Running away, except her feet had planted themselves firmly, and as tingles raced down to curl her toes, she found herself not wanting to move. Ever.

Sam pulled back and pressed his forehead to hers. She gazed up at him, her eyes lazily refocusing, mostly on those lips.

"Lucy. . ." he began, his voice a husky whisper.

Then his mouth firmed. A muscle jumped in his jaw. He gripped her wrists and pulled her hands free of his neck.

What—? Then she saw it. On the ground between them. The wanted poster had fallen to the ground, his likeness staring up at them in a hastily folded square.

"Wait. Sam. . ." She wanted to explain why she'd come. Wanted *him* to explain why the poster existed. But his face turned cold, impassive, and he turned to face the door as rapid footsteps approached.

"Well done, Miss Frederick," he said, low and tight. "I hope your story wins what you seek most."

Sheriff Frank burst in, pistol drawn and shaky, flanked by his deputy and Mr. Thorp, with more coming behind.

"Sam Brazos! Yer under arrest!" The pistol shook harder. "Don't give us no trouble, you hear me?"

Lucy quaked in her Adelaide boots. They couldn't take him! He was innocent. She *knew* he was good. She'd sensed it, tasted it, saw it in his eyes. "Sam?"

"Get out of the way, Lucy," he muttered, his fierce stare trained on the sheriff.

"You heard the man, Miss Lucy," Mr. Thorp said.

If she got out of the way, what would happen to Sam?

Stinkeye reared. The sheriff's gun hand jerked. Someone shoved Lucy, and she faceplanted into a hay bale as the echo of a shot thundered through the rafters.

Moments later, Lucy surfaced to chaos. Spitting hay and crouching next to the wall, she tried to assess the situation, to stay calm and collected like she was following a lead. . .like Sam had accused her of doing. She filed away Stinkeye's pounding hooves against a shuddering stall door. The stable boy's rounded eyes as he leaned out of Dellarosa's enclosure, hair askew and lines on his cheek as if he'd been napping.

Men shouted. Women screamed. Rufus howled. Checkers sat in the middle of the livery, casually observing everything, his tattered tail moving in languid swipes across the floor.

Then she saw the blood. On the hay near her. On the floor.

And on the shirt of Sam Brazos as they dragged him away.

Chapter Eight

She had no time to come up with a plan. All Lucy knew as she raised herself from the livery floor was that she had to free Sam. But first, she had to heal him. How badly had he been hit?

"You're not allowed to die, Sam Brazos," she muttered to no one in particular, her voice cracking.

After helping Dusty calm Stinkeye, Lucy swept up the wanted poster and tore it into bits as she rode Dellarosa to the boardinghouse. Aunt Margret met her at the kitchen door, arms folded as she watched the townspeople milling around the boardwalk.

"Whatever you're thinking," Aunt said, "it's probably a bad idea."

"I need a gun."

"A catawampusly bad idea."

"I can handle one. I promise."

"Now where would Henry Frederick's daughter learn to shoot a gun?"

"Research, Aunt. I'm a writer."

"Yes. That you are." A wry smile twisted one side of Aunt Margret's generous mouth. "I saw what happened, and I think the sheriff's being unreasonable, as is typical. There's a shotgun in my room, under the pillow. Shells are on the dresser, but I trust you won't be using them."

"Likely not. I'm going to fetch the doc first." Lucy swung down and raced to retrieve the sawed-off shotgun then returned to the kitchen and hugged Aunt Margret.

"You be careful out there, brave girl," the older woman whispered in her ear.

Lucy thanked her aunt and mounted Dellarosa. Minutes later, she eased the mare to a halt in front of the doctor's house. She marched up to the stoop, the shotgun tucked against her side, not caring whether she presented a ladylike picture as she pounded on his door.

After all, she had a cowboy to save.

◆　◆　◆

The stark look Lucy had worn burned Sam far worse than the bullet that tore a furrow through his side.

She'd turned him in—played him for a story, gave him a Judas kiss, and turned him over to his death when she was through.

How had he misjudged her so badly?

Even then, with her freckles standing out against white skin, she'd appeared innocent. Breathless with his kiss. But it had all been one great adventure, playing with fire in hopes of getting a story sensational enough to earn the respect of her infamous father.

Maybe win a ticket back home, back into Henry Frederick's good graces.

At the expense of Sam's sunburned but still-rather-beloved neck.

As the sheriff shoved him into the lone cell in the jailhouse, bitterness welled up inside Sam, throbbing along with his wound. Even though in some ways he'd expected it, Lucy's betrayal hurt worse than he'd reckoned it would. The whole town's betrayal. Had he not shown himself honorable? Was a poster and a rumor enough to erase the kind of man he tried to be?

"Ripple was a right good town, a quiet town to fall in love in." Sheriff blinked love-lorn eyes. "A place to get married, retire." He shook his shaggy head. "Now this. . ."

"I'm not the one who just shot someone, unprovoked." Sam's voice came out more peeved than he meant it to.

"You shoved Miss Lucy."

"To make sure you didn't shoot her by mistake." The scene replayed in his mind. The sheriff—out of practice or inexperienced, his hand shaking, his trigger finger too twitchy for the comfort of anyone within range. Lucy, standing between Sam and the others, frozen in place.

"Your horse was about to attack."

Sam scoffed. "Stinkeye wasn't going anywhere, and it was *your* dog who upset him."

A mite red-faced, Twitchy-Fingered Frank hemmed and hawed before spitting out a weak, "I did what I had to do," and retreating outdoors. No doubt to assure onlookers that the dangerous criminal had been subdued and imprisoned by their humble but mighty lawman.

Breathing in the stillness, Sam lowered to the cot and examined his side. The bullet had ripped a hole in his shirt and paved a painful path along his ribs. The blood still ran but had slowed. The wound was dirty, and he bore more cuts and bruises from his rude escort to the jailhouse. But he wouldn't die.

Not from this, anyway.

Removing his shirt completely, he rolled it and pressed it tightly against the wound. The best he could do for now, as it seemed Sheriff Frank had no intention of sending for the doctor. Lying on his good side, Sam stared at the floor and tried to erase Lucy's face from his mind.

How had it come to this? How had he fallen so far?

Once upon a time, he'd owned a homestead, had friends and prospects. A partner he loved like a father, and a fortune about to be made. They'd been preparing to buy an impressive spread, build a cattle empire with the gold they'd earned by the sweat of their brow and a bit of luck. Then, in a lightning-quick turn of events, everything had changed.

George Keene, shot in the back by a yellow-bellied coyote. Nearly their entire fortune stolen. . .and somehow Sam's name became attached to the cowardly deed.

The lawman stomped back inside and shoved a bucket of water inside the cell then propped his feet up on the desk.

Sighing, Sam ripped a sleeve from his bloodied shirt, dunked it in the water, and gritted his teeth as he attempted to cleanse the wound.

The gold didn't matter to him. He only wanted justice for George and his own name cleared, and maybe the love of a fiery redhead while he was at it. All he needed was for someone to give him the benefit of the doubt. To listen long enough for him to explain his side of the story. To earn a couple more weeks to find the one who'd done this and prove his own innocence.

Was that so much to ask?

But Lucy—

His wound twinged, halting all thought as he drew in air with a hiss. When the pain receded, Sam rested his head against the log wall and looked up. . .where he should have been looking all along.

All right, God. I reckon I'm listening.

For a long time, he'd been moving from project to project, building on his success. Then when everything crashed around him, he'd chased after justice.

Or was it revenge?

It had been too long since he'd stayed still. Sam closed his eyes and breathed in the quiet.

He wanted others to listen to him, to hear his story before casting judgments. But had he offered the same to others? To Lucy? Had he allowed God a chance to speak?

The forced silence soothed him, and Sam gradually relaxed his shoulders and felt tension release from the rest of his aching body. Praying, he asked God for forgiveness, and for the strength to forgive.

But that didn't mean he had to forget. Someone had killed George. That person's greedy and cowardly acts might cost Sam his life. If he could think hard enough, maybe he could stop it there.

The trail ended in Ripple. The killer lived in the area. But who?

Each face presented itself to him. The ones with alibis he'd already established. The ones he didn't find capable of the act for one reason or another. The ones he needed to investigate more thoroughly, if only he'd had the chance.

Of the men in town, only three fell in that last category. And the true criminal *was* a man, of that Sam was certain. If not, by the sunken prints he'd found of the killer's boots the only woman in town big enough was Mrs. Thorp. And. . .no.

So. *Mr.* Thorp.

The elderly mercantile owner had held his Colt with a steady hand, his eyes steely, easily the most dangerous of the men who'd confronted Sam in the livery stable. But he was lean and wiry. Slightly stooped. A good chance he wasn't heavy enough to fill the boot prints left at the scene or strong enough to carry away the loot. Besides, the mercantile seemed to be doing well enough—no apparent motive for robbery.

No evidence either way, but Sam reckoned the man was innocent.

Doc Smith. The man had curious timing, arriving in town shortly after the death of the only doctor in half a day's ride. But maybe he'd been traveling through the area and caught wind of an opening. Pure coincidence. Though on the lean side, the doc was tall with a paunch. There was a chance he might weigh enough to make a matching boot print. He'd been unaccounted for during the time of George's murder, and he kept to himself. Friendly but quiet, with chipped and dirty fingernails suggesting he'd done some digging of his own. . .along with the rest of the town. The big question was, would a man who healed for a living kill? Could he?

Lastly, there was Jasper Groth. The former actor had a whiny disposition. He wanted attention, wanted the best of everything. The gold could come in handy for a flashy man like him. He'd accosted Lucy. Maybe he wouldn't have harmed her, but he'd been improper in any case. Taking advantage of a lady—that was a mark of a coward. And his weight. . .well, the man would sink a few inches in muddy ground, that was a sure bet.

Had he been bunking next to the killer? The Jasper he knew wouldn't hide the fact he had a trunk full of gold. But how well did Sam actually know him? Had the clumsy, loudmouthed exterior been an act?

Of the three, Jasper had his vote. But he could be letting his dislike of the man—his disgust at his treatment of Lucy—dictate his suspicions. There might be a way to know for sure. . .

As if on cue, the man himself entered the jailhouse, his beady gaze darting from Sam to the lawman and back again. Remaining outwardly relaxed, Sam analyzed his every move as Jasper approached the desk, catching Sheriff Frank midsnore.

"I sent Dusty to get word to a ranger," Jasper reported once the other man snorted to attention.

The sheriff cleared his throat. "That's fine, that's fine."

Even Dusty had turned on him? Fighting against another wallowing session, Sam concentrated on Jasper.

The man grinned at nothing in general, seemingly elated. Buoyant, even. Due to excitement? Revenge for Sam's earlier rebuke? Or relief that Sam would now be executed and the crime wiped off the books, with Jasper going free and clear?

He stomped closer to Sam's cell, *tsk*ing all the while. "I knew there was something fishy about you, Brazos. All cocky and playing up to the ladies, but evil deep down to the bone. Well, now you're gettin' jist what you deserve."

"Even condemned men get last wishes," Sam said coolly, angling for the kill. He would look Jasper in the eye, and he would know. All it took was one question—

"Is your wish a kiss from the delectable Miss Lucy perhaps?"

Sam bristled. "Speak what you want of me, but you show respect to Miss Frederick."

Jasper laughed. "Says the man who shot someone in the back."

Swallowing hard, Sam held back a sharp retort.

"So if not the redheaded Yankee, what?"

Sam caught the actor's gaze and held it, wanting Jasper to know that *he* knew— that Sam had trailed the killer to the town of Ripple partially by the nutshells Jasper's thoughtless hands had left where he'd waited and at various stops along the way.

Wanting to see the flicker of guilt.

"Pecans," Sam said. "I'd like a handful of pecans."

There was no change in Jasper's gleeful expression other than a touch of blankness. "No slab of beef for a last meal? No letter to a sweetheart or your poor mother?"

"Nope." Sam's eyes narrowed. "That's it."

"It's a simple enough request," the sheriff said. "Think you can scrounge some up, Groth? I'm busy. . .guarding."

"No, siree. Even if I wanted to help a condemned man, which I do *not*, I cain't touch those pesky nuts with a ten-foot pole. Break me out in hives, they do."

Sam blinked back his surprise. Allergic? It could be another part of the act. But if not, that meant. . .

"Sorry, Brazos." A slow, oily smile. "Guess you're on your own."

Sam felt his chest tighten. His wound twinged again, and his thoughts instantly leaped to Doc Smith. "Sheriff, could you send for Miss Frederick?"

"Now see here, Brazos—"

"I'm not going to take advantage of the lady." Anger colored his tone. "She can stand across the room, but I need to see her." She needed to know what he suspected.

Doc was the killer. He had to be.

The lawman hesitated.

"She'll want to talk to me. For her article." The wheels were turning now, along with that same feeling Sam had at Rockin' R when he'd heard about Dillehay going missing.

Sheriff Frank nodded. "I see your point. Jasper?"

The actor growled, but he turned, promising to find Margret Frederick and have her fetch Lucy.

Except Margret couldn't. The boardinghouse owner rushed over to the jailhouse to tell Sam to his face.

Lucy was gone.

Chapter Nine

Doc pulled the door open, and his stare shifted from Lucy's face to the gun. The testy expression he wore morphed into pure rage, his skin stretching across his cheekbones and turning his bulbous nose three shades of purple.

"I threw you a bone. Why didn't you take it and leave me be?"

Blinking, Lucy backed up a step, half-raising Aunt's shotgun. "I'm here on behalf of Sam Brazos."

"Of course you are, and here's what I think about that." After a furtive look down the empty road, Doc grabbed the barrel of the gun and hauled Lucy inside, slamming the door behind him and yanking the weapon away.

"What on earth—?" The shotgun pointed straight at her heart, which was currently doing a polka dance.

"It's too late to pretend, Lucy. I know you started those rumors about me, trying to ferret out a story for your father."

Doc backed her up to the wall and rummaged inside a nearby pack.

She should be fighting. Screaming. Running for the hills. But all she could do was gape in shock as he pulled out a length of rope.

"Hold out your hands."

"No!"

"Lucy, I'm warning you."

"Are you *crazy*?"

"You're the one who came here by your lonesome." He laughed—surprisingly high-pitched and wheezy—and Lucy noticed for the first time how evil it sounded. How his teeth actually resembled a badger's in the right light.

"Now, out the back. You and me are taking a little trip."

No, they weren't. Please, no. Sam could be bleeding out as she made like a Grecian statue for the second time in less than an hour. Or the sheriff could get overzealous and hang him this very night! She choked on the thought. She had to escape. Had to get to her cowboy.

Lucy held out trembling hands, wrists up. The doctor would need both hands to tie hers. When he set the shotgun on his propped-up knee, she lunged for the door, tripping over her skirts.

Something heavy and cold and scary pressed into the back of her neck before she could crawl to the door.

"Roll over," Doc snarled. "Hold out your hands. Now."

If only she'd read more of those dime novels, instead of turning up her nose. Surely the brawling heroes would have given her some clue as to how to overcome this situation.

Instead, she obeyed, finding she had no choice in the matter as Doc prodded her along like a wayward cow.

"I think you misunderstand—"

"I know everything." He pushed her down a dark path to his wagon.

He'd been at the sheriff's office earlier. Had Doc been the one to turn in Sam? Did he know the truth about Sam's past?

Lucy bit her tongue, but the words spilled out anyway. "What—ow!—what exactly do you know?"

"About your articles, for one. How you think you've got the town hoodwinked as you tell all their secrets to your rich father back home."

In an ungentlemanly fashion, he helped her onto the wagon seat. Next, he hitched up his buckskin Buttermilk and landed beside Lucy.

"That's right," he continued. "Gus Wiley reads every one before he sends them off. Tells his lady love, who then tells the blacksmith's wife. So on and so forth. We *all* know, Lucy Frederick. Even if you didn't write my name, I know *you* know and that you'll spill the truth about me sooner or later." His dark, glittering eyes found hers. "Unless I stop you."

Lucy's mouth hung open wide. She closed it. Swallowed. Tried to speak. Finally, she managed a high-pitched, "Gus reads my letters?"

Doc heaved an exasperated sigh. "I think you're missing the point here. I gave you an escape—planted that poster where your Royal Nosiness was sure to find it. You didn't take your out. You should have."

So that's why he'd talked to her about the posters. It had all been a setup. If bouncing all over the road hadn't already given her a headache, Lucy would be tempted to pound her forehead against the nearest hard surface. Which just might have been the doctor's skull.

"If you wanted Sam in jail, you succeeded," she said.

"Is that what that ruckus was about?" A smile slid across his pockmarked face. "Good for the sheriff. I didn't think he had it in him to take Brazos down."

"Well. . ." Lucy frowned, picturing the bloody cowboy being dragged away, and after he'd so gallantly protected her, too. "He did. A bit unfairly, to tell the truth. So why are you kidnapping me, if you got what you wanted?"

"I don't just want him caught. I want him picking turnips with a stepladder, and the whole George Keene case buried along with him."

"What's it to you?"

"It's a confession you want, eh? Fine. I'll give it to you. *I* killed Keene. Stole the gold and framed Brazos. I came to this no-account town to bide my time until Sam Brazos got himself caught and took my place with a rope around his neck. Then my real life would begin. At least, that was the plan before you came nosing around, spreading tales too close to the truth."

Lucy shifted in her seat, not sure if she was more disgusted by his rank breath or the reminder that Gus had been peeking at her mail.

She cringed at the sudden realization that Gus knew about Sam—that the mysterious cowboy had played the infuriating and swoon-worthy hero in every story written after his arrival. Did the whole town know of her infatuation?

Did the cowboy himself?

Doc droned on as Lucy gnawed her lower lip. Finally, she cut in. "You killed Doc

Dillehay, didn't you?" Things began to click. Sam had been right—something was off about that story. "You found a quiet town with a lazy sheriff, so you made a reason for the town to accept you, few questions asked. Is Smith actually your name?" She turned on him, fuming. "Are you even a doctor?"

"Ira Moledord, at your service." He bent low in a mocking bow. "And yes, I'm a doc. Of sorts, not that it's any of your concern. But I'm fixing to be a rich man, free and clear, no longer needing to play nursemaid to snotty-nosed brats and complaining old nags. You're the only one standing in my way. And pretty soon, well, you won't be standing."

He flipped the reins, and Lucy bounced a little harder against the seat. The sun had begun to set as they trotted away from town. Who would come after her? The only one who might save her was bleeding out in a jail cell.

And he believed *she* was the one who'd put him there.

◆　◆　◆

Sam paced his cell in short, angry strides. "No one's seen Doc?" he asked again.

Twitchy-Fingered Frank shook his head, seemingly unconcerned. "You ain't even bleeding anymore. What's got you so fired up?"

Besides the fact that he'd been wrongfully incarcerated, shot by a lawman who didn't know how to use a gun, and betrayed by the woman he loved?

Sam stopped in his tracks.

Loved? Lucy Frederick?

She was beautiful and witty and smart and in a class far above him. But when she wasn't driving him crazier than a rabid coyote or delivering him to a lynching bee, he enjoyed bantering with her. Watching her. Being around her.

He knew he'd been too drawn to her. Knew she could betray him at any point. But still he'd fallen, and the thought of her at the mercy of the man who'd killed his partner—

"Sheriff, I'm telling you." He gripped the bars, rattling them to snag the man's attention away from the window. "Someone needs to find Lucy. She may be in serious danger."

Or maybe she'd been in cahoots with the doctor all along?

Casting the thought away as soon as it entered his mind, Sam fought his rising panic. He refused to believe that of her. But the fact that she wasn't here—asking questions for the story she'd fought so hard to get. . .

She was in trouble. He knew it, but he could do nothing, not stuck here behind bars. Which meant it was time to escape. Somehow.

An image of the doc's hands sprang to mind. Picking pecans from their hard hulls would explain the ragged fingernails. If he dared to lay one of those dirty hands on Lucy. . .

Eyeing the lock on the cell, Sam casually worked his way closer to it as Margret Frederick returned, pushing her way inside the jailhouse door with Gus Wiley following immediately after.

"Well, Margret, to what do I owe the pleasure of seeing you again so soon?" The sheriff bobbed his head around as if looking for hidden treasure.

"I'm not here for you, gunslinger." She lifted the basket she held, which didn't contain the hoped-for pie. Just as well, considering any accompanying dessert would likely have been shoved into the clueless lawman's face. "I'm here with real bandages to take care of your prisoner, since you haven't bothered to send for the doc."

"Dadgum it, Margret, I sent for him! I did!"

"He shore did," Gus echoed. "Right after he had Jasper send a message to the Texas Rangers."

"Is it my fault Doc chose this particular time to go digging for gold like everyone else in this addle-brained town?"

Sam tested the cell door as Margret turned up her nose. "Give me the key or you're never tasting my cooking again, and the next time your coon dog finds its way into my kitchen, I'm feeding him to my boarders."

Gus and the sheriff both recoiled, and Margret took the opportunity to grab the keys from Sheriff Frank's desk.

Narrowing his eyes, Sam eased back and watched. Could it really be that easy?

"Now see here—"

"*You* see here. I'm going to take care of this boy's wounds. You're going to look at whatever mail Gus took the time to hand-deliver, and then you're going to find my niece, else you've no claim to that gold star. None at all."

Turning the key, she let herself into the cell, closing the door behind her.

Grumbling all the while, Twitchy-Fingered Frank aimed his rifle in Sam's direction. "No bright ideas, boy, or the next shot will be fatal."

"Yes," Margret muttered. "But to whom?"

Sam remained still and watchful as the woman jerked him around a bit, slopping fresh water over him and roughly patching him up again. Uncertain if she was trying to help or maim, he braced against the pain and watched for any opening. The sheriff stayed with Gus, his rifle gradually drifting away as the man became engrossed in whatever news Gus had brought his way.

"Boy," Margret said as she gathered her things. "I don't know who you really are or what you've done, but my girl's out there and she needs you. So go find her and bring her back safe, or I'll string you up myself." She laid out a clean shirt. "But put that on first. Modesty and all that."

With that, she let herself out of the cell, closing it behind her. . .failing to lock it before laying the key on the sheriff's desk.

Gus had started an argument. Something about hunting dogs versus mousers. The lawman grew animated, finally reaching for pen and paper to draw a diagram to solve the problem once and for all. Sam allowed the cell door to swing open a foot or two and waited. Nothing. Picking up his hat, he sauntered toward freedom, earning the slightest of nods from Wiley on his way out.

Sprinting toward the barn, he found Dusty holding Stinkeye at the ready.

"Thank you kindly. I thought you set the Rangers after me." Sam palmed the reins.

"Nah." Dusty handed over Sam's pistol and Winchester rifle. "I took Admiral out for a run, that's all."

Sam swung onto Stinkeye. "Did you see Miss Lucy? Or Doc Smith?"

"Thought I saw Doc's wagon headed down the river way, but I ain't certain—"

"Thanks, Dusty." Sam urged his horse into a full gallop. They had a good lead on him, and Sam wasn't at full strength. But if he could find them—if he was in time—nothing would keep him from saving Lucy.

He hoped.

Sensing Sam's urgency, Stinkeye extended his stride like a racer pushing to the finish. "Come on, boy," Sam muttered. When they rounded the last bend and the river sprang into sight, Stinkeye gave a final burst of speed. . .just in time to hear a scream.

Chapter Ten

Lucy was willing to sacrifice many things for a story. Ruining her favorite pearl-buttoned boots in a filthy river was not one of them. She kicked and screamed and writhed and prayed, but the doctor flung her over his shoulder like a living fox stole and trudged toward the water.

"Unhand me, you cad! You yellow-bellied fraud! You murderer!" Her lack of imaginative insults infuriated Lucy.

Father was right all along. She didn't have what it took, and for the first time she was okay with that—perfectly resigned to the fact that she'd never write a published story—as long as she could make sure Sam would be all right. Tell him she hadn't set him up, she believed him, and had even before the crazy killer confessed.

She loved him.

"Go ahead, missy," Ira Moledord said. "Waste your last words calling me names. There's no one around to hear you."

If only she'd known his true name to begin with, she would have realized he was a villain. How could any Ira Moledord not be?

The doctor let out a laugh far too jolly for their predicament. "They're too busy getting ready to hang Sam Brazos."

They stood on the edge now, the rocky surface tilting at a sharp angle until it met a rush of brown water. Moledord grunted, his muscles coiling. Lucy shrieked louder, kicked harder. And still felt herself falling. . .falling. . .

◆ ◆ ◆

As Sam watched Lucy tumble from the bank, his heart fell with her. Shouting her name, he leaped from Stinkeye's back and drove his fist into the surprised doctor's face. Doc grabbed for his gun too late as momentum carried them both over the edge. The outlaw twisted away as they hit the water. Sam wanted to follow. To take him down. But he lunged for the surface, fighting with his own need for revenge as Doc kicked completely free and was caught by the current.

Lucy was all that mattered now. . .and she hadn't come up for air.

"Lucy!" The shout came out half-choked by river water and dread. Sam spotted the yellow fabric of her skirt billowing underneath the surface and dove for her. Closing his hand around her arm, he frantically hauled her up.

As she cleared the water, Lucy let out an impressive imitation of a rebel yell and brandished a small rock. Her hands were bound by coarse rope, her eyes wild.

Fury rising within once again, Sam grabbed her face and tried to hold her gaze. "It's me, Lucy. Sam. I'm not going to hurt you." What had Doc Smith done to her?

Sputtering, she dropped the rock and swiped at the water running down her face, stark in the fading light. "Is he. . .gone?"

"Downriver. I didn't get a chance to. . ." Defeat tugged at Sam as surely as the current. But he'd done the right thing. "Are you all right?"

"I heard the splash, was certain he was coming after me. So I stayed under, tried to find a weapon, my shoe got stuck. I prayed for deliverance, and then"—she panted for breath, gave him a dazzling smile—"and now here you are."

"I'm here."

"I—I thought you were dying."

"Only a flesh wound."

"Are you certain we're not both dead?"

A smile worked its way across Sam's face. "Not yet."

"Is this where you sweep me into your arms, and we ride off into the sunset?"

He reached for her hands and freed them from their bonds, holding them a moment longer than necessary. "Has someone been reading more of those dime novels?"

"Why, I never." Her nose lifted, but her words were breathy as she patted her ruined curls with trembling fingers.

Sam laughed and helped her up the steep bank. Emotions churned inside as he scanned the water for signs of the doctor. He'd failed in his mission, but he knew the identity of the killer now. Lucy was safe, but why had she betrayed him?

Or had she?

He should take off after Doc, but all he wanted to do was hold her in his arms and—

"This isn't the way I wanted to do this," Lucy said, staring at the ground, her hands twisting in her sodden skirts.

"Do what?" Sam asked, concern drawing the words out. She sounded fine. Prim, proper, with a touch of sass. But he pulled back, turned away, afraid of what was coming. Her confession about the stories she'd written about him? Her reasoning for turning him in?

"To tell you—" She broke off with a sharp cry.

Sam whirled to find Gus Wiley standing behind her, a gun pressed to her head.

The postmaster smirked. "How 'bout you tell me instead?"

◆　◆　◆

This couldn't be happening. Not again. Especially not when she'd been about to declare her undying love.

Lucy tried not to dwell on the irony, considering she might be about to die after all.

"What are you doing, Gus? You wouldn't really shoot Lucy, would you?" Sam's words were terse, frustration evident on his strained features.

"Shore would." The cool muzzle pushed harder into her temple.

"So that's why you helped me escape," Sam muttered.

Lucy cast him a quick glance.

"Everyone would blame you for her death, after all," Gus said.

"But why?" Lucy asked. "What do you want?"

"I want you to stop playin' games and tell me where the gold is."

The gold? With a shock, it all came back. "You!" Lucy fumed. "You've been reading my letters!"

"Yes, ma'am, and I'm shore tired of the wild goose chase. Where is the gold?"

Lucy shook her head, ignoring the weapon. "I can't believe it. What kind of person reads another's private mail, anyway?" The anger built until her wet skin was fairly steaming with it.

"Lucy. . ." Sam's eyes warned.

"No, I will not calm down! This sad excuse for a postmaster has been violating my privacy, and it's totally unacceptable! If there's been a crime committed anywhere, surely—"

"Lucy!"

"Well, then." Lucy pursed her lips and lifted her chin in the air. "It serves you right, Gus Wiley, to know there *is no gold*. I made those stories up. Every. Single. One."

Gus hissed in her ear. "I don't believe you. Tell me where—"

"Then you're a fool." She dared turn to face him, the gun now fastened on the center of her forehead. "There. Is. No. Gold."

Gus trembled, his face turning varying shades of red and purple.

"Lucy. . ." Sam's voice was low. Another warning, one that required obedience without question.

Woodenly, she turned back around, suddenly afraid of what she'd done. The postmaster was a coward, yes. But he wanted that gold, and she'd just taunted him, antagonized him, humiliated him.

"One more chance." Gus spit at Lucy's feet, wrapped a wiry arm around her neck. "Where is it?"

"I told you—"

"I know where it is," Sam said.

"What?" Gus said.

"What?" Lucy echoed.

"There *is* gold hidden around Ripple. I think I can tell you where to find it."

How was that possible? Lucy stared at Sam, eyebrows raised. He looked back, opened his mouth as if to explain, took a step forward.

"Don't move!" Gus shrieked. "Not a step closer!"

Sam held up his hands, empty of weapons. "I can show you where it is. But first, let Lucy go."

There was movement behind Sam. A form crawling up the bank.

"Sam," Lucy whispered.

"Not another word out of either of you!" Gus brandished his weapon. "Let me think!"

The form inched closer, moving toward Sam, who had his eyes fastened on Gus.

Lucy mouthed, "Behind you," but Sam didn't see, completely intent on Gus. On saving her life.

How could she possibly save his? She was only a writer, and not a good one at that. Someone who had nearly caused Sam's death and might still. Someone who created misunderstandings and rumors and had nearly ruined this good town without even knowing it. A writer who—

A writer who always, *always* carried her lucky fountain pen.

The figure was closer. Ira Moledord, alive and well. . .with the glint of a knife in his hand. Lucy carefully reached into her hidden pocket, fishing around until her fingers met cold nickel plating. It was now or never.

"Behind you, Sam!" she shouted, at the same time whirling to jab the pen into Gus's scrawny bicep.

With an indignant yell, the postmaster dropped his gun and clapped a hand over the wound, staring in consternation as Lucy scooped up his weapon.

"The pen is mightier than the sword?" she offered then glanced over to see Sam twisting a rope around the doctor's wrists.

Safe. They were safe. Now she could tell Sam—

A cloud of dust heralded the approach of several horsemen. The sheriff and a hurriedly assembled posse.

"Lucy, give me the gun," Sam said. His jaw was chiseled granite as he held out his hand.

"Not on your life."

"I'm not going to shoot anyone."

Doc Moledord lifted his head, eyes hopeful.

"Except maybe the doctor. But if you have the gun—"

"If *you* have the gun, the sheriff will shoot you. Again."

His eyes gentled, and the faintest hint of a smile softened his mouth. "Twitchy-Finger Frank couldn't get lucky twice, could he?"

"Fine. Then he'd shoot me. On accident."

Gus spoke up from his fetal position. "Maybe you should give it to me."

"Not a chance."

Sam took a step closer to Lucy. "You should leave. Take Stinkeye and get out of the line of fire."

"Are you jesting? I'm not going anywhere without you."

"Right." His voice flattened. "Your story."

"Not because of a story—Gus broke my pen, after all."

The postmaster muttered an angry protest and started to rise. Lucy cocked the pistol and let it dangle in his direction before turning back to the handsome cowboy.

"Not my story," she repeated. "Because I love you, Sam Brazos."

He locked eyes with hers but shook his head slightly. "I reckon I want to believe you. I love you, Lucy. But the rumors. And back at the barn—"

"I believed in your innocence even before Doc confessed. I didn't betray you—I was there to warn you."

"Not because of a story?"

"No," she said, hoping he was finally getting it. Men could be a bit dense, after all. "The articles I wrote were fake—something to amuse a friend while I searched for a real story to send my father. And you always played the hero. Always." Lucy glanced at her captive. "Right, Gus?"

The postmaster grunted. "He was too perfect. I knew he'd turn out to be an outlaw."

Lucy rolled her eyes. "Anyway. I love you. I'm staying. And—"

"Sam Brazos!" the sheriff called. "You are under arrest. Again."

Lucy stepped in front of her cowboy. "Ira Moledord, a.k.a. Doc Smith, killed George Keene. Doc Dillehay, too. He confessed to me this evening before trying to kill me."

Sheriff shook his head and turned to Mr. Thorp. "Load 'em both in Doc's wagon. We'll sort it out at the jailhouse."

Sam cleared his throat. "Reckon you'll want to grab Wiley, too."

The sheriff flung his arms into the air, seemingly unaware when everyone in firing range ducked. "What the deuce did Gus do?"

"He threatened to kill Lucy," Sam said.

"Him, too?"

"He wanted her to tell him where the gold was."

"And what does Miss Frederick know about—never mind." With an exasperated sigh, Sheriff Frank turned to his deputy. "Thorp, load 'em all in the wagon. We're gonna have a full house tonight."

Chapter Eleven

S am stepped into darkness outside the jailhouse, breathing in the air that smelled twice as sweet tonight. His name was cleared, or well on its way. The real murderer locked up inside, being held for his crimes.

Sam was free. He could go anywhere he liked. Start over fresh. Be anyone. Anywhere.

Lucy stepped out beside him, shivering in her still-damp clothes but smiling in pure triumph. Sam knew—despite the misunderstandings and his stinging bullet wound and muddy boots—there was nowhere he'd rather be.

"There's something I've been pondering. How did you know to look for me?" Lucy turned to Sam. "Why did you bother, after what you thought. . .?"

"I knew there'd be nothing that kept you from the biggest story yet. Assuming your meddling heart too kind to allow me to bleed out while you pumped me for information, I figured you went to get the doc."

Lucy took that in then shook her head. "My 'meddling heart'?"

Chuckling, Sam held out his good arm and escorted her toward the boardinghouse as he searched for the right words. Finally, he cleared his throat. "I hear gals like flowers. Poetry. Pretty little baubles."

"Most gals. At times."

"Like when a man is courting her."

"That's a good time."

"Lucy. . ." He stopped in the circle of light near the door. "Right now I don't have any of those things."

"Do you love me, Sam?"

"I do."

"I'm not most gals."

"True." A smile snuck across his face. "Which is why I have something better to offer."

Her eyes sparkled. "I'm listening."

"Marry me, and—"

"Yes."

Sam blinked. "You didn't hear the offer."

"I was hoping to get to the part where we seal the deal with a kiss. But if there's more. . ." She stepped back and gave him a mischievous grin.

"There's more. The story of a lifetime. An exclusive. *My* story." Maybe the things he'd gone through could be used to give her the chance she needed to prove herself to her father. Everything could work together for good after all. "And of course, there's the lost gold."

She frowned. "What gold do you keep talking about?"

"*My* gold. The money Doc stole from my partner and me. He buried it somewhere nearby. . .and I think I can find it."

Lucy stepped into the circle of his arms and placed a finger over his lips. "Careful, Sam. Don't want to start any rumors."

He laughed then sobered, searching her face in the dim light. "You'll marry me, then?"

"Since I first laid eyes on you, you've been the hero in all my stories. Sticking with you for the happily ever after. . .well, it would be a dream come true."

His arms tightened around her, since offering some of his warmth was only gentlemanly under the circumstances. "What about your father?"

"Didn't you hear?" She blinked up at him, all wide eyes and playful innocence. "I've secured Henry Frederick an exclusive with a former outlaw, thanks to you. The editor will be pleased."

"Well, if that's what it'll take. . ." He leaned his forehead against hers, his hat lost somewhere during the excitement of the past several hours. "Sweet Lucy. You're not who I thought you would be."

"Really? And here I thought the rumors were all about you, Mr. Pinkerton Agent."

"Is that why Polly cornered me in the mercantile and told that random tale? Something about a section of her granddaddy's crops being mysteriously cut down in the middle of the night?" Sam chuckled. "She was sure that elusive, nameless outlaw had a hankering for fresh corn and no sense of direction."

"Pinkerton, schminkerton," Margret hollered from the open window. "Polly cornered you because she thought you two lovebirds were engaged, and she wanted to be quoted in Lucy's next article!"

Sam raised his eyebrows and leaned closer, lowering his voice. "I think I'm going to need to see these articles."

"Too late," Lucy whispered back. "But for the record, in real life you're every inch the hero I thought you to be when you first rode into town on your mustang."

"Stinkeye manages to look somewhat noble when he wants to make an impression."

A smile lit Lucy's face then gradually faded. "How did you figure it out?"

"Figure what?" He tucked a strand of her wet hair behind her ear. She needed dry clothes and warm food as the night grew cool, but he found himself reluctant to release her. "That I love you?"

"Well, that." Her eyes turned dreamy for a moment then snapped back to the present. "And who the real killer was. Where he hid the gold. And—"

"You want an interview? Now?"

"I have to know what I missed. I've been hunting for a story, and it's been right in front of me all along."

"Lucy!" Margret hollered from a closer window this time. "What's right in front of your pretty little face is love, the best story there is. So shut your clapper and claim it already. The cowboy proposed!"

"I'll fill you in," Sam whispered. "But let's move somewhere a little more private-like. What do you say?"

"I'd say you're as smart as you are heroic."

Sam took her arm and ushered her toward the garden. "Now that you're being nice, I can't help thinking you're buttering me up for that interview."

"You might be right." She giggled then bit her lip. "I'm sorry." Her skirts still dripped, mixing with the dirt as they sloshed toward a stone bench. "The nosiness—it's who I am. Who I was raised to be, whether Father intended it or not." She took a deep breath. "Maybe you should reconsider."

Were those tears sparkling in the moonlight? Sam stopped and tipped up her chin. "I reckon I like who you are. That's why I proposed."

"Writing and all?"

"You bet. Although I figure if you ever hang up the fiddle on those articles, you should consider giving dime novel writing a shot."

Lucy gasped, her green eyes wide in the moonlight. "Goodness, Sam. What a thing to say!"

He leaned close, his mouth hovering above her scandalized lips. "You have to admit," he said softly, "there's something mighty fine about a happily ever after."

When their lips touched, she sighed softly. "I'll think on it," she whispered. "But not right now."

Lucy drew him down for another kiss, and that was just fine with him.

Epilogue

Dear Amelia,

In the unnamed town in Texas, the waters have calmed down so there's nary a ripple. Something as simple as a hankering for pecans—found at the original scene of the murder and various stops along the way—blazed a trail to the stolen gold and the true criminal. With the brave Sam Brazos serving as the newly appointed sheriff, trouble has fled, or has been escorted away by the legendary Rangers.

After finishing the rest of the article, the postmistress slid her spectacles in their holder and tucked the pages back inside their envelope.

She'd had no earthly idea the sheriff had been replaced. In fact, she wondered if Sheriff Frank himself knew. She'd have to ask Aurilla next time the widow stopped in.

Sighing happily, she tossed the letter into a bag with the rest of the outgoing mail. With people like Lucy Frederick in town, she had a feeling her new job would never be boring, and that was a fact you could take to the bank. . .if the bank was still safe. Hadn't the article mentioned a foiled heist?

She'd have to find out about that, too.

Jenness Walker lives in South Carolina with her website-designer husband, their toddler, and their hungry hound. Her lifelong love of books is evidenced by her day jobs, which have included freelance editing, managing an independent Christian bookstore, and even cleaning a library. Jenness's short stories have appeared in *Grit* and *Woman's World* magazines as well as in Guidepost's *A Cup of Christmas Cheer* collections. She is a former ACFW Genesis contest winner, Carol Award finalist, and her debut novel, *Double Take*, received 4.5 stars and a Top Pick rating from RT Reviews.

The Battlefield Bride

by Renee Yancy

Chapter One

Paducah, Kentucky
February 10, 1862

T he moans of the wounded soldiers inside the sanctuary of Grace Episcopal Church struck Katherine Wilkes like a punch to the gut.

There would be no turning back now.

She straightened her spine and climbed down from the wagon to stand next to Horace, her faithful old donkey, giving him a vigorous scratch. Discarded pews littered the front yard of the church, and the army's mules were sharpening their teeth on them. The nearest mule, a shaggy gray and smaller than the others, pricked its long ears and brayed an enthusiastic welcome.

Dear Lord, what had she gotten herself into?

Her heart thrummed like a bee in a bottle as she walked toward the wooden church, commandeered by the Union Army for use as a hospital after the recent battle to retake Fort Henry. A foul miasma of old blood and unwashed bodies escaped when she opened the door, and she wrinkled her nose. A raised platform stood at the far end of the rectangular room, and on the sanctuary floor about thirty men lay on cots crowded close together. Muted light filtered through the diamond-shaped panes of colored glass in the windows, throwing jeweled bands of blue, purple, and green across their pallets. She slowly walked the narrow aisles between them. All were dirty, bloodstained, many missing arms or legs, some with their pitiful faces still blackened with soot from cannon discharges. Most were sleeping or semiconscious, but one grizzled soldier noted her presence.

"Howdy do, ma'am," he said, reaching out a bruised and bloodstained hand.

She took it and pressed his fingers gently. "Good morning, sir. How are you?"

He shook his head, and moisture came into his eyes. "To be honest, ma'am, I'm feelin' almighty blue today."

"I'm sorry to hear it. Is there anything I can do?"

"No, ma'am." He lifted the grimy wool blanket and gestured to the empty place where his leg should have been. "Cannonball." He dropped the blanket and smiled lopsidedly. "The doc says I'm lucky to be alive." He sat up straighter on the cot. "What's a fine lady like you doing in this place?"

She smiled. "I've come to see what I can do to help you boys."

A grin cracked through the grime on his face, and the years fell away from him. "Jumpin' Jehosophat, ma'am, just the sight of you's done chirked me up good. We need a woman's hand around here. Look at this." From the crate that served as a bedside table he plucked a tin plate that held the congealed remains of some previous dinner.

She lifted it to her nose, recoiled, and hastily dropped it back onto the table. "I shall do my best to bring it, Mr. . . ."

"Private Benjamin Norton, Ninth Illinois Cavalry Volunteers."

"Thank you, Private Norton. I must see if I can find someone in charge."

"Out that door, ma'am." He pointed to a door off the side of the dais at the back of the former sanctuary.

Two tiny rooms off the main building comprised the rectory, and in one of them, a door led outside. Neat lines of canvas tents populated the grassy field, and farther off a larger tent flying a red flag nestled in a grove of crepe myrtle bushes. Close to the back door stood another tent with a makeshift cookstove, with provisions and foodstuffs stocked on rough board shelves. Near it a lanky soldier in a stained apron lay sprawled under a tarp, clutching a long spoon in his hand and snoring with his mouth open. She touched the stove, stone cold, and nothing else for dinner in the works. Kate frowned and nudged the soldier rather hard with the toe of her boot, whereupon he promptly sprang up, sputtering.

"Are you the cook?" she asked.

The soldier blinked several times. "Yes, ma'am," he muttered, rubbing his eyes.

"Then put some kindling into that stove and heat it up. Fetch the chickens in the wagon out front and wring their necks. Then turn my mule loose with the others." She pointed to an iron pot. "Fill that with water, and heat it quick as you can. Then unload the wagon." She paused. "What's your name, soldier?"

He looked at her sideways and took a step back, no doubt wondering where on earth she had appeared from to torment him. "Private Cletus Bennett, ma'am."

"Are you the only help available?"

"I work in the kitchen, ma'am."

"Who takes care of the injured men?"

"There be some orderlies, ma'am, but they ain't here right now. They's helping the sawbones with the amputations in the medical tent."

He pointed to the red-flagged tent a quarter-mile away. A shudder rippled through Kate at the memory of Henry's leg, amputated above the knee.

Private Bennett frowned and pursed his lower lip. "Ma'am?"

Kate swallowed. "It's nothing." She filled her lungs with fresh air to dissipate the memory. "I'm here to help. I'm fixin' to make soup. You can help me feed the men when it's done."

Thirty minutes later, five chickens stewed in a huge cauldron with the onions and carrots she had brought. She found the water firkin and one by one gave each man a good draught of clean water.

Armed with a bucket of hot water and some soft flannel cloths, she returned to the sanctuary. Most of the sleeping or moaning men looked devastatingly young. One soldier in the far corner wept, his face turned to the wall. She poured some water into a pan and chose him first. She dragged a stool to the edge of the bed and gently touched his shoulder.

"There, now. Are you in pain?"

The young man turned and gaped at her, his mouth open. A bloody bandage covered his left eye. He couldn't be more than eighteen. His beard had barely come in.

"Am I dreaming, ma'am? Are you an angel?"

She smiled wryly. "No, indeed. Far from it. I'm going to wash your face and try to make you more comfortable."

She dipped the rag into the warm water and gently sponged his face. "What's your name, soldier?"

"William Thornton, ma'am. But everybody calls me Billy."

"Where are you from, Billy?"

"Virginia, ma'am."

The water in the pan soon turned black and Kate changed it several times until Billy's face, arms and chest were clean. She dropped the sodden mass of his filthy shirt into an empty bucket and covered him with a clean sheet. Then she moved on to the next man.

Late afternoon sun slanted through the west windows when she had finished bathing each wounded man. In the kitchen tent, she boned the chicken and returned it to the broth.

"Have you any crackers? Or rusks?"

Private Bennett shook his head. Kate sighed and pointed to a large metal box holding the bread she had baked early that morning. "Bring that."

After the men had been fed, Kate raised the windows a few inches to let the fresh air wash away the fetid odors in the makeshift ward. It was a start. She rubbed her aching back.

A mournful whistle pierced the air, and the hiss of steam announced a train's arrival two blocks away at the station near the confluence of the Ohio and Tennessee Rivers. Kate winced. Six months ago, Henry had returned on the same train, but she couldn't think about him right now, couldn't think about his last days, even though she was here because of him. Her Union views had ostracized her from most of her friends and neighbors, and with Henry dead, she had decided to offer her services as a nurse, so that no man would have to go through what her husband had suffered alone. After collecting a wagonload of food and supplies for the soldiers from the few Union sympathizers in Paducah, she had shut up their tiny farmhouse on the outskirts of town, hidden the key in the well, and driven her wagon to the temporary Union hospital. There was nothing to go back to.

She pulled a gold locket out from her bodice and ran a finger over the glass covering the curl of blond hair. "Henry," she whispered, "I'm so sorry."

◆　◆　◆

Chief Surgeon Major James Logan mopped blood and sweat from his face as he stepped out of the surgical tent. Groaning, he straightened his back and stretched his tired muscles, first one shoulder and then the other, feeling the joints pop. The effort of bending over the operating table all day had taken its toll. The rain had stopped, and after the hellish scene in the tent, the cool air washed over him like a soothing balm. But his work wasn't finished. The wounded men in the sanctuary needed to be seen. His left leg, or what was left of it, had pained him all day, and his limp was decidedly more pronounced this evening. Cursed Confederate minié ball. Inevitably it crushed the tissues and shattered the bones of any unfortunate arm or leg it entered during battle. He'd lost his leg to one at Bull Run and now sported a crude wooden prosthesis attached to his thigh with buckles and braces.

He passed the cook tent and paused. A huge pot of soup simmered on the stove, and his empty stomach reminded him with subterranean growls that he hadn't eaten all day.

"Hmm," he muttered, "when did Bennett start cooking like this?" He found a bowl and ladled out rich golden broth, full of tender chicken, rice, and carrots. "Well, I'll be hanged if it's not delicious!" After another large bowlful he entered the ward, replete.

Someone hummed nearby, and then he blinked, astonished. A petite redheaded woman moved among the men on the cots, adjusting a pillow there, arranging a leg more comfortably here, and offering sips of water.

What in Sam Hill?

He strode toward the woman, who gave him a wary glance as he approached. "What in the world do you think you're doing here?"

She calmly smoothed her apron. "Ministering to these men."

"By whose orders?" he demanded. "Women aren't allowed in here."

"The Lord God Almighty has given me my orders," she said with a challenging glare. "Have you anything that ranks higher than that?"

"Madam, that. . .that is sacrilegious," Major Logan stammered.

"I hardly think so." She turned away and offered water to the next man.

He noticed her wedding ring and the black armband. A widow then.

"Madam," he barked, "I demand you leave immediately—" He stopped. Several of the men were gazing at her with unquestionable thankfulness on their faces. Then he realized their faces were clean and they were covered with fresh linen. Tin bowls at every bedside stood empty, and the foul odor had noticeably dissipated.

"Who are you, madam?"

She turned to face him. Her hair had been tightly constrained into a bun, but along her hairline tiny russet curls had escaped. Her eyes were a clear gray, and she barely reached his shoulder.

"Why, you're no bigger than a minute," he said. "What can you do here?"

"I'll thank you to kindly refrain from comments about my person, sir," she said acidly. "I am Mrs. Katherine Wilkes," she said. "And I've already done it."

◆ ◆ ◆

Shortly before midnight, Kate made a pallet for herself in a corner of the ward. She could be useful here if Major Logan would allow her to stay. In better days he would be considered a handsome man with that square jaw and shock of black hair, but exhaustion had aged him, his face lined, his eyes heavy-lidded and bloodshot. He had quite a noticeable limp as well.

There was no reason he shouldn't allow her to stay. The secretary of war had appointed Dorothea Dix as superintendent over the female nurses assigned to the US Army. Miss Dix had established strict criteria for any woman who desired to serve. She had to be above thirty years of age, wear only plain dark colors, and have no "ribbons, curls, bows, or hoops" about her person.

Kate laughed quietly. She fit all the criteria except one. Her father had always said she had curls so tight even God couldn't straighten them.

She had nursed both her parents before their deaths from consumption and influenza, so she had plenty of experience. And Henry. She gritted her teeth, powerless to stop the surge of memories that arose unexpectedly day and night at the most unexpected times—a young soldier with a smile like Henry's or a certain manner of walking. A drift of pipe tobacco.

For three days she had nursed him, more dead than alive after being furloughed from the Confederate prison camp and sent home to die. When she shaved off his matted beard, his face was so gaunt she'd barely recognized the dashing soldier she had sent off to war twelve months earlier.

Now he lay with the other two tiny graves in the pine grove at the back of the farm, forever silent and cold.

◆　◆　◆

Major Logan removed his wooden leg, blew his candle out, and lay back on the cot, staring into the darkness. He'd heard about women nursing injured soldiers at other camps, but he'd never thought to actually see one. He would send her packing tomorrow. She didn't belong here.

His calf ached, and he automatically reached down to rub it but found only empty space. Even after a year he hadn't completely realized his leg was gone, and through some cruel trick of nature, he could still feel his toes.

He groaned, sat up, and reached to relight his candle. Slowly he pulled the crumpled letter from his haversack. Even though he'd already memorized every line, he couldn't stop himself from reading it again, if only to see the letters and words she had formed with her own hand on the paper:

> Buffalo, New York
> October 2, 1861
>
> Dearest James,
>
> It is with much trepidation that I write to you now. I have spent much time pondering our future since your terrible injury. I thought I should be able to accept your limitations, and that it would have no impact on our life together, but I was wrong. I'm weak, James. I've always had an aversion to blood and illness, and after much prayer and contemplation I have come to the conclusion that I must break our engagement. I am sorry to do this now while the war still rages but thought it much crueler to have you believe I am waiting for you here at home, only to return and find that we cannot marry.
>
> I hope in time you will come to forgive me. I will pray for God's richest blessings on your life.
>
> Sorrowfully,
> Beth

A fresh ache pierced his heart. He pictured himself traveling home to Buffalo after the bloody war ended, going straight to Niagara Falls and throwing himself over the brink like Sam Patch, the "Yankee Leaper." Then he laughed grimly. With his luck he'd probably survive.

He had to stop torturing himself.

He groped for a lucifer, struck it against the table, and lit a corner of the pale blue letter. The flame burned through the elegant script and consumed the paper. Only when his fingers scorched did he fling it to the grass and stamp on it.

It was over. Finished.

Done.

Chapter Two

Before dawn in her dark corner of the sanctuary, Kate lit a candle, helpfully supplied by Private Bennett, and splashed some water on her face. Perhaps later she could find a place to have a proper wash. Amazingly, Private Bennett had risen even earlier than she and had the fires kindled and a pot of farina cooking. She picked up a can of Borden's condensed milk and considered the bucket of eggs on the counter. Perhaps the men would enjoy a rice pudding.

"I need an extra-large cauldron, Private Bennett. Filled with water and brought to a boil."

"Will that do?" Bennett jerked his head toward the immense iron pot that that stood outside the tent.

"That will suit excellently."

His face lit up. "What are you going to cook today, ma'am?"

"The men's laundry," she said. "Best get to it."

Bennett started to salute and then dropped his arm, his sallow complexion coloring red. Kate suppressed a smile. At least Private Bennett had accepted her presence.

Shouts and the clatter of wheels drew Kate out of the tent. A string of wagons, each carrying its load of limp figures, stretched beyond the picket lines of the camp. Here and there an arm or leg stuck out, and piercing screams of agony tore from the patients when the wagons lurched over a rut.

Private Bennett came to stand beside her. "One of the gunboats has come into the harbor, ma'am, bringing the injured from a battle downriver in Tennessee, most likely."

"Is Major Logan the only surgeon here?"

"Yes, ma'am."

That would account for the exhaustion she had witnessed yesterday. Another reason to stay.

Bennett eyed the long line of wagons. "Bless their hearts. It's gonna be a mighty long day for the doc. But I heard tell there's another sawbones coming."

The tall figure of Major Logan detached itself from the swarm of men and limped toward them, his black brows drawn together in a fierce frown.

"Mrs. Wilkes," he shouted, still a good distance away, "I have urgent need of your help."

She sniffed. Quite a different tune from yesterday.

The major reached her and paused. "The army has taken Fort Donelson, the wounded are coming in, and my surgical assistant is down with dysentery. I need you to assist me in the tent." He lifted his chin as if daring her to refuse.

"I would be happy to, Major," she said, pretending a calmness that she didn't feel. She had to be strong and capable, even though her knees were shaking under her skirts. "Will you be able to feed the men by yourself?" she asked Bennett.

"I can give him some men to help." Major Logan said. "Come with me."

A line of stretchers waited outside the tent, each containing a moaning, bloodied figure. Some called for their mothers, others their wives or sweethearts. Flies crawled over their bloody wounds, and the stink of blood, feces, and fear rolled over her like a wave. Her throat constricted, and for a moment she couldn't breathe.

"Mrs. Wilkes?" The major watched her, his face inscrutable. "Are you ready?"

"Y–yes" she managed to gasp, hating the tremor in her voice.

He shrugged and entered the tent. She followed.

A waist-high wooden table ran down the middle. Bandages and surgical instruments lay on a smaller table to the side: scissors, knives of varying lengths, needles, and saws. There were other instruments like awls and long slender tools with small hooks at the end. Bloodstains, some fresh, some rusty, spattered the walls of the tent and soaked the flattened grass underneath her feet.

"Put this on." He threw her a bloodied leather apron, which reached to her ankles.

With trembling fingers, she tied it on as best she could.

"You will administer the chloroform. Stand here."

She took her place at the head of the battered table as indicated, trying to close her ears to the screams of agony outside the tent.

"You will follow my instructions completely."

She nodded and stiffened her spine. *Dear Lord, be my strength.*

He took a paper cone and stuffed some cheesecloth loosely into the point then nodded to the waiting orderlies, who swiftly picked up the first stretcher. The soldier screamed and grabbed for his leg as they deposited him on the table.

"No!" shrieked the soldier. "Don't take my leg! Don't you do it, Doc. Please! No, no!"

Jagged ends of white bone protruded from the mangled flesh above the knee, the leg already nearly severed in two. The orderlies grunted as they labored to restrain his thrashing limbs.

Major Logan seemed oblivious to the wounded soldier's struggles. "Hold the cone like this." He placed the open end of the cone over the man's contorted face. "Leave several inches of space for air to circulate." He picked up a brown glass bottle and, with a dropper, carefully administered eight drops onto the pointed end, then eight more, until the patient's thrashing diminished. The administration of the chloroform continued over the next minute or two, when a sudden muscle contraction shook the soldier and his limbs relaxed into blessed unconsciousness.

He handed her the cone and the bottle. "Be ready to do exactly as I did when I tell you."

Silently she nodded her assent. Sweat trickled down her back and dampened her forehead. Furtively she wiped her face on her sleeve and hoped she could do what he expected of her.

The major chose a scalpel, quickly severed the shredded skin and sliced through muscle and tendons. One of the long slender implements with the hook at the end was used to pull arteries out of the bloody flesh and tie them off. Then he picked up the bone saw as the patient started to stir. "Four drops now."

Trying to control her shaking hands, Kate managed to properly drop the chloroform onto the cone, while maintaining the space for air to circulate. Once again, the patient's limbs relaxed as anesthesia was achieved.

"Now then."

Kate shuddered as Major Logan sawed through the bone and then used a file to smooth the rough ends. An orderly took the amputated limb and tossed it onto the grass outside the tent. Moving with great speed, the major sutured the flaps of skin over the stump and took the bandages held at the ready by the orderly. In crisscross fashion he expertly bound the stump as the patient began to wake.

"Done."

Major Logan lifted his hand, and a pair of orderlies swiftly removed the patient while others lifted the next soldier to the table, this one with a shattered arm.

"Are you ready, Mrs. Wilkes?"

The severed leg lay discarded on the grass outside with the poor soldier's boot still on the foot. She would never forget when she'd unwrapped Henry's bloody dressing for the first time. Pus had oozed from the swollen angry flesh, and the wound crawled with maggots. And the smell—she gagged at the memory. Henry had suffered this same barbarous surgery. Had writhed in agony on a hard bloody table like this. Had he had chloroform? *Oh, dear God, dear God, I pray he did.* If only she hadn't—

"Mrs. Wilkes!"

The intrusion of Major Logan's stern voice dissolved the image in her head. With a start, Kate realized the major and the orderlies were staring at her.

"I said, are you ready to proceed?" Major Logan asked in a tight voice.

"I'm s—sorry. Yes. I'm ready."

She clenched her jaw and took a breath, steeling herself for the next amputation.

The major nodded to the orderlies, who took a firm grip of the soldier. Kate raised the cone above the patient's nose and mouth.

"Ten drops."

Carefully, Kate concentrated on measuring out the chloroform as the patient convulsed, his arms and legs twisting.

"Ten more."

The patient's body went limp.

The same surgery then repeated in a rapid, dizzying fashion. A scalpel to the skin to form the flaps, the muscles and tendons divided and the bone saw separated the arm from the body.

Hours later a stack of amputated arms and legs lay piled outside the tent. Her head throbbed, and she had completely sweated through the bodice of her dress. Her arms ached from holding the cone upright for hours. Morning had blurred into afternoon, a mindless maze of blood, body parts, and screams of agony.

"Just one more, Mrs. Wilkes." He hesitated. "You've done well."

"What is a woman doing in here?" an angry voice roared, and a moment later the owner of the voice lunged into the tent, a portly officer with pendulous cheeks and a belly that threatened to burst the double row of brass buttons on his coat. Bald on top, with stringy hair at the back and a tiny, cruel mouth, he stood with his arms akimbo and glared at Kate like a basilisk. Her nostrils flared at the strong odor of alcohol that clung to him.

"Pity you didn't arrive sooner, Major Drake," said Major Logan calmly. "I could have used the help. Four more drops."

Kate administered the chloroform, trying to ignore the blustering man staring at her a few feet away.

Major Drake stamped his foot, splattering her apron with bloody mud. "I demand to know what she's doing here." He took an unsteady step closer, and Kate barely managed to keep the cone in place and not shrink away from him.

Major Logan paused. "She is assisting me with this amputation." He fixed the man with a stern glare. "We will speak later."

"We'll speak now, James—"

Something snapped inside Kate, and she whipped her head around. "You're drunk, sir, higher than a Georgia pine!" It certainly wasn't the first time, as evidenced by the purplish web of tiny burst veins that covered his nose and cheeks. "You need to leave." Kate held his furious gaze, willing herself not to look away.

Major Drake's lips closed into a perfect circle, soundlessly opening and closing like a flabbergasted fish. Then he shut his mouth and straightened stiffly. "You haven't heard the last of this," he snarled. He clapped his hand to his mouth and stumbled out of the tent. A moment later they heard him vomiting into the crepe myrtles.

"Almost finished. Hold steady." Major Logan tied off the last suture, bandaged the stump, and then nodded to the orderlies, who took the stretcher off to the makeshift hospital ward.

Kate let out a long breath as a sudden dizziness passed over her. No wonder she was lightheaded. As the roaring of her heartbeat filled her ears, she realized she hadn't had anything to eat or drink this entire day.

"Mrs. Wilkes?"

When she didn't answer, Major Logan gripped her arm and dragged her to a camp chair outside the tent. "I'm afraid you may have inhaled some chloroform. I had forgotten how short you—" He stopped abruptly. "Bring some water!"

It felt like heaven going down her parched throat.

Refreshed, she stood to her feet. "I'm perfectly fine. I didn't have time for breakfast before you summoned me. That's all. I must get back. . .back to the men." Quickly she drew her skirts together and hurried toward the makeshift hospital. She wanted to forget what she'd seen in the surgical tent. What Henry had suffered—because of her.

"Mrs. Wilkes!"

She didn't turn around when he called her name but hurried faster. He caught her at the back door. "Mrs. Wilkes. What's wrong?"

She refused to look at him. "Nothing."

"Why are you running away?"

"I'm doing no such thing. Let me pass."

"You're crying."

"I'm not."

The major snorted. "I knew it. It's too much for a woman, exactly as I suspected."

She lifted her chin defiantly. "It's nothing of the kind. I'm sorry to disillusion you, but I am perfectly capable of taking care of these soldiers."

"Then why the tears?"

"It's Major Drake you should be questioning, sir, as to his fitness for his chosen profession."

"I will deal with Major Drake. Now then."

She clenched her fists. "I was thinking of my husband, if you insist on knowing. He suffered the same operation to amputate his leg. The surgeries today gave me a terrifying vision I'd rather forget. I hadn't realized how agonizing it must have been for him—" She groaned inwardly. And she had caused it. She dug her fingernails harder into her palms until she gasped at the pain. She deserved it, and more.

The arrogant look on the major's face softened slightly, only to be swiftly replaced with a scowl. "Mrs. Wilkes, this is no place for a woman. Pack your things and go home."

Kate pressed her lips together. If she hadn't given the water cup back to the orderly, she could have smashed the imperious look off his face. But that wouldn't help her cause, so she turned on her heel instead and stalked around the building.

"I'm leaving for Illinois tonight," he shouted after her, "and you'd better be gone when I get back!"

She tossed her head and didn't deign to look back. Insufferable man.

A breeze off the river cooled her flushed face as she sat on the wooden front steps of the church to simmer down. Hadn't she proved herself in the surgical tent? She knew she'd surprised him. Once or twice she had caught him studying her.

The stench of blood still filled her nostrils, as well as plastering most of her dress and face. The major had to contend with this after every battle. How did he do it? Bodies torn apart, piles of amputated limbs, the screams of the wounded, all coalescing into one long bloody nightmare until the last man had been operated on. And then to wash off the blood and try to forget what he'd seen, what he'd done until the next transport of injured and dying men arrived.

The mules were still on the front lawn, and the wooden pews had taken a beating. Idly she wondered what the church's congregation would think when the battered seats were back in their proper places. Horace whinnied at the sight of her and wandered over. She ruffled his bristly mane, and he pressed closer, nudging her hand when she stopped petting him.

"Well, Horace," she said, giving his neck a good scratch, "it's been a hair-raising day."

Private Bennett came around the corner at that moment and raised his eyebrows when he saw her talking to the mule. "Howdy, ma'am."

"Good afternoon."

Bennett stopped in front of her and recoiled. "Ma'am, could I get you some hot water?"

She smiled wryly. "I'm a sight, I know." Every muscle in her body ached, but she needed to return to the boys. "Thank you, Private." Kate gave Horace one last pat. "Time to get to work."

Horace brayed his disappointment when she left him to wash her face.

She had absolutely no intention of obeying Major Logan's demand.

◆ ◆ ◆

Major Logan rubbed his forehead wearily as he walked toward his tent. Of all the surgeons Washington could have sent it had to be Benjamin Drake. When sober, he performed as an adequate surgeon. But rumors had recently surfaced of problems arising wherever Drake had been sent. And then Mrs. Wilkes had piped up. Drake had an apoplexy when she called him out. What nerve that woman had. Surely there would be hell to pay.

It proved that women didn't belong here, and that was that. He had told her to leave, and she had better be gone when he returned from Cairo. He didn't want to deal with her or any other woman, anywhere, ever again.

Chapter Three

The next morning after a proper wash, clean clothes, and a fresh apron, Kate readied to face the day. She found Bennett in the cook tent, bent over a pot on the stove.

"What's for breakfast, Private?"

Bennett jumped and pressed a hand to his heart. "Well, fry me in butter and call me a catfish, ma'am! You skeered the daylights out of me." He gulped. "What are you doing here, anyhow?"

Kate frowned. "Why shouldn't I be here?"

Private Bennett goggled at her. "Well, I thought. . .that is. . .I heard. . .the major. . ."

"Were you eavesdropping yesterday, Private?"

"Beggin' your pardon, ma'am," he said indignantly, "the whole camp heard the major yelling after you. Bellowed like a bull."

Kate smiled. "I suppose he did. I apologize." She sniffed the air. "Your oatmeal is scorching, Private."

He hurriedly pulled the pot off the fire and poured most of it into a bucket. "Saved it." He opened his mouth then hesitated. "So, you ain't going to leave then, ma'am?"

"Does it look like it?"

He studied her, and his thin face broke into a beaming smile. "Well, I'll be hornswoggled. You're stayin', ain't you?"

"Yes." It would take more than Major Logan to make her quit.

"Bully for you, ma'am. I'd take a bet the major will cotton to you afore long. I know the men would be fair sorry to see you go. You've chirked them all up."

She felt her face flush. It did her heart good to hear it. Whether Major Logan agreed or not, her efforts hadn't been in vain. "Thank you, Private Bennett."

"Aw, call me Cletus, ma'am."

Kate smiled. "So be it, Cletus. Let's begin."

◆　◆　◆

Three days later, Kate stood in the ward and surveyed her domain. With Major Logan away and Major Drake temporarily working at the Marine Hospital at Fort Anderson a few blocks away, she had wasted no time putting things into order in the ward. At her direction all the cots had been taken out, the floors swept and bleached, and all the linen cleaned. She had worked with the two orderlies assigned to the ward, McCracken and Livingston, to establish set times for bathing and shaving and for the boiling of bandages and the men's laundry. The windows had been washed and all the mattresses aired. Cletus and the orderlies had done such a fine job that she had time to sit with the men, helping them write letters home. Recently arrived Private George Sutton, well enough to sit and play his fiddle, had helped pass the last two evenings pleasantly, especially once the men found out Kate could sing. Then there was nothing for it but to sing all the popular songs, everything from "Goober Peas" to "Tenting Tonight on the Old Campground."

But the attitude in the ward had muted this evening. The men conversed quietly among themselves, every so often casting furtive glances her way. Cletus had told her Major Logan had arrived back on the post earlier this afternoon.

Her insides felt like a twisting nest of snakes ready to strike. Why didn't he come and get it over? Surely he had discovered she had ignored his order.

She strode resolutely into the ward. "Private Sutton, won't you get your fiddle out and play us some tunes?"

"Certainly, ma'am," he said and led them a rousing rendition of the "Anderson March." Then he moved on to "Yankee Doodle" and "Camptown Races."

The men joined in raucously, clapping their hands:

"Camptown ladies sing a song
Doo dah, doo dah
Camptown racetrack five miles long
Oh the doo dah day
Going to run all night
Going to run all day
Bet my money on the bob-tailed nag
Somebody bet on the bay."

Two of the men who could walk started an impromptu jig, and the men hooted and hollered when Private Welch dragged her into it. "C'mon, ma'am! Right hand around!"

She laughed as he swung her through the steps while the men clapped harder and stamped their feet with a deafening noise that rattled the rooftop. "I'm getting dizzy."

The fiddle cut short with a jarring screech, and Private Welch lurched to a halt as the singing died away. She staggered, trying to regain her balance, when a hard hand clamped onto her arm and spun her around.

Major Logan's eyes blazed like blue lightning. "What are you still doing here?"

She wrenched her arm out of his grasp and stepped back, raising her chin. "And where else should I be, but here taking care of my boys?"

He gritted his teeth. "I gave you an order, madam."

Some of the men rustled their feet and muttered under their breath. She smiled prettily with a confidence she didn't feel. "Orders? But, sir, I'm not in the army."

"Don't play coy with me." He exhaled hard through his nose. "You know exactly what I mean. Why aren't you gone?"

"Aw, sir, let her stay," called out Private Welch. "She sings beautifully."

"She's wonderful to us," said Private Sutton. "My own ma couldn't have done better."

A general chorus of agreement and "Let her stay, sir" and "Please, sir," went up.

Major Logan's lips tightened. "Come outside to discuss this, madam," he snarled, his face formidably grim, "if you'd be so kind."

He gestured her ahead of him, and with her head held high, she walked to the front door and sent a silent prayer heavenward for help.

He didn't speak immediately but paced back and forth on the walkway. Then he turned to glower at her and shook his head. "Is your command of the English language somehow wanting, madam? Did you not clearly understand what I said to you three days ago?"

She nodded. "I did."

His eyes narrowed. "Then what is wrong with you? Why didn't you obey?"

"As I said, sir, I'm not under your orders. I take mine from God."

"Ah, yes," he said. "You mentioned that the day you came here." His fists were clamped at his sides as if he didn't trust himself, so she said nothing, sensing his rising frustration.

"I don't want you here, Mrs. Wilkes."

"You've made that quite plain, Major. But the men need me." She hesitated, not wanting to make him any angrier. "Perhaps we could take this matter to General Sherman?"

Something had prejudiced Major Logan against her. Maybe someone with a better sense of practicality would see her skills and experience as an asset.

His head snapped up. "Out of the question!"

"Why?"

"General Sherman has neither the time nor the inclination to deal with such a trivial matter."

She stiffened. "It isn't trivial in the least. It's important to the men. Anyone with common sense could see it. Why can't you, sir?" She spoke more sharply than she had intended and immediately regretted it.

"How dare you speak to me in such a tone?"

She raised her chin defiantly. "How dare you turn away help and succor for those poor injured men, some of whom you know will never see their loved ones or their homes again? How dare you deny them comfort and kindness? What is wrong with *you*?"

Major Logan stood stock still, breathing hard. Then he stepped closer. "You will leave tomorrow, Mrs. Wilkes, do you hear me?" He towered over her, but she stood her ground, refusing to be intimidated. He pointed his finger in her face. "Answer me."

"I'm not leaving, Major."

He gasped, incredulous.

"I'm sorry, Major, but whether you like it or not, I'm staying."

"I'll have you removed, by force if necessary."

"You'll have to," she said coolly. "Because I'm not going anywhere."

◆　◆　◆

Major Logan stalked away, seething. What an infuriating woman! He'd never met anyone so stubborn. He'd fully expected her to be gone when he returned. He couldn't remember the last time he'd been this angry. And the men. Traitors. They wanted her to stay.

After three hard laps around the camp perimeter, his pace slowed. He was being irrational. Of course the men wanted her to stay. She reminded them of home and of a mother or wife's loving care. Why had he allowed her to affect him so?

He entered his tent, declining to light the lantern, and dragged his cot closer to the open tent flap. Overhead the starry constellations wheeled slowly across the night sky while a chorus of early spring peepers sang in the oak forest that edged the camp, a promise of spring. The tightness in his chest eased. Maybe, after all, it wasn't his to decide. He slid off the cot onto his knees and bowed his head for the first time in many months. In anguish, he poured out the burdens of his heart before God. The daily battle with life and death. The waste of young lives on the battlefield. The bitterness and the torment of feeling half a man after the loss of his leg. The death of his future with Beth wiped out as a heavy rain erases footprints on a path. Only emptiness lay ahead.

When he finished, spent, he rested his head against the edge of the cot. "Now what, Lord?" he said aloud in the peaceful stillness. A small voice answered gently in the darkness.

"Wait on Me."

◆ ◆ ◆

Kate sang softly to herself as she went about her daily business. Major Logan had apparently changed his mind about sending her home, and she silently gave thanks for this. Things were running smoothly on the ward. That is, when Major Drake wasn't around. She repressed a frown as he entered the sanctuary, blustery and cold as the March wind outside. As usual, the major pointedly ignored her as he made his rounds, and as usual she stayed out of his way, while keeping a wary eye on him from a distance. He first stopped to see Private Moore, recovering from a minor head injury. Next he examined Private Clemens, whose fractured arm had nearly mended. Then he arrived at the bedside of Private Kelly, who had become apathetic after the amputation of both legs below the hips three days ago. His state of mind especially concerned her. The major pulled up a stool to examine the dressing.

A shrill scream erupted through the ward a moment later, and Kate hurried over. The major prodded at the bandages and roughly unwound them. His hands were nasty with blood and grime and who knows what else under his fingernails.

"Major Drake!"

The major narrowed his small piggy eyes as Kate quickly inserted herself between him and the patient. "You're too rough, Major. He's in a lot of pain." She glanced down at Drake's hands. "And I'm sorry, but your hands are filthy. Would you mind washing before you see the patients?" She pointed to a washstand in the corner, with clean towels and soap. "Everyone washes their hands before they touch a patient."

A pulse throbbed at his temple as his face turned crimson. He bunched his fists together and sprang to his feet, knocking the stool over.

"I have never been so insulted in my life." He shook a finger in her face. "And by a miserable chit like you, who thinks she knows better than a physician how to treat patients." He narrowed his eyes. "Don't think I don't know what's going on between you and Major Logan." He smirked in her face. "You're an adventuress who's charmed her way in here and so bewitched the man, he thinks whatever you want to do is wonderful."

Kate gasped. What a pompous toad of a man. Private Kelly's eyes bulged, and rumbles of discontent rose from the other beds.

She sniffed. "How many adventuresses do you know, Major, who empty bedpans, boil bloody bandages, and go without sleep to minister to these boys? It's you who have insulted me."

Many of the men were sitting up in their beds scowling at the major, and she realized that she mustn't let this go any further. With an effort she softened her voice. "Perhaps we could take this conversation outside, so the boys will not have to be privy to it."

"The boys?" he sneered. "You're one of those women that can't have a child, is that it? So you're pouring out your misplaced maternal instincts here."

His words stabbed deep, and she recoiled, turning away to hide the pain on her face.

"Leave her alone!" Private Moore lurched out of bed and stumbled toward them, as muttered words of disapproval rose through the room.

"Get back in bed, Private!" snapped Major Drake, whirling around. "Or I'll see to it that you're court-martialed."

Private Moore's face whitened, and he groped his way back to his cot.

The major turned back to Kate, his lips twisted. "You've even got these men under your thumb, don't you? Ready to stand up and defend you. Well," he snorted, "the few with legs, anyway."

Kate stiffened as a gasp went around the room. The man was impossible. "Perhaps they appreciate being treated with kindness and respect." She couldn't keep the derision out of her voice. "Something you obviously know nothing about."

The major laughed grimly. "You're nimble witted, I'll say that for you. But you don't fool me." He poked her in the shoulder with his beefy finger, and she groped in her pocket for the butt of the Colt Baby Dragoon revolver hidden there. "I'll have you dismissed today, madam," he spat out, his lips twisted. "If you were a man," he said, lowering his voice, "I'd knock you down and tear you apart!" He viciously kicked the stool out of his way, narrowly missing her, and left.

Kate let out the breath she had been holding, weak in the knees, and sank onto the end of Private Kelly's cot.

"I heard what he said, Mrs. Wilkes," said the soldier weakly. "And I ain't afraid of him. I'll tell Major Logan how he threatened you."

"That's right," said Private Moore. "We'll all speak to Major Logan for you." Then he laughed. "You sure rumpled his feathers, ma'am."

"I wish I had my pigsticker," said Private Clemens. "I'd show him what's what."

"Thank you, boys," she said, warmed by their words. "But I don't think that will be necessary. I will go and speak to the major myself."

◆　◆　◆

Major Logan moved his feet closer to the brazier at his feet to ward off the March chill. In Buffalo they probably still had three feet of snow. But perhaps that was preferable to the muddy ruts in camp that caught one's boot and wrenched the ankle.

He bit the end of his pen and looked out of the tent flap, considering the crucial supplies needed for the camp hospital. Mrs. Wilkes exited the back of the church, her cloak pulled closely about her and her head down against the wind. What a determined woman she was. She'd been here three weeks and had already accomplished more in the ward than any orderly or physician had been able to.

As she turned first down one path and then another, he realized she was headed toward his tent. He quickly shrugged into his coat and smoothed his hair.

She stopped outside the tent flap. "Major Logan?"

"Come in, Mrs. Wilkes." He unfolded a camp chair and set it near the brazier.

"Thank you," she said, sitting down and clutching the cloak about her. The rough wind had loosened her hair, and burnished red-gold ringlets streamed down her back. Then he realized there were tears in her eyes and her hands trembled.

He pushed the brazier closer to her feet. "Are you cold? Is everything all right?"

She swallowed and shook her head. "No, Major. I'm afraid I have made a terrible mess about something."

"I doubt it. You're usually cleaning them up, not making them."

She blinked, as if she hadn't expected such a positive response, and pulled at a loose thread on her cloak. "I've had an awful scene in the ward with Major Drake."

"Hmmm." Drake again. The man was a scalawag. "What's he done now?"

"It's not what he has done, but what I've done." She shrugged. "I asked him to wash his hands before he examined the patients."

Major Logan whistled softly. "I can guess at his reaction."

"His fingernails were filthy, Major. And he had food in his beard! He always appears unkempt, greasy as fried lard. And he's rough with the men." She wrung her hands. "He doesn't seem to care if he causes them pain or not. I had to say something."

"Go on."

"He said he'll see to it that I am dismissed today." She hesitated. "I know that initially you wanted the same thing, and I don't know why you've changed your mind, but—" She broke off. "I've severely angered Major Drake."

He could imagine. "Mrs. Wilkes, I can't discuss another officer with you. But after all you've done for the men, I will do my best to ensure that you stay."

Her beautiful gray eyes widened. For the first time since she'd arrived she smiled at him, and his heart did a somersault. "Thank you, Major."

When she left, he returned to his supply list, but a quarter of an hour later, Major Drake loomed large in the tent opening. "James."

"Come in, Benjamin," he said, repressing a groan. "What can I do for you?"

"No need to be so polite," said Major Drake as he deposited his considerable bulk on the chair recently vacated by Mrs. Wilkes. "I'm sure you know why I'm here. I saw that infernal woman leaving your tent." He leered. "I don't know what you two lovebirds have going on, but I want her dismissed immediately. You can carry on your affair somewhere else."

Major Logan scowled. His hands itched to wipe the smug look off Drake's pugnacious mug. "There is no affair, and I take offense at that statement."

Drake laughed. "Tell yourself whatever you want, but don't lie to me. Get rid of her. You know as well as I that women don't belong in an army hospital."

"She's made our position here easier, Benjamin. It would send the men into the doldrums if we dismissed her now."

Drake's piggy eyes lit up. "You're sweet on her. I knew it."

"I respect her and what she has accomplished. That's all."

"I knew I wouldn't get any support from you." Drake stood and smoothed his stringy hair. "I'll have to do it myself."

Logan shook his head, frowning. "I don't agree. Suppose we put the matter before General Sherman when he returns." How ironic. Exactly what Mrs. Wilkes had originally proposed. "And let him decide."

Drake sniffed. "Why delay the inevitable, James? You know he'll send her away. And won't the parting be even more painful?"

"You're mistaken. There is no affair. Are we agreed then?"

Drake approached and stuck out his hand, and they shook on it. Major Logan had to swallow a smile at the remnants of eggs and toast in Drake's beard.

Chapter Four

March 25

Kate rose at 4:00 a.m. and dressed by the light of the kerosene lantern in the tiny rectory room that had become her bedroom, although she spent little time there. It had been six weeks since her arrival at Grace Episcopal. Major Logan had accepted her presence, although she often caught him studying her with an enigmatic look on his face.

Major Drake maintained an icy reserve around her, but he had managed to stay sober for a month after his arrival. Unfortunately during the last fortnight he had arrived on the ward several times in an intemperate state. And she knew why. Someone had been pilfering the store of medicinal brandy meant for the patients. Three days ago she had hidden it in a canned milk crate and stuffed it in a pile of wool blankets on the dais. But even hidden there, brandy had still gone missing. The orderlies in the ward overnight swore they had neither seen nor heard anything.

She tied her apron on as she reflected on Private Kelly. He'd been feeling poorly and feverish when she retired at midnight, still in despair over the loss of both his legs, and worried about his mother. Lantern in hand, she walked through the darkened rectory toward the ward. A stealthy scuffling noise stopped her at the door to the sanctuary, and she strained to listen. From the other side came a scraping sound and heavy breathing, then a muffled oath.

Quickly she swung open the door and raised her lantern. The burly figure of a man turned and squinted against the sudden brightness. "Get that blasted light outta of my eyesh! Whoosh there?"

Just as she had suspected. The milk crate sat on the floor in its nest of blankets, and Major Drake held a half-empty bottle in his hand.

"Major, have you no shame?" She gave him a scathing look. "That brandy is for the patients!" From the alcohol reek that surrounded him like a fog, he'd already polished off at least one bottle.

The orange glow of a lantern flared in the ward below as several of the patients raised sleepy heads, blinking. McCracken and Livingston sat up on their pallets in the corner, rubbing their eyes.

"Git outta my way, w–w–woman," bellowed Drake. He dropped the bottle on the carpeted dais and pushed her aside. She lifted the lantern dangerously close to his face, and he shrank away. She'd catch a weasel asleep before she let him have that brandy. "That's not for your personal consumption, Major."

"Why, you brazen—" He struck the lantern out of her hand with his fist. It sailed across the dais in a perfect arc and crashed into a basket of cotton bandages, which immediately caught fire. McCracken shouted a warning as he and Livingston dashed toward the steps, pulling up their suspenders. Kate gasped and tore off her apron to muffle the burning basket while the orderlies grabbed blankets, but the flames, accelerated by the brandy spilled on the carpet, had already leaped to the back wall.

"Get help," she yelled to McCracken. "Most of the men can't walk." McCracken nodded and bolted for the door.

"Fire!" screamed Kate. "Help! Fire!"

Together she and Livingston beat at the flames as black smoke swirled through the sanctuary. The heat inside the building intensified as the flames consumed the wood of the back wall. Drake had lurched to a chair and sat, stupefied, staring slack-mouthed at the fire.

"Help us!" she shouted at Drake. Her lungs burned, and the billowing smoke made it hard to see. Livingston moved ahead of her to attack a fresh burst of flames in the corner. Someone seized her arms from behind, and she was spun around. Drake's demonic pupils mirrored the flames behind her and focused on her with diabolic intent. Before she could scream, he seized her by the throat with both hands. She flailed on the tips of her toes and desperately scrabbled to pry his fingers from her neck. Private Monroe stumbled from his pallet, got his crutch under his arm, and stumbled toward the dais as Drake squeezed harder and her vision darkened. A fiery explosion shattered the air, and Drake screamed and released her, falling back with his hands clamped to his face. The milk crate had caught fire, exploding the brandy bottles and spraying the dais curtains, which ignited with a blazing whoosh. On her belly Kate slithered toward Livingston. Below, the men coughed and choked and cried out as the flames roared to the top of the wall and curled along the vaulted wood ceiling, crackling as it consumed the wood like a living creature.

Kate reached Livingston and pulled his pant leg. "Get help," she shouted over the roar of the fire.

Livingston nodded and turned for the door then stopped as Major Drake came out of the smoke and lunged at her once again. Her sleeve ripped as she twisted out of his grasp and screamed hoarsely through her bruised throat. Livingston tackled Drake, pinioning his arms, and wrestled him to the floor as Major Logan burst into the sanctuary.

"Make a line! Make a line!" He tore down the flaming draperies and stamped on them. Other soldiers poured into the building and efficiently established a bucket brigade to the river while vile oaths and imprecations spewed like vomit out of Major Drake's mouth. Slowly but surely the men brought the fire under control until only smoldering heaps of charred wet wood remained. Cold air poured in through the gaping, burned-out wall. The major put men to work to temporarily close the hole with tarpaulins hastily brought from the fort.

Kate's legs collapsed, and she sat down with a thump on the wet floor. Shivering, she pulled her knees to her chest. Her throat hurt terribly, and her body shook like she had an ague.

Major Logan bent over her, dressed in trousers and his shirt loose. "Are you injured?"

"Not badly," she managed to croak through her bruised throat, so tired she couldn't move.

"Major Drake attacked her, sir," said Private Kelly weakly, from his cot below the dais. "Like a mad man. He tried to strangle her. I seen it with my own eyes."

Major Logan's face darkened as he lifted her chin and inspected her neck. His lips pressed into a hard line as he glanced at her torn dress and the purple bruises showing through her ripped sleeve. He helped her to her feet and settled her on a stool.

"He'll be court-martialed for this," he said grimly. "If I don't kill him myself first."

"He's been. . .stealing the brandy. . .meant for the men," she said. Her throat throbbed as if Major Drake's hand still gripped it in a vise, her voice raspy. "Only this morning. . .did I get my proof."

"Shesh's lyin'," shouted Drake as the orderlies struggled to lash him to a chair. "I demand to be released at once!"

"Shut him up," said Major Logan.

"Yes, sir." McCracken obligingly stuck a massive roll of bandages in Drake's mouth, effectively cutting off the fountain of profanities. Drake's eyes bulged while he tried to shout around the gag and tossed his head from side to side like a madman. Blood dripped from the cuts on his face, giving him a ghoulish appearance.

A soldier rushed in, slipped on the wet floor, righted himself, and saluted the major smartly.

"Yes, Private?"

"General Sherman, sir," the soldier stuttered, "General William Tecumseh Sherman has docked on the river at Fort Anderson. He's proceeding here now."

"Thank you." Logan sighed and pushed his hair out of his eyes. In the chaos of the fire he had forgotten the telegram that had arrived yesterday from Cairo, Illinois, informing him of General Sherman's visit. He glanced about the dripping walls, the ruined ward, and the charred remains of the dais draperies. The riverfront lay two blocks away. General Sherman would get a firsthand look at the damage. He tucked his shirttail in and rubbed the stubble on his jaw. What a way to greet his commanding officer.

A few moments later, Kate noticed the two orderlies spring to attention. Major Logan followed suit. A tall officer strode in and saluted in return. His reddish hair lay curiously short and ragged on his head. He possessed an aquiline nose and thin lips in a dark beard clipped close. The shadows around his eyes gave him an implacable appearance. Even in her dazed state, Kate caught the air of strength and determination that emanated from him.

"At ease, men." The general scrutinized the damaged wall and the smoldering piles of scorched wood. He nodded to her, but his gaze lingered on Major Drake, bound and gagged in the corner.

"Well, Major Logan, I can see this isn't an ordinary morning."

"Not at all, sir."

General Sherman turned to her. "General William Tecumseh Sherman, at your service, ma'am." He bowed. "No, please remained seated," he said, as she tried to rise.

"Mrs. Katherine Wilkes," she whispered hoarsely, sinking onto the stool. "It's a pleasure to meet you, sir, even under these conditions."

"You're injured, Mrs. Wilkes. Do you require medical attention?"

"I will see to it that she's taken care of, sir," said Major Logan.

The general nodded. "I've been hearing some interesting reports about this camp hospital, Major," he said briskly, "which I wish to discuss with you. But first," he glanced toward Major Drake, once more struggling against his bonds and growling against the gag, "why is Major Drake bound?"

"He's been stealing the brandy meant for the men, sir," said Major Logan. "When

Mrs. Wilkes attempted to stop him this morning, he attacked her and tried to strangle her. Somehow a fire started."

General Sherman's lips hardened, and he turned a calculated gaze on Drake, who wilted and quieted under the imperturbable assessment.

"He knocked my lantern. . .into some bandages. . .which caught fire," she said haltingly, her voice hoarse. "It spread from there."

General Sherman turned to one of the lieutenants with him. "Put Major Drake in the stockade."

The veins in Drake's neck bulged as two soldiers released him from the chair and rebound his wrists behind him. He looked thoroughly disreputable and capable of further violence as he glared at her, and she shuddered, glad to see him taken away.

Drake managed to spit out the gag as the soldiers dragged him away. Beet-red in the face, he shouted at Major Logan. "I'll have y–you court-marthialed for thith!"

General Sherman shook his head. "Gag him again."

After the soldiers removed Drake, General Sherman glanced around the ward. "All these patients will be transferred to the fort, Major Logan. Lieutenant Gordon, please see to it immediately." He glanced at Kate. "That will give Mrs. Wilkes a few days to recover. After you've seen to her, come to the fort. I need to speak with you privately."

"Yes, sir." Logan saluted General Sherman, who returned the salute and left.

"Are you feelin' poorly, Mrs. Kate?" Private Kelly gazed at her anxiously.

She nodded, not wanting to speak unless absolutely necessary, but smiled faintly at his method of address. The men had taken to calling her that in the last few days.

His pale face lit up. "You did real good, ma'am, standing up to that old wrangler."

Around the room, the soldiers nodded at her.

"Serves him right," said another. "He's lower than a snake in a rut. I hope he does get court-martialed."

"Meaner than a whole sack of rattlesnakes, plumb sure," said Private Monroe.

Kate straightened and took careful stock of the men. "No one hurt?" she croaked.

"No, ma'am," they chorused. "Take more than that to hurt us."

The Fort Anderson soldiers had returned with litters to transfer the men. The boys were in good hands for the time being. She couldn't have done much for them at the moment anyway. The rush of strength while fighting the fire had dissipated, leaving her spent and weak as a baby.

◆ ◆ ◆

Major Logan seethed inside. He should have reported Drake before this. Now Mrs. Wilkes had paid the price. She slumped on the stool, exhausted, her face streaked with soot and her dress singed with charred holes. The print of Drake's thumbs showed clearly on her throat. He gritted his teeth.

"Mrs. Wilkes, let me help you to your room."

She opened her eyes and nodded. Her first step was unsteady, and when she stumbled, he picked her up like a rag doll. She couldn't weigh more than ninety pounds soaking wet.

"At the far end," she pointed to the end of the hallway, farthest away from the sanctuary.

He carried her to the tiny room and laid her gently on the cot. After placing a pillow behind her head, he lifted the roller shade to examine her by the sunlight streaming through the window. Her eyes were clear, no hemorrhages. He poured a glass of water and held it out. "Try a swallow."

Obediently she took a cautious sip and shook her head, her face pained. "Hurts."

He placed the glass on the table. "You have some internal swelling, but I don't think you'll have any permanent damage. Your vocal cords have been injured, and you need to rest. I'll make a draught of slippery elm for your throat."

She nodded wearily and pulled the pins out of her hair, releasing the mass of curls and ringlets down her back. In the sunlight her hair glowed a fierce reddish gold.

He hesitated. "There isn't any woman here to help you, Mrs. Wilkes. Shall I send to St. Mary's and ask one of the sisters to come?"

She shook her head. "I'll manage," she whispered. "Thank you." She laid her head on the pillow.

"I'll bring you some hot water." He took the pitcher to the cook tent and picked up some towels. He couldn't imagine that she would want to stay after what had happened today.

Her eyes were closed when he returned. Although she looked tiny and helpless, she'd already proven her value. But what had happened this morning might be enough to cause her to give up nursing the men. With a start, he realized he didn't want her to go.

She didn't stir when he sat down on the edge of the bed. He wet a corner of the towel and took a gentle hold of her chin. Carefully he wiped the soot off her face and neck. Then he smiled. Tiny freckles were sprinkled across her nose and cheeks. Her eyes opened then—gray eyes so clear he could get lost in them. He gave himself a mental shake. *Get hold of yourself, Logan.*

"Major," she said hoarsely.

"Yes?"

She gazed at him. "Why have you changed your mind about me?"

His mouth fell open. He hadn't expected such a point-blank question. The obvious reason was that the Lord had told him to wait. But if he were to be brutally honest, there was more to it. Because he'd never met another woman with the grit she possessed? The temerity to stand up against a man twice her size when he interfered with the care of her 'boys'? An unexpected and powerful impulse surged through him to gather her in his arms and protect her.

"I prayed," he said gruffly. "I trusted that the Lord had another plan." He stood and pulled the roller shade down. "Now get some rest."

"Yes, Doctor," she said meekly and closed her eyes.

◆ ◆ ◆

Major Logan posted a guard outside her door, left orders to fetch him when she awoke, and walked the two blocks toward Fort Anderson on the Ohio riverfront. Sunlight glittered off the water-filled ditches that surrounded the fort on three sides. Another officer showed him to General Sherman's study, and he and the general descended to the stockade, a small windowless room in the lowest level of the fort. Four small cells stood empty at one end of the room, each furnished with a cot and a wooden slop bucket.

Major Drake had been handcuffed to a chair, with a burly guard on each side.

Someone had washed the blood off his face. Although the gag had been removed, he didn't speak as they entered the room but glowered daggers at Logan.

General Sherman seated himself at a battered desk in the corner, and Logan took the only other piece of furniture in the room, a wooden stool. The general considered each of them in turn, his dark eyes determined. "I want an explanation of what happened in the ward this morning. You may go first, Major Logan."

Logan nodded. "As I told you, sir, Mrs. Wilkes caught Major Drake stealing the medicinal brandy. When she tried to stop him, he assaulted her."

Drake sprang to his feet, dragging the chair with him, his face livid. "You're taking her side against me?" The soldiers pushed him back into the seat. He turned to face the general and lowered his voice. He had regained control of his faculties, no longer slurring his words. "Sir, that woman is disrespectful. She back-talked me constantly and thought she was as good as any physician."

Major Logan exhaled hard through his nose, incredulous. "Do you remember anything about this morning? In your enraged and inebriated state you tried to strangle her!" He glanced at the general. "If the orderlies hadn't managed to restrain him, he might well have accomplished the deed."

"I hardly touched her."

"The bruises on her throat and arms say otherwise, Major."

"I wanted to teach her a lesson."

"While fire destroyed the ward and the lives of our injured soldiers were at risk? If you hadn't been stealing the brandy, none of this would have happened. You've lost your mind. And you will lose your commission now, if I have anything to say about it."

General Sherman pulled a case from his jacket and took out a cigar. "There are witnesses to this, Major Logan?"

"Yes, sir. Several."

Drake tried to get out of the chair again, but this time the soldiers were ready and clamped him firmly in his seat. His fleshy jowls shook with rage. "I knew you'd take her side, Logan. Maybe General Sherman should ask what you've been doing with Mrs. Wilkes, hmm? I'll bet you haven't mentioned your little affair with that woman to the general. I should have reported you at once."

General Sherman turned his inexorable gaze on Major Logan. "Is this true?"

"Absolutely not, sir, on my word as an officer."

General Sherman leisurely lit his cigar and took a puff. "How long *has* Mrs. Wilkes been here?"

"About six weeks, sir."

"Interesting." The general put his cigar down on the end of the desk and drew a paper out of his pocket. "I have here the official mortality reports for this camp hospital for the past three months." He tapped the paper. "Some curious numbers. The mortality rate in this particular hospital dropped dramatically for the month of February." He eyed the men. "What can we attribute this to?"

Major Logan sat up straighter.

General Sherman smiled. "Yes. You've arrived at the same conclusion I have, Major Logan. It has to be the nursing the men have received at the hands of Mrs. Wilkes."

Major Logan blinked. And he'd wanted to send her away.

Drake clenched his meaty fists. "You don't mean to say you're going to let her stay, General? That's outrageous."

"I disagree." The general shook his head. "To successfully fight this war, I need every man I can get, as strong as he can be. Mrs. Wilkes has accomplished a small miracle here, one I wish to see repeated in other hospitals. As a matter of fact, I'm going to ask her to accompany my army in a few days when we move south to Tennessee."

Major Logan's chest tightened. Of course she would say yes, and that realization left a surprising void inside him. He struggled to keep his face stoic as Drake leered knowingly at him.

"You'll be coming with me as well, Major Logan. The sanctuary is going to be returned to its congregation, and the Marine Hospital should be able to handle the patient load as the army moves farther south."

Logan couldn't hold back the grin that cracked his face. "Yes, sir."

Drake gasped. "You can't be serious, General," he sputtered.

"To the contrary, I'm quite serious." General Sherman stubbed his cigar out and stood. "But you needn't worry about it, Major." The general's lips pursed in a faint moue of distaste as he scrutinized Drake's sweat-stained uniform, the corpulent paunch over his belt, and the bloodshot eyes. "You'll be on a train to Washington for your court-martial." He nodded to the soldiers. "Put him in a cell."

◆　◆　◆

Kate awoke to a pink sunset outside her window. Why was she in bed at dusk? Her throat hurt, and still groggy, she swung her legs over the side of the cot and wrinkled her nose at the harsh scent of charred wood and smoke that rose from her ruined dress. The altercation with Major Drake, the flames of fire—it all came rushing back, and she blushed, remembering how Major Logan had swept her up and carried her to the tiny bedroom, sat on the cot, and tenderly washed her hands and face. The intimacy of that moment had taken her breath away. Her face grew hotter at the memory of his strong arms holding her close, the heat of his body against her wet, chilled flesh.

Then she blinked. He'd probably noticed she wasn't wearing a corset. What would he think of her?

This wouldn't do. She clamped her jaw, got out of bed, and reached for the water glass, taking a cautious sip. Not quite as painful as this morning. She needed a wash and change of clothes. She emptied the cold water from the pitcher out the window and went to the door, where she ran into the guard.

The soldier snapped to attention. "Howdy, ma'am," he said. "You're awake now."

"I am. Going to fetch some hot water."

"I'll be happy to do that for you, ma'am." He took the pitcher from her.

"Thank you."

Back in her room, she pulled fresh clothing from her trunk and found her brush. A gentle knock sounded at her door and the guard peeked in. "Here's your hot water, ma'am. I'll be off to report to Major Logan now. He asked to be notified when you woke."

Once he left, she stripped off her sooty clothes and washed her face and body, giving thanks for soap, hot water, and clean towels. Carefully she brushed tiny pieces of glass out of her hair. After dressing with fresh clothing from her unmentionables out to her dress and with her hair pinned up, she felt herself again. Then she left her room and made her way to the front of the churchyard to sit on one of the shabby wooden pews. Venus twinkled low on the horizon in the rosy sky, and the pungent smell of charred wood wasn't as pervasive. Horace wandered over and pushed his nose against her shoulder. She was giving him a vigorous scratch when General Sherman and Major Logan came along the road and approached her.

The general bowed. "Mrs. Wilkes, I will come straight to the point. I have direct evidence that your care for my men here has borne joyful fruit, despite what many say about a woman in the hospital camps. You've single-handedly reduced the mortality rate here by half."

A thrill ran through her, hastily tempered by the knowledge of why she was there to begin with. "Thank you, sir," she said hoarsely.

"Major Drake will bother you no longer. He's been placed under arrest. I sincerely apologize for his actions."

"Thank you." Now he couldn't hurt anyone else.

General Sherman studied her, his fine dark eyes seeming to miss nothing. "I'm moving my forces to Tennessee in a few days. Would you consider accompanying me? I will give you all the assistance and support you need."

Kate blinked. Henry would have been proud of her. Then her gut twisted, and she tried to keep the agonizing pain off her face. If only she hadn't—

She bowed her head. "I would be honored, General. Thank you." The expiation of her terrible sin could continue in Tennessee.

General Sherman bowed to her and left.

"May I?" Major Logan glanced at the seat next to her.

"Of course."

"How are you feeling?"

"Better."

Silence stretched between them as the sky darkened and a white mist appeared over the river.

"I want to offer my congratulations," Major Logan said suddenly. "You've done some fine work with the men." He hesitated. "I know. . .I know I was harsh when you came."

"You were."

"I had a reason, Mrs. Wilkes." He gazed out at the river. "The horrors I've seen, the waste of life, the blood, the dirt, and the despair." His voice rose, impassioned. "Why should you have to see it? Endure it?" His voice broke. "Forgive me, I—it's wrong of me to burden you."

"I have my own burdens, Major," she said quietly. "Things in my past I'd rather forget." Such as Henry's eyes, dulled with fever and pain, yet still full of love for her. Love she didn't deserve. Forgiveness she didn't—

Major Logan shifted on the seat to look at her. "I knew there was something different about you right from the start. A certain. . ." He paused, searching for the right word. "Intransigence. Yes, that's it." He smiled. "No compromise."

She smiled bitterly, glad the darkness hid her face.

If only he knew.

Chapter Five

At midnight, Major Logan sat at the desk in his tent by the battlefield, wearily writing a letter to his mother. So many amputations today, so many lives lost. The rebels had charged the Union forces early this morning with initial success, resulting in thousands of Union casualties. General Sherman had been wounded twice— in the hand and the shoulder—and had three horses shot out from under him. When reinforcements arrived later that afternoon, the tables had turned, the Confederates had been forced back, and a Union victory declared.

At a terrible cost.

Through the narrow opening of the tent flap, a flickering orange glow appeared on the battlefield, flitting in and out. Logan turned his lantern down and peered through the darkness. Midnight had passed. There shouldn't be anyone out there at this time of night.

He stepped outside the tent as the light disappeared and then reappeared farther down the field. Looters? He didn't see any other lights. Looting the dead and injured was strictly forbidden, but there were always blackguards who didn't hesitate to break the law and had no respect for the dead.

He approached the nearest sentries and pointed out the light. "Investigate that."

"Yes, sir."

They saluted and went out into the darkness. A few moments later, the orange light bounced crazily about and went out. Footsteps approached, jostling, and grunts from the men. The sentries stepped into the tent with a small struggling figure between them.

A pair of baleful gray eyes glared at him. "What is the meaning of this?"

"You!" He snapped his sagging jaw closed. "What are you doing out on the battle-field? In the dark. An active battlefield, may I remind you, Mrs. Wilkes."

"I'm well aware of what it is, Major." She glared at the two soldiers holding her. "Take your hands off me."

At a nod from him, they quickly let go and stepped away, one furtively rubbing his shin.

She raised her chin, her cheeks flushed, and the outraged glare she leveled at him made him shrivel inside. He cleared his throat. "I repeat, Mrs. Wilkes, what are you doing?"

She straightened her back. "If you must know, I'm searching the bloody ground because I can't rest until I know there is no living man left on it."

He gasped, struck speechless for a moment. "Have you no regard for your own safety? There might be enemy soldiers still alive out there."

"That's the idea."

"You could be killed. A woman with no protection."

She smiled faintly. "I'm not stupid, Major." She plucked the baby Dragoon Colt from her pocket and cocked it. He ducked instinctively as the soldiers yelped and fell back. "Mrs. Wilkes! Please! Put that away."

She lowered the hammer and pocketed the pistol.

"Do you even know how to use that?" he asked indignantly.

She shot him a withering look. "Why else would I be carrying it?" Then she pointed toward the battlefield. "It's lovely having a midnight conversation with you, Major, but while we're speaking, a wounded soldier is lying out there. Best get to bringing him in."

He bristled and then exhaled hard. "Get a stretcher and fetch the man," he said to the two sentries.

The soldiers saluted and quit the tent.

Mrs. Wilkes turned to go.

"A moment, please."

"Why? I need to attend to that injured man."

"Please take a seat."

She plunked down on the camp chair. "What now?"

He didn't answer immediately, exhausted after a long day performing amputations. How she had the energy to be out at midnight on the battlefield when she had been awake since 4:00 a.m. mystified him. She had more energy in her little finger than most of his surgical assistants. He thought back to the evening sitting outside the burned-out sanctuary of Grace Episcopal Church.

"Intransigence," he said slowly. "I thought that was it." He studied her, noting the clenched fists and the high color in her cheeks. "But it's more than that, isn't it?"

She stiffened.

"The risks you take, the fearlessness. It's not really altruism, is it, Mrs. Wilkes?"

She lifted her chin. "I'm sure I don't know what you mean."

His eyes narrowed as he studied her. "There's a desperation about it, as if you don't care if you live or—"

"Flummadiddle!" She sprang up so quickly the chair crashed over backward. Her brows slanted together in a ferocious scowl. "Who do you think you are, sir? Ascribing the basest of motives to what I am trying to do here? Good night!"

She stalked out of the tent.

He waited to be called for surgery, but the summons didn't come. Just as well. He needed to rest before the next round of battle-injured men arrived. But sleep wouldn't come, and he found himself thinking of Mrs. Wilkes and the elusive hunch about her that had occurred to him while she sat fuming in his tent. She had a deeper reason for being here than simply ministering to the men.

Something that drove her to do dangerous things.

Chapter Six

Memphis
June 2

Kate stood in the middle of her well-appointed tent kitchen. General Sherman had been true to his word, supplying her with assistants. Two older women, Mrs. Blake, a tall, gray-haired widow, and Mrs. Ennis, who reminded Kate of a plump brown wren, had joined her to help run the camp hospital. She had managed to avoid Major Logan in recent weeks after—after whatever had transpired in his tent after the battle at Pittsburg Landing. She steadfastly refused to think about it, up before dawn and never going to bed until midnight or later. Only the present existed. Nursing the men, washing their clothes, boiling bandages, cooking them special treats. There was no time to dwell on the past. It was gone.

If only that were true, said a tiny voice in her mind.

"No!" she said aloud.

Mrs. Ennis turned from kneading a bowl of bread dough and shot her an inquisitive look.

"Sweets have gone missing," Kate said hastily. "We have a thief on our hands. Last week an entire batch of blanc mange disappeared, and yesterday two apple pies vanished."

Mrs. Ennis nodded and returned to her work while Kate considered the peck of early peaches on the counter, donated by a local family. Then she went into the ward to fetch her medicine chest, a gift from General Sherman. Cunningly crafted from walnut, with brass end handles, it had three shelves fitted with compartments for vials and bottles, with a drawer below for bandages and lint. She ran her fingertips over the middle row of bottles, labeled variously camphor, quinine, rhubarb, castor oil, tincture of opium, and then stopped. Calomel. That would do. She pocketed it and returned to the kitchen, where she prepared a large bowl of peach pie filling. When none of the kitchen workers were watching, she surreptitiously sprinkled a good portion of the calomel into the peaches then added more cinnamon. She left the filling on the wooden counter nearest the tent flaps and went back into the ward.

An hour later she returned to the kitchen, and sure enough, the bowl of peach filling had disappeared. She casually took a seat outside the back of the hospital tent as if to rest for a bit. She had an excellent view of the center of camp and the sea of canvas tents that surrounded it. Then she waited.

It wasn't long before a soldier passed her at a fast trot, his face twisted in a grimace. "Good afternoon, Private Murphy," she called pleasantly. He didn't answer but increased his pace and dashed past the tents to a scrub of bushes where one of the camp latrines stood.

Then she straightened as Major Logan approached her. She hesitated, trying to decide whether to bolt, but she waited too long.

436

He stopped in front of her. "I don't usually see you sitting down, Mrs. Wilkes. Is all well?"

"Yes, indeed," she said shortly, avoiding his gaze.

Then she suppressed a smile and tried to keep a straight face as a couple of young soldiers from two different tents burst through the flaps and headed toward the latrine. One actually had a hand clutching his posterior as he ran, his eyes bulging, and she couldn't stop from laughing.

Logan turned to see what had caused her laughter. "Mercy me," he exclaimed as the panicked men disappeared behind the bushes. "What's going on?" he demanded.

Distant groans emanated from the latrine, and Kate doubled up, tears streaming down her face. The moaning, now accompanied by gasping curses, grew louder, alarming Major Logan. "I'd better see what the ruckus is about."

"No, Major." She recovered and wiped her eyes. "They will be perfectly all right in an hour or so."

Major Logan squinted sternly at her. "What did you do?"

She hesitated.

"Mrs. Wilkes?"

My, he was handsome as he gazed down at her. His skin had tanned in the southern sun, making his blue eyes even more intense.

She averted her gaze and smoothed her skirts. "Some varmints have been stealing food from the hospital kitchen."

"Go on."

"After the last episode, I couldn't tolerate it any longer. So I fixed some peaches for pie filling. And then I spiked it with calomel."

His eyes widened. "You didn't."

"I did," she said calmly.

Major Logan looked toward the latrine, bemused. "So that's why they're doing the quick step. Well, those boys have only got one oar in the water if they try to pilfer anything else from your kitchen after that."

"I don't suppose they will."

"Rather unorthodox way to deal with food thieves." Then he turned to her. "But then, you're a rather unorthodox woman."

Their gazes locked.

"Good afternoon, Major." She stood and turned to go.

"Wait, please." He pulled an envelope from his pocket. "I have a message from the general for you."

"Thank you." She pocketed the envelope and walked away.

Once inside the ward, she opened the small note:

Dear Mrs. Wilkes,

I hope I may presume upon you to visit with the women of Calvary Baptist Church in Memphis tomorrow evening. They are Union supporters and have made inquiries as to what aid they might provide for our wounded soldiers. I can think of no better person to undertake this request than you.

I have asked Major James Logan to accompany you.

Please reply at your earliest convenience if you are able to speak to the ladies.

Your servant,
W. T. Sherman

◆　◆　◆

The next day Kate stood in front of the cracked mirror Private Bennett had scrounged somewhere for her. For months, she hadn't worn anything but her practical cotton dresses and the huge aprons that covered them. It had been an age since she'd had a complete bath and washed her hair—which may have been a mistake. Freed from the pins and netting and freshly washed, her hair streamed past her shoulders in a wild cascade of curls and ringlets. The Tennessee humidity had doubled its volume, and she wasn't sure she'd be able to get it back up correctly.

She had debated whether to ask General Sherman for a different escort than Major Logan. But he had more serious things to worry about, so in the end she had sent an affirmative response to the general and left the ward in the capable hands of Mrs. Blake and Mrs. Ennis.

Kate had brought only one dress proper enough to wear in polite society. After Henry's death, she had spent two days dying her dresses and cloaks black. This particular dress had originally been a rich aubergine silk, a special favorite of Henry's. "It makes your hair look like flames, my love," he had said. If she concentrated hard, she could remember the feel of his lips on hers before the familiar pain surfaced.

She was thankful that all these weeks of hard work with her "boys" had allowed her no time to think about Henry. She pulled the locket from her bodice, warm from her skin. Since the first night sleeping on the floor of the sanctuary in Paducah, she hadn't opened it. Slowly she unlatched the filigreed gold oval. The lock of his blond hair still curled underneath the glass. Scripture told her she must forgive others, in order to be forgiven her own sins. But what about forgiving yourself? So far she hadn't been able to do that. Would she ever be able to look at the locket without the terrible guilt and regret that cleaved her heart like an ax and turned her blood cold? It felt like an albatross around her neck, and before she knew it, she had taken it off and hidden it in a pocket of her valise.

Time to get dressed.

And that meant putting on her corset. If Mrs. Ennis and Mrs. Blake knew that she taken to leaving it off during the days she labored in the ward they would be scandalized. But a woman couldn't bend or move freely in a corset. They were absolutely not suited to hospital work. So one day she let out the waists of her work dresses and decided to simply leave the corset off. With an extra chemise over the first, her dress, and the bibbed apron she wore, no one was the wiser. Kate picked up the detested thing. There would be no avoiding it tonight in this dress.

First the chemise, then the corset, fortunately laced in front. Then the drawers, the under-petticoat, the hoop skirt, the ruffled petticoat, and the plain petticoat. Then the silk skirt and the bodice. She put on her pearl earbobs and placed a white lace collar at her throat, as the first year of her mourning had passed. Amethyst hat pins secured the spoon bonnet to her curls. The bonnet had been a bit crushed in her valise, but it would have to do. She didn't have the time or inclination to steam it back to its original shape.

Major Logan waited for her next to a covered carriage he'd commandeered from somewhere. Clad in his dress uniform, with gold oak leaves on the epaulettes at his shoulder and a ceremonial sword thrust through the emerald green silk sash around his waist, he cut quite a dashing figure. His eyes widened at the sight of her, and her cheeks grew warm at his admiring look. He offered his hand to assist her in, and why in the world would she now be aware of the warmth of his fingers after all these months?

The major had brought four soldiers to accompany them in case of trouble on the road, but they had a peaceful ride. Wild roses lined the lane to the church, their sweet scent on the evening air powerfully evocative of home, where she'd had her own rose garden. The day's heat had softened into a mellow warmth, and she realized that she hadn't been outside the hospital wards for at least three months.

"Mrs. Wilkes," Major Logan said suddenly, and she jerked on the seat next to him.

"Yes, Major?"

"I've been meaning to speak to you about that—that night in the tent at Pittsburg Landing."

"Oh?" she said stiffly. "I'd quite forgotten about it."

He stole a sideways look at her. "That can't be true, Mrs. Wilkes, for you haven't spoken to me since. But let me finish." He rushed on. "I want to apologize for speaking out of turn. I never meant to offend you. . .and I was wrong."

Actually he'd been far more perceptive than he knew, unnervingly close to the truth. But she wouldn't—couldn't—give him the satisfaction of knowing it. She inclined her head graciously. "I accept your apology, Major."

"Thank you."

He clucked to the horses and whistled a tune. "Camptown Races." How ironic, since the fiddle had played that song the night he returned from Cairo and found her still in residence at the camp hospital. But he had noticeably relaxed, and she found herself glad that he had made the effort to smooth things over.

Calvary Baptist Church was a grand old building in Southern style, with great white pillars rising two stories to a gracious pediment. A tiered balcony ran along both sides of the sanctuary to a soaring roof supported by barrel vaulting. A stained-glass oriel window in the apse poured jeweled sunlight over a sanctuary filled with women of all ages.

A dignified gentleman with an impressive gray mustache approached Kate. "Mrs. Wilkes?"

She nodded.

"I'm Rev. Obadiah Morris. This is my wife, Penelope," he said, indicating the plump blond woman beaming next to him. "We are so pleased to have you with us tonight."

Kate introduced Major Logan.

"If you are ready, Mrs. Wilkes, I will introduce you now."

She nodded and followed him to the podium in the middle of the stage. The buzz of feminine voices filled the air, and her stomach lurched. It had been so long since she had been in "polite" society that she'd forgotten what it was like.

After the pastor introduced her, she stepped forward, wishing she had thought to write out her remarks beforehand. The crowd quieted, and a sea of raised, expectant faces waited.

Then she was speaking, telling the story of her arrival at Grace Episcopal Church in Paducah, Kentucky. Of what she was able to do for the men. She kept it light, leaving out the terrible realties of severed limbs, gangrene, infection, and death.

"The men love packages from home. I try to have a sweet for them every day. Gifts of coffee are always welcome, fresh fruit, jams, and jellies. Then there are certain things we are chronically short of, especially sheets and bandages."

She paused as a harebrained idea went through her head. It was an eminently practical thing, something specific and valuable she could take back with her to the camp hospital and put to immediate use. But did she dare?

"Ladies, you're here tonight because you want to help." Heads nodded throughout the sanctuary. "And I have a practical, and rather unusual, suggestion for something you can do right now. But first, Reverend Morris, would you mind leaving the sanctuary for a moment?"

The pastor's eyes goggled, and he glanced at his wife, who nodded approval. While he stood and made his way down the aisle she searched the crowd. "Major Logan?" she called. He stood at the back of the sanctuary. "Would you join Reverend Morris, please?"

He bowed and exited through the front door, as a swirl of excited apprehension swept through the room.

"Ladies, please rise to your feet."

Kate swallowed hard as they complied. If the women took her suggestion the wrong way, it could cause her discharge from the camp hospital. The reverend might be outraged, and she could even be permanently banned from polite society. But for the heartsick men lying on their pallets in the hospital wards she would risk her reputation.

"Now." She took a deep breath. Once the words left her lips she couldn't take them back. "If you can spare a petticoat, please take it off and drop it on the floor."

Shocked silence met her words. Women glanced sideways at their neighbors, eyebrows raised. Whatever they had been expecting, it wasn't this. In polite society one never spoke about their "unmentionables."

She tried again. "I know it's an unconventional request, but think of all the bandages you would be supplying for our wounded men."

One brave young matron in the first pew uttered a giggle, bent over, and lifted her skirt. Little screams and titters broke out, and laughter. Then gamely, most of the women, some helping each other, reached under their voluminous skirts, shimmied this way and that, and managed to wriggle out of a petticoat.

"Ladies, would you bring them here to the front?"

With wide smiles on their faces, the women trooped to the front and, one by one, piled their petticoats on the dais. When they were finished, the pile of white undergarments surrounding Kate reached her waist.

"Thank you so much for your gracious contribution to the care of our sick and injured soldiers. May our Lord richly bless you. And now, good night."

◆ ◆ ◆

Major Logan waited outside in the warm summer air with Reverend Morris. The soldiers who had accompanied them stood off a bit, smoking cheroots. Crickets chirped in the grass, and over the crest of a distant hill, a waxing silver moon rose, but Mrs. Wilkes's voice inside the church held the greater part of his attention. When she asked the ladies to stand and drop one of their petticoats, Reverend Morris choked as if he'd swallowed a rattlesnake. His accusatory gaze darted to Logan as if he'd brought some horrible corrupter to church instead of a God-fearing woman.

Logan smiled faintly and shrugged. She had surely raised a ruckus. The pastor crossed his arms over his chest and frowned, tapping his foot. There wasn't anything he could do to stop her now, for he couldn't enter the church if the women were shucking their underwear.

A few minutes later, the ladies streamed out of the church, chattering to one another.

Penelope Morris exited last, and she chuckled at her husband's grim face. "There, there, Obadiah," she said as she took his arm. "It's for a good cause."

Logan didn't wait to see the reverend's response and went into the church. There the miscreant stood, surrounded by heaps of white.

"Well, Mrs. Wilkes, I've said it before. You definitely have some unorthodox ideas."

Kate beamed at him. "Do you have any idea how many bandages I can get out of these?"

"Knowing you, I'm sure you'll multiply them like the loaves and fishes."

She laughed as if she didn't have a care in the world, and the sound of it pierced his heart. Her eyes sparkled, and for an awful moment he had a terrible impulse to kiss her right then and there.

"Let's get these loaded," he said brusquely. "We need to get back."

He lit the lamps on the carriage, and they stuffed most of the petticoats behind the bench seat. The rest were tied down behind the soldier's saddles, much to their amusement.

The major let the horses take their lead as they ambled down the lane. Mrs. Wilkes seemed lost in her thoughts and made no attempt to initiate a conversation. So he remained silent, too, wondering if she had truly forgiven him.

They were close to camp when she shifted on the seat and looked at him. "Major," she asked hesitantly, "have you a family back home?"

He transferred the reins to one hand and adjusted his sword more comfortably. "No. Just my mother, in Buffalo, New York. My father is dead."

"No wife?"

He snorted. "No."

"A sweetheart then?"

He sighed. "No."

"I don't mean to intrude. We've worked together all these months, and I've never known if you had a family. You never speak of it."

"You never speak of yours, either, Mrs. Wilkes."

She caught her breath. "I don't suppose I do."

"If you tell me your story, I'll tell you mine."

She hesitated. "I haven't spoken about it to anyone. I've tried to forget."

He turned to look at her. "Perhaps it would unburden you to speak of it?"

The positive response of the Calvary Baptist women and the mellow summer dusk had lulled her into a serenity she had rarely experienced since Henry's death. That and the underlying note of real interest and concern in Major Logan's voice. Perhaps it would help if she could relax her guard and speak of it. She could give him the basic facts without revealing the terrible thing she had done to her husband.

"My husband, Henry, was taken prisoner in late 1861 and sent to a camp in Georgia. I received a telegram that he was being released. I hadn't seen him in a year, and I stood on the platform in Paducah as the train pulled into the station, searching every window for a glimpse of him." She cleared her throat. "After the passengers had disembarked, one of the porters approached me. They had Henry in a special car at the rear of the train. They carried him off on a stretcher—" She choked and pulled a handkerchief from her pocket. "I didn't recognize him. He was filthy and emaciated, delirious with fever. Blood-stained bandages covered the stump of his leg. Somehow I got him home. Cleaned the vermin from his body. Fed him beef tea through a mouth with bleeding gums and teeth missing from scurvy." She sighed. "When I shaved off his matted beard, his cheekbones were sharp enough to cut paper. The fever broke on the second day, and he recognized me. We had one day together before the fever returned. I held him against me all night, trying to stop the chills that racked his body." Her voice thickened. "But it was no use. He died in my arms shortly before dawn."

She clenched her fists in her lap. "His suffering was over. But I couldn't forget the stories he told me. Of the sick and injured soldiers left to fend for themselves without a covering to protect from the cold night of winter or the blazing Georgia summer sun. Of rations so rotten they were inedible. Of the nights that he felt so alone that only calling out to God kept him sane, while others around him raved in the fury of fever and hunger."

She relaxed her fists and leaned back. "At the end, he was grateful to be able to come home to die in the peace and warmth denied to those men still interned in prison camps and hospitals. That's why I came, Major Logan. I had to do something, anything to alleviate the pain."

"And you have done some remarkable work, Mrs. Wilkes," he said gruffly.

"Even though you were ready to send me home the first day?"

"Yes. I admit it now. You've proved a blessing to the men." *And me,* he thought. When had it begun, this awakening in the morning with his first thought about her? Seeing her face. Knowing she was there.

"Your turn," she said.

"Pardon me?"

"You said you'd tell me your story, if I told mine."

"Yes." He shrugged. "There isn't much to tell. I lost my leg at Bull Run. Minie ball. Like so many other men."

She nodded.

"I was engaged to be married to a girl back in Buffalo. Beth." A pang went through him as he spoke her name. "I wrote to tell her of my injury. Of course, she was horrified and said she would do her best to take care of me after the war. After the wedding we would live with her parents until we could have our own home. She had plans, she said. She was sewing tablecloths and embroidering napkins. Collecting things for the house."

He pulled a pipe out his pocket. "Do you mind?"

She shook her head. "Go on."

He lit the pipe, puffed, and blew a smoke ring into the air. "The strange thing was, while she sounded happy, planning our future, it struck me wrong somehow. As if she was trying to convince herself. It didn't ring true." He snorted. "Turned out I was right. I didn't have a letter for a solid month, and then one finally came. After much prayer and contemplation," he said, in a sarcastic tone, "she had come to realize that it wouldn't work. She attributed the fault to herself, said she was weak. That she'd never been good around blood or illness. So that was that."

"I'm so sorry, Major."

"So was I." He smiled faintly. "Perhaps it was for the best. I couldn't have borne it if she had married me out of pity."

"She doesn't know what a good man she's put aside. You deserve better."

"Thank you for that."

"I mean it," she said. "I have no use for insincere flattery." She smiled then, and his heart turned over in his chest. She was so beautiful.

When the carriage pulled into camp, he dismounted and helped her down, resisting the urge to let his hands linger about her waist. Together they stacked the petticoats on a long table in the camp kitchen.

"Thank you, Major," she said when they had finished. She hesitated and then smiled at him. "There is someone special out there for you, Major. I know it."

I know it too, he thought, watching the petite redhead walk away.

Chapter Seven

General Sherman marched farther south and Kate, Major Logan, Private Bennett, and the portable hospital moved with him. President Lincoln's Emancipation Proclamation on January 1, 1863, had deprived the South of much of its labor force, and the tide of war was slowly turning in the Union's favor. The siege of Vicksburg, the "Gibraltar of the South," had begun. Army units surrounding the city reported heavy casualties, and the camp hospital overflowed with the wounded.

Extra pots of beef stew and corn bread had been made for the units passing by the camp all day, and Kate and her ladies fed every soldier they could. With no time to think and barely time to eat or sleep, the nurses took shifts around the clock to attend the sick and injured.

A young soldier was brought in soaked with blood from head to toe. A bullet had ploughed a furrow along the side of his head, and he remained unconscious, although the wound had been field bandaged and the bleeding had stopped. As Kate washed the blood off his still form, the gray color of his bloodstained jacket became visible.

A Confederate boy.

Kate swiftly removed his uniform and hid it under the thin mattress. Across the aisle a soldier stirred and rose up on his elbow. "Well," he drawled, "whatcha got there, ma'am? Looks like a Johnny Reb."

It was Lieutenant Baldwin, a grizzled, foulmouthed farmer from Missouri brought in a week ago with a compound fracture of the tibia. Although Major Logan had set it, the wound became gangrenous and the leg had to be amputated above the knee. Each day Baldwin became more bitter and morose and less interested in anything going on in the ward. Until now.

She turned and shot him a fierce glare. "You don't have a dog in this fight, Lieutenant."

He smirked back at her. "Couldn't find his own people, I guess. We jes' might have to do somethin' about that."

"You will do nothing," she said in a low voice, not wanting to attract any more attention. "He's a boy."

"A boy who carried a gun." Baldwin lifted his right leg and obscenely waved the stump around. "Old enough to do this."

"Enough, soldier. Sit there and sip your tea."

He raised his hands in a mock gesture of surrender. "Yes, ma'am," he said, lying down on his pallet and turning his back to her.

But as she worked in the ward that morning Lieutenant Baldwin returned to watching the unconscious boy like a cat waits at a mouse hole. Uneasy, she sought out Major Logan in the amputation tent. His face lit at the sight of her, and her heart gave an answering thump. "Kate."

"I need to speak with you," she said, trying to ignore the flash of joy that rose up at his smile.

"Certainly. Give me a minute to finish here," he said, returning to his patient.

She nodded and walked away until the stench of blood diminished. After a wet, rainy winter, the creamy white flowers of Solomon's seal nodded in the damp places under the trees, along with airy Queen Anne's lace and orange jewelweed. A mockingbird sang nearby, and she counted the number of his songs and trills. How difficult to reconcile that in the midst of this green and fertile beauty, men were bleeding and dying a few feet away.

"Kate." He'd taken off his bloody apron and washed his hands. A shock of his black hair had fallen over his forehead, and her heart tripped faster. "You needed to see me?"

"Yes," she said, smoothing her skirt as she always did when nerves threatened to overcome her. "One of the patients brought in this morning is a Confederate, the boy with the head wound."

Logan frowned. "Unfortunate."

"And Lieutenant Baldwin knows. He wants to cause trouble. Can you have him sent somewhere else?"

"I can try. Or we could send the Reb back to his own side."

She shook her head. "He's too sick to be moved."

Logan nodded. "So be it. I'll have Baldwin transferred out."

"Thank you."

"How are you holding up?" His blue eyes were concerned. "It's been so chaotic."

"Yes." She felt the welcome warmth of the sun on her face and sighed. "I wonder sometimes if this war will ever be over. I can barely remember my life before it started." Which wasn't entirely true. The excruciating memory of what she had done to Henry never left her.

"It will end. We're moving toward it now. When it's over. . ." He gazed at her with such intensity she had to look away from the promise there, her breath coming faster.

"I need to get back." She turned to go.

"I'll wait," he said.

A tremor went through her, but she didn't turn, afraid of what her face might reveal. She couldn't allow herself to give him any hope.

◆ ◆ ◆

Bless Major Logan. He transferred Baldwin out that afternoon. The rebel boy hadn't recovered consciousness, but Kate breathed easier knowing Baldwin had left.

She had taken some supper and returned to the hospital later that evening, writing letters home for the men by lantern light, when a demanding voice cut through the quiet ward.

"Lemme by." Supported by another soldier, Lieutenant Baldwin limped toward her, a crutch in one hand and a revolver in the other. His collaborator carried a heavy coil of rope looped around his shoulder, and both hard faces were set like rock, grim and relentless.

Baldwin jerked his head toward the Confederate boy in the corner. "We're here to take the Reb."

Kate stood and shook her head. "This isn't the way, Lieutenant. He's already dying." Slowly she inched her way toward the boy. "There's no need to hasten his end by violent means. Hasn't enough been done to each of you?"

Baldwin shook his head. "We're takin' him, ma'am, so get out of the way."

The edge of the cot bumped her knees. "You'll have to go through me first." She lifted her chin. "And if I can't persuade your hardened hearts, then perhaps this will." She pulled the Colt Baby Dragoon from her pocket.

"I've treated you with love and respect," she said firmly, leveling the Colt at Baldwin, "and I would hate to see my good work mean naught to you. But if you intend to murder this boy in cold blood, you'll have to kill me, too."

Behind Baldwin, Major Logan had entered the ward. He shook his head at her and crept toward them on cat feet.

Baldwin hesitated then raised his revolver and took aim, giving Major Logan enough time to tackle the two men as Baldwin pulled the trigger.

Misfire.

Baldwin's crutch skittered off under a cot. Logan kicked the smoking gun out of the stunned Baldwin's hand and scrambled to his feet. Baldwin's accomplice threw off the rope and took off running. Logan tackled him to the floor amid the general pandemonium among the men and dragged him outside. Two of the wounded men had gotten out of their beds to restrain Baldwin as three sentries entered the ward to arrest him.

Kate returned the Colt to her pocket with trembling hands. She could have been killed. And for the first time since Henry had died, she wanted to live.

◆　◆　◆

After Lieutenant Baldwin and his accomplice had been locked in the temporary stockade, Major Logan marched back to the hospital tent. This was it. He was going to have it out with her one way or another. If she refused him, well. . .he didn't want to think about that.

When he entered the tent, there she was, ministering to the men as if nothing had happened. Anger rose up inside him like a boiling flame. He came up behind her. "Kate," he said tersely. "Come with me. Now, please."

She nodded and put aside the book she had been reading to one of the men.

"Come outside."

Silently she complied. Once outside, she stood and looked up at him with a tranquil expression, which outraged him.

"Kate," he barked, gripping her arms and giving her a shake. "Don't you care if you live or die?" He shook her again, hard. "And even if you don't care, let me tell you something, I do!"

Her eyes widened, and he thought her icy reserve had been broken as her breathing quickened. "Here's the thing, Kate. I love you. I love you! Do you hear me?"

Now his breathing grew ragged, and his fingers tightened on her arms. He kissed her, warm and urgent, and he didn't stop for a long moment.

She wrenched out of his grasp. "You won't love me when you find out who I really am."

"I doubt that," he said quietly. Her shoulders shook and she looked wildly about, as if deciding whether to bolt. "Tell me then."

◆　◆　◆

She moved closer to the lantern light and steeled herself. This would be the last time he looked at her with unabashed love and longing on his handsome face. What she was about to tell him would destroy it.

"My husband didn't want to join the army," she said harshly. "He was a meek and gentle man who loved his farm and his books. When war was declared, he thought it would blow over quickly. He didn't believe the South could stay away from the Union for long."

He stood silent, a shadow in the night.

"We'd only been married two years. In those two years, I lost two babies. When the war began, I was still angry over those losses. Henry didn't know how to console me, so he retreated to his study and his books. And that made me angrier."

Her voice shook, and he made an instinctive move toward her.

"No!" she cried, waving her hands to ward him away. "You have to know the truth. Why I'm here." Angrily she brushed away the welling tears. "Most of our friends and family joined the Union Army. I waited for him to do the same. When it didn't happen—" She stopped, choking, as the flood of memories arose. "I told him he was a coward who didn't deserve to live!"

Her chest heaved with wracking sobs. "He left the house that night and joined the Union forces in Tennessee." She turned away. "I didn't see him again until he arrived on the Paducah train, near death." She fell to her knees and wept.

"Kate," he said gently, touching her shoulder.

She wrenched away. "Are you blind? I goaded him into it, and now he's dead. Dead! It's all my fault." She managed to get to her feet, pushing him away when he tried to help her. "That's why I came. I had to atone for what I'd done."

"Kate, someone has already made atonement for you. You don't have to do it yourself."

"You know what the worst thing was?" She pushed her hair out of her face. "He still loved me. And forgave me."

"So, it is well then."

She shook her head. "It will never be well," she whispered. "Because I can't forgive myself." She bowed her head. "And the most terrible thing of all is. . .I love you. And now that you know what I've done, I'll lose that, too."

He pulled her into his arms. "You're wrong, Kate. Look at me."

She met his gaze. The look of love and compassion mingled on his face brought a fresh rush of tears.

"You're forgiven, Kate, as I have been forgiven. This is a second chance for you. For us." He took her face in his hands. "All these long months with no light shining through the clouds," he kissed her lips softly, "you've been my beacon of hope in a dark and weary world."

She couldn't breathe. It wasn't possible. "Can you still love me. . .with. . .all that you know about me? What I've done?"

He grinned, and her heart came alive with a painful thump. "I can. And that's why, by all that's holy, I want you to stop taking these dangerous chances!" He reached for her hands and got down on one knee. "And I'm not going to wait another moment. Kate, will you marry me?"

Her head felt incredibly light as the vise of darkness clamped around her heart dissolved. She had been forgiven. *Thank You, Lord*, her heart cried out.

She collapsed onto his knee and he tightened his arms around her. She laid her cheek against his chest, feeling his heartbeat, and realized she had been set free. "Yes," she said. "Oh, yes!"

Renee Yancy is a history and archaeology buff who works as an RN when she isn't writing historical novels. She has visited Ireland, Scotland, and England to stand in the places her ancient historical characters lived. She lives in Kentucky with her husband, two dogs, and her ninety-five-year-old mother-in-law. Check out her blog at www.reneeyancy.blogspot.com or visit her website: www.reneeyancy.com.